Cast in terms of its embeddedness in two successive 'constellations' of economic, political and socio-cultural power (the first driven by Northeast Asia, the second by China), the chapters of this volume contain materials, ideas and arguments vital to rethinking Southeast Asia's global significance. For anyone seeking cutting-edge knowledge about contemporary Southeast Asian development – including both the opportunities and dangers inherent in its future prospects – this is the book you need.

Jeffrey Henderson, *University of Bristol*

This volume contains gems on East Asian economies including China as well as for those interested in comparative analysis. Nederveen Pieterse, Rahman and Tham have provided editorial coherence to the chapters which reflect on the region's miracle, debacle, trajectories and options for the future.

Jomo Kwame Sundaram, *former economics professor, UN Assistant Secretary General, 2007 Wassily Leontief Prize for Advancing the Frontiers of Economic Thought*

This is a most enlightening book about contemporary Southeast Asia. Readers will profit immensely from the useful comparisons between ASEAN and Northeast Asia, thoughtful analyses of the role of domestic institutions on socio-economic performance, and insightful projections of future China-ASEAN relations. I am proud that scholarship on Southeast Asia has advanced so impressively.

Wing Thye Woo, *University of California Davis, Fudan University, Shanghai; President of Jeffrey Cheah Institute on Southeast Asia, Sunway University, Kuala Lumpur, Malaysia*

Changing Constellations of Southeast Asia

Southeast Asia is among emerging economies that have become important drivers of the world economy. ASEAN has furthered the region's economic integration. Growth, however, remains dependent on foreign investment. Inequality has grown or remains high. Democracy, instead of consolidating, has stalled or regressed.

Changing Constellations of Southeast Asia seeks to:

- shed light on the gap between Northeast Asia and Southeast Asia from a variety of viewpoints, across trade and industry, services, and education and language policies;
- examine institutions and elite capture to understand why middle-tier Southeast Asian countries have failed in matching the 'East Asian miracle';
- examine China's increasing influence and how this growing role affects Southeast Asia as a constellation.

Contributing to critical political economy and comparative development studies in East Asia, this timely volume will appeal to undergraduate and post-graduate students interested in Southeast Asia studies, international political economy, development sociology and economics, social policy and Asian politics.

Jan Nederveen Pieterse is Duncan and Suzanne Mellichamp Distinguished Professor of Global Studies and Sociology at University of California, Santa Barbara, USA.

Abdul Rahman Embong is Emeritus Professor in Sociology of Development and Principal Research Fellow at the Institute of Malaysian and International Studies, Universiti Kebangsaan Malaysia, Malaysia.

Siew Yean Tham is a Senior Fellow at ISEAS-Yusof Ishak Institute, Singapore.

Routledge Studies in Emerging Societies

Series editor: Jan Nederveen Pieterse

University of California, Santa Barbara

The baton of driving the world economy is passing to emerging economies. This is not just an economic change, but a social change, with migration flows changing direction towards surplus economies; a political change, as in the shift from the G7 to G20; and, over time, cultural changes. This also means that the problems of emerging societies will increasingly become world problems. This series addresses the growing importance of BRIC (Brazil Russia India China) and rising societies such as South Korea, Taiwan, Singapore, Indonesia, South Africa, Turkey, the UAE and Mexico. It focuses on problems generated by emergence, such as social inequality, cultural change, media, ethnic and religious strife, ecological constraints, relations with advanced and developing societies, and new regionalism, with a particular interest in addressing debates and social reflexivity in emerging societies.

1 **Global Modernity, Development, and Contemporary Civilization**
Towards a Renewal of Critical Theory
José Maurício Domingues

2 **Globalization and Development in East Asia**
Edited by Jan Nederveen Pieterse and Jongtae Kim

3 **Brazil Emerging**
Inequality and Emancipation
Edited by Jan Nederveen Pieterse and Adalberto Cardoso

4 **Higher Education in the Global Age**
Policy, Practice and Promise in Emerging Societies
Edited by Daniel Araya and Peter Marber

5 **Critical Theory after the Rise of the Global South**
Kaleidoscopic Dialectic
Boike Rehbein

6 **Changing Constellations of Southeast Asia**
From Northeast Asia to China
Edited by Jan Nederveen Pieterse, Abdul Rahman Embong, Siew Yean Tham

Changing Constellations of Southeast Asia

From Northeast Asia to China

Edited by Jan Nederveen Pieterse, Abdul Rahman Embong, Siew Yean Tham

Routledge
Taylor & Francis Group
LONDON AND NEW YORK

First published 2018 by Routledge

2 Park Square, Milton Park, Abingdon, Oxfordshire OX14 4RN
52 Vanderbilt Avenue, New York, NY 10017

Routledge is an imprint of the Taylor & Francis Group, an informa business

First issued in paperback 2019

British Library Cataloguing in Publication Data
A catalogue record for this book is available from the British Library

Library of Congress Cataloging in Publication Data
A catalog record for this book has been requested

ISBN: 978-1-138-05921-4 (hbk)
ISBN: 978-0-367-35990-4 (pbk)

Typeset in Bembo
by Wearset Ltd, Boldon, Tyne and Wear

Contents

Figures

Tables

Contributors

Abdul Rahman Embong is Emeritus Professor in Sociology of Development and Principal Research Fellow at the Institute of Malaysian and International Studies (IKMAS), Universiti Kebangsaan Malaysia, UKM. He was President of the Malaysian Social Science Association 2000–2010 and is currently the Association's Advisor. He has published numerous journal articles and book chapters and authored/edited more than 20 books. The latter include *State-led Modernization and the New Middle Class in Malaysia*; *Development and Wellbeing*; *Malaysian Studies: Looking Back Moving Forward*; *Southeast Asian Middle Classes: Prospects for Social Change and Democratisation*.

Edmund Terence Gomez is Professor of Political Economy at the Faculty of Economics and Administration, University of Malaya. He specializes in state–market relations and the linkages between politics, policies and capital development. He has held appointments at the Universities of Leeds, Murdoch (Australia), Kobe, Michigan (Ann Arbor) and California (San Diego) and as Research Coordinator at the United Nations Research Institute for Social Development in Geneva, Switzerland. His publications include nine single-authored books on political economy of Malaysia and Asia and many articles.

Sufian Jusoh is Senior Research Fellow at the Institute of Malaysian and International Studies, UKM; Senior External Fellow of the World Trade Institute, Switzerland; and Distinguished Fellow at the Institute of Diplomacy and Foreign Relations, Malaysia. His expertise is in international trade, international investment and intellectual property management and he serves as an Investment Law and Policy Expert at the World Bank and ASEAN. He is a Barrister-at-Law of Lincoln's Inn, London and holds a Doctor in Law (summa cum laude) of the University of Bern, Switzerland.

Andrew Jia Yi Kam is a research fellow at the Institute of Malaysian and International Studies, UKM. He graduated First Class in BSc Economics specializing in Econometrics at the National University of Malaysia, MSc Economics from Warwick University and PhD from the Australian

National University (ANU). His research interests include international trade, industrialization and economic growth. He was the recipient of the Chevening Scholarship in 2005, the Australian Endeavour Postgraduate Fellowship in 2008 and the Malaysian Fulbright Scholarship in 2016.

Elsa Lafaye de Micheaux is a political economist, an associate professor at Rennes 2 University, France, and a member of the Paris Centre of Southeast Asia Studies, CASE (CNRS). Dr Lafaye de Micheaux analyses the current transformation of Malaysian capitalism in a comparative perspective and has been Associate Researcher at the Faculty of Economics, University of Malaya between 2014 and 2016. She is the author of *The Development of Malaysian Capitalism: From British Rule to the Present Day* (SIRD, Petaling Jaya, 2017). Following her *Asian Capitalisms and Chinese Power* (co-edited with P. Alary, in French; Paris, Presses de Sciences Po, 2015), she has conducted an in-depth study of the Malaysia-China 'precious' relationship with D. Delfolie and N. Fau (Irasec, 2017; English version forthcoming). She now co-directs the *Institut Pondok Perancis* with D. Delfolie in Kuala Lumpur and leads the *Asean-China-Norms* international research network.

Jan Nederveen Pieterse is Duncan and Suzanne Mellichamp Distinguished Professor of Global Studies and Sociology at University of California Santa Barbara. He held the Pok Rafeah Distinguished Chair of international studies at National University of Malaysia, 2014–2015. He specializes in globalization, development studies and cultural studies. His recent books include *Multipolar Globalization: Emerging Economies and Development* (2017); *China's Contingencies and Globalization* (co-edited, 2017); *Capitalism in Asia* (co-edited, 2017); *Globalization and Culture: Global Mélange* (2015); *Development Theory: Deconstructions/Reconstructions* (2010). He edits book series with both Routledge and Palgrave Macmillan.

Tim Rackett is Associate Professor and heads the Centre for Development Studies at HELP (Higher Education Learning Program) University, Kuala Lumpur, Malaysia. His earlier research explores western psychiatric powers of truth-telling about racism, culture and madness in colonial and post-colonial metropolitan situations. He has lived and taught philosophy and international relations in Thailand and Malaysia for 20 years. He has published on Buddhist nationalism, racism and violence, recently focusing on the performance of ethnic and religious identities in the Southern Thailand conflict.

Rashila Ramli is Professor of Political Science at the Institute of Malaysian and International Studies, UKM. Her areas of specialization are political development, gender and politics, and international politics focusing on global governance. Her current research is on the governance of the South China Sea and its implications for ASEAN and Promoting Social Inclusion through Public Policies (funded by UNESCO). Recent publications are *Human Security in Archipelagic Southeast Asia*, 2015 (with Sity Daud and

Zarina Othman) and *Social Constructivism and Malaysia's International Relations*, 2011 (with Nor Azizan Idris and Zarina Othman).

Fazal Rizvi is Professor in Global Studies in Education at the University of Melbourne. A collection of his papers has been published in *Encountering Education in the Global* (Routledge, 2014).

Marc Saxer is the Resident Representative of the Friedrich Ebert Stiftung (FES) in Delhi, India, and the Regional Coordinator of the Asia–Europe Economy of Tomorrow project. His work focuses on transformation and democratization processes. His work has been published in nine languages and has been featured in major news outlets around the world. He headed the FES Thailand office and coordinated the global security, democracy promotion and climate policy working lines of the FES Dialogue on Globalization program. Marc holds a Masters of Law from Hamburg University and MA in Political Science from the Free University of Berlin.

Siew Yean Tham is a senior fellow at ISEAS-Yusof Ishak Institute, Singapore. She was formerly Director and Professor at the Institute of Malaysian and International Studies, UKM. As an economist, she has served as a consultant to several national agencies in Malaysia and international agencies, including among others, the World Bank, Asian Development Bank and Asian Development Bank Institute. She has published extensively on foreign direct investment, international trade and trade policies, industrial development, and trade in services in Malaysia and ASEAN. She has a PhD in economics from University of Rochester, US.

Zawiah Yahya was head of department, faculty dean, professor of postcolonial literature and critical theory, and guest scholar at the School of Language Studies and Linguistics, UKM. She was Asian Public Intellectuals senior fellow and conducted research in Tokyo and Bangkok before becoming Professor and Principal Researcher at the Institute of Malaysian and International Studies, UKM. Her publications include *Malay Characters in Malaysian Novels in English* (1994); *Resisting Colonialist Discourse* (2nd ed. 1994); *Reading Approaches in Malay Literature: Critical Theory in the Making* (2010); and *Border Crossings* (2013); and she was editor of *Western Perspectives of Mahathir's Anti-West Policy Positions 1981–2003* (2015).

Acknowledgments

This volume is a collaborative research project of the faculty of the International Studies Institute of Malaysian and International Studies (IKMAS) at Universiti Kebangsaan Malaysia (National University of Malaysia, UKM) and international colleagues. It is the outcome of a series of workshops conducted when Jan Nederveen Pieterse held the Pok Rafeah Distinguished Chair of international studies at IKMAS, UKM in 2014 and 2015.

Chapters 1 and 8 are modified versions of the author's inaugural Pok Rafeah Chair lecture, November 2014 and second PRC lecture, November 2015. An earlier version of Chapter 1 was previously published in the *Canadian Journal of Development Studies* (63, 3, 2015: 263–282). I thank the journal for kind permission for publishing a modified version in this volume.

I thank colleagues at IKMAS for sharing critical perspectives, in particular the co-editors of this volume, Professors Abdul Rahman Embong, who initiated this cooperation, and Siew Yean Tham. In addition, I thank Rashila Haji Ramli, Andrew Kam, Helen Ting and Zawiah Yahya. For valuable comments I further thank Paul Chan, Nguyen Van Chinh, Fara Edayu, Hans-Dieter Evers, Terence Gomez, Jeffrey Henderson, Wendy Liow, Jin-Ho Jang and Jong-Cheol Kim, Omar Merican, Aashish Mehta, Neilson Ilan Mersat, Sophal Ear, Ratna Nepal, Tim Rackett, Marc Saxer, Bob Terpstra, Jane Tong, Yin Shao Loong, Wing Woo and colleagues at Universiti Malaysia Sabah, Universiti Malaysia Sarawak and Seoul National University. For research assistance I thank Muhamad Azwan bin Abd Rahman, Mohd. Hariszuan Jaharuddin, Daniel Zorub, Andrew Kam and Lan Xuan Le. Mistakes and omissions are entirely mine.

Chapter 2 is a different edited version of a paper that is published in the *Journal of Contemporary Asia* (http://dx.doi.org/10.1080/00472336.2017.1322628). Andrew Jia Yi Kam thanks the journal for kind permission to publish this version of the paper. The author would also like to thank his sponsors, the Bureau of Educational and Cultural Affairs (ECA) of the United States Department of State and the Malaysian-American Commission on Educational Exchange (MACEE) for the Fulbright Visiting Scholar Program grant (G-1–00005) and the National University of Malaysia for the traveling grant under GGPM-2014–002.

Chapter 5 is a different edited version of a paper that is published in the *Journal of Contemporary Asia* (http://dx.doi.org/10.1080/00472336.2017.1322629). Edmund Terence Gomez and Elsa Lafaye De Micheaux thank the journal for kind permission to publish this version of the paper.

Chapter 6: Marc Saxer thanks Jan Nederveen Pieterse for useful comments on his initial draft chapter.

Chapter 7: Tim Rackett thanks Dr Andrew Jia Yi Kam, Jan Nederveen Pieterse and his half-Thai sons Ben and Dan.

Chapter 10 is a different edited version of a paper that is published in the *Journal of Contemporary Asia* (http://dx.doi.org/10.1080/00472336.2017.1310273). Siew Yean Tham thanks the journal for kind permission to publish this version of the paper. She also thanks her co-editors, Jan Nederveen Pieterse, Abdul Rahman Embong and other members of the book project for useful comments on her initial draft chapter.

Introduction

Jan Nederveen Pieterse, Abdul Rahman Embong and Siew Yean Tham

The cohesiveness of Southeast Asia as a region has been questioned; the region has been viewed as a 'contingent category' (Kratoska *et al.* 2005). Nevertheless, Southeast Asia has distinctive features that have endured over time. It is an ancient seafaring region where maritime commerce goes back to the fourth millennium BCE (Hodos 2017). It is a region of archipelagos, island worlds, Nusantara and a region where the 'globalization of food' goes back to the second millennium BCE. The region has long supplied spices, notably to China. It is a geostrategic region astride major sea-lanes, in particular the Strait of Malacca. It sits astride the land bridge between South and East Asia, between India and China. As a region in-between monsoon zones and cycles, it has served as a shelter and way station for seafarers. It is a region where monsoons, civilizations and religions meet – Indic, Sinic, Hindu, Buddhist, Muslim and Christian, a confluence that has shaped the character of the region.

Southeast Asia has experienced historical periods during which a distinctive constellation held sway and influenced much of the region, constellations with distinctive political, economic and cultural features. This volume focuses on two such constellations, the period 1980–2000 when Northeast Asia with Japan and the tiger economies were in the lead, and the period from 2000 that is increasingly marked by the rise of China. To situate our discussion as part of transformations in the *longue durée* and to introduce regional constellations as an analytical tool, we first briefly review constellations of Southeast Asia over time. Salient periods of historical cohesion of the region include, in brief:

- The era of Indic and Sanskrit influence from 200 BCE until the fifteenth century CE.
- The era of maritime empires – Srivijaya (650–1377), Majapahit (1293–1500), the Malacca Sultanate (1400–1511), and mainland empires and kingdoms such as the Champa kingdom (192–1832), the Khmer empire (802–1431) and Ayutthaya (1351–1767).
- During the 'age of commerce', *c.*1400–1700, the region was a major trade hub connected to the Indian Ocean trade and the Levant trade

(Abu-Lughod 1989; Reid 1990, 1995). As the hub of spice routes and as central nodes in maritime Silk Routes, the region was a force in the world economy and attracted Chinese traders and settlers, Arab and Hadramaut merchants and settlers and European colonizers (Portuguese, Dutch, British and French; Sien and Church 2012).

- During the nineteenth and twentieth centuries, the region – which by then was under western colonial rule – again was a hub in the world economy, now as a supplier of raw materials for industry in Europe and the United States, tin and later rubber and timber, which brought migrant labor from afar to the region. Tin and rubber produced in the region fueled different phases of European and American industrialism, and was the largest and most significant compared to any part of the world.
- In the twentieth century the region was an arena in the Second World War and a frontier of decolonization with conflicts such as the Indonesian revolution against Dutch rule and the armed struggle against British rule during the Malayan Emergency.
- With the Cold War came ideological and political divides in the region. Southeast Asia became a theater of American-led counterinsurgency operations and a protracted people's war in Vietnam against American aggression.

Regional formations or constellations arise from the interaction of external and internal forces and dynamics. This differs fundamentally from Ruth Benedict's (1935) notion of configurations, the idea of cultures as stable cohesive wholes, 'patterns of culture' that should be understood 'from within'. In contrast, regional constellations involve the dynamic interplay of external and internal dynamics and institutions, relations that change over time. Each formation represents different patterns of interdependence, different ways in which social forces in the region interact with wider and global forces.

Constellations are *layered* in that traces and legacies of prior constellations continue to exercise influence. Each constellation, then, is also a recombination of strands of previous formations. Thus, the imprint of Indic civilization in language, culture and religion has been lasting in the region. For instance, several Southeast Asian countries, also Muslim countries, continue to perform the Ramayana in many variations. Chinese influence and presence have endured over centuries. As seafaring continues, so does the mingling of peoples and cultures. The legacies of maritime empires and trade routes endure in notions such as Nusantara, and the role of seafaring peoples such as Bugis across the island world. The trading religions Buddhism and Islam have left lasting imprints.

Owing to its central and geostrategic location, seafaring and trading history, Southeast Asia is probably the world's most ethnically and culturally diverse and mixed region (Hefner 1997, 2001). Precolonial and colonial legacies remain in evidence in architecture and urban design, law (adat, customary law), administration, religion, customs and cuisine. Anti-communism and the Cold War have left the imprints of security states, security laws, a prominent role of armed forces, and so forth. Thus, Southeast Asian modernities are typically mélange modernities (Nederveen Pieterse 1998), more so and more complex than most other modernities. Capitalisms in the region are, likewise, bricolage capitalisms, uneven combinations and recombinations of diverse strands.

The nature and meaning of regional constellations change over time. The basic meaning of a regional constellation is a formation of salient historical cohesiveness – as during the era of the influence of Indic civilization. In addition, constellations refer to dominant political and economic formations that lend character to an epoch – as during the era of the maritime empires. As connectivity becomes increasingly dense and complex over time, inter-regional economies and the world economy play a greater part and formations take on more complex patterns – as during the age of commerce. Rulers and sultans at the time balanced the interests of short- and long-distance traders, of local farming communities that reorganized their production, as well as security concerns. At this stage, constellations became expansive opportunity structures in which external and internal forces and institutions interact, bringing challenges as well as opportunities. Each constellation, then, is a composite, a different mix of external forces and conditions, arising from trends in the region and the world economy, and internal agency and institutions.

During the second half of the twentieth century, dynamics that have affected Southeast Asia include, first, the Cold War and its geopolitical and ideological ramifications. Second, the worldwide trend of regionalization, a marked change in the general political profile of globalization. Third, with the shift from industrial mass production to flexible production has come the splicing up of production in global value chains (GVC) and increasing economic interweaving across regions.

The Cold War divided Southeast Asia into large ideologically profiled groupings, with the US attempting to impose its version of liberal democracy while other countries and China resisted American domination. With the Treaty of Rome (1956) that established the European Community (now the European Union) regionalism took on a global momentum. The Association of Southeast Asian Nations (ASEAN) was established in 1967. Five countries (Malaysia, Indonesia, Thailand, the Philippines and Singapore) charted a new course under the banner of ASEAN by upholding principles of nonalignment in a Zone of Peace, Freedom and Neutrality (ZOPFAN, 1971).

ASEAN has grown to a grouping comprising 10 member nations that for the first time unifies the entire region and has overcome the Cold War divide in the region. Thus, Southeast Asia as a category is contingent no more. With the establishment of the ASEAN Economic Community (AEC, 2015), the political economy of regional cooperation has moved to the foreground. With a population of 630 million and a combined GDP of over US$4 trillion,

ASEAN is an important trade partner of China, the US and the EU and is in sustained dialogue with Australia, Canada, India, New Zealand, Russia and other parties. ASEAN plus Three (Japan, Korea, China) is the cooperation framework of a major economic powerhouse.

The elimination of tariff barriers under the ASEAN Free Trade Area (AFTA, 1993) has contributed to the expansion of intraregional trade. Openness to trade and investment have helped to shape the economic significance of the region, although there are differences among countries and over time in the outlook on these variables. Inflows of foreign direct investment helped to progressively integrate countries in the region with global value chains (GVC), which is a defining feature of contemporary economic globalization. Southeast Asia has become an important source of intermediate goods in East Asia with intraregional trade growing over time.

Regionalism plays an important role in consolidating the economic significance of the region. Within the region, ASEAN is pushing forward its 'One Vision, One Identity, One Community'. State-led initiatives in ASEAN countries continue to deepen their economic integration. Although progress toward the AEC has been slow and laborious, the region inches its way forward to a regional economic grouping, which differs from the EU in substance and intent. The establishment of the AEC is a milestone and the ASEAN Vision 2025 signals a continuing drive toward establishing an economic community.

The US, Japan, the EU and China court ASEAN as the emerging power in Asia. The ASEAN-China Free Trade Agreement (ACFTA), China's first FTA with foreign trade partners, signed in 2002, has grown in importance. ACFTA is the world's largest free trade area in terms of population and the third largest in terms of GDP. The EU is resuming its stalled negotiations with ASEAN on a free trade agreement between the two regions. The US has abandoned its proposed Trans-Pacific Partnership (TPP) that included some ASEAN countries (2017). In its stead come intensified efforts to conclude the Regional Comprehensive Economic Partnership (RCEP) agreement, which will include China as well as India. Despite criticisms of ASEAN as a 'talk shop' and the 'long-winded and indecisive' 'ASEAN way', the efforts of trade partners to engage with ASEAN as an economic entity attest to ASEAN's evolution as a cohesive formation and to its strategic importance.

This volume focuses on two major recent constellations of Southeast Asia. The first is the period of broadly 1980–2000, the era of the rise of the Asian tigers, which the World Bank dubbed the 'East Asian miracle' (World Bank 1993). During this period, the middle four Southeast Asian countries, Malaysia, Thailand, Indonesia and the Philippines, showed high growth rates and the World Bank coined the term the 'Miracle Eight', grouping the four tiger economies (South Korea, Taiwan, Singapore, Hong Kong) and the middle four Southeast Asian economies together. In Malaysia, Prime Minister Mahathir adopted the 'Look East' policy in 1981. The period after 2000 to the present is marked by the rise of China.

Looking back, we can note the following. The rise of the tiger economies has continued and consolidated. They continue to be *the* major successes of the entire postwar epoch of development. Not just Southeast Asia but virtually all developing countries have been looking to Northeast Asia as guiding lights. The achievements of South Korea and Taiwan (leaving aside Singapore and Hong Kong as city-states) were threefold. They achieved advanced industrialization and developed country status with relatively egalitarian economies while also consolidating their democracies. Many assessments slated the middle-tier Southeast Asian countries, Thailand, Malaysia, Indonesia and the Philippines, for similar achievements. Financial media ranked them as high-growth emerging markets. Assessments of democracy viewed them as poised for achieving democratic reforms. However, by many accounts, Southeast Asian countries have not been able to match any of the three achievements of Northeast Asia – industrialization has been based on FDI and low wages, inequality remains high, and democracy remains work in progress (Studwell 2007, 2013; Chapters 1, 8, this volume). The question where Southeast Asia is headed is significant because it is part of rising Asia and is part of emerging economies, which have become drivers of the world economy (Nederveen Pieterse 2017).

Chapters in this volume shed light on the gap between Northeast and Southeast Asia from a variety of viewpoints and across several dimensions such as trade and industry, services and education policies, and institutions. Several chapters adopt a comparative development studies approach. Some scholars offer nuances and shy away from blanket assessments such as convergence or divergence of Northeast and Southeast Asia. Some seek to map and others also to explain the gap or to consider options that might bridge the gap.

Outline of the book

This volume is organized in three parts and around three problematics. The first problematic is the 'Miracle Eight' and the comparison of Southeast and Northeast Asia, which four chapters in Part I address. The second problematic arises from Part I – the 'Miracle Eight' has not materialized and, by many assessments, the main reason why tiger cubs have not become tigers is governance and institutions. The three chapters in Part II take up this key question. The third problematic is how the rise of China affects Southeast Asia and gives rise to a new regional constellation. The five chapters in Part III focus on relations between Southeast Asia and China.

Nederveen Pieterse's opening chapter in Part I sketches the historical background of oriental globalization and compares trends in Northeast and Southeast Asia in agriculture, industry, services, the state and political institutions.

Andrew Kam in Chapter 2 groups Northeast, Southeast Asia and China together as East Asia and 'Factory Asia', which is connected by regional value chains that are part of global value chains. Focusing on the trade patterns of the 'Factory Model', Kam discusses the dynamics of trade with a view to value added and technology upgrading and how countries try to diversify and upgrade their manufacturing activities in an effort to capture more added value in GVC. Although the findings of this study show that the 'Factory Asia' model still holds, it is slowly changing as different East Asian countries continue to upgrade at different rates. The gaps in the rates of upgrading are mainly attributed to differences in government policies and market competition. However, the dependency on foreign input remains an important part of high technology production in East Asian countries, hence the idea that East Asia is evolving from a 'factory' into a 'R&D hub' is still far from reality.

Fazal Rizvi in Chapter 3 engages with higher education in Southeast Asia, a prerequisite for training human capital to promote development. Higher education systems across Southeast Asia have expanded rapidly in the last two decades. Rizvi discusses the factors behind this expansion, such as growing student demand for postsecondary education and the widely held conviction that for nations to participate effectively in the global knowledge economy they need a highly skilled, technically proficient and globally oriented workforce. However, despite developing a range of strategies to both expand and transform their higher education systems, these have met with little success and have faced major obstacles as the development of a higher education space in Southeast Asia has been more difficult than policy makers have imagined.

Chapter 4 by Zawiah Yahya continues the questions raised in Chapter 3 with a focus on the rise and spread of English as a global language and how it affects the language policies and practices in the educational systems of East Asian countries. Focusing on four countries, China and Japan in Northeast Asia, and Malaysia and Thailand in Southeast Asia, the chapter examines how these countries have generally responded through changes in their language policies and practices, to the new linguistic realities that accompany the forces of globalization, thus enabling links between impact and response. While the chapter is comparative, it however does not make generalizations as changes in policies are country-specific and each country has its own distinct profile of political and educational systems, historical trajectories, ethnic population mix, English language environment, and contending native or national language demands.

A key question that arises from Part I is *why* the expectations for Southeast Asia have not been met. Chapters in Part II examine questions of institutions and governance, which may explain why mid-tier Southeast Asian countries have failed to meet the challenge of the Miracle Eight. The critical question of institutions is addressed in chapters on Malaysia and Thailand, which is meaningful because both have often been regarded as the strongest among the middle-tier Southeast Asian countries.

Chapter 5 by Terence Gomez and Elsa Lafaye de Micheaux discusses the varieties of capitalism and politics of enterprise development in Southeast Asia with Malaysia as a case study. Identifying both theoretical and empirical gaps in the literature on varieties of capitalism, the authors argue that theories based on Western or OECD experience and contexts are ill equipped to deal with power and state-business nexuses when the political system is not democratic in nature and ruling politicians distribute government-generated rents on a selective basis. Such practices have resulted in diverse business systems such as highly diversified conglomerates, state-owned companies and small- and medium-scale enterprises. Adopting the framework of regulation theory, this chapter unravels the implications of evolving state-business configurations for the political system and enterprise development.

Marc Saxer in Chapter 6 views the middle-income trap as, rather, a social transformation trap. He deals with the question of how to escape the transformation trap by taking a forward position – what does it take to build social consensus for sustainable development? Amidst social and political conflict, what is necessary to graduate from the middle-income trap may not be implementable politically because innovation-led growth requires a skilled workforce. The greatest challenge is to unleash the dynamic of creative destruction while maintaining political stability, which requires a social compromise between established and aspirational classes. Only this can generate the political stability needed to move up the value chain. According to Saxer, a progressive transformation project needs to lay the social foundation for sustainable development and the discourse needs to shift from communalist patronage and identity politics to social empowerment and economic development.

One of the case studies that underlies Saxer's argument is Thailand (where he was resident director of the Friedrich Ebert Foundation for a number of years). Tim Rackett in Chapter 7 also discusses Thailand (where he lived and taught for many years), as a case study of political factors that impede socio-economic development. While Thailand ranks as a regional economic success story, it faces multiple institutional failures: legal, constitutional and parliamentary along with a history of serial coups, military dictatorships and states of exception. Rackett argues that, in Thailand, the authoritarian tradition is the norm, not the exception.

Against this backdrop, we turn to Part III and the question how the growing role of China affects the equations. Does it add to the gap in East Asia, the gap between an advanced and highly industrialized North and a sputtering Southeast Asia, or does it mitigate the gap by generating new economic complementarities? Does it offer sputtering regimes a way out? Do China's initiatives such as Belt and Road, the Maritime Silk Road, the Silk Road Fund and the Asian Infrastructure Investment Bank light up Southeast Asia's economic horizons? Alternatively, does the gap also run *within* China, in terms of the quality of growth, wealth and income gaps, uncertain property laws and legitimacy of rule? The China dream is also work in progress (e.g. Guo *et al.* 2017).

How does this emerging constellation differ from the previous constellation of Southeast Asia? How does the ASEAN Economic Community engage the new challenges and opportunities? During the previous constellation of Southeast Asia, the mid-tier countries in the region were grouped together with Northeast Asia. Arguably, Southeast Asian countries have missed the boat, or have only partly been able to grasp the opportunities of this constellation. Now a new constellation is taking shape, driven by the rise of China and the question is what opportunities and challenges does this constellation pose? Will Southeast Asia be able to rise to the challenges this constellation poses and be able to grasp its opportunities, different challenges and opportunities for different parts of Southeast Asia? What if Southeast Asian countries miss the boat of this constellation, as they did during the previous one? If the opportunities of the previous constellation were missed because of weak institutions and governance and if, according to Part II, institutions and governance remain weak, the starting position is weak. Addressing this involves not just examining China's role in the region but also taking a new look at internal institutions and forces.

Part III focuses on relations between Southeast Asia and China. The argument of Chapter 1 was the Miracle Eight; Chapter 8 resumes this argument under the heading Goodbye Miracle Eight and resumes the question of institutions and governance. Chapter 8 by Nederveen Pieterse examines the differences between Northeast and Southeast Asia as regional pattern differences, which are historically rooted and embedded in social structures and institutions. Southeast Asian political systems include the world's longest ruling parties, rule by majority ethnocracies and elite capture of major institutions, often in combination with neoliberal business policies. Part of this is shifting economic complementarities. The rise of Northeast Asia took place as part of different geoeconomic constellations than the rise of Southeast Asia. The latter is now increasingly part of a China-centered regional economy, which presents a different set of development challenges.

In Chapter 9, Abdul Rahman Embong engages with one dimension of the changing regional formations, China's One Belt One Road (OBOR) megaproject and its relations with Southeast Asia. Rahman argues that China's OBOR, including the Maritime Silk Road, evokes not only a deep sense of history and civilizational romance, but a new hope for development and cooperation between China and her neighbors, including ASEAN. Given ASEAN's development gaps and its aspirations to build economic integration, China's Maritime Silk Road initiative is an opportunity that should not be missed by ASEAN countries, particularly Malaysia and Indonesia. Such positive perceptions make it easier for both China and ASEAN to connect the 'dots', although there are concerns about China's global ambitions and the need to maintain ASEAN's neutrality.

Siew Yean Tham in Chapter 10 compares Malaysia and China's shift from manufacturing to services by examining why the shift takes place, the role of policy in the shift, and the challenges and prospects of such a shift. Malaysia's shift occurred earlier than China's and was prompted by the failure of its manufacturing sector to deepen as it has not produced any world-class domestic technology firms. China's shift is more recent and is accompanied by ongoing upgrading in its manufacturing sector while some global domestic technology firms have emerged. Both countries used similar policies to drive this shift in response to domestic and external changes. It remains to be seen whether the shift to services can also bring about a shift to knowledge-intensive services as the current service sector development in both countries is still focused on labor-intensive services.

China's OBOR megaproject requires governance of trade and investments. China's early steps toward global governance seek to match international UN standards of inclusive and sustainable development (Cheng 2017). Chapter 11 by Sufian Jusoh takes up the question of governance in a discussion of economic diplomacy in ASEAN and China. His chapter compares the investment reforms in Myanmar and China, which are important trade and investment partners. Domestic political reform, ASEAN membership as well as the push to diversify sources of investment and the quest to be part of the international community contributed to investment policy reforms in Myanmar. China's reform in investment policy is driven by the need to address investors' concerns and to diversify types of investments. Myanmar's adoption of international and ASEAN investment policy standards may well affect the way investors from China conduct their businesses in Myanmar. Whether it also affects the economic relations and economic diplomacy practice between the two countries remains to be seen.

Rashila Ramli's chapter, the final chapter in the volume attempts to shift the perspective on the South China Sea from the dominant, much-talked about 'security' perspective to that of 'desecuritization' along with a political development perspective. The chapter maintains that while the security approach of overlapping claims assumes a conflict- and tension-ridden situation, the desecuritization perspective is more open-ended. As the basis for desecuritization, she adopts the 'Nusantara' approach. Such an approach will enable stakeholders to see different sets of opportunities besides risks, such as how China and ASEAN member states can narrow the gap in finding an agreeable mode of governing the regional commons as this can provide benefits for all states through negotiated plans for peace and joint development.

This volume fills a major lacuna in comparative development studies of Southeast and Northeast Asia and how, with the rise of China, the changing regional constellation affects the development of Southeast Asia. In the process it raises major questions.

References

Abu-Lughod, Janet L. 1989. *Before European Hegemony: The World-system* A.D. *1250–1350*. New York: Oxford University Press.

Benedict, Ruth. 1935. *Patterns of Culture*. London, Routledge and Kegan Paul.

Cheng, Dawei. 2017. One Belt One Road: China's trade governance. University of California, Santa Barbara, Mellichamp Global studies lecture.

Guo, Changgang, Debin Liu and Jan Nederveen Pieterse, eds. 2017 *China's Contingencies and Globalization*. London: Routledge.
Hefner, R.W., ed. 1997. *Market Cultures: Society and Morality in New Asian Capitalisms*. Boulder, CO: Westview.
Hefner, R.W., ed. 2001. *The Politics of Multiculturalism: Pluralism and Citizenship in Malaysia, Singapore, and Indonesia*. Honolulu: Hawaii University Press.
Hodos, Tamar, ed. 2017. *The Routledge Handbook of Archeology and Globalization*. London: Routledge.
Kratoska, P.H., R. Raben and H. Schulte Nordholt, eds. 2005. *Locating Southeast Asia: Geographies of Knowledge and Politics of Space*. Singapore: Singapore University Press.
Nederveen Pieterse, Jan. 1998. Hybrid modernities: mélange modernities in Asia. *Sociological Analysis* 1(3): 75–86.
Nederveen Pieterse, Jan. 2017. *Multipolar Globalization: Emerging Economies and Development*. London: Routledge.
Reid, Anthony. 1990. *Southeast Asia in the Age of Commerce, 1450–1680, Vol. 1*. New Haven: Yale University Press.
Reid, Anthony. 1995. *Southeast Asia in the Age of Commerce, 1450–1680, Vol. 2*. New Haven: Yale University Press.
Sien, Chia Lin and Sally K. Church, eds. 2012. *Zheng He and the Afro-Asian World*. Melaka, Melaka Museums Corporation.
Studwell, Joe. 2007. *Asian Godfathers: Money and Power in Hong Kong and Southeast Asia*. London: Profile Books.
Studwell, Joe. 2013. *How Asia Works*. London: Profile Books.

Part I

Southeast and Northeast Asia

1 What happened to the Miracle Eight?

Looking East in the twenty-first century

Jan Nederveen Pieterse

Consider the cityscapes of Seoul, Taipei, Bangkok, Kuala Lumpur, Jakarta, etc., and there seems to be little difference – corporate high rises, multilane traffic, traffic jams, high-modern facilities, transnational and signature architecture, advanced mass transit systems, bustling shopping streets, ritzy malls, international brands and banks, a mobile WiFi populace. The differences lie elsewhere. In Northeast Asia, per capita GDP is high and inequality is low while in Southeast Asia per capita GDP is low and inequality is high. Is this a temporary deviation, just a time lag, or is there a pattern of differences between Northeast and Southeast Asia? This is the central question.

Why is the question important and how should it be addressed?

All developing countries have been 'looking East' since the rise of the Asian tigers simply because, during decades of development, the tiger economies, especially South Korea and Taiwan, have been the most successful and accomplished. In the 1990s, the World Bank grouped the region's eight high-growth economies together under the heading of the 'East Asian Miracle'. In the Malaysian context the question resumes Mahathir's Look East perspective. The comparison is implied in the term 'tiger cubs' for Southeast Asian economies. Can would-be tigers become tigers? If Southeast Asian countries are to escape the 'middle-income trap' this question has policy relevance. A further appeal is that it concerns Asia–Asia (East–East) research, rather than the well-worn problematic of Orientalism, the western gaze, North–South relations, and so forth.

There is a considerable literature on both regions, which differs in emphasis. Literature on Northeast Asia (NEA) deals with the developmental state, NICs (newly industrialized countries), an East Asian model, gender, democracy and subsequent developments such as neoliberal trends in South Korea and Taiwan's industrial development and investments in south China. In Southeast Asia (SEA), early perspectives have often been culturalist, such as Asian values, Lee Kuan Yew's Confucian ethic and Mahathir's Melayu Bharu (New Malay). They echo Weber-in-reverse. According to Weber,

Confucianism hampers progress; according to the new Confucian ethic, it enables progress. Asian dependency thinkers have all along questioned the success of the tiger economies and have criticized fast-lane growth in China and the region (Bello 1992, 2013; Jomo 1999, 2001).

While both regions have been the subject of vast swaths of literature, literature that compares NEA and SEA is relatively sparse, with a slight uptick in the wake of the Asian crisis of 1997–1998. Several studies compare specific terrains (such as agriculture, corruption, Buddhism) but few take on a wide-ranging comparison (Booth 1999, 2002; Park 1997, Park 2000; Wu 2001; Perkins 2013). Of interest are two books by Joe Studwell, *Asian Godfathers: Money and Power in Hong Kong and Southeast Asia* (2007) and *How Asia Works* (2013) about Northeast Asia. When put side by side they offer a penetrating account of stark differences. If we compare the Northeast–Southeast Asia discussion with the interminable India–China debate, it has a much lower profile. Yet the comparison is important and meaningful not just within Asia but also with a view to the general debate on emerging economies – the leading economies in the twenty-first century. While they are often lumped together as emerging markets, or under the cheerful heading of 'rising Asia', they actually refer to quite different political economies.

Methodological considerations that guide this inquiry include the following.

- *Avoid presentism*: to avoid a short-term, episodic approach it is important to take into account the depth of the historical field, also with a view to capturing structural transformations in the *longue durée*. In addition, the problematic involves temporal disjunctures. Comparisons don't refer to outcomes but to processes so they are intrinsically dynamic. NEA is now no longer at the stage of the rising tigers, has entered different stages, including 'second modernity' and is facing the challenges of success. Options that were available to NEA countries at an earlier stage are now no longer open to SEA because dynamics of globalization have moved on. As Alexander Gerschenkron noted, it matters not just whether development occurs but also *when* it occurs, at which juncture in geoeconomic dynamics.
- *Avoid one-dimensionality*: previous discussions have often been biased toward particular perspectives or dimensions. Twenty-first century research should be multidimensional and wide-angle (while short of encyclopedic).
- *Avoid economism and culturalism*: an emphasis on institutions is constructive in that it bridges multiple dimensions; in addition, institutions play a central role in contemporary development studies (Rodrik 2007, Acemoglu and Robinson 2012).
- *Avoid in-built ideology*: to avoid that a comparison is biased by fixed assumptions, say about capitalism, a comparative capitalisms approach is helpful (cf. Lim *et al.* 2017). Paradigm consciousness should extend to the concepts and categories used.

This chapter addresses history by way of a brief review of oriental globalization and reflects on the geographical categories used. The discussion then turns to a sectoral comparison of trends in agriculture, industry and services in NEA and SEA. It follows from an institutional approach that the state and political institutions are a key part of the comparison. The closing section deals with China's effects in the region.

Oriental globalization, past and present

For 18 out of the past 20 centuries Asia was the main driver of the world economy, notably from 1000 to 1800 (Frank 1998; Pomeranz 2000; Hobson 2004). While South Asia and China were major forces in this constellation, so was Southeast Asia, particularly as a midpoint and center of maritime commerce and the spice trade (Gunn 2003). According to Abu-Lughod, 'Venice survived because Egypt survived, sustained by the persistence of the southern route to Asia'. She quotes the sixteenth century Portuguese writer Tomé Pires: 'Whoever is lord of Malacca has his hands on the throat of Venice' (Abu-Lughod 1989, 215, 291). This places Southeast Asia center stage in the transformations of the 'long sixteenth century'. Anthony Reid observes that in Southeast Asia after 1400,

> Whole communities devoted themselves to cultivating pepper, clove, cotton, sugar, and benzoin [a resin used for making incense], and became dependent on the international market for their livelihood … The peak of the boom in Southeast Asia's trade occurred during the period 1580–1630, as a result of the exceptional demand from China, Japan, India, and Europe. Price levels were high throughout the world during this period, largely as a result of unprecedented exports of silver from the Americas and Japan, and competition for Southeast Asia's valuable products was intense.
>
> (Reid 1992, p. 467)

During Southeast Asia's 'age of commerce' Melaka was 'a Southeast Asian entrepôt par excellence' (Reid 1997, p. 63). Pires and others described it as a city larger than the Iberian cities. The motivation of the Portuguese in annexing Melaka included a wide assessment:

> if they were only to take Malacca out of the hands of the Moors, Cairo and Mecca would soon be entirely ruined and Venice would then be able to obtain no spices except what her merchants might buy in Portugal.
>
> (Ting 1999, p. 45, n. 65)

Venice at the time held the monopoly of the spice trade in the Mediterranean. Traders in Lisbon then cornered the spice trade, until the expulsion of the Jews, when the trade moved to the Low Countries.

A related variable is the combination of the Atlantic and Pacific exchanges. According to the economists Flynn and Giraldez (2006, p. 244), 'The birth of globalization occurred in 1571, the year that Manila was founded as a Spanish entrepôt connecting Asia and the Americas.'

As occidental globalization took the lead from circa 1800, Asia's role as driver of the world economy receded. Asia's comeback occurred gradually from the late nineteenth century onward; the significant episodes are familiar and include the Meiji Restoration in Japan (1868) and among postwar developments, decolonization, the Bandung conference (1955), the establishment of ASEAN (1967), Japan's 'economic miracle', the rise of the Asian Tiger economies, China's reform (1978) and the rise of Southeast Asian economies, along with ideas of the 'Pacific century' and the 'Asian century', cut short by the Asian crisis (1997–1998) and IMF influence.

Contingent categories

The categories Southeast Asia and Northeast Asia are 'contingent devices'. Southeast Asia is a recent notion: 'The concept of Southeast Asia evolved from the need of Europe, America and Japan to deal collectively with a set of territories and peoples that felt no particular identification with one another' (Kratoska *et al.* 2005, p. 11; Sutherland 2005). According to McVey (2005, p. 309), 'Southeast Asia is neither a region of the heart nor of ambition'.

It is often noted that Southeast Asia as a category is a modern notion and is wedded to the paradigm of modernizing states (i.e. nation building and economic growth) (McVey 2005; Owen 2005). In fact there are 'many Southeast Asias' which intersperse in layers of precolonial, colonial and postcolonial cosmopolitanisms, in uneven assemblages of 'networks and transitions' (Sutherland 2005), of commerce and diasporas, of state regionalism (ASEAN with modernizing states as core components), of market regionalism (ASEAN repurposed for economic cooperation), global connectivity, consumer and knowledge culture.

East Asia in a geographical sense comprises China, Japan, North and South Korea and a broader definition includes Taiwan, Mongolia and the Russian Far Northeast. East Asia in the 'East Asian model' and the World Bank's 'East Asian miracle' refers mainly to Japan, South Korea and Taiwan but at times also includes Southeast Asia (Nederveen Pieterse and Kim 2012). *Northeast Asia* is a term of recent vintage, used in economic research and World Bank categorizations. It implies a distinction with Southeast Asia. Then 'East Asia' widens into an umbrella category comprising a South and North, and stands in contrast to South Asia and West Asia; all of which have also been referred to as the Far East (i.e. further than the Near East and Middle East), obviously in relation to Europe. While there is great depth to the historical field in the region, it holds different meanings in Northeast Asia than in Southeast Asia (Arrighi *et al.* 2003; Cohen 2000).

East Asia and Southeast Asia are recognized in literature and databases so these notions are meaningful as tools to analyze development trajectories

– with provisos. Since East Asia often refers to both Northeast and Southeast Asia, this chapter uses the term Northeast Asia. And since Japan belongs to an earlier wave of industrialization, in this discussion Northeast Asia mostly refers to South Korea and Taiwan, and China is viewed as a separate case.

In terms of GDP per capita, Southeast Asia is tiered, with Singapore and Brunei in the first tier, Malaysia, Thailand, Indonesia, the Philippines in the second, and Vietnam, Cambodia, Laos and Myanmar in the third. In this discussion 'Southeast Asia' mostly refers to second tier countries, the ASEAN-4. Mainland SEA further differs from the archipelagos, Indonesia and the Philippines. SEA has been strongly influenced by Hindu and Sanskrit culture of the subcontinent (Coedès 1996) while Vietnam ('Indo-China') has long been exposed to Chinese influence.

Some discussions refer to the ASEAN-5, meaning Singapore, Malaysia, Thailand, Indonesia and the Philippines. However, Singapore is a city state, like Hong Kong. Both function as Free Trade Zones (FTZs), entrepôt ports, intermediaries in globalization dynamics, offshore financial hubs and tax havens for neighboring states. This includes a Monaco effect of low tax, low regulation havens, hospitable to tycoons and the rich. Theirs are the highest living standards and the highest Gini index in the region (besides China), 0.45 and up, and they host the richest Asians, such as Li Ka-shing. Crony capitalism is institutionalized with property as a key variable along with trade licenses and resource monopolies (Seagrave 1996, Studwell 2007). In terms of development profile they are outliers. They don't face the core problematic of modernity that all countries in the region face – how to integrate the peasant majority. Brunei is an oil-rich sultanate, like the Gulf emirates. Yet, although or because they are outliers they exercise influence in the region.

Singapore is like a 'gated community' in the region, a dreamscape for Asia's middle class, and is described as 'a nice piece of real estate in a lousy neighbourhood' (Wu 2001, p. 74). It comes with apartheid for unskilled migrant workers, similar to the Gulf emirates (Nederveen Pieterse and Khondker 2010). Singapore is a hybrid of a strong developmental state with a liberal market ideology. Hong Kong with a history of labor and social activism acts as a counterpoint to China's party rule. Hong Kong is also a media and film capital. With the rise (comeback) of Guangdong and the Pearl River delta, and financial services in Shanghai (Pudong) and Shenzhen, Hong Kong's importance to China has receded and the 'one state two systems' structure may come under pressure, although the larger question of Taiwan looms on the horizon.

Sectoral comparison of Northeast and Southeast Asia

This comparison of trends in NEA and SEA considers agriculture, industry, services and state institutions. Table 1.1 offers general comparative data on NEA and SEA. Of note are the Gini indices for the different countries. Those

Table 1.1 Northeast Asia and Southeast Asia comparative data[1]

	South Korea	Taiwan	Japan
Population (million)	50.22	23.4	127.3
GDP (US$)	1.305 (trillion)	474 (billion)	4.902 (trillion)
GDP per capita (US$)	25,977	31,900 (2008)	38,492
HDI (Rank)	15/187	n.a.	17/187
Literacy rate (%)	97.9	96.1	99.0
Gini index	0.31 (2011)	0.34	0.376 (2008)
CPI (level)	107.67		100.4

	Malaysia	Thailand	Indonesia	Philippines
Population (million)	29.72	67.01	249.9	98.39
GDP (billion US$)	312.4	387.3	868.3	272.0
GDP per capita (US$)	10,514	5,799	3,475	2,765
HDI (Rank)	62/187	89/187	108/187	117/187
Literacy rate (%)	93.1	93.5	92.8	95.4
Gini index	0.42 (2014)	0.39 (2010)	0.41 (2011)	0.43 (2012)
CPI (level)	107.2	109.28	116.91	111.20

of NEA approximate the Gini indices of Northwest Europe (in the high 0.20s) while those of SEA are in a much higher league.

Table 1.2 offers general data on third-tier Southeast Asian countries. In relation to these countries the second-tier countries look good, so this is a soft comparison while the comparison with Northeast Asia is a tough comparison.

Table 1.2 Cambodia, Vietnam, Laos and Myanmar (2013)

	Cambodia	Vietnam	Laos	Myanmar
Population (million)	15.14	89.71	6.77	53.26
GDP (trillion/billion US$)	15.25	171.4	11.14	n.a.
GDP per capita (US$)	1,008	1,911	1,646	n.a.
HDI (rank)	136/187	121/187	139/187	150/187
Literacy rate (%)	74	94	72.7	93 (2012)
Gini index	31.8 (2011)	35.6 (2012)	36.2 (2012)	n.a.
Urban population (%)	20	32	36	33
Urbanization rate (%)	2.13	3.03	4.41	2.49
Work in agriculture (%)	51	47	n.a.	n.a.
Productivity per ha (kg/ha)	3,097	5,430	4,046	3,551
Agriculture as share GDP	35.56	18.38	27.98	48.35
Industry as share GDP	24.25	38.31	36.21	16.21
Services as share GDP	40.19	43.31	35.81	35.44
Work in industry (%) (M, F)	19 M	25 M	n.a.	n.a.
	18 F	17 F (2012)	n.a.	n.a.
Consumption as share GDP	82 (2011)	63	69 (2012)	n.a.
Workforce in services (%)	27.3	31 (2012)	20.6	23 (2001)

Agriculture

Japan, South Korea and Taiwan all underwent postwar land reform with major ramifications. Land reform boosted agricultural productivity and, accompanied by broad educational and fiscal reform, instilled a fundamental egalitarianism in social structures.

According to Anne Booth, the agricultural development that occurred in much of SEA since the 1960s has been less egalitarian than in NEA, notably Taiwan,

> because it has taken place in the context of an unreformed or partially reformed agrarian structure, where the distribution of land and incomes are more skewed, the labour intensity of agricultural production is lower, and linkages between on-farm and off-farm income growth are less pronounced … no country in Southeast Asia has pursued an integrated rural development policy.
>
> (Booth 2002, p. 41)

Much of SEA has been marked by large landholdings and low agricultural productivity, generating little surplus to fund industrialization. Aristocratic strata or their functional equivalents continue to influence local and national politics (as was the case in Latin America until fairly recently). 'Land reform programmes in Southeast Asia have been partial in coverage and hesitant in execution' (Booth 2002, p. 43) with the Philippines as a notorious case of continuing landlordism. In Thailand,

> About 90% of the total privately owned land is owned by 10% of the population or about 6 million people … while 90% of the total population is owners of land of less than 1 rai (0.16 hectare). For Bangkok, the ratio between land owned by the top and bottom 50 owners is astronomically high at 291,608. These result in the problems of insufficient farmland for the poor in agricultural sector and unutilized land held speculatively by the rich. Since there is neither inheritance tax nor wealth-based land tax, the cost of holding unexploited land plots is almost non-existent and the severity of the problem tends to escalate. There is now a debate on a need to have land and other property taxes in order to stem further wealth concentration. But there is strong resistance from property owners, many of whom are MPs and senators.
>
> (Phongpaichit and Benyaapikul 2012, p. 22)

Phongpaichit and Benyaapikul note, 'In Malaysia under the New Economic Policy after 1969, a land distribution project managed to redistribute public land (about 5 acres) to more than 500,000 landless households to grow oil palm' (Phongpaichit and Benyaapikul 2012, p. 22). In this regard Bumiputra affirmative action policies have paid off.

Modernization of the countryside (cash crops, plantations, mechanization, timber, mining) has been regionally diverse and uneven. The former socialist countries of Vietnam and China reflect different itineraries with major land distribution, intensive agriculture and higher agricultural productivity than in SEA.[2]

A comparison of agricultural productivity in NEA and SEA shows a distinct pattern: intensive agriculture in NEA with high productivity per hectare (double the yield of most of SEA); larger landholdings, extensive agriculture (plantations, swidden cultivation) and lower productivity per hectare in SEA (Table 1.3). An outlier is Indonesia with much higher yields per hectare, which is mostly due to Java where high population density has long given rise to intensive cultivation.[3]

Industry

Japan and South Korea invested in heavy industry, following the German model. In Japan this included a military industry and navy. Investment in heavy industry meant long-term state investment and support, in short the developmental state (cf. Johnson 1982; Woo-Cumings 1999; Chang 2003). As Studwell observes, industrial policy fostered *competition* among enterprises and 'weeding out losers' (rather than 'picking winners'), *export discipline*, with government subsidies directly tied to exports, and financial prudence. Critical copying and, over time, technological upgrading and indigenous innovation have generated international brands (such as Samsung, LG, Hyundai, Acer, Asus), which all involve major and growing investments in R&D.

In SEA, in contrast, assembly industries that are part of global value networks (GVN) predominate alongside light domestic industries (such as garments, agro processing). The 'Singapore model' of industrial development led by FDI shaped trends in the region. Singapore chose FDI because of its small

Table 1.3 Agriculture in Northeast Asia and middle-tier Southeast Asia

	South Korea	*Taiwan*	*Japan*	
Urban population (%)	82.0	78.0 (2011)	92.0	
Urbanization rate (%)	0.71	n.a.	0.57	
Work in agriculture (%)	7	5.2	4	
Productivity per ha (kg/ha)	6,489	n.a.	6,105	
Agriculture as share GDP (%)	2.34	n.a.	1.22	
	Malaysia	*Thailand*	*Indonesia*	*Philippines*
Urban population (%)	73	48	52	45
Urbanization rate (%)	2.49	1.6	2.45	2.16
Work in agriculture (%)	13	40	35	32
Productivity per ha (kg/ha)	3,834	3,223	5,085	3,532
Agriculture as share GDP	9.33	11.98	14.43	11.84

size while a capacious and capable state sought to integrate FDI with policies of skills development and tech transfer.[4] In Malaysia,

> Successive Malaysian governments chose to mobilize foreign, rather than domestic, capital … this choice was probably seen as a way of limiting further capital accumulation among wealthier Malaysian Chinese, as it was they who would have been the primary beneficiaries of the state's mobilization of domestic capital for industrialization purposes. Thus the use of foreign capital represented a way of avoiding politically sensitive ties between the state and local Chinese capital, as well as a means of 'crowding out' the latter's influence on the Malaysian economy.
>
> (Henderson and Phillips 2007, p. 83)

FDI was concentrated in the electronics sector. Move the clock forward 40 years and Malaysia's industrialization has stalled. Rather than moving up the ladder of productivity, the industry remains locked in low-skill, low value-added activities, which is further reinforced by the large scale import of migrant workers: 'Rather than seeing a decisive increase in the demand for technical and engineering personnel, the Malaysian electronics industry has become increasing dependent on the import of lower skilled migrant workers' (largely from Indonesia) (Henderson and Phillips 2007, p. 91). While high-tech exports are a sizeable part of Malaysia (56.9 percent) and Thailand's manufacturing exports (31.1 percent, 2001), these countries' R&D expenditures are a mere 0.5 percent and 0.1 percent respectively.[5] Henderson and Phillips find that after 35 years of specializing in electronics Malaysia is by and large no further than low-value added assembly industry, even in the most advanced electronics industry in Penang. Recent research by Malaysian economists confirms this trend and notes an ongoing decline in the country's exports of electronic parts and components (Tham *et al.* 2014). Malaysia also invested in heavy industry, iron, steel and automobiles, but state support was crisscrossed by ethnic and party political considerations. In Malaysia the share of manufacturing in GDP stood at 27 percent in 1990, 37 percent in 2000 and 27.5 percent in 2011 (services 58.6 percent, agriculture 7.3 percent, mining 6.3 percent and construction 3.2 percent; see Table 1.4).

Thailand's specialization in automotive industry has not paid off either. Phongpaichit and Benyaapikul (2012) find Thailand 'Locked in the middle-income trap'. 'As Thailand has been in the middle-income trap for more than 20 years since 1987 … the country faces a challenge in sustaining growth and continuing to benefit from globalization'. Both countries, the most industrially advanced of SEA, now face growing competition from China. For Malaysia,

> This limited upgrading in Malaysian electronics means that it is now exposed to the competitive pressure of China's export 'machine' … by 1990, China had exceeded Malaysia in terms of all FDI inflows, capturing

Table 1.4 Industrial sector in Northeast and Southeast Asia

	South Korea	*Taiwan*	*Japan*
Industry as share of GDP	38.55	n.a.	25.64
Services as share of GDP	59.11	n.a.	73.15
Work in industry (%) (M, F)	20 M	n.a	33 M
	13 F (2010)	n.a.	15 F (2010)
Consumption share GDP (%)	52	n.a	61
Workforce in services (%)	69.4	n.a.	69.8
Exports/share of GDP (%)	53.92		14.73
Tertiary education enrolment (%)	98 (2012)		61 (2012)

	Malaysia	*Thailand*	*Indonesia*	*Philippines*
Industry as share GDP (%)	40.61	42.55	45.69	31.09
Work in industry (%) (M, F)	33 M	23 M	25 M	19 M
	20 F	18 F	16 F	10 F
Services as share GDP (%)	50.07	45.47	39.87	57.07
Workforce in services (%)	53.5	48.2	47.9	53
Wages as share of GPD (%)	32.3			
Consumption share GDP (%)	51	54	59	73
Exports share of GDP (%)	81.87	73.57	23.74	27.92
Tertiary education enrolment	36 (2012)	51	32	28 (2009)

> 9 per cent of the world total, as against Malaysia's 7 per cent. By 2002, China's share of FDI inflows had increased to 33 per cent while Malaysia's share had dropped to a mere 2 per cent.
>
> (Henderson and Phillips 2007, p. 95)

In Thailand,

> There is also a concern about Thailand's relatively low technological capability in industry. Increased demand from China has been a positive factor in recent years, but already China's market is racing ahead, with consumers developing more sophisticated consumption patterns ... Thailand may not be able to supply the increasingly sophisticated markets in China because Thailand is facing a middle-income trap, a situation where its technological development is too low to develop new products and move up the value chains.
>
> (Phongpaichit and Benyaapikul 2012, p. 11)

For political reasons state policies often fostered costly, inefficient monopolies rather than competition and did not apply export discipline. In Indonesia, experiments such as aerospace ('an expensive failure'; Perkins 2013) and automobiles have foundered. One near-exception, Malaysia's Proton Saga, survives, barely, thanks to a joint venture with Mitsubishi and is sold only in neighboring countries. Despite ample 'technological populism' in the region

(Mee 2012), R&D, science and innovation are at a much lower level in SEA than in NEA (Marginson 2014), which is reflected in tertiary education enrolment data. 'Attempts by government agencies to promote technology transfer cannot succeed in the absence of a strong commitment to education, especially at the post-primary and vocational levels' (Booth 1999, p. 315). A common observation is that no SEA economy has generated internationally known industrial brands.

Kunio (1998) characterizes SEA industry as 'technology-less industrialization'. Since there is no technology transfer to speak of and decision making is in the hands of multinational companies (MNCs) it may be viewed as dependent industrialization.

Look closer, however, and there *is* a difference in cityscapes: in SEA cities the salient corporate logos are of international brands and banks (and hotels), rather than national industries (besides Petronas, commodities and retail conglomerates). Compare the skyline of Seoul with the neon logos of Samsung, SK, LG and Daewoo towering over the city. So while both NEA and mid-tier SEA are factory economies, they are different kinds of factory economies: national ownership, international brands and high tech in NEA, foreign ownership and low tech in SEA. If we were to compare the value added and profits of manufacturing accruing domestically or to overseas firms in NEA and SEA (aggregate data are hard to get), the outcome would likely be to the significant disadvantage of SEA countries.

Export-oriented industrial economies often practice wage repression in order to sustain competitiveness (as in Germany, China, Japan), and also in SEA. In Malaysia, the share of wages in GDP has been a low 32.3 percent (the share of corporate and business profits is 64.8 percent and the government share is 2.9 percent; averages during 2009–2013; Wong 2014). Also, 'Thailand may be classified in the "low wage" policy approach' with a 'low and declining share of wages in factor income' (Phongpaichit and Benyaapikul 2012, p. 19).

The low-wage regime matches methods of labor control (with dormitories and curfews; Kelly 2002). Yet, the share of private consumption in GDP in NE and SEA is broadly at the same level (with the Philippines at 73 percent, even higher than the US' high rate of 72 percent). This is to a large extent enabled by private debt, which is made possible by low interest rates (similar to in the US). (In the Philippines remittances also weigh in.)

The situation in SEA industry generates a twofold problem. First, industrial production has become more competitive and less profitable worldwide. With accelerated globalization, the industrial sector has become increasingly dynamic with tight margins so the era of industrial export-led growth is coming to a close, except in high-end brand and original equipment industries. China's competition in manufacturing adds pressure. Second, wage repression limits the domestic market, which is counterproductive at a time when export-led growth is drawing to a close.

Services

In NEA countries, industry as a share of GDP is shrinking, the service sector is growing and these countries are headed toward post-industrialism, where western countries have gone before. Besides logistics and finance, services in South Korea include design, marketing, entertainment and culture (Hallyu, K-wave). In South Asia, India's software and back office services represent a major niche.

Services are the largest economic sector in SEA (58.6 percent of GDP in Malaysia, 2011). With manufacturing mostly left to FDI, much wealth in SEA has gone into property and finance, or is invested outward. The FIRE (finance, insurance, real estate) sector is large in SEA. Malaysia developed a substantial financial sector and stock exchange and ranks third in the world's Islamic banking assets with a 10 percent share.[6]

Most services are non-tradable so the sector is not dynamic, productivity is low and the inflow of labor is large so wages are low (McJobs), except in the upper echelons, which is a worldwide trend. In SEA the informal sector is large. With industry winding down as a driver of growth, what is the potential of service specializations for development? In SEA, urbanization still has considerable growth ahead, unlike in NEA, and will be a major driver of demand for services.[7] Yet education and human capital pose barriers to higher service sector productivity.

In NEA, banks have generally been under strict state regulation (reminiscent of the German tradition of public service banking). South Korea and Taiwan are rated investment grade in international finance. In SEA, banks have often been subject to elite capture and state patronage has been driven by political considerations rather than long-term horizons (Studwell 2007). As the saying goes, 'the best way to rob a bank is to own one'.

States

Northeast Asian societies show greater cohesion and states show greater continuity over time compared with those of Southeast Asia. Arguably, traditions of Confucian bureaucracy and meritocracy contribute to dedication to public service in Japan, Korea, Taiwan and China, to the developmental state and the idea of the intelligent state (Connors 1997). Here 'Sinic circle' arguments are relevant (Cohen 2000; Kang 2010; Katzenstein 2012).

Marginson discusses the 'post-Confucian heritage zone' in relation to science and higher education and notes 'four common features that have facilitated the take-off: the comprehensive Sinic state, Confucian education in the home, an effective response to Western modernization, and economic growth sufficient to pay for educational infrastructure and research' (Marginson 2014, p. 91). This affects science systems in the region.

SEA political cultures have been markedly different. SEA states have often been analyzed from a modernization point of view and Weber's notion of patrimonialism (ruler or patron-centric economic regulation) echoes in many accounts. This approach views SEA societies as premodern holdovers with traits resembling European feudalism, so modernity in the region is a mix of patrimonial and modern traits. According to Wim Wertheim (1993, p. 79),

> What distinguishes the patron-client relationships in a 'new state' from their counterparts in a 'feudal' one, either colonial or pre-colonial, is the integration of these followings within formal organizations at a supralocal or national level, such as political parties or all kinds of unions.

Marc Saxer views 'transformation societies' as configurations with political institutions based on rural holdovers of patronage and kinship that are out of sync with a complex pluralistic economy. In such societies corruption both lubricates transition (by coopting new groups into the political system) and slows it down by eroding legitimacy (Saxer 2014, p. 3).

The SEA states have been historically fundamentally different from European feudalism. States such as Srivijaya, Melaka, Ayutthaya were maritime trading kingdoms or empires in which rule was based on the control of trade and duties from trade were the main source of revenue. Unlike feudal Europe they were urban, not rural, and port cities (such as Palembang, Malacca, Makassar, Aceh, Penang, Ayutthaya, Patani) played a key role. War played a significant part but they were trading formations, not military formations like Europe's castle system. They have much more in common with the Mediterranean world of maritime trade (such as the Levant trade of Renaissance Europe) than with rural medieval Europe. The central task of rulers was balancing competition (rival trade networks) and cooperation (with groups representing diverse trade networks) while keeping conquerors at bay. The task of rulers was to shelter and benefit from trade, from through-flow, rather than from production or manufacture. Abu-Lughod characterized Srivijaya as a 'comprador state'. Cash crop production played a significant part and was linked to the trading networks. The trading religions of Buddhism and Islam exercised a major influence in the region along with migrants and diasporas such as the Hadrami. To paraphrase Anthony King's (1995) ironical observation, they were postmodern formations (heterogeneous, multicultural, hybrid, outward-looking) long before Europe became modern.

The NEA societies were state-centric and Confucianism is a state-centric outlook. Already from the second century BCE onward, during the Han Empire, China sidelined feudalism and the aristocracy so there was no elite independent of the state. The Confucian bureaucracy was founded on competitive written examinations, a system that was finely honed by the time of Song China, and was established in Europe only in the nineteenth century. In contrast, the SEA states were ruler-centric and the relationship between rulers and subjects was hierarchical. In much of SEA, ascribed status and the influence of traditional elites still looms large, such as the sultans as heads of states in Malaysia. Thus, the SEA states were historically different *both* from feudal Europe and from state-centric NEA.

According to Park,

> Southeast Asian countries do not have the strong tradition of a powerful and capable indigenous bureaucracy as did Japan and later Korea. The state could thus not play a dominant role in national economic development in Southeast Asian nations as it did in Northeast Asia even if it were willing to do so, for the simple reason that it was less able to do so … Therefore, they relied to a greater extent on market forces to dictate the evolution of their economies.
>
> (Park 2000, pp. 237, 252)

Thailand is a case in point: 'Thailand has never had an active industrial policy. Thailand's lively and influential business sector operates under what is arguably the most laissez-faire business environment in Asia outside Hong Kong' (Park 2000, p. 240; cf. Phongpaichit and Benyaapikul 2012).

Contemporary SEA states have been variously described 'as "corporate-paternalist", "neo-patrimonial", "quasi-democratic", "soft-authoritarian", "repressive-responsive" or generally "authoritarian but developmentalist" states' (Saravanamuttu and Loh Kok Wah 2004, p. 363). They combine liberal market economies with pervasive patron–client relations along with strategic groups and business lobbies. Thompson (2010, p. 179) defines strategic groups as 'social networks connected by a common interest in the expropriation of key resources (not only material) and capable of collective action'. Where institutions are weak, social networks fill the gap. The role of money politics and crony capitalism in the region has been extensively discussed (Jomo 2001). It comes through in marked differences in the Corruption Perception Index in NE and SEA (Sang-hwan 2004). Between the older literature on money politics in SEA and now, there has been little change in variables and perspectives.[8]

According to Saravanamuttu and Loh Kok Wah (2004, p. 263), 'the Southeast Asian developmental state … thrived on KKN (*korupsi*, *kolusi* and *nepotisme*)'. However, this is a contradiction in terms; it isn't possible to have a developmental state *and* KKN because the two institutions collide. Traditional elites (sultans, landlords, priyayi) colluding with strategic groups (business lobbies, ethnic Chinese entrepreneurs, compradors, the military) through formal political institutions, yields alignments that don't add up to the kind of state autonomy and policy competence a developmental state requires. It may be possible to adopt the rhetoric of the developmental state but not to deliver the product. Thus, the region is marked by a structural mismatch between ambitions and institutions. The region's developmental aspirations cannot be realized with the existing political institutions. Elites derive legitimacy from their developmental claims and objectives, here as elsewhere, but institutions and politics are out of step with development agendas. Mahathir's administration is a case in point. Lest we fall back on culturalist interpretations (Confucianism works, look at Singapore), this requires institutional analysis. In each SEA country there are different reasons why developmental states don't or barely function.

It is a general understanding that 'the "flying geese" of Pacific Asia were developmental dictatorships' (Thompson 2010, p. 185). In NEA, this applies in the past tense (although democracy remains a major discussion in the region) and development has been successful by many measures; in SEA, rates of growth have been high but development has been limited and democracy is quasi or pseudo, fragile or fledgling. The specifics of KKN vary by country, such as ethnocracy in Malaysia, the 'network monarchy' in Thailand, landlordism in the Philippines, military rule and its legacies in Indonesia and Myanmar, etc.

In Thailand, conservative elites have been clustered around the monarchy (sheltered by the archaic *lèse majesté* law) and the military with support of much of the urban middle class. According to a report,

> It helps that the bureaucracy and most of the wealthiest Thai families back the military government. These rich Chinese-Thai families, along with the Thai elites, control much of the country's assets. In the course of the 20th century a small group courtiers and businessmen have played their cards right with the monarchy and managed to join them. The result is that 0.1% of Thais own half the nation's assets, a concentration of wealth that makes America's mind-bogglingly unequal wealth distribution (where 0.1% of citizens own 22%) look like a socialist dream come true.[9]

In Malaysia ethnic cronyism plays a key role. Nativist redress in Malaysia institutionalized ethnic cronyism in political institutions, produced 'Bumiputra conglomerates' and a Malay rentier class in the economy, and permeates education and civil society (Gomez 1994; Woon 2011; Milner *et al.* 2014). A *Financial Times* report notes that wealthy Malaysians are investing in Europe and the UK rather than in local companies and that 'the one factor business people say holds back economic development are "pro-Bumi" policies' (Bender 2013).

Malaysia's National Culture Congress convened in 1971 set forth the following platform:

> 1) The National Culture must be based on the indigenous culture of this region. 2) Suitable elements from the other cultures can be accepted as part of National Culture. 3) Islam is an important component in molding the National Culture.
>
> (Ishimatsu 2014, p. 81)

In 2017, the key elements of the ruling party's platform are no different: Malayness, Islam and the monarchy.

China effects

In the twenty-first century we enter an era of 'globalization with Chinese characteristics' (Henderson *et al.* 2013). Between Mahathir looking East in 1981 and looking East now, what has changed is that China has replaced Japan. Mahathir's East Asia Economic Caucus, proposed in 1990 didn't materialize because Japan resisted the exclusion of western countries. Now several projects of regional cooperation and 'new Silk Roads' are ongoing and 'China effects' crosscut several of them. Institutions that bridge North and Southeast Asia are ASEAN plus Three, the ASEAN Economic Community and FTAs with ASEAN, the Asian Development Bank, the Chiang Mai Initiative, China's Asian Infrastructure Investment Bank, Silk Roads projects, the FTA of the Asia-Pacific, and US-backed APEC and Trans Pacific Trade Partnership (TTP). These initiatives involve diverse centers of influence and types of capitalism. To explore their significance it is appropriate to discuss how China fits into the NE and SEA problematic.

China straddles and displays features of both North and Southeast Asia, which loosely overlaps with China's internal north–south divide, the Yangtze River. In terms of GDP per capita, HDI rank, Gini index and urbanization rate China broadly parallels middle-tier Southeast Asia (see Table 1.5). Ethnic diversity in Yunnan and western border-zones parallels conditions in neighboring SEA. Chinese diasporas crisscross Asia and have exercised a major influence in SEA. South China matches features of SEA with assembly industries led by FDI (the 'Singapore model'), massive investments by ethnic Chinese enterprises and tycoons in Special Economic Zones (since Deng Xiaoping), most of which are family-owned enterprises.

At the same time, in terms of agriculture (land reform, high productivity), industry (long-term state support, export-oriented growth), finance

Table 1.5 China data (2013)

Population (billion)	1.357
GDP (trillion US$)	9.240
GDP per capita (US$)	6,807
HDI (rank)	91/187
Literacy rate (%)	95.1
Gini index	42.1 (2010), 47.0 (2013)
Urban population (%)	53
Urbanization rate (%)	2.85
Workforce in agriculture (%)	35
Productivity per ha (kg/ha)	5,934
Agriculture as share of GDP (%)	10.01
Industry as share of GDP (%)	43.89
Services as share of GDP (%)	46.09
Workforce in industry (%) (M, F)	n.a.
	n.a.
Consumption as share of GDP (%)	34
Workforce in services (%)	36.1

(macroeconomic targeting) and state institutions (quasi-Confucian bureaucracy), many Chinese trends and institutions parallel those of NEA. China's strong emphasis on science, innovation and tertiary education, long-term investments in Science and Industrial Parks (with strategic emphases on nanotech, biotech, aerospace and integrated circuits) parallels trends in South Korea and Taiwan. Major Chinese companies and SOEs now seek to emulate South Korea's chaebol, to 'go global' and become 'new champions'.

China's economic coordination has been termed market Leninism, a socialist developmental state, socialism with Chinese characteristics, market socialism, capi-communism, Sino-capitalism, state capitalism, power-elite capitalism, party-state neoliberalism, an idiosyncratic coordinated market economy ('nearer to France than to the US'), capitalism beyond categorization, capitalism-with-no-name – the literature counts no less than 17 contending labels (Peck and Zhang 2013, p. 367). However, for a nation that comprises a fifth of humanity should there be a single label? Why not rather recognize the coexistence and interspersion of multiple and contending capitalisms? Hybrid China comprises three different strands of capitalism. SOEs are the largest sector; second are family-owned SMEs that practice 'network capitalism', similar to ethnic Chinese-owned SMEs in SEA; the third strand is the public–private corporations of local governments, which are termed 'clan capitalism' (Redding and Witt 2010; Nederveen Pieterse 2014b).

The Chinese state has been termed polymorphous and multi-organizational and as 'moving in several, contradictory directions at the same time' (Peck and Zhang 2013, p. 378). China's central state institutions are crosscut by decentralization and local government power. China faces many major contingencies and is undergoing multiple major transitions (Roach 2009; Chi 2010).

As China is plural, so are its outward effects. Its multi-pronged effects range across the state and SOEs in infrastructure, financial and aid initiatives, which overlap with but are not identical to geopolitical forays of China's security state; the local government corporates that vie for market niches across the world and compete with one another; and the 'network capitalism' of family-owned SMEs, which is also termed guanxi transnationalism (Crawford 2000, Beh 2008, Wang and Lin 2008). China effects vary with the international institutional setting; where norms are strong and institutions are dense, China adjusts (Reilly 2012; Gu *et al.* 2014).

In the twenty-first century, China has begun to shift its export-led model of growth to an investment and domestic-demand led growth model. The 'harmonious society' platform (2003) involved major infrastructure investments inland, changes in labor law and improvements in social security, followed by massive stimulus spending in the wake of the 2008 crisis. Infrastructure investment has been occurring at an unprecedented scale in China, with variable benefits depending on the design of infrastructure. 'In just two years – 2011 and 2012 – China produced more cement than the US did in the whole of the 20th century' (Anderlini 2014). This is part of China's economic rebalancing, part of putting its foreign currency reserves ($3 trillion in

US dollar holdings alone) to use, and part of 'globalization with Chinese characteristics'.

China is exporting its investment-led growth model in loans and infrastructure development in Latin America and Africa, in the BRICS' New Development Bank and Contingency Reserve Arrangement and in the Asia Infrastructure Investment Bank (all established in 2014). China's new initiatives include the major One Belt One Road (OBOR) program (discussed in Chapters 9 and 10). In SEA, this includes plans for a high-speed rail from Yunnan via Laos, Thailand and Malaysia to Singapore, along with projects of resuming the Maritime Silk Road, from Guangzhou to Indonesia and beyond. Japan competes with China in infrastructure and bullet train development in India and SEA. Chinese plans for new Silk Roads and fast-trains to Central Asia, Europe and SEA will alter economic horizons, boost trade opportunities for SMEs, and attract FDI. It breaks with regional center–periphery and south–south relations. Erstwhile peripheries (such as Xinjiang in western China) become pivotal locations in new cross linkages.

As China is investing in rising Asia, how should SEA engage these developments? China's overall effects in SEA broadly parallel those in Latin America and Africa, in brief: winners in comparative advantage are commodities and energy exporters and losers are exporters of low-end manufactures who stand to lose also in third markets (Beeson 2010) – *unless* they meet China's challenge by moving up the ladder of technology, improving productivity and speed-to-market, which among others Mexico, South Africa, Kenya and Tunisia have been able to do. Thus, China effects are (a) diverse yet with an overall momentum; (b) boost growth that may come at a cost of deindustrialization and resource depletion; (c) are a challenge that requires agency rather simply an impact; and (d) should be viewed dynamically over time.

Conclusion

In sum, there is a pattern of difference between Northeast and Southeast Asia in agriculture, industry, and state institutions. Two dynamics landed SEA in the group of the Miracle Eight – growth and industrialization. Both have been in question for some time. Growth is no longer the main lode star and navigation has moved on (in China it is called 'GDPism'). With the rise of emerging economies growth is more widely shared and now the leading question, also in Asia, is the quality of growth – is growth sustainable, is it inclusive and broad-based, does it bring wellbeing? (Nederveen Pieterse 2014a).

Growth in SEA was initially based on commodities exports (such as tin, rubber, palm oil, cocoa, timber and petrol in Malaysia). Next, the inflow of FDI in industry maintained above-average growth rates. But just as there is growth and growth, there is industry and industry. For instance, in the US there is a significant difference between the old industries of the Northeast

(Fordist, unionized, high wages) and the industrial investments in the South and Southwest, the sunbelt (flexible production, low taxes, low wages, no unions), which I have termed 'Dixie capitalism' (Nederveen Pieterse 2004), a form of plantation capitalism with industrial technology. Most FDI in SEA, participating in global value networks (GVN) with low-value added assembly production, belongs to the latter category and doesn't have much future. Where next is growth going to come from? In Malaysia, 'Islamic finance' and 'Islamic economics' are among the narratives of redemption, along with innovation. China also features as an economic dreamscape, amid mixed reports. When countries such as Malaysia and Indonesia perform their usual balancing acts of the USA, Japan and China, they should take into account the development models that these entail. The Anglo-American liberal market economy approach relies on market forces while the coordinated and state-led market economies of NEA and China are fundamentally different. While the twenty-first century comeback of oriental globalization opens new horizons, major challenges lie ahead.

What are the implications of the differences between NEA and SEA outlined in this chapter? First, the differences are regional pattern differences, not merely differences among countries. Second, they are to a significant degree historically rooted and embedded in social structures and institutions. Thus, the comparison cannot be taken in a mechanical fashion but rather in a signal and alert fashion. While the differences are ultimately political in nature in the sense that they can be changed by political action, this isn't a simple matter of social engineering.

What SEA countries need to do to move beyond the middle income level includes, in brief, (a) land reform to curb large landholdings and increase agricultural productivity; (b) fiscal reform toward progressive taxes, and (c) overhaul of the industrial model. In each SEA country there are different reasons why such measures aren't likely to be adopted (Bello 2015). Land reform has been on the agenda in the Philippines for decades but hasn't been implemented. In Thailand where the uprising of 'red shirts' from the agricultural Northeast has been countered by military rule aligned with the monarchy, it isn't likely to be adopted. In Malaysia, likewise, the monarchy and the sultans are central political forces. In Indonesia and Myanmar the military are major landholders. Thus, agricultural reform is blocked by holdovers of feudalism, or of conservative Cold War modernization, or combinations of both.

Overhaul of the industrial model would entail gradually reducing reliance on FDI; negotiating better terms with MNCs, including tech transfer and joint ventures; providing incentives for domestic capital to invest in domestic industries, and establishing science and industrial parks to foster niche industries and startups. At a time when industry has become increasingly competitive and countries experience 'premature deindustrialization', these are not easy options. Meanwhile, the political reasons why industrial policy in SEA hasn't worked out (such as UMNO rule in Malaysia) have not changed over the years.

The ongoing economic cooperation of ASEAN plus Three (China, Japan, South Korea) is more likely to institutionalize existing differences than to provide a structural way forward for Southeast Asia (the same would apply to ASEAN plus Six). Cooperation with China comes with economic and political asymmetries.

If political forces and elites in Southeast Asia are not able to turn economic models around, the likely course is muddling through (i.e. the status quo), which will gradually lead to a cul-de-sac of stagnation at a low level of development. Large countries such as China and India can attempt to climb out of the middle income level by 'buying brands' and technology (Tata bought Land Rover and Jaguar; Lenovo bought ThinkPad; Geely bought Volvo, etc.). Such options are not open to firms in Southeast Asia. For the majority of the population in Southeast Asia, the middle-income level still represents an improvement of living standards in comparison with the past generation, but this sense of relative achievement will not last long. Chapter 9 takes this analysis further.

Notes

1 Sources of Tables 1–6 are: http://data.worldbank.org/country (accessed on 23 October 2014). http://data.worldbank.org/indicator/NY.GDP.PCAP.CD (accessed on 23 October 2014). http://hdr.undp.org/en/countries (accessed on 23 October 2014). www.cia.gov/library/publications/the-world-factbook/fields/2103.html (accessed 23 October 2014). http://data.worldbank.org/indicator/SE.ADT.LITR.ZS (accessed on 23 October 2014). http://data.worldbank.org/indicator/SI.POV.GINI (accessed on 23 October 2014). http://data.worldbank.org/indicator/SP.URB.TOTL.IN.ZS (accessed on 23 October 2014). www.cia.gov/library/publications/the-world-factbook/fields/2212.html (accessed 23 October 2014). http://data.worldbank.org/indicator/SL.AGR.EMPL.ZS?page=2andorder=wbapi_data_value_2009%20wbapi_data_value%20wbapi_data_value-firstandsort=asc (accessed on 23 October 2014). http://data.worldbank.org/indicator/AG.YLD.CREL.KG (accessed on 23 October 2014). www.quandl.com/c/economics/agriculture-share-of-gdp-by-country (accessed on 25 October 2014). www.quandl.com/c/economics/industry-share-of-gdp-by-country (accessed on 25 October 2014). www.quandl.com/c/economics/services-share-of-gdp-by-country (accessed on 25 October 2014). http://data.worldbank.org/indicator/SL.IND.EMPL.MA.ZS (accessed on 23 October 2014). http://data.worldbank.org/indicator/SL.IND.EMPL.FE.ZS (accessed on 23 October 2014). http://data.worldbank.org/indicator/NE.CON.PETC.ZS (accessed on 23 October 2014). www.cia.gov/library/publications/the-world-factbook/fields/2048.html (accessed 23 October 2014).

2 Booth notes 'Only in Vietnam has land reform created a more egalitarian land distribution than prevailed in the colonial era … and in recent decades [Vietnam] had a faster growth of per capita agricultural output than other countries in the region' (Booth 2002, p. 49; cf. Khondker 2011).

3 See Geertz's (1963) classic study of agricultural involution in Java.

4 Cf. Connors (1997), Mahiznan (1999), Park (2000).

5 See Table 1.2 Technology indicators for selected East and Southeast Asian Countries, in Henderson and Phillips (2007, p. 90).

6 In 2012, Iran accounted for 43 percent of the world's Islamic banking assets, with Saudi Arabia (12 percent) and Malaysia (10 percent) ranking second and third. 'Islamic finance: Big interest, no interest' (*The Economist* 13 September 2014, p. 79).

7 McKinsey Insight, Michael Zink, The keys to succeeding in ASEAN, October 2014.
8 See, for example, Hewison *et al.* (1993), Gomez (1994, 2014), Jomo (1995, 2001) and Jomo and Hui (2014).
9 'Thailand's political future: Changing of the garb', *The Economist* 2 October 2014.

References

Abu-Lughod, Janet L. 1989. *Before European Hegemony: The World-system A.D. 1250–1350.* New York: Oxford University Press.

Acemoglu, Daron and James A Robinson. 2012. *Why Nations Fail: The Origins of Power, Prosperity and Poverty.* New York: Crown.

Anderlini, J. 2014. Housing slowdown a 'major risk' to China. *Financial Times* 26 August: 20.

Arrighi, G., T. Hamashita and M. Selden, eds. 2003. *The Resurgence of East Asia: 500, 150 and 50 Year Perspectives.* New York: Routledge.

Beeson, Mark. 2010. Asymmetrical regionalism: China, Southeast Asia and uneven development. *East Asia* 27: 329–343.

Beh, Loo See. 2008. Developmental state and Chinese capitalism: Competition and collaboration. In Emile Kok-Kheng Yeoh and Joanne Hoi-Lee Loh, eds. *China in the World: Contemporary Issues and Perspectives.* Kuala Lumpur, University of Malaya, Institute of China Studies, 185–209.

Bello, Walden. 1992. *People and Power in the Pacific.* London: Pluto/Food First.

Bello, Walden. 2013. *Capitalism's Last Stand? Deglobalization in the Age of Austerity.* London: Zed.

Bello, Walden. 2015. The left in power. *The Nation*, April, 112–115.

Bender, Yuri. 2013. Asia's secret millionaires. *FT.Com/Wealth*, Winter: 31–33.

Booth, Anne. 1999. Initial conditions and miraculous growth: Why is South East Asia different from Taiwan and South Korea? *World Development* 27(2): 301–321.

Booth, Anne. 2002. Rethinking the East Asian Development model. *ASEAN Economic Bulletin* 19(1): 40–51.

Chang, Ha-Joon. 2003. *Globalisation, Economic Development and the Role of the State.* London: Zed Books.

Chi, Fulin, ed. 2010. *Change of China's Development Models at the Crossroads.* Beijing: China Intercontinental Press.

Coedès, G. 1996. *The Indianized States of South-East Asia.* Honolulu: University of Hawaii Press (orig. 1964).

Cohen, Warren I. 2000. *East Asia at the Center: Four Thousand Years of Engagement with the World.* New York: Columbia University Press.

Connors, M. 1997. *The Race to the Intelligent State: Charting the Global Information Economy in the 21st Century.* Oxford: Capstone.

Crawford, Darryl. 2000. Chinese capitalism: Cultures, the Southeast Asian region and economic globalization. *Third World Quarterly* 21(1): 69–86.

Flynn, D.O. and A. Giraldez. 2006. Globalization began in 1571. In B.K. Gills and W.R. Thompson, eds. *Globalization and Global History.* London, Routledge, 232–247.

Frank, A.G. 1998. *ReOrient: Global Economy in the Asian Age.* Berkeley: University of California Press.

Geertz, C. 1963. *Agricultural Involution: The Processes of Ecological Change in Indonesia.* Berkeley: University of California Press.

Gomez, E.T. 1994. *Political Business: Corporate Involvement of Malaysian Political Parties.* Townsville: James Cook and University of North Queensland.
Gomez, E.T. 2014. Malaysia's political economy: Ownership and control of the corporate sector. In Sophie Lemière, ed. *Misplaced Democracy: Malaysian Politics and People.* Petaling Jaya: Strategic Information and Research Development Centre, 245–282.
Gu, Jing *et al.* 2014. *Understanding China's Approaches to International Development.* IDS Policy Briefing, Issue 75.
Gunn, G. C. 2003. *First Globalization: The Eurasian Exchange, 1500–1800.* Lanham, MD: Rowman and Littlefield.
Henderson J. and R. Phillips. 2007. Unintended consequences: Social policy, state institutions and the 'stalling' of the Malaysian industrialization project. *Economy and Society* 36(1): 78–102.
Henderson, J., R. Appelbaum and S.Y. Ho. 2013. Globalization with Chinese characteristics: Externalization, dynamics and transformation. *Development and Change* 44(6): 1221–1253.
Hewison, K., R. Robison and G. Rodan, eds. 1993. *Southeast Asia in the 1990s: Authoritarianism, Democracy and Capitalism.* St Leonards, NSW Australia: Allen and Unwin.
Hobson, John M. 2004. *The Eastern Origins of Western Civilization.* Cambridge: Cambridge University Press.
Ishimatsu, Noriko. 2014. Shifting phases of the art scene in Malaysia and Thailand: Comparing colonized and non-colonized countries. In *Engage! Public Intellectuals Transforming Society.* Bangkok: Chulalongkorn University and Nippon Foundation, 78–87.
Johnson, C. 1982. *MITI and the Japanese Miracle.* Stanford, CA: Stanford University Press.
Jomo, K.S, ed. 1995. *Privatizing Malaysia: Rents, Rhetoric, Realities.* Boulder, CO: Westview.
Jomo, K.S., ed. 1999. *Tigers in Trouble.* London: Zed Books.
Jomo, K.S., ed. 2001. *The Malaysian Eclipse: Economic Crisis and Recovery.* London: Zed Books.
Jomo, K.S. and Wee Chong Hui. 2014. *Malaysia@50: Economic Development, Distribution, Disparities.* Petaling Jaya: Strategic Information and Research Development Centre.
Kang, David C. 2010. Civilization and state formation in the shadow of China. In Peter J. Katzenstein, ed. *Civilizations in World Politics: Plural and Pluralist Perspectives.* London: Routledge, 91–113.
Katzenstein, Peter J., ed. 2012. *Sinicization and the Rise of China.* New York: Routledge.
Kelly, Philip F. 2002. Spaces of labour control: Comparative perspectives from Southeast Asia. *Transactions of Institute of British Geographers NS* 27: 395–411.
King, A.D. 1995. The times and spaces of modernity or who needs postmodernism? In M. Featherstone, S. Lash and R. Robertson, eds. *Global Modernities.* London: Sage, 108–123.
Kratoska, P.H., R. Raben and H. Schulte Nordholt, eds. 2005. Locating Southeast Asia. In P.H. Kratoska, R. Raben and H. Schulte Nordholt, eds. *Locating Southeast Asia: Geographies of Knowledge and Politics of Space.* Singapore: Singapore University Press, 1–19.

Kunio, Yoshihara. 1998. *The Rise of Ersatz Capitalism in South-East Asia*. Singapore: Oxford University Press.

Lee, Kuan Yew. 2000. *From Third World to First: The Singapore Story, 1965–2000*. New York: HarperCollins.

Lim, Hyun-chin, Suk-man Hwang and Jan Nederveen Pieterse, eds. 2017. *Capitalism in Asia*. Seoul: Seoul National University Press.

Mahiznan, A. 1999. Smart cities: The Singapore case. *Cities* 16(1): 13–18.

Marginson, Simon. 2014. Emerging higher education in the post-Confucian heritage zone. In Daniel Araya and Peter Marber, eds. *Higher Education in the Global Age: Policy, Practice and Promise in Emerging Societies*. New York: Routledge, 89–112.

McVey, Ruth. 2005. Afterword: In praise of Coelacanth's cousin. In P.H. Kratoska, R. Raben and H. Schulte Nordholt, eds. *Locating Southeast Asia: Geographies of Knowledge and Politics of Space*. Singapore: Singapore University Press, 308–319.

Mee, Wendy. 2012. Technology, culture and modernity in Malaysia. In W. Mee and J. Kahn, eds. *Questioning Modernity in Indonesia and Malaysia*. Singapore: NUS Press, 225–246.

Milner, Anthony, Abdul Rahman Embong and Tham Siew Yean, eds. 2014. *Transforming Malaysia: Dominant and Competing Paradigms*. Singapore: ISEAS Publishing.

Nederveen Pieterse, J. 2004. *Globalization or Empire?* New York: Routledge.

Nederveen Pieterse, J. 2014a. Asia rising: Welcome to the multipolar world. In H-C. Lim, W. Schäfer, and S-M. Hwang, eds. *Global Challenges in Asia: New Developmental Models and Regional Community Building*. Seoul: Seoul National University Press, 31–62.

Nederveen Pieterse, J. 2014b. Rethinking modernity and capitalism: Add context and stir. *Sociopedia Colloquium* (e-journal).

Nederveen Pieterse, J. 2015. Hybrid China. In *Globalization and Culture: Global Mélange*, 3rd ed. Lanham, MD: Rowman and Littlefield.

Nederveen Pieterse, J. and Habibul H. Khondker, eds. 2010. *Twenty-first Century Globalization: Perspectives from the Gulf*. Abu Dhabi: Zayed University Press.

Nederveen Pieterse, J. and Jongtae Kim, eds. 2012 *Globalization and Development in East Asia*. New York: Routledge.

Owen, N.G., ed. 2005. *The Emergence of Modern Southeast Asia: A New History*. Honolulu: University of Hawaii Press.

Park, Donghyun. 2000. The dichotomy between Northeast Asian capitalism and Southeast Asian capitalism. *Journal of the Asia Pacific Economy* 5(3): 234–254.

Park, Sang-Chul. 1997. The transformation of the South Korean economy and international economic development in East and Southeast Asia. *International Planning Studies* 2(2): 241–255.

Peck, J. and J. Zhang. 2013. A variety of capitalism … with Chinese characteristics? *Journal of Economic Geography* 13(3): 357–396.

Perkins, Dwight H. 2013. *East Asian Development: Foundations and Strategies*. Cambridge, MA: Harvard University Press.

Phongpaichit, Pasuk and Pornthep Benyaapikul. 2012. *Locked in the Middle-Income Trap: Thailand's Economy between Resilience and Future Challenges*. Bangkok: Friedrich Ebert Stiftung.

Pomeranz, K. 2000. *The Great Divergence: China, Europe and the Making of the Modern World Economy*. Princeton, NJ: Princeton University Press.

Redding, G. and M.A. Witt. 2010. *The Future of Chinese Capitalism: Choices and Chances*. Oxford, UK: Oxford University Press.

Reid, Anthony. 1992. Economic and social change, *c.*1400–1800. In N. Tarling, ed. *The Cambridge History of Southeast Asia, from Early Times to c.1800, Vol. 1.* Cambridge, UK: Cambridge University Press, 460–507.
Reid, Anthony, ed. 1997. *The Last Stand of Asian Autonomies.* Hampshire: Macmillan.
Reilly, James. 2012. A norm-taker or a norm-maker? Chinese aid in Southeast Asia. *Journal of Contemporary China* 21(73): 71–91.
Roach, Stephen S. 2009. *The Next Asia: Opportunities and Challenges for a New Globalization.* Hoboken, NJ: Wiley.
Rodrik, Dani. 20.07. *One Economics, Many Recipes.* Princeton, NJ: Princeton University Press.
Sang-hwan, Lee. 2004. An empirical comparison of corruption in Northeast Asia. *East Asian Review* 16(1): 97–109.
Saravanamuttu, Johan and Francis Loh Kok Wah. 2004. Development and democracy in Southeast Asia. In Abdul Rahman Embong, ed. *Globalization, Culture and Inequalities.* Selangor: Penerbit Universiti Kebangsaan Malaysia, 352–376.
Saxer, Marc. 2014. *Fighting Corruption in Transformation Societies.* Bangkok: Friedrich Ebert Stiftung.
Seagrave, S. 1996. *Lords of the Rim.* London: Corgi Books.
Studwell, Joe. 2007. *Asian Godfathers: Money and Power in Hong Kong and Southeast Asia.* London: Profile Books.
Studwell, Joe. 2013. *How Asia Works.* London: Profile.
Sutherland, Heather. 2005. Contingent devices. In P.H. Kratoska, R. Raben and H. Schulte Nordholt, eds. *Locating Southeast Asia: Geographies of Knowledge and Politics of Space.* Singapore: Singapore University Press, 20–59.
Tham, Siew Yean, Andrew Kam Jia Yi and Nor I. Abdul Aziz. 2014. *Moving up the Value Chain in ICT: ASEAN's Trade with China.* University of Malaya conference paper.
Thompson, Mark. 2010. The dialectic of 'good governance' and democracy in Southeast Asia. In H-C. Lim, W. Schäfer and S-M. Hwang, eds. *New Asias: Global Futures of World Regions.* Seoul: Seoul National University Press, 175–208.
Ting, Helen. 1999. *A Historico-systemic Analysis of the Development Process in Malaya between 1400–1940.* University of Louvain la Neuve, Thesis.
Wang, Wangbo and Zhiqing Lin. 2008. Investment in China: The role of Southeast Asian Chinese businessmen. In Emile Kok-Kheng Yeoh and Joanne Hoi-Lee Loh, eds. *China in the World: Contemporary Issues and Perspectives.* Kuala Lumpur: University of Malaya, Institute of China Studies, 147–160.
Wertheim, W.F. 1993. *Comparative Essays on Asia and the West.* Amsterdam: VU University Press.
Wong, Pauline. 2014. Malaysia's income gap problem. *The Heat* (Kuala Lumpur), 27 September – 3 October, 20.
Woo-Cumings, Meredith. 1999. *The Developmental State.* Ithaca, NY: Cornell University Press.
Woon, Toh Kin. 2011. Coping with disintegration in a fragmented society: The case of Malaysia. In V. Somboon, ed. *Coping with Disintegration: From the Perspectives of Local to Global.* Bangkok: Chula Global Network, Chulalongkorn University, 9–30.
Wu, Friedrich. 2001. The emerging Northeast-Southeast Asia divide and policy implications. *World Economics* 2(1): 169–118.

2 Dynamics of trade in *Factory Asia*

Value added

Andrew Jia Yi Kam

Introduction

East Asia's trade[1] has shown remarkable changes over the past five decades. It has emerged as a manufacturing powerhouse, with Japan becoming one of the main global exporters of electronics and consumer goods since the 1960s. Following the flying-geese industrialization pattern,[2] Taiwan, Hong Kong, South Korea and Singapore (or, Newly Industrialized Economies, NIEs) appeared as manufacturing hubs due to their consistent focus on export-oriented policies from the 1970s onwards. In the 1990s, the Association of Southeast Asian Nations (ASEAN) countries launched the ASEAN Free Trade Area (AFTA) to foster greater competitiveness in the region. In tandem with these developments, China initiated economic reforms in the late 1970s to gradually open up its economy. Aided by the development of production networks, shades of 'supply in East, consume in West' slowly surfaced in the late 1980s (Choi and Rhee 2014). By 1990, emerging economies in East Asia had moved from being peripheral players to major hubs of global trade (IMF 2012). When the global trading system formally integrated China in 2001 through its accession into the World Trade Organization (WTO), the production and trade patterns of East Asia slowly solidified into a well-known moniker called *Factory Asia*.

Factory Asia represents a model where factories in different Asian economies are linked through regional production networks, producing parts and components that are then assembled and exported as finished products to advanced economies (Ando and Kimura 2005). This model came to the fore owing to the extensive international fragmentation of production through investment and trade in parts and components within regional and global value chains (GVC). The advancement in production, communication and transportation technology, and reduction in service link costs have increased cross-border dispersions of vertically integrated production processes. Outsourcing and distributing production processes to different locations consequently opened up opportunities for exploiting gains from specialization brought about by cost competitiveness. However, some studies have pointed out that the distribution of gains in terms of value added through intra-industry trade is uneven across countries that are engaged in GVC (Banga, 2014).

The international fragmentation of production in East Asia has witnessed a growth in the use of foreign intermediaries, and off-shoring of production processes means that a finished export good may contain a high percentage of foreign value added content, with the exporting country capturing only a small percentage of value added in the network.[3] Several studies have shown that developing host countries often continue to remain as export platforms over time for low-value added, labor-intensive goods unlike industrialized countries with high technology that are able to extract more gains in terms of the domestic value added (DVA) in their exports from their participation in GVC. For example, Oikawa (2008) argues that it is the multinationals (MNCs) that decide on the extent of value added that is to be contributed by host economies. Likewise, Koopman and Wei (2012) and Powers (2012) indicate that only advanced countries have substantial DVA in their gross exports, while Newly Industrialized Economies (NIEs) and emerging Asian countries have the lowest DVA in the world.

The debate therefore, points to the manner in which participation in GVC can help to increase the DVA in their gross exports across countries. Banga (2014) argues that in order to reap the gains from participating in GVC, a country's policy focus should not only emphasize linking its economy with GVC alone. Instead, it should be designed to raise forward linkages,[4] that is, by exporting DVA content to other countries rather than just enhancing exports in gross terms. As GVC become increasingly complex, the question arises to what extent a country participates in GVC through its exports and what are its DVA gains from this participation. This question is timely in light of recent claims that trade patterns in *Factory Asia* are changing in terms of trade composition and technological sophistication. Helble and Ngiang (2014) observe a shift from parts and components trade to trade in finished goods. Hence, they claim that East Asia is evolving from a 'global factory' into a 'global mall' – whereby East Asia is itself becoming an important consumption destination for exports of finished consumer goods rather than just as an export platform in a 'global factory'. For example, improvements in the quality of ASEAN ICT exports to China and an upward shift in ICT value chain of ASEAN countries (Tham *et al.* 2016) further implies that *Factory Asia* may no longer be just an outsourcing location that merely manufactures goods at competitive prices for exports to advanced economies.

This chapter, therefore, investigates the distribution of DVA gains between countries in the changing landscape of *Factory Asia*. The aftermath of the two economic crises (1997 and 2007) have weakened demands from advanced countries, and together with the internal erosion of comparative factor price advantage, the notion of substituting foreign input for domestic inputs embodied in their exports is becoming one of developing nations' policy goals in 'moving up the value chain' (Baldwin 2014). Specifically, this chapter seeks to identify patterns in DVA in the manufacturing exports from key participants in the *Factory Asia* model. It does this by examining the DVA content of exports and its technological sophistication over time to identify changes in the trade patterns in key *Factory Asia* economies. The chapter is organized as follows: first it summarizes the current literature and highlights salient features of the *Factory Asia* model, followed by the methodology and variables used to measure trade flows and gains in DVA in this chapter. The next section examines patterns in key economies in *Factory Asia*'s trade and technological structure while the conclusion includes policy implications.

Salient features in *Factory Asia* model

Global Value Chains (GVC)

The mechanics of international production and distribution networks can be summarized using three theories (Ando and Kimura, 2005). First is the 'fragmentation theory', where advancements in communications/transportation technology and reductions in service link costs have enabled production to be spliced up to different fragments. Second is the internalization theory, which addresses firms' decisions on product specialization (internalization decision), and where these products should be manufactured (locational decision). Finally, the combined networks of these fragmented processes are held together by the agglomeration theory through industrial clustering and locational advantages of production bases. Thus, with the combination of these theories, specialized tasks are created across borders linking suppliers, manufacturers and distributors into integrated production networks that are also known as GVC.

Factory Asia is a part of GVC, with China positioned as the core factory that imports intermediate goods from production bases around the world (namely, Japan, Korea, and Southeast Asia) before processing and exporting them as finished goods to the European Union and the USA.[5] The exchanges in input and output of goods depend on the trade specialization of countries based on a comparative advantage framework. For example, wage differentials in the internalization theory suggest that multinationals (MNCs) relocate labor-intensive production segments to locations with lower wages retaining capital-intensive production segments at home. Rising labor costs in Japan and the NIEs pushed MNCs to seek opportunities to exploit gains from specialization by relocating production tasks to locations with a comparative advantage of cheaper labor such as China and Southeast Asia (SEA). However, as explained earlier, this trend is changing. China and, to some extent, certain SEA countries have not remained in the low-wage production activities and have instead moved up GVC by upgrading their domestic industrial structure.

Industrial upgrading in GVC

Industrial upgrading is a process whereby an economy improves its capabilities and capacities and moves into more profitable and/or technologically sophisticated capital- and skill-intensive economic niches along a GVC (Gereffi 1999). Studies often point to this movement using the U-shaped 'smiling curve' logic (Shih 1996). In an illustrated graph with value-added measured on the vertical axis, and GVC activities (or stages of production) along the horizontal axis, the curve shows different value-added potential of different segments along a value chain. The curve implies that both ends of the value chain indicate higher value added content of a product compared with the middle.[6] Therefore, a country's position in a value chain is an issue of concern to many policy makers. Emerging economies are often stuck at the bottom of the curve, creating or capturing little value added from their manufacturing activities. A movement up the value chain requires an upgrade in the stages of production or a shift in manufacturing activities from low to high value-added activities. This includes *process* upgrading through increased efficiency in GVC activities; *product* upgrading, namely switching from low to high value-added products in similar activities; *functional* upgrading, namely moving to higher-value activities along a value chain; and *chain* upgrading, which is a shift to an entirely new value chain (Kaplinsky and Morris, 2002; and OECD, 2013).

Functional upgrading is commonly interpreted as 'moving up the value chain', which is a shift beyond manufacturing and standardized services activities to the tails of the 'smiling curve' (OECD 2015). Extraction of value involves increasing DVA, such as adding new activities to existing activities along the GVC. Using this definition, domestic industries[7] gain more value-added in their trade in GVC when they upgrade their capabilities to substitute previously imported with domestically produced inputs for the production and manufacture of export goods. This may imply an upgrade in skills and product sophistication to supply higher-quality inputs. For example, Tham *et al.* (2016) argue that improvements in quality will imply that goods exported from ASEAN countries are moving up the information and communications technology (ICT) value chain, thereby enabling ASEAN economies to improve their trade competitiveness. In the *Factory Asia* model, industrial upgrading involves moving to more technologically sophisticated and higher value-added niches in GVC to create new sources of competitive advantage in trade. It includes cross-border *inter-industry* upgrading; a movement from domestic backward-to-forward linkage activities (Banga 2014), and shifting from bilateral (or asymmetrical) intraregional production and trade to a more fully developed intraregional division of labor in production in the value chain (Gereffi, 1999).

New measurements in trade patterns, data and methodology

A value chain consists of a sequence of functional activities needed in the process of creating values across different industries and/or countries. As the distribution of value-added gains are uneven across a GVC, the increasing fragmentation of production has challenged the standard interpretation of trade data. Traditional total trade measures only record finished goods crossing borders in gross values. Increasing flows of trade in intermediate goods along a value chain may cause problems in 'double counting' and therefore the country of final producer appears to capture most of the value of goods that are traded. A high percentage of foreign value added and a corresponding small percentage of DVA from the exporting country raises the question as to who has truly benefited from trade in GVC. Therefore, indicators based solely on gross export data may misrepresent the real specialization of countries, meaning they may merely reflect that a country is specialized in final assembly, with a high import on intermediate inputs, but may add only marginal or no value to the exported good. This misrepresentation in specialization of production challenges the notion of a country's trade competitiveness as well. Price and cost competitiveness hinge on the costs of imported components, and high-technology exports no longer imply a corresponding increase in the technological capabilities in the exporting country as the upstream economies keep the technology within.

To mitigate this 'double-counting' problem, the WTO and the Organization for Economic Cooperation and Development (OECD) have developed a Trade in Value-added (TiVa) database.[8] Using intercountry and world input–output tables, goods are classified according to their use as intermediate or final demand goods, and they are compiled based on their value added by source countries. The methodology and construction of matrices will not be discussed here but are well documented (OECD 2013) for the years 1995, 2005 and the latest available year of 2011.[9] This study focuses only on two commodity groups, namely intermediate and consumption/final goods, to represent the composition of trade in GVC, since the TiVA database does not include value-added data for capital goods.[10] The measure of DVA is the value of a domestically produced good net of its direct and indirect imported input. This means that a decline in DVA in the production of a good is also an indication of an increase in the use of foreign inputs in its production. DVA is also a better representation of the contribution of exports to a country because its increase implies an increase in the contribution of local economic activities[11] to the export good of a country. At the country level, this provides a clearer picture on which countries within *Factory Asia* have gained from trade in GVC.

In line with the objectives of this study, the chapter also investigates the DVA in industries of different technological levels since an economy's technology level is reflected in part in the technology sophistication of its exports

(Kuroiwa, 2014). An increase in DVA of high-technology exports implies an increase in domestic production of the inputs with the quality that can meet the needs of technology-intensive exports. The technological intensity of goods is classified by OECD (2013) based on the International Standard Industrial Classification (ISIC) Rev. 3 Technology Intensity Definition.[12] OECD's classifications of high, medium and low technology are based on research and development (R&D) expenditure per value-added, and R&D expenditure per 12 OECD countries from 1991 to 1999 (recalculations in 2003 exhibit identical results). Owing to data limitations, only two-digit ISIC Rev. 3 by industry and partner country is available and not all products are covered. Therefore, the results have to be interpreted with caution, meaning, that this study is only able to analyze the variation *within* a technology product group and not *between* groups. The full list of available technological products and description of variables is given in Table A2.1.

Finally, the study controls for the competitiveness level of exports to identify the significance of DVA gained in the GVC. The Bilateral Revealed Comparative Advantage[13] (BRCA) indicator is used to measure trade competitiveness. Examining trade competitiveness using DVA allows the study to identify more accurately the comparative advantage of countries in *Factory Asia*. A high BRCA and DVA implies that domestic producers have more local advantages (e.g. labor, capital, trade policy regimes) to specialize in exports in comparison with others countries. This is similar to Hildago and Hausmann (2009) concept of significant exporter, where the aim is to identify the trends in domestic contributions in the production of competitive exported goods. However, analyzing the increase in DVA alone is insufficient to examine gains from participating in GVC. Therefore, we analyze trade competitiveness in tandem with the technological level of goods. In this study, we define *significant DVA gains* when DVA increases and BRCA switches from less than 1 to more than 1 or, if BRCA remained at more than 1. If a product has an increase in competitiveness and an increase in DVA, it means that the increase in competitiveness is due to domestic contribution in DVA. An increase of these two conditions in high technology industries further indicates significant DVA capture in competitive and high value (technology) markets.

Factory Asia: who gained?

This study first examines the gross trade patterns in East Asia.[14] One concern on examining the trade nexus between East Asian countries is the role of China as the assembly core of *Factory Asia*. Aggregating China with Korea and Japan may therefore bias the results. In keeping with the *Factory Asia* trade structure, China is maintained as an individual country for analysis since its trade spans from labor-intensive manufacturing products to products from high-technology industries.

Patterns of gross trade

Table 2.1 shows total gross manufacturing exports and its decomposition into intermediate and final (finished) goods by destination. The time frame of analysis covers three benchmark years: 1995 is used to represent trade patterns before China's accession into WTO; 2005 covers China's post-accession year, and also the year when the implementation of The Agreement on Trade in Goods in the ASEAN–China FTA (ACFTA); and 2011 represents the current trade scenario (which is also the latest year available from TiVA). This chapter will first analyze the trade patterns between Northeast Asia (NEA) and Southeast Asia (SEA) in gross terms before examining the trade pattern in value-added terms.

First, we explore NEA's and SEA's trade with China.[15] Exports from both regions share two commonalities: first, a high share of intermediate goods and a decreasing share of finished goods in total exports. Since 1995, more than 70 percent of NEA's exports to China are in intermediate goods. SEA came close to 67 percent in 1995 but it increased its share by 10 percent after China's accession into the WTO. Although both NEA and SEA have somewhat stagnated in their share of intermediate exports to China from 2005 to 2011, this still respectively amounts to 79 percent and 77 percent for both regions in 2011. Both regions however, have decreasing share of final goods exports to total exports to China. China on the other hand, also exports a higher proportion of intermediate goods to NEA and SEA compared with the share of finished goods. Therefore, Table 2.1 suggests that intraregional trade within SEA, NEA and China is mostly trade in intermediate goods.

By comparison, China's extra-regional trade (to the USA and EU) has a higher portion of final goods compared with its trade within East Asia. SEA and NEA export more final goods, in total, within the region than to the USA, EU and the rest of the world in 2011. This indeed supports the notion that China operates as the core assembly hub in *Factory Asia*, processing intermediate goods within the region and exporting them to high-income countries around the world. There is, however, an interesting diversion from the model. As mentioned earlier, the composition of products in SEA, and NEA's exports to China has not changed since 2005, especially in intermediate goods. NEA, instead, has increased its exports share of intermediate goods to the USA and EU; which suggests market diversification by NEA into intermediate goods markets outside of China since 2005.

Table 2.1 therefore suggests that China dominates (in comparison with SEA and NEA) in the final goods market of the USA (in trade value). SEA, however, is the only region that has made the shift from exporting more intermediate goods to exporting more final goods to the US market since 1995. SEA is also the only East Asian region with a share of final goods exports higher than intermediate goods in the US market after 2005. It is almost as if SEA is establishing itself as a secondary assembly factory in *Factory Asia* that focuses more on US demand for consumable goods. This supports

Table 2.1 Manufacturing trade (US$ billion) and share of intermediate and final goods in total manufacturing

From	*To:*																	
	NEA			*China*			*SEA*			*ROW*			*EU15*			*USA*		
	Year:																	
	1995	*2005*	*2011*	*1995*	*2005*	*2011*	*1995*	*2005*	*2011*	*1995*	*2005*	*2011*	*1995*	*2005*	*2011*	*1995*	*2005*	*2011*
China	**21.6**	**107.2**	**231.0**	**0.0**	**0.0**	**0.0**	**3.6**	**24.8**	**75.9**	**6.2**	**47.9**	**170.8**	**16.9**	**102.5**	**233.7**	**25.3**	**180.0**	**327.8**
Intermediate	0.53	0.61	0.63				0.67	0.78	0.69	0.51	0.52	0.51	0.50	0.50	0.51	0.54	0.50	0.52
Final	0.47	0.39	0.36				0.30	0.21	0.29	0.41	0.44	0.41	0.49	0.49	0.48	0.46	0.48	0.47
EU15	**57.0**	**69.8**	**97.5**	**15.0**	**68.3**	**181.6**	**29.2**	**27.2**	**41.9**	**107.3**	**193.5**	**296.0**	**0.0**	**0.0**	**0.0**	**114.7**	**241.8**	**269.6**
Intermediate	0.57	0.66	0.70	0.58	0.71	0.72	0.49	0.72	0.66	0.56	0.57	0.58				0.62	0.57	0.59
Final	0.42	0.33	0.29	0.38	0.28	0.27	0.49	0.27	0.32	0.37	0.38	0.34				0.38	0.42	0.40
NEA	**41.8**	**58.7**	**90.0**	**24.7**	**151.6**	**320.9**	**48.9**	**52.1**	**97.7**	**30.0**	**50.9**	**107.9**	**67.9**	**86.9**	**82.4**	**118.4**	**144.7**	**142.9**
Intermediate	0.62	0.74	0.78	0.71	0.79	0.79	0.53	0.75	0.74	0.46	0.52	0.52	0.50	0.49	0.54	0.63	0.52	0.56
Final	0.38	0.26	0.21	0.27	0.21	0.20	0.44	0.23	0.25	0.43	0.42	0.35	0.49	0.50	0.45	0.37	0.47	0.42
ROW	**9.6**	**16.5**	**34.2**	**2.9**	**13.1**	**35.7**	**2.7**	**7.6**	**19.3**	**0.0**	**0.0**	**0.0**	**36.2**	**90.3**	**127.8**	**21.1**	**66.8**	**63.4**
Intermediate	0.71	0.73	0.75	0.75	0.86	0.87	0.74	0.78	0.79				0.58	0.55	0.56	0.52	0.50	0.48
Final	0.29	0.27	0.24	0.21	0.13	0.12	0.23	0.20	0.19				0.41	0.45	0.43	0.48	0.49	0.51
SEA	**23.7**	**41.1**	**61.9**	**3.3**	**40.5**	**101.3**	**8.5**	**27.1**	**58.3**	**5.0**	**20.6**	**48.2**	**22.8**	**29.5**	**38.1**	**31.8**	**52.5**	**49.6**
Intermediate	0.60	0.65	0.69	0.67	0.77	0.77	0.55	0.72	0.69	0.43	0.53	0.52	0.51	0.50	0.52	0.59	0.49	0.49
Final	0.40	0.34	0.30	0.29	0.22	0.21	0.43	0.27	0.30	0.53	0.45	0.43	0.48	0.49	0.47	0.41	0.50	0.50
USA	**68.7**	**73.9**	**87.8**	**8.0**	**37.8**	**88.3**	**18.1**	**25.0**	**32.2**	**50.9**	**64.9**	**136.8**	**92.5**	**132.3**	**177.0**	**0.0**	**0.0**	**0.0**
Intermediate	0.55	0.63	0.66	0.66	0.76	0.75	0.54	0.76	0.70	0.53	0.55	0.57	0.56	0.54	0.58	0.0	0.0	0.0
Final	0.45	0.37	0.33	0.31	0.24	0.23	0.44	0.23	0.29	0.39	0.41	0.34	0.43	0.45	0.41	0.0	0.0	0.0

Source: calculated from Trade in Value Added (TiVA) database.

Notes
NEA = Northeast Asia (Japan and Korea), SEA (Southeast Asia – Malaysia, Indonesia, Philippines and Thailand). ROW is Rest of the World (outside of the list).
Figures in bold are in US$ billions, values are different due to rounding up.

Helble and Ngiang's (2014) observation that SEA is becoming a 'regional mall', or supplier of final goods to the USA, as observed in the earlier section.

Patterns of value-added trade

We analyze value-added trade and break down the analysis in Table 2.1 to examine the contribution of domestic input to gross exports. Table 2.2 mirrors Table 2.1 except that the figures now represent the shares of DVA content in gross exports. Although Table 2.1 shows a significant increase in gross exports of NEA to China, the DVA share has decreased by almost 20 percent since 1995. There is also a gradual decline in the shares of DVA content for both intermediate and final exports (with the former holding a larger share). On the other hand, China's DVA content in its gross exports to NEA has increased for both intermediate and final goods from 2001 to 2005. There is therefore a gap in the balance of trade between China and NEA on the use of domestic input. This means that China is capturing more DVA content from its exports to NEA in comparison with NEA where more imported inputs are used in its exports to China.

In comparing NEA and SEA's exports to China, the difference in DVA content is substantial. In 2005, NEA was the only region with a high DVA of over 50 percent of its gross export value in intra-regional East Asian trade in intermediate goods. This is expected as NEA countries with a higher home-grown knowledge in capital stock are likely to capture more value-added by producing goods that use more local inputs. This pattern, however, has changed. Since 2005, DVA content of NEA's intermediate exports to China has decreased from 57 to 52 percent of its gross export value compared with SEA's DVA that has increased from 37 to 39 percent from 2005 to 2011. As compared with SEA, NEA is increasingly reliant on foreign inputs in the production of intermediate exports to China. This suggests that domestic industries in SEA are gaining more value-added from its trade with China compared with NEA. In addition, SEA has not only increased its DVA content of intermediate goods exports to NEA and China but has also increased its share of final goods in its total exports to the USA, EU and the rest of the world (ROW). This reinforces the role of SEA being a secondary 'factory', hence, creating another production system within *Factory Asia* whereby, after 2005, domestic industries in SEA are reorienting SEA's trade of parts and component exports to China to final goods that are traded outside East Asia.

SEA's DVA content of its exports follows a distinct pattern: the DVA in its gross exports declined from 1995 to 2005, followed by an increase from 2005 to 2011. This 'U'-shaped graph suggests that SEA economies have been increasingly relying on imported inputs in their trade from 1995 until 2005. Baldwin (2014) confirms this by noting that most nations relied on imports to export (I2E) during this period, in a phenomenon known as the second unbundling – North–South production, and knowledge sharing. In the later stage of this phenomenon, some countries have attempted to achieve self-reliance in intermediate inputs. For example, from 2005 to 2011, there are signs of SEA increasing its DVA in intermediate trade in its exports to trade partners. Although foreign content is still high, empirical work by Taguchi and Ni (2015) complements this finding by explaining that SEA has moved beyond the turning point of the estimated 'smile curve', indicating some industrial upgrading has occurred and thereby increasing modestly the DVA of its exports. The decline in the share of NEA's intermediate exports to SEA (Table 2.1), in tandem with the rise of SEA's DVA in intermediate exports to NEA (Table 2.2), suggests that SEA is slowly moving away from its subcontracting (I2E) role for the region.

China's DVA content in its gross exports can be summarized into two distinct patterns. First, the DVA content in China's exports since 1995 is generally low due to its role as a 'processing trade' center. Being deeply integrated into the GVC through FDI, MNCs in China also have higher foreign content in their intermediate imports. This contributes to the low DVA shares of China's exports. However, due to the need to remain competitive, China is slowly upgrading its GVC activities in an effort to move away from volume-oriented trade to a greater focus on quality in its production of exports. Table 2.2 shows that since 2005, all shares of DVA content in China's gross exports have increased, be it in intermediate or final goods.

According to OECD (2013), the rise in China's DVA implies a decreasing importance in the country's processing trade. Domestic activities in China's processing zones now focus on capturing more value from trade by shifting from simple contract assembly operations into higher value-added activities that have a greater control over all stages of production from procurement of raw material to product designs (Pilat *et al.* 2012). This DVA export pattern is also consistent with Koopman and Wei (2012) who found that progressively more locally supplied inputs are used in China's exports to high-income countries, while the opposite holds true for its exports to developing countries. The findings in this study confirm that these locally supplied inputs are used mostly in the production of final goods.

In Table 2.1, we can see that the share of exports of intermediate goods from China to the USA and NEA has increased since 2005, compared with the share of US and NEA intermediate exports to China. This signals some decline in the dependence of China on foreign input in its export of final goods. The increase in China's DVA is confirmed in Table 2.2 which indicates that China's domestic industries have gained more from its trade with the world at large. One overall observation on final goods is that trade in final goods among Asian countries has very low DVA. However, in comparison, the share of DVA content in export of final goods from China to NEA and SEA is higher than that of these two regions' DVA content in their exports of final goods to China. In other words, there is a gap in trade benefits, and China has gained more in trade value by exporting final goods to SEA and

Table 2.2 Compcsition of Domestic Value Added (DVA) shares of intermediate and final goods in manufacturing

From	*To:*																	
	NEA			*China*			*SEA*			*ROW*			*EU15*			*USA*		
	*Yea*r*:*																	
	1995	*2005*	*2011*	*1995*	*2005*	*2011*	*1995*	*2005*	*2011*	*1995*	*2005*	*2011*	*1995*	*2005*	*2011*	*1995*	*2005*	*2011*
China	**0.55**	**0.53**	**0.60**				**0.55**	**0.49**	**0.59**	**0.55**	**0.58**	**0.64**	**0.49**	**0.52**	**0.62**	**0.50**	**0.51**	**0.58**
Intermediate	0.3C	0.33	0.37				0.39	0.38	0.40	0.28	0.31	0.33	0.24	0.25	0.31	0.25	0.25	0.29
Final	0.25	0.21	0.23				0.16	0.11	0.18	0.26	0.27	0.31	0.25	0.27	0.31	0.24	0.25	0.28
EU15	**0.77**	**0.71**	**0.68**	**0.77**	**0.72**	**0.68**	**0.76**	**0.71**	**0.68**	**0.77**	**0.71**	**0.66**				0.76	0.69	**0.64**
Intermediate	0.44	0.47	0.47	0.45	0.51	0.49	0.38	0.51	0.45	0.43	0.41	0.38				0.47	0.40	0.38
Final	0.33	0.24	0.21	0.32	0.21	0.19	0.39	0.20	0.23	0.34	0.30	0.28				0.29	0.30	0.26
NEA	**0.84**	**0.75**	**0.66**	**0.86**	**0.74**	**0.68**	**0.89**	**0.78**	**0.68**	**0.87**	**0.77**	**0.71**	**0.89**	**0.78**	**0.72**	**0.89**	**0.80**	**0.74**
Intermediate	0.52	0.56	0.52	0.60	0.57	0.52	0.47	0.58	0.49	0.40	0.40	0.36	0.45	0.38	0.38	0.56	0.41	0.41
Final	0.32	0.19	0.14	0.26	0.16	0.15	0.42	0.20	0.19	0.47	0.37	0.35	0.44	0.40	0.33	0.33	0.39	0.32
ROW	**0.84**	**0.85**	**0.88**	**0.76**	**0.82**	**0.85**	**0.79**	0.81	0.83				**0.80**	**0.80**	**0.80**	**0.80**	**0.81**	**0.84**
Intermediate	0.59	0.62	0.66	0.56	0.71	0.75	0.58	0.64	0.67				0.46	0.44	0.45	0.42	0.41	0.41
Final	0.25	0.23	0.22	0.20	0.11	0.10	0.21	0.17	0.16				0.34	0.36	0.35	0.38	0.40	0.43
SEA	**0.71**	**0.58**	**0.62**	**0.75**	**0.47**	**0.51**	**0.67**	**0.56**	**0.60**	**0.74**	**0.63**	**0.62**	**0.69**	**0.57**	**0.63**	**0.64**	**0.51**	**0.58**
Intermediate	0.43	0.38	0.43	0.50	0.37	0.39	0.37	0.40	0.41	0.31	0.33	0.32	0.35	0.28	0.32	0.36	0.24	0.27
Final	0.28	0.19	0.19	0.25	0.11	0.12	0.30	0.16	0.18	0.43	0.30	0.31	0.34	0.29	0.31	0.28	0.27	0.31
USA	0.84	0.83	0.82	0.85	0.83	0.81	0.84	0.82	0.82	0.84	0.82	0.78	0.84	0.82	0.79			
Intermediate	0.46	0.52	0.54	0.56	0.63	0.61	0.46	0.62	0.57	0.45	0.45	0.44	0.47	0.44	0.46			
Final	0.38	0.31	0.28	0.29	0.20	0.20	0.38	0.20	0.25	0.40	0.37	0.34	0.36	0.38	0.33			

Source: calculated from Trade in Value Added (TiVA) database.

Notes
NEA = Northeast Asia (Japan and Korea), SEA (Southeast Asia – Malaysia, Indonesia, Philippines and Thailand). ROW is Rest of the World (outside of the list).
Figures in bold are in US$ billions, values are different due to rounding up.

NEA than vice versa. In the case of final goods, the share of DVA of gross exports of final goods from NEA and SEA to the USA and EU is higher compared with China's DVA in its gross exports of final goods to NEA and even SEA. Therefore, domestic industries in SEA and NEA have gained more DVA from their exports of final goods to the USA and EU than to China.

Patterns in upgrading: technology trade and significant domestic value-added gain

While Table 2.2 shows signs of increasing use of domestic input in exports of different product categories from different East Asian economies, we have yet to ascertain whether the increase in domestic input is from low- or high-technology production. This section examines the technology composition of trade in *Factory Asia* in order to determine whether countries have moved up the value curve (functional upgrading) through the production of higher technological and competitive exports. Table 2.3 shows the pattern of technology that is embodied intermediate goods across countries, while Table 2.4 displays the same for final goods. In this study, high-/medium-/low-technology goods consist mostly of products produced by high-/medium-/low-technology-intensive industries as categorized by OECD (2013). High-technology goods include ICT products, while medium-technology goods are a mixture of electrical, chemical and automotive products. Low technology refers to food, textiles and paper products. Table 2.5 summarizes the trade flows, product composition and competitiveness, and the previously discussed criterion on significant domestic value-added gains.

In Table 2.3, NEA exports of intermediates to China from 1995 to 2005 are concentrated in high-technology goods, while the share of exports of intermediates in low-technology goods have decreased. Since 2005, the DVA share of NEA's high-technology intermediate exports to China is around 40 percent, which is relatively high compared with other high-income countries (USA and EU). NEA's intermediate exports to the ROW and EU are mainly concentrated in medium-technology goods. Value-added gain in domestic medium-tech industries is significant (see Table 2.5), as NEA has remained competitive in medium-tech exports since 1995. NEA's exports to SEA also remained specialized (with increasing DVA) in low technology for intermediate goods and medium technology for final goods.

DVA content of NEA's medium technology final goods exports is the highest (above 50 percent) to SEA in consumer electrical and automotive goods. This increase was driven by progressive liberalization in motor vehicles, machinery and equipment, and basic metals since the 1990s along with a growing demand from emerging East Asia, including China (IMF, 2011). Unlike medium technology final goods, NEA lost its competitiveness in high-technology exports to the EU market since 2005. Only NEA industries producing high-technology final goods for China have remained competitive after 2005. NEA's loss of shares in high-technology exports from 2005 to 2011 warrants closer specific country analysis. Japan's high-technology exports have stagnated since the 1990s. IMF (2011) suggests that Japan's loss in competitiveness in this sector may have contributed to the rise in its focus on the medium- and lower-technology sectors. Trade liberalization in these sectors, in combination with increasing demand from China, has spurred an increase of 10 percent in the exports of lower- and medium-technology goods from Japan between 1995 and 2010.

Another reason for the loss of high-technology exports is the rise of outsourcing and GVC. While R&D activities are performed domestically, Japanese firms in high-technology sectors have transferred production operations to other East Asian countries. Hence, the value captured from flows of high-technology trade is redirected to the host economies of Japanese MNCs in East Asia. The increase in Japan's R&D expenditures since the mid-1990s, and the increase in inflows of royalties and license fees in its balance of payment further confirm that Japanese direct investment in East Asia is the main reason for the loss of high-technology exports from Japan. The gap in the development of new technologies for export between Japan and Korea is caused by the difference in the amount of R&D spent between the countries (Fukuchi 2010). South Korea's R&D spending in 2007 (3.5 percent of GDP) is above that of Japan, USA and the EU. Initially, only 25 percent of R&D spending was directed toward developing new technologies. However, in the years following 2009, Korea has increased its R&D spending and narrowed its technology gap against other technology-creating countries such as Japan (Wakabayashi 2012).

Similar to NEA, SEA also exhibit high DVA (over 40 percent) in its high-technology intermediate exports to China. SEA countries are also switching to the production of high-technology intermediate goods by reducing their production of low-tech, less competitive and foreign input-dependent intermediate products. This is highlighted in numerous studies in the electronics and electrical industries in SEA. Studies on Malaysia (Tham and Kam 2015) and Philippines (Aldaba 2015) in the electronics industry show some evidence of industrial upgrading in the ICT sector with a shift into high-growth potential areas of electronic semiconductor manufacturing services and manufacturing services. Firm-level interviews of the electronics cluster in Penang, Malaysia, indicate that domestic upgrading has occurred with MNCs increasing their operations using domestic supply firms and local talent (Edgington and Hayter 2015). Further evidence of using local talent points to the collaboration between local universities and the Thai Microelectronics Center (Patarapong *et al.* 2016). Opened in 2004, the Center specializes in microelectronic research, and collaborates with experts in the university to create commercially viable high-tech prototypes. The collaboration, in return, increased domestic knowledge, and thus, upgraded Thailand's domestic ICT industry.

Final goods from SEA to NEA, on the other hand, have comparative advantage in all the three technology categories. Final goods have a higher

DVA compared with intermediate goods of low-technology products, as the former accounts for an almost 45 percent share of gross final products exported to NEA from SEA. The increase in DVA has been significant, as low- and high-technology exports of consumer goods to the USA remained competitive. There is a distinct gap in DVA content of final goods traded between SEA countries and China. SEA has increased the DVA in its exports of low-technology goods to China but not vice versa. Market competition seems to be the key factor accounting for this gap. As minimum wage levels have doubled between 2009 and 2014 (China Labour Bulletin 2014) and are up to four times higher than SEA (KPMG 2011), China, while still maintaining its lead in trade shares, faces stiff competition from SEA as a source of textile, footwear and certain electronics inputs.

Gaps in technology product exports between China and SEA can also be attributed to differences in government policy directions. China's Five-Year Plan has indicated a shift in emphasis toward infrastructure and higher-technology industries, while some SEA countries still emphasize textiles as strong contributors to poverty alleviation and economic development. A combination of relatively lower production costs, strong capabilities in textiles dyeing in Malaysia, and specialization of apparel manufacturing in Indonesia are among the reasons as to why the region continues to focus more on trading in final goods in low-technology activities in its trade with the USA and the EU.

Table 2.3 shows that even though China specializes in exports of high-technology intermediates to SEA, its domestic contribution is very low as it has a DVA of only around 30 percent. Although China is the only country with an increase in the DVA share of high-technology intermediates exports to NEA, its domestic contribution is not enough to compete in NEA's high-tech goods market as its BRCA is less than one. China has yet to be able to compete with products from the USA and EU in the NEA market (both countries have BRCA values greater than 1 compared with China). China however, is able to compete in exporting high-tech intermediate products to SEA. In 1995, China's DVA content in its intermediate exports to SEA amounted to only 2 percent of total gross exports; this number later increased to 26 percent in 2005, and high-tech Chinese intermediate goods have become increasingly competitive in the SEA market. China has, therefore, increased its specialization in producing exports of high-technology goods to SEA. Interestingly, China's intermediate high-tech export to the USA, on the other hand, has the highest DVA (32 percent), and has remained competitive since 2005. This suggests that China has evolved from the role of a mere assembler to becoming a high-technology parts provider in key high tech sectors. This holds true for industries such as radio, television and communication equipment, electronics machinery and office automatic data processing (ADP) equipment (OECD 2013).

The overall increase in technology exports from China may be attributed to the country's strong focus on industrial R&D development. Already the second largest spender on R&D in 2009 (after the USA), Chinese R&D

investments also occupy 73 percent of the global business sector (OECD 2011). This is in line with the rapid increase in triadic patents[16] held by Chinese residents at an average annual rate of almost 30 percent from 1999 to 2009. The gap in industrial upgrading between China and other East Asian countries hinges on the role the countries play in the knowledge segments of GVC. The rise of large export-oriented Chinese ICT companies such as Huawei and ZTE (Eberhardt *et al.*, 2011) and Xiaomi as global OEM players, further separates China from other Asian emerging economies in terms of technology leadership. China's upgrading also differs from other East Asian emerging economies, in part, due to its ability to tap its own rapidly growing domestic market. Unlike other East Asian countries, China is able to leverage its own large domestic market to utilize technology-spillovers as well as technology copied from MNCs operating in its country. The learnt technologies are subsequently adapted to develop new products for the domestic market, which, in turn, creates the demand for another cycle of absorption, reverse engineering and innovation.

This is only possible due to the attractiveness of China's large domestic market, which also creates a competitive environment for fostering MNCs and domestic firm collaborations. MNCs are also expected to localize more segments of their GVC to facilitate access into the Chinese market (Brandt and Thun 2010). Domestic market competition with MNCs further exacerbates the gap in upgrading between China and SEA countries, as Chinese state-owned enterprises and other state-controlled enterprises have incentives and finance to invest in technology and knowledge-based assets. This is somewhat in contrast to the more protectionist approach taken by the government-linked companies in most SEA countries in this study.

Conclusion

The main findings show that SEA, NEA and China have somewhat moved up the value chain in the production and export of different technology products to extra-regional markets such as the USA, EU and ROW. For China and SEA, industrial upgrading seems to focus more on final goods at different levels of technology, for export. This implies that different regions within East Asia have comparative advantages in different markets and the rise of one region does not necessarily impede trade expansion of the other. This development model is reshaping the flying-geese model, whereby, the 'geese' seems to 'fly' in parallel.[17] The diversification in export profile also relaxes the main assembler 'role' of China in *Factory Asia*. Interestingly, while SEA has increased the DVA content of its exports to China in high-technology goods, its exports of neither intermediate nor final products have a comparative advantage in China. This means that domestic industries in SEA may have been able to upgrade for the production of high-technology exports to China; however, these exported products have yet to be able to compete in the domestic Chinese markets.

Table 2.3 Technology composition and RCA (in value added terms) in DVA exports of intermediate goods

From	*To:*																	
	NEA			*China*			*SEA*			*ROW*			*EU15*			*USA*		
	Year:																	
	1995	*2005*	*2011*	*1995*	*2005*	*2011*	*1995*	*2005*	*2011*	*1995*	*2005*	*2011*	*1995*	*2005*	*2011*	*1995*	*2005*	*2011*
1 China	**6.5**	**34.9**	**86.0**	**0.0**	**0.0**	**0.0**	**1.4**	**9.4**	**30.7**	**1.8**	**14.9**	**56.1**	**4.0**	**25.7**	**72.4**	**6.4**	**45.6**	**96.5**
Low tech	0.39	0.24	0.18				0.13	0.08	0.10	0.26	0.15	0.10	0.28	0.20	0.16	0.28	0.16	0.12
Medium tech	0.01	0.01	0.01				0.00	0.01	0.02	0.17	0.14	0.21	0.01	0.02	0.03	0.00	0.00	0.01
High tech	0.03	0.17	0.21				0.02	0.26	0.20	0.02	0.05	0.05	0.11	0.23	0.20	0.15	0.24	0.32
RCA	**0.91**	**0.98**	**1.01**	**0.00**	**0.00**	**0.00**	**0.85**	**1.09**	**1.00**	**0.91**	**1.37**	**1.22**	**0.87**	**1.03**	**0.97**	**0.95**	**1.35**	**1.11**
Low tech	1.14	1.29	1.37	0.00	0.00	0.00	0.85	0.27	0.54	1.81	0.69	0.68	1.84	0.69	0.84	2.00	0.69	0.75
Medium tech	0.26	0.49	0.36	0.00	0.00	0.00	0.04	0.35	0.84	4.03	9.66	11.88	0.23	0.93	1.41	0.12	0.29	0.36
High tech	0.42	0.82	0.98	0.00	0.00	0.00	0.08	3.87	1.01	0.07	0.85	0.30	0.45	3.19	0.96	0.63	4.34	1.74
2 EU15	**25.0**	**32.7**	**45.8**	**6.8**	**34.9**	**88.7**	**11.0**	**13.9**	**18.7**	**46.0**	**78.9**	**112.7**	**0.0**	**0.0**	**0.0**	**54.2**	**96.0**	**101.8**
Low tech	0.18	0.15	0.14	0.08	0.09	0.08	0.11	0.10	0.11	0.15	0.13	0.11				0.11	0.10	0.07
Medium tech	0.03	0.01	0.02	0.05	0.03	0.02	0.04	0.03	0.05	0.11	0.14	0.16				0.04	0.02	0.03
High tech	0.09	0.12	0.10	0.13	0.18	0.14	0.10	0.28	0.19	0.04	0.05	0.03				0.13	0.09	0.09
RCA	**0.90**	**0.93**	**1.00**	**1.04**	**1.00**	**1.09**	**1.06**	**0.89**	**0.92**	**1.31**	**1.13**	**1.15**	**0.00**	**0.00**	**0.00**	**1.04**	**0.79**	**0.86**
Low tech	1.02	1.10	1.23	0.51	0.57	0.67	1.09	0.55	0.77	1.81	0.91	1.02	0.00	0.00	0.00	1.03	0.49	0.48
Medium tech	0.59	0.32	0.52	1.20	0.81	0.63	0.86	0.69	1.11	3.22	3.87	4.37	0.00	0.00	0.00	0.81	0.38	0.69
High tech	0.86	1.20	1.30	1.51	2.02	1.59	1.36	2.83	1.79	0.72	0.62	0.30	0.00	0.00	0.00	1.78	0.78	0.79
3 NEA	**21.5**	**32.7**	**46.7**	**14.9**	**87.1**	**167.7**	**22.9**	**30.2**	**47.6**	**12.1**	**20.4**	**39.1**	**30.4**	**33.3**	**31.4**	**65.9**	**59.5**	**59.0**
Low tech	0.07	0.03	0.03	0.16	0.05	0.03	0.05	0.02	0.04	0.08	0.04	0.02	0.02	0.02	0.02	0.02	0.02	0.02
Medium tech	0.01	0.01	0.01	0.00	0.00	0.00	0.02	0.02	0.01	0.28	0.20	0.40	0.06	0.10	0.12	0.01	0.02	0.02
High tech	0.26	0.27	0.15	0.19	0.44	0.41	0.17	0.32	0.18	0.08	0.03	0.02	0.38	0.32	0.18	0.45	0.22	0.19
RCA	**0.99**	**1.01**	**1.03**	**1.02**	**1.11**	**1.07**	**0.98**	**1.06**	**1.06**	**1.01**	**1.10**	**1.12**	**0.91**	**0.87**	**0.85**	**0.97**	**1.00**	**0.95**
Low tech	1.48	0.95	1.21	3.16	1.19	1.00	1.80	0.50	1.14	2.93	0.79	0.75	0.72	0.27	0.58	0.77	0.46	0.60
Medium tech	0.26	0.27	0.11	0.12	0.06	0.04	0.39	0.44	0.17	5.71	5.36	12.06	1.13	2.01	2.78	0.24	0.48	0.54
High tech	0.81	0.90	0.61	0.62	1.50	1.45	0.69	1.04	0.62	0.31	0.12	0.07	1.42	0.86	0.51	1.79	0.70	0.58

4 ROW	**5.6**	**10.3**	**22.6**	**1.6**	**9.3**	**26.6**	**1.6**	**4.9**	**12.9**	**0.0**	**0.0**	**0.0**	**16.8**	**39.8**	**57.7**	**8.9**	**27.4**	**26.0**
Low tech	0.12	0.08	0.06	0.33	0.18	0.12	0.21	0.10	0.07				0.30	0.25	0.23	0.28	0.22	0.20
Medium tech	0.00	0.01	0.03	0.00	0.00	0.00	0.00	0.01	0.02				0.01	0.02	0.05	0.00	0.00	0.00
High tech	0.00	0.01	0.00	0.01	0.02	0.01	0.00	0.03	0.04				0.01	0.03	0.01	0.00	0.01	0.02
RCA	**0.65**	**0.50**	**0.60**	**1.32**	**0.72**	**0.71**	**1.27**	**0.67**	**1.04**	**0.00**	**0.00**	**0.00**	**1.18**	**0.80**	**0.83**	**1.16**	**0.73**	**0.72**
Low tech	0.34	0.23	0.28	1.93	0.56	0.49	1.98	0.30	0.44	0.00	0.00	0.00	2.62	0.87	1.12	2.43	0.72	0.85
Medium tech	0.67	0.39	0.69	0.08	0.03	0.06	0.11	2.28	2.31	0.00	0.00	0.00	0.54	3.16	5.20	0.01	0.02	0.13
High tech	0.12	0.13	0.12	2.58	3.07	0.25	0.04	3.67	1.45	0.00	0.00	0.00	0.41	4.58	0.31	0.21	2.03	0.38
5 SEA	**10.1**	**15.8**	**26.4**	**1.6**	**14.8**	**39.7**	**3.2**	**10.9**	**24.0**	**1.6**	**6.8**	**15.3**	**8.0**	**8.3**	**12.1**	**11.5**	**12.8**	**13.6**
Low tech	0.47	0.24	0.26	0.61	0.19	0.15	0.31	0.18	0.22	0.50	0.39	0.41	0.37	0.32	0.32	0.27	0.26	0.28
Medium tech	0.00	0.00	0.01	0.00	0.00	0.00	0.01	0.02	0.01	0.03	0.04	0.08	0.02	0.03	0.02	0.00	0.00	0.00
High tech	0.11	0.14	0.10	0.03	0.44	0.42	0.10	0.14	0.06	0.02	0.01	0.01	0.21	0.18	0.12	0.43	0.32	0.26
RCA	**0.68**	**0.77**	**0.71**	**0.91**	**1.30**	**0.95**	**1.06**	**1.11**	**1.01**	**1.30**	**1.41**	**1.30**	**1.16**	**0.99**	**0.84**	**1.49**	**1.40**	**1.14**
Low tech	0.89	0.74	0.75	1.54	0.69	0.55	1.32	0.55	0.89	2.65	1.55	2.15	1.75	0.89	1.07	1.61	1.01	1.29
Medium tech	0.23	0.25	0.32	0.16	0.11	0.04	0.53	1.85	0.89	2.85	5.12	7.91	2.09	2.78	1.25	0.25	0.32	0.21
High tech	0.33	0.48	0.39	0.10	2.53	1.82	0.60	0.69	0.29	0.18	0.09	0.08	1.35	0.79	0.45	3.56	1.98	1.34
6 USA	**31.8**	**38.3**	**47.3**	**4.5**	**23.8**	**54.2**	**8.3**	**15.6**	**18.3**	**22.7**	**29.1**	**59.7**	**43.8**	**58.3**	**82.0**	**0.0**	**0.0**	**0.0**
Low tech	0.21	0.17	0.21	0.14	0.22	0.23	0.14	0.10	0.13	0.13	0.19	0.14	0.14	0.15	0.14			
Medium tech	0.05	0.09	0.05	0.04	0.04	0.03	0.03	0.03	0.04	0.18	0.22	0.23	0.08	0.15	0.10			
High tech	0.23	0.24	0.18	0.17	0.26	0.23	0.30	0.53	0.36	0.07	0.06	0.03	0.29	0.18	0.11			
RCA	**0.87**	**0.98**	**0.93**	**0.95**	**1.15**	**1.20**	**1.27**	**1.16**	**1.18**	**1.39**	**1.08**	**1.27**	**0.89**	**0.60**	**0.62**	**0.00**	**0.00**	**0.00**
Low tech	1.23	1.03	1.26	0.87	1.68	1.72	1.20	0.78	0.98	1.20	1.35	1.13	0.81	0.58	0.53	0.00	0.00	0.00
Medium tech	0.76	1.02	0.62	0.59	0.83	0.40	0.65	0.48	0.58	3.63	3.81	3.55	1.12	1.43	0.75			
High tech	1.02	1.42	1.43	0.85	1.58	1.71	3.29	3.19	2.60	0.88	0.31	0.23	2.22	0.55	0.44	0.00	0.00	0.00

Source: calculated from Trade in Value Added (TiVA) database.

Note
Figures in bold are in US$ billions, values are different due to rounding up.

Table 2.4 Technology composition and RCA (in value added terms) in DVA exports of final goods

From:	*To:*																	
	NEA			*China*			*SEA*			*ROW*			*EU15*			*USA*		
	Year:																	
	1995	*2005*	*2011*	*1995*	*2005*	*2011*	*1995*	*2005*	*2011*	*1995*	*2005*	*2011*	*1995*	*2005*	*2011*	*1995*	*2005*	*2011*
China	**5.4**	**22.3**	**52.2**	**0.0**	**0.0**	**0.0**	**0.6**	**2.8**	**13.8**	**1.6**	**12.7**	**53.3**	**4.3**	**27.7**	**72.5**	**6.1**	**45.4**	**92.8**
Low tech	0.79	0.52	0.43				0.32	0.19	0.18	0.48	0.32	0.18	0.49	0.43	0.40	0.52	0.33	0.33
Medium tech	0.07	0.17	0.20				0.36	0.31	0.34	0.11	0.24	0.22	0.09	0.14	0.15	0.09	0.15	0.15
High tech	0.02	0.13	0.17				0.03	0.09	0.14	0.02	0.10	0.13	0.06	0.12	0.12	0.04	0.16	0.22
RCA	**1.00**	**0.96**	**0.95**				1.06	0.79	0.89	0.89	**1.07**	**1.12**	**1.15**	**1.05**	**1.03**	**1.15**	**1.07**	**1.04**
Low tech	1.40	1.32	1.34				0.60	0.40	0.51	0.75	0.92	0.66	1.00	1.19	1.34	1.06	0.95	1.14
Medium tech	0.67	0.91	0.90				3.53	1.36	1.46	0.93	1.47	1.20	0.99	0.85	0.76	0.92	0.90	0.74
High tech	0.64	0.95	1.01				0.68	0.67	0.85	0.45	0.73	0.80	1.64	0.95	0.71	1.03	1.22	1.33
EU15	**18.7**	**17.0**	**20.4**	**4.8**	**14.1**	**35.4**	**11.3**	**5.5**	**9.6**	**36.1**	**58.5**	**82.8**	**0.0**	**0.0**	**0.0**	**32.8**	**71.8**	**70.5**
Low tech	0.31	0.30	0.31	0.07	0.07	0.07	0.08	0.14	0.13	0.26	0.16	0.16				0.25	0.17	0.17
Medium tech	0.39	0.39	0.39	0.67	0.64	0.68	0.59	0.39	0.42	0.30	0.35	0.31				0.31	0.36	0.31
High tech	0.07	0.09	0.08	0.09	0.11	0.09	0.07	0.10	0.08	0.06	0.11	0.06				0.05	0.06	0.06
RCA	**0.98**	**0.94**	**1.02**	**1.36**	**1.31**	**1.43**	**1.21**	**0.93**	**1.01**	**1.00**	**1.17**	**1.15**				**0.85**	**0.89**	**0.86**
Low tech	1.33	1.55	1.77	0.40	0.48	0.58	0.40	0.69	0.75	1.14	0.99	1.05				0.93	0.82	0.82
Medium tech	0.95	0.90	0.93	2.28	2.07	2.25	1.81	0.89	0.99	0.77	1.00	0.84				0.67	0.78	0.62
High tech	1.04	1.20	1.59	1.42	1.41	1.62	1.01	1.33	1.57	0.92	1.49	1.18				0.79	0.83	1.13
NEA	**13.5**	**11.2**	**12.6**	**6.4**	**24.9**	**49.4**	**20.6**	**10.3**	**18.9**	**14.0**	**19.0**	**38.1**	**30.1**	**34.9**	**27.5**	**39.5**	**56.6**	**46.4**
Low tech	0.21	0.12	0.15	0.15	0.06	0.04	0.04	0.04	0.07	0.10	0.05	0.03	0.04	0.02	0.04	0.06	0.04	0.04
Medium tech	0.34	0.31	0.41	0.45	0.40	0.48	0.63	0.54	0.58	0.42	0.59	0.36	0.41	0.44	0.45	0.46	0.53	0.57
High tech	0.19	0.24	0.16	0.21	0.36	0.31	0.10	0.11	0.11	0.10	0.07	0.04	0.28	0.22	0.13	0.23	0.17	0.15
RCA	**0.93**	**0.88**	**0.93**	**1.04**	**1.09**	**1.07**	**1.03**	**0.87**	**0.94**	**1.08**	**1.06**	**1.10**	**1.05**	**1.06**	**1.03**	**1.01**	**0.99**	**0.94**
Low tech	2.54	2.45	3.19	2.06	1.45	0.94	0.55	0.85	1.53	1.40	1.12	0.66	0.55	0.58	0.92	0.85	0.90	0.96
Medium tech	0.70	0.54	0.75	1.03	0.86	0.99	1.42	0.93	1.05	0.98	1.24	0.76	0.93	0.92	0.91	1.01	1.04	1.03
High tech	0.95	1.28	1.10	1.03	1.87	2.11	0.51	0.57	0.72	0.49	0.39	0.30	1.37	1.15	0.85	1.17	0.90	1.02

ROW	**2.4**	**3.8**	**7.4**	**0.6**	**1.4**	**3.7**	**0.6**	**1.3**	**3.1**	**0.0**	**0.0**	**0.0**	**12.1**	**32.2**	**45.1**	**8.0**	**26.7**	**27.1**
Low tech	0.54	0.37	0.33	0.80	0.72	0.55	0.65	0.34	0.28				0.59	0.55	0.59	0.62	0.61	0.59
Medium tech	0.01	0.03	0.01	0.05	0.03	0.06	0.04	0.06	0.05				0.03	0.05	0.06	0.02	0.04	0.03
High tech	0.00	0.01	0.01	0.01	0.03	0.02	0.00	0.01	0.02		0.00	0.00	0.01	0.02	0.01	0.01	0.01	0.01
RCA	**0.34**	**0.78**	**1.02**	**0.92**	**0.65**	**0.59**	**0.72**	**0.69**	**0.78**		**0.00**	**0.00**	**1.00**	**1.08**	**1.05**	**0.97**	**1.05**	**1.07**
Low tech	0.78	0.58	0.71	1.27	0.94	0.68	0.81	0.47	0.46		0.00	0.00	1.02	1.19	1.31	1.05	1.28	1.34
Medium tech	0.13	0.29	0.13	0.67	0.26	0.38	0.47	0.52	0.45		0.00	0.00	0.51	0.64	0.71	0.31	0.44	0.39
High tech	0.63	0.54	0.56	1.65	1.21	1.13	0.39	0.40	1.46		0.00	0.00	1.04	1.06	0.56	1.07	0.59	0.84
SEA	**6.7**	**7.9**	**11.8**	**0.8**	**4.3**	**12.0**	**2.5**	**4.3**	**10.7**	**2.1**	**6.1**	**14.8**	**7.7**	**8.6**	**11.9**	**8.9**	**14.0**	**15.4**
Low tech	0.55	0.37	0.45	0.79	0.32	0.34	0.43	0.29	0.33	0.76	0.61	0.62	0.53	0.52	0.56	0.52	0.47	0.54
Medium tech	0.13	0.20	0.21	0.09	0.12	0.11	0.25	0.37	0.34	0.06	0.15	0.12	0.06	0.12	0.11	0.05	0.06	0.08
High tech	0.11	0.13	0.10	0.02	0.29	0.22	0.06	0.04	0.03	0.02	0.03	0.03	0.12	0.11	0.06	0.16	0.19	0.13
RCA	**1.07**	**1.03**	**1.08**	**1.14**	**1.03**	**0.96**	**0.94**	**0.94**	**1.05**	**0.94**	**0.99**	**1.07**	**1.09**	**1.10**	**1.10**	**1.17**	**1.04**	**1.12**
Low tech	1.09	0.87	1.03	1.67	0.76	0.71	0.75	0.62	0.75	1.33	1.38	1.42	1.08	1.30	1.32	1.13	1.12	1.30
Medium tech	1.49	1.33	1.31	1.12	0.80	0.63	2.57	2.19	2.09	0.60	0.97	0.74	0.66	0.87	0.69	0.67	0.39	0.51
High tech	1.05	1.10	1.16	0.21	2.37	2.57	0.62	0.33	0.39	0.20	0.23	0.32	1.17	0.87	0.69	1.53	1.55	1.57
USA	**26.2**	**22.9**	**24.4**	**2.3**	**7.4**	**17.4**	**6.9**	**5.0**	**8.0**	**20.3**	**24.1**	**46.5**	**33.6**	**50.3**	**58.6**	**0.0**	**0.0**	**0.0**
Low tech	0.26	0.25	0.32	0.15	0.15	0.19	0.10	0.17	0.22	0.19	0.16	0.14	0.14	0.14	0.16			
Medium tech	0.26	0.18	0.17	0.41	0.31	0.31	0.38	0.21	0.22	0.29	0.21	0.18	0.23	0.15	0.14			
High tech	0.13	0.12	0.11	0.12	0.16	0.13	0.17	0.17	0.15	0.10	0.10	0.07	0.17	0.08	0.06			
RCA	**0.86**	**0.81**	**0.78**	**0.98**	**1.07**	**1.04**	**1.12**	**0.99**	**1.08**	**1.07**	**1.10**	**1.13**	**0.87**	**0.84**	**0.89**			
Low tech	1.26	1.21	1.36	0.86	0.92	1.09	0.63	0.98	1.34	1.15	1.02	0.91	0.71	0.69	0.78			
Medium tech	0.69	0.49	0.49	1.23	1.13	1.18	1.30	0.73	0.87	0.94	0.80	0.76	0.61	0.44	0.45			
High tech	0.93	1.41	1.60	0.84	1.84	1.95	1.20	1.92	2.18	0.69	1.16	1.02	1.18	0.96	0.91			

Source: calculated from Trade in Value Added (TiVA) database.

Note
Figures in bold are in US$ billions, values are different due to rounding up.

Table 2.5 Summary of trade patterns: DVA intermediate and final goods exports by technology composition, competitiveness and significant upgrading (2005–2011)[a]

		Types of good	*Share/DVA*			*RCA*			*Significant upgrading industries*
			Low	*Medium*	*High*	*Low*	*Medium*	*High*	
NEA	China	Intermediate	D	U	D*	C	N	C	
		Final	D	I*	D	N**	N	C	
	EU	Intermediate	U	I	D*	N	C	N	Medium
		Final	I	I*	D	N	N	N**	
	NEA	Intermediate	U	U	D*	C**	N	N	
		Final	I	I*	D	C	N	C	
	ROW	Intermediate	D	I*	D	N	C	N	Medium
		Final	D	D*	D	N**	N**	N	
	SEA	Intermediate	I	D	D*	C**	N	N**	Low
		Final	I	I*	U	C**	C**	N	Low and medium
	USA	Intermediate	U	U	D*	N	N	N	
		Final	U	I*	D	N	C	C**	Medium
SEA	China	Intermediate	D	U	D*	N	N	C	
		Final	I*	D	D	N	N	C	
	EU	Intermediate	U*	D	D	C**	C	N	
		Final	I*	D	D	C	N	N	Low
	NEA	Intermediate	I*	I	D	N	N	N	
		Final	I*	I	D	C**	C	C	Low and medium
	ROW	Intermediate	I*	I	U	C	C	N	Low and medium
		Final	I	D	U	C	N	N	Low
	SEA	Intermediate	I*	D	D	N	N**	N	
		Final	I	D*	D	N	C	N	
	USA	Intermediate	I	U	D*	C	N	C	Low
		Final	I	I	D	C	N	C	Low

China	EU	Intermediate	D	I	D*	N	C**	N**	Medium
		Final	D*	I	U	N	C	N	Medium
	NEA	Intermediate	D	U	I*	C	N	N	
		Final	D*	I	I	C	N	C**	High
	ROW	Intermediate	D	I*	U	N	C	N	Medium
		Final	D*	D	I	N	C	N	
	SEA	Intermediate	I	D	D*	N	N	C	
		Final	D	I*	I	N	C	N	Medium
	USA	Intermediate	D	U	I*	N	N	C	High
		Final	U*	U	I	C**	N	C	High

Summary (total number of sig upgrade)

	NEA			*SEA*			*China*		
	Intermediate (Int.)	*Final*	*Total*	*Int.*	*Final*	*Total*	*Int.*	*Final*	*Total*
Low tech	1	1	2	2	4	6	0	0	0
Medium	2	2	4	1	1	2	2	2	4
High	0	0	0	0	0	0	1	2	3
Total	3	3	6	3	5	8	3	4	7

Source: calculated from Trade in Value Added (TiVA) database.

Notes

* Indicates the largest share of the product across categories, whether it increases (I), decreases (D) or remained unchanged (U).

** Indicates a switch from Competitive (C) into Non-competitive (N) and vice versa.

a Significant upgrading is measured when DVA increases and RCA switches from less than 1 to more than 1 or, if RCA remained more than 1. Improvements in competitiveness when DVA is decreasing imply the increase in competitiveness due to foreign input or increased in foreign content. We do not consider these as domestic industrial upgrading.

While remaining as the core of the 'factory', China is also diversifying its production into higher-quality goods for the US and EU markets. China is, however, not the only country diversifying its activities. SEA is also slowly moving into higher value-added goods especially in the ICT industry after 2005, in the wake of China's accession to the WTO and the formation of the ASEAN-China Free Trade Agreement (ACFTA). These small changes show an increasingly blurry role of China as the main assembler, and China's claim as core 'factory' is no longer entirely exclusive. Instead, there is another claimant, as SEA is emerging as a secondary assembly 'factory', producing competitive, low- and medium-technology consumer goods for NEA, EU and ROW. NEA on the other hand, has a partial decline in exports of high-technology goods, and it has moved into the production of medium- and low-technology goods that are highly demanded by China. This partial decline, however, does not fully represent a decline of Japan and Korea's trade in high-technology goods, as both countries have redirected their production of high-technology goods to other parts of East Asia.

It is also important to add a caveat to the above analysis. Despite some promising signs that upgrading has occurred in high-technology industries, the share of DVA content in exports in general is still very small. This means that dependence on foreign imported input remains an important part of high-tech production for East Asian countries. Hence, the idea of East Asia evolving from its current *Factory Asia* status into a region of high-technology trade and innovation or a 'Global R&D hub' is still far-fetched. Intra-regional trade in East Asia mostly involves intermediate goods except among SEA countries where there is an increase in the share of final goods traded. Given the latest available data are only until 2011, SEA itself is evolving into a supplier of consumer goods à la 'regional mall', where trade in final low-technology and low value-added goods has increased within the region. The study also confirms that even if upgrading is ongoing, there are gaps in the level of upgrading that are driven by market forces and government policies.

Policies on local sourcing that promote industrial upgrading require a need to strike a balance between increasing the benefits of trade for the domestic economy and creating policies that support knowledge generation in GVC. Government policy directions and industry focus must effectively promote the development of domestic capabilities and productivity. The key to successful domestic industrial upgrading should be linked to market competitiveness. Continuous upgrading and market competitiveness are important factors that can sustain the future of East Asian growth. However, the *Factory Asia* model has to enhance cooperation to maintain global competitiveness in comparison with other countries or regions. Since a low-cost base for global manufacturing is unsustainable, East Asia has to focus on other comparative advantages, one of which is to create knowledge-sharing initiatives within the region. A good example is the creation of China–ASEAN Technology Transfer Centers (CATTC) across ASEAN. The centers host a series of technology partnership programs such as joint-laboratory program, forums and human capital development such as scientist exchange programs. One suggestion for SEA countries is to adopt a similar model and move as a collective bargaining unit to set up collective institutions with remaining NEA countries such as Japan and Korea, along with countries from other regions.

As demand from the developed West has become increasingly unpredictable, interdependence between countries in East Asia is vital in creating competitive forward and backward linkages to cater to supply and demand within the region. The goal is also to support the production of goods made within *Factory Asia*. One way to encourage the use of inputs within the region is to improve the quality of production. Another way is the promotion of *Factory Asia* products through branding. This means that East Asian manufacturers have to focus on long-term quality considerations rather than a short-term focus on cost competitiveness.

In terms of future research, one limitation in this study is that the non-availability of capital data may have excluded an important component that affects the industrial upgrading narrative. In addition, although the chapter highlighted the changes in East Asia (NEA, SEA and China), a country-specific focus on sub-regions has not been considered extensively and needs further in-depth research.

Appendix

Table A2.1 Technology classifications of industries by OECD

High-technology

- Pharmaceuticals (ISIC 2423) – unavailable
- Office, accounting and computing machinery (ISIC 30)
- Radio, television and communication equipment (ISIC 32)
- Medical, precision and optical instruments, watches and clocks (ISIC 33)
- Aircraft and spacecraft (ISIC 353) – unavailable

Medium-high technology

- Chemicals excluding pharmaceuticals (ISIC 24 less 2423) – unavailable
- Machinery and equipment not elsewhere classified (ISIC 29)
- Electrical machinery and apparatus not elsewhere classified (ISIC 31)
- Motor vehicles, trailers and semi-trailers (ISIC 34)
- Railroad equipment and transport equipment not elsewhere classified (ISIC 352 plus 359) – unavailable

Low-technology

- Food products, beverages and tobacco (ISIC 15–16)
- Textiles, textile products, leather and footwear (ISIC 17–19)
- Wood and products of wood and cork (ISIC 20)
- Pulp, paper, paper products, printing and publishing (ISIC 21–22)
- Manufacturing not elsewhere classified and recycling – unavailable

Gross export data are calculated by the row sum of the international trade flows in the OECD Inter-Country Input–Output (ICIO) tables. They are consistent with official National Accounts estimates of total exports and imports of goods and services, as well as estimates for GDP adjusted for re-exports. Exports industry estimates, here presented, are based on the balanced trade system drawn from the global input–output database. Unspecified export destination is included in partner WORLD, but not as an individual partner.

Gross exports of intermediate goods and services is calculated from domestic industry *i* in country *c* to partner country *p*.

Domestic value added embodied in exports by industry *i* in country *c* covers value added generated anywhere in the domestic economy

Domestic value added in gross exports of intermediate products as a percentage of total gross exports. It reveals, by industry *i* in country *c*, the share of gross exports that is domestic value added destined for further production within direct partners' economies – either to meet partners' final demand or to be embodied in exports by direct partners. It can be considered as a measure of forward linkages in global value chains (GVC).

Domestic value added in gross exports of final demand products as a percentage of total gross export.

Notes

1 While trade in services is equally important within East Asia, this study focuses only on merchandise trade. The paper attempts to understand trade flows within the region while bilateral trade data on services (especially for developing Southeast Asian countries) is unavailable.
2 The flying-geese pattern of industrialization explains the shift in the stages of industrialization of East Asian countries based on international division of labor and a country's comparative advantage. Due to an increase in labor cost, the 'lead goose (Japan)' moves its labor-intensive activities to less advanced Asian countries while focusing on capital intensive and high productivity industries. The cycle repeats itself when less advanced countries began to upgrade their industrial activities. The model is understandably Japan-centric as the country became an industrial powerhouse in the late nineteenth century.
3 In the often cited case study by Dedrick *et al.* (2008), for each Apple iPod sold, the value added captured in China is less than 3 percent of the factory gate price.
4 Banga (2014) made a distinction between forward and backward linkages in a country's participation in GVC. The former explains a country's participation in GVC by producing inputs into exports of other countries whilst the latter measures imports of intermediate inputs used in its exports. Gains are measured in terms of 'net value-added' by participation in GVC meaning the higher the proportion of forward linkages compared with backward linkages increases such gains.
5 Eighty percent of imported intermediate goods (including high technology ones) originate from East Asia economies. They are used for assembly with at least 45 percent of the final products assembled in China exported to the USA and the EU (OECD 2013).

6 From the left to the right of the x-axis, value chain activities are separated into three groups: pre-production tangible (R&D, Design, Logistics purchases), production tangible (Production and Assembly) and post-production tangible (Logistics, Marketing and Services).
7 We focus on domestic industrial upgrading in the GVC. The reason is that the heavy dependence on imported high technology goods as inputs (as the first source explained above) for the production of high-technology exports may merely be a statistical artefact and does not necessarily reflect the technology levels in the local industry of a country. The lack of technology transfer is attributed to a few reasons. The common adage is that 'there has not been much [technology] to spill' (Menon, 1998) due to MNCs' focus on low technology labor-intensive assembly activities in developing countries. Other reasons include low absorptive capabilities of local firms or insufficient quality and choice of domestic manufacturing suppliers. The highlighted absence of technology transfers from the MNCs suggests the need to examine homegrown technologies in driving industrial upgrading. This is consistent with Banga (2014) who argued that policy should be designed to raise forward linkages, that is, exporting domestic value added content.
8 This study acknowledges that much research has been done on measuring trade in value-added. However, there are no harmonized data collection, techniques, standard reports and reporting standards that enabled a consistent large pool of cross-country analysis. The availability of Trade in Value Added (TiVA) data mitigates these limitations.
9 While it is ideal to obtain annual value-added trade flows, we are constrained by the use of the input–output table, which is published at 'snapshot' years. We acknowledge this constraint and leave longer time series for further studies.
10 Flows of capital goods played an important role in the formation and the future of 'Factory Asia' for they (may) have been embedded with new technologies for industrial upgrading. Since they are not available for this study, flows of products classified in Table A2.1 will be used as a proxy for technology-embedded goods. We leave capital goods for future research upon data availability.
11 These activities may not be conducted by local firms and can also include foreign firms operating in the host economy.
12 United Nations industry classification system where data is classified according to the kind of economic activity in the fields of production, employment, gross domestic product and other statistical areas. Industries are based on codes and their disaggregation are coded according to digit-levels. The higher the digit number, the finer the category of industries. Rev. 3 means the classification has gone through the third revision.
13 Bilateral RCA = (DVA Exports of product X_i from Country A to Country B/All DVA manufacturing exports of A to B)/(All DVA exports of X_i from A/All DVA manufacturing exports of A). A value above one represents comparative advantage of product X_i in B's manufacturing sector.
14 The countries of interest here are China, Japan and Korea for Northeast Asia (NEA) while developing Southeast Asian countries are represented by Malaysia, Indonesia, the Philippines and Thailand (SEA). East Asia refers to the combination of both these regions. While we acknowledged Singapore's role in the formation of global production network in the region since the 1970s (see Athukorala and Kohpaiboon 2015), Singapore has moved some, if not most of the activities in the 1990s into services trade (Wong, 2007). Hence it is not within the scope of the study, which examines the GVC partially on the production and trade of manufacturing goods after 1990. We left Brunei out for similar reasons as it is an oil-rich sultanate.
15 The discussion focuses on regional blocks (NEA and SEA) in part due to the notion that supply-chain trade is not global, but is marked by regional blocks (Johnson and Noguera, 2012; Baldwin and Lopez-Gonzalez, 2014).

16 Patents filed at the European Patent Office (EPO), the United States Patent and Trademark Office (USPTO) and the Japan Patent Office (JPO), for the same invention, by the same applicant or inventor.

17 Some may term this as 'bamboo network' or 'bamboo capitalism' (Xing, 2007) whereby the region grows together (in a parallel development model) using the extensive production network and exhausting resources vertically and horizontally across the network. However, bamboo capitalism commonly refers to enterprises of Chinese diaspora across East Asia.

References

Aldaba, R. 2015. The Philippines in the electronics global value chain. Paper presented at the Second EIA Workshop on Levelling up Southeast Asia's Value Added, 24–26 April 2015, Okura Hotel, Japan.

Ando, M. and Kimura, F. 2005. The formation of international production and distribution networks in East Asia. NBER Chapters in *International Trade in East Asia, NBER-East Asia Seminar on Economics*, 14: 177–216. National Bureau of Economic Research, Inc.

Athukorala, P. and Kohpaiboon, A. 2015. Global production sharing, trade patterns and industrialization in Southeast Asia. In I. Coxhead (ed.), *Routledge Handbook of Southeast Asian Economics* (pp. 139–161). Abingdon and New York: Routledge Taylor & Francis Group.

Baldwin, R. and Lopez-Gonzalez, J. 2014. Supply-chain trade: A portrait of global patterns and several testable hypotheses. *The World Economy* 38(11): 1682–1721.

Banga, R. 2014. Linking into global value chains is not sufficient: Do you export domestic value added contents? *Journal of Economic Integration* 29(2): 267–297.

Brandt, L. and Thun, E. 2010. The fight for the middle: Upgrading, competition, and industrial development in China. *World Development* 38(11): 1555–1574.

China Labour Bulletin. 2014. www.clb.org.hk/en/content/three-major-cities-china-raise-minimum-wage (accessed 18 January 2016).

Choi, B.I. and Rhee, C. 2014. *Future of Factory Asia*. Asian Development Bank and Korea Economic Research Institute (KERI). http://hdl.handle.net/11540/52. License: CC BY 3.0 IGO.

Dedrick, J., Kraemer, K.L. and Linden, G.. 2008. Who profits from innovation in global value chains? A study of the iPod and notebook PCs. *Industrial and Corporate Change* 19 (1): 81–116.

Eberhardt, M., Helmers, C. and Yu, Z. 2011. Is the dragon learning to fly? An analysis of the Chinese patent explosion. University of Oxford, CSAE Working Paper 2011/15.

Edgington, D. and Hayter, R. 2013. The in situ upgrading of Japanese electronics firms in Malaysian industrial cluster. *Economic Geography* 89(3): 227–259.

Ernst, D. 2001. Global production networks and industrial upgrading – a knowledge-centered approach, *Economics Study Area Working Papers 25*, East-West Center, Economics Study Area.

Fukuchi, A. 2010. South Korea's export competitiveness: Critical to overcoming the global crisis and issues going forward. *Bank of Tokyo-Mitsubishi UFJ Economic Review* 5(2): n.p.

Gereffi, G. 1999. International trade and industrial upgrading in the apparel commodity chain. *Journal of International Economics* 48(1): 37–70.

Helble, M. and Ngiang, B.-L. 2014. From global factory to global mall: East Asia's changing trade composition. *ADBI Working Papers 496*. Asian Development Bank Institute.

Hildago, C.A. and Hausmann, R. 2009. The building blocks of economic complexity. *PNAS* 105(26): 10570–10575.

IMF. 2011. Changing patterns of global trade. *IMF Departmental Paper No. 12/1*, Washington.

IMF. 2012. *Changing Patterns of Global Trade*. Washington, DC: International Monetary Fund.

Kaplinsky, R. and Morris, M. 2002. *A Handbook for Value Chain Research*. Canada: International Development Research Center (IDRC).

Koopman, R.W.Z. and Wei, S-J. 2012. Estimating domestic content in exports when processing trade is pervasive. *Journal of Development Economics* 99(1): 178–189.

KPMG. 2011. *Product Sourcing in Asia Pacific New Locations, Extended Value Chains*. KPMG.com.

Kuroiwa, I. 2014. Value added trade and structure of high-technology exports in China. *IDE Discussion Papers 449*. Institute of Developing Economies, Japan External Trade Organization (JETRO).

Menon, J. 1998. Total factor productivity growth in foreign and domestic firms in Malaysian manufacturing. *Journal of Asian Economics* 9(2): 251–280.

Johnson, R.C. and Noguera, G. 2012. Fragmentation and trade in value added over four decades. *Working Paper 18186*. Cambridge, MA: NBER.

OECD. 2011. *Attractiveness for Innovation: Location Factors for International Investment*. Paris: OECD Publishing. DOI: 10.1787/9789264104815-en.

OECD. 2013. *Interconnected Economies: Benefiting from Global Value Chains*. Paris: OECD Publishing. DOI: http://dx.doi.org/10.1787/9789264189560-en.

OECD. 2015. *Diagnostic of Chile's Engagement in Global Value Chains*. Paris: OECD Publishing.

Oikawa, H. 2008. Empirical global value chain analysis in electronics and automobile industries: An application of Asian input–output tables. *IDE Discussion Paper No. 172*. Chiba, Japan: Institute of Developing Economies.

Patarapong, I., Pun-Araj, C. and Preeda, C. 2016. Global production networks and host-site industrial upgrading: The case of the semiconductor industry in Thailand. *Asia Pacific Business Review* 22(2): 289–306.

Pilat, D., Yamano, N. and Yashiro, N. 2012. Moving up the value chain: China's experience and future prospects. In OECD, *China in Focus: Lessons and Challenges*. Paris: OECD.

Powers, W. 2012. The value of value added: Measuring global engagement with gross and value added trade. *Office of Economics Working Paper, No. 2012–11A*. Washington, DC: International Trade Commission.

Shih, S. 1996. *Me-too Is Not My Style: Challenge Difficulties, Break through Bottlenecks, Create Values*. Taipei: The Acer Foundation.

Taguchi, H. and Ni, L. 2015. Global-value-chains participation and industrial upgrading in Asian developing economies. *MPRA Paper 65708*. University Library of Munich, Germany.

Tham, S.-Y. and Kam, A.J.Y. 2015. Trade in value-added: Case of Malaysia. Economic Research Institute for ASEAN and East Asia (ERIA). *Discussion Paper No. 2015–58*. Jakarta: ERIA.

Tham, S.-Y., Kam, A.J.Y. and Izzatina, A.A. 2016. Moving up the value chain in ICT: ASEAN trade with China. *Journal of Contemporary Asia* 46(4): 680–699.

Wakabayashi, Daisuke. 2012. How Japan lost its electronics crown Sony, Sharp and Panasonic fixated on hardware breakthroughs. 'Sometimes, it's easier to run from behind'. *The Wall Street Journal*. www.wsj.com/articles/SB10000872396390444840104577551972061864692 (accessed 24 December 2015).

Wong, H.K. 2007. The remaking of Singapore's high-tech enterprise system. In Henry S. Rowen, Marguerite G. Hancock and Lilliam F. Miller, eds. *Making IT: The Rise of Asian in High Tech* (pp. 123–174). Stanford, CA: Stanford University Press.

Xing, Li. 2007. East Asia regional integration: From Japan-led 'Flying-geese' to China-centered 'Bamboo Capitalism'? *CCIS Research Series No. 3*. http://comtrade.un.org/. http://data.worldbank.org/data-catalog/world-development-indicators.

3 Higher education in Southeast Asia

Fazal Rizvi

Over the past three decades, systems of higher education in Southeast Asia have expanded rapidly, with a spectacular rise in gross enrolment rates (GER). The growing demand for higher education reflects an increasing level of economic, social and political confidence within the region. As the countries of Southeast Asia become increasingly integrated within the global economy, they have taken advantage of the global flows of capital and shifting modes of production. This has created a strong middle class, which widely perceives higher levels of education to be a good investment in protecting and extending its economic gains and social status. With the region showing every sign of political stability and improving economic conditions, a large number of new universities have been created in Southeast Asia, while the competition for places in the region's older higher education institutions (HEIs) has also intensified.

At the same time, governments throughout Southeast Asia have been prepared to allocate large sums of public money in higher education, facilitate greater private investment in the development of new universities and programs, and encourage the public to view an investment in higher education as an outlay that is likely to bring good returns to both the individuals and the nation. There has emerged a strong rhetoric about the ways in which an expansion of higher education is necessary if nations are to meet the requirements of the new global economy that is increasingly knowledge-based. Effective participation in such an economy, it is assumed, demands a steady supply of human resources, which possess knowledge and skills to carry out the complex tasks inherent within the operations of the global supply chains in which Southeast Asian economies have now become embedded. In this way, the expansion of higher education is now inextricably linked to the goals of national social and economic development.

Growth in student enrollments in higher education is, however, not sufficient. Also important is the need for the renewal and reform of higher education policies, programs and practices – not only to bring about system efficiency, but also to ensure greater relevance and effectiveness. HEIs have thus been asked to align their curriculum to the shifting requirements of a new knowledge-based economy. Throughout Southeast Asia, governments have embraced the notion that higher education should not only work toward the goal of improving the livelihood of individuals but also become more responsive to the requirements of the changing labor market, as well as to the shifting national priorities.

This chapter explores some of the ways in which countries in Southeast Asia are working toward the realization of these ambitious goals. It suggests that many of their policies and programs draw heavily on certain globally circulating discourses about the nature of the global knowledge economy and how systems of higher education should engage with it (Rizvi and Lingard 2010). In developing their systems of higher education, the chapter points to some of the ways in which countries of Southeast Asian have sought to collaborate at the regional level, and have looked to the Association of Southeast Asia Nations (ASEAN) to develop instruments of reform, share examples of good practice and 'harmonize' their policies across the region. It is argued in this chapter that while various national and regional initiatives have been successful in increasing the ratio of students attending HEIs, their contribution to forging and sustaining robust systems of higher education that are responsive to the shifting requirement of the global economy has been, at best, limited. I contend that higher education in Southeast Asia continues to face a range of challenges, some of which are specific to national systems while others apply generally to the region.

Higher education expansion

Over the past three decades, higher education enrolments in Southeast Asia have expanded at an explosive rate. According to the World Bank Data (2014), GER in Southeast Asia grew by 2.5 times, from just over 10 percent in 1995 to almost 25 percent in the 2010. Between 2003 and 2012, the number of students enrolled in higher education institutions in Malaysia, for example, grew from just over 600,000 to almost 1 million (UNESCO Institute of Statistics 2014). The World Bank Data also show that in Vietnam there are now over 2.2 million students enrolled in higher education representing over 25 percent of the relevant age group. In Thailand, more than 35 percent of young people attend higher education. In Indonesia, the number of students attending higher education institutions has similarly increased.

The growth in smaller countries in Southeast Asia has been no less impressive. Brunei's GER has, for example, increased from 10 percent in 1998 to 24 percent in 2012. In Cambodia, it has gone up from 1 percent in 1995 to 16 percent in 2011, while in Myanmar, the increase has been lower but no less significant, increasing from 5 percent in 1995 to 15 percent in 2012. Figure 3.1 (UNESCO Institute of Statistics 2014) illustrates the rapid growth in higher education enrollments in Asia since 1980, indicating, in particular, South Korea's spectacular success in transforming its higher education sector – something to which most Southeast Asian countries now aspire and try to emulate.

Figure 3.1 shows how most countries in Southeast Asia have moved from their previously elite status to systems that are 'massified'. Trow (2006) suggests that higher education growth may be classified as following three phases – elite, mass and universal access – based on the proportion of the relevant age group enrolled in HEIs. In the elite phase, less than 15 percent of the relevant age group attends higher education, while the massification phase is characterized by GER that is between 15 percent and 50 percent. The universalization phase is reached when GER is above 50 percent (Trow 2006). In line with Trow's classification scheme, most systems of higher education in Southeast Asia are now massified. As for now, only Singapore provides universal access to higher education, with an expectation that almost everyone in Singapore who can, will attend higher education (Mahbubani and Chye 2015). The speed with which systems of higher education in Southeast Asia have become massified is truly remarkable. In less than three decades, throughout the region, higher education has begun to be viewed as a norm rather than an exception.

It needs to be noted that Trow's definition of massification refers to access to undergraduate programs only, and does not speak of graduate education. In graduate enrollments, the contrast between Singapore and its neighbors is even starker. As a high-income country, Singapore has a mature system of graduate education, with robust programs of research and extensive academic networks with leading universities in the United States and Europe.

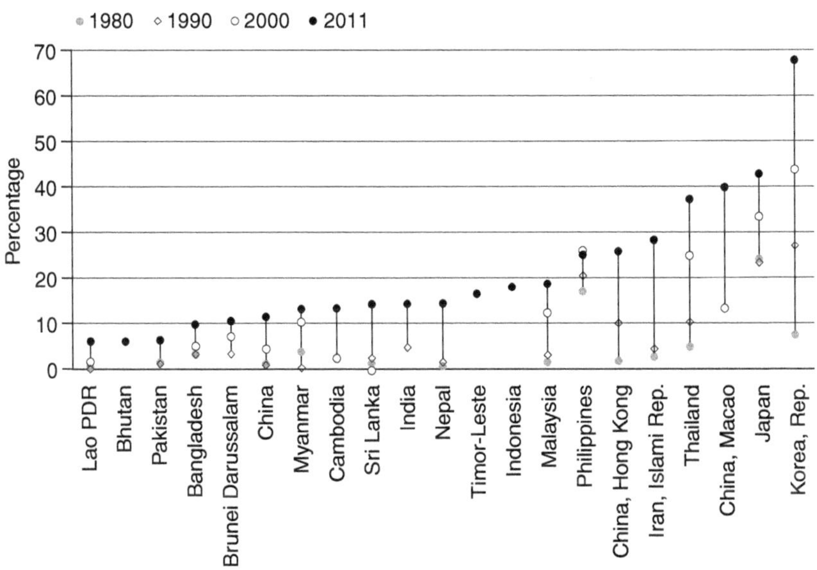

Figure 3.1 Gross enrollment ratios for Bachelor's programs by country or territory, 1980–2011.

Source: UNESCO Institute for Statistics, http/dx.doi.org/10.15220/2014/ed/sd/2/f1.

In middle-income countries such as Malaysia and Thailand, graduate enrollments are rising but not at the rate Singapore experienced. In Malaysia, the number of research students has grown from 21,000 in 2000 to 85,000 students in 2010. Malaysia has set itself the highly ambitious goal of producing at least 100,000 PhD graduates by 2020 (UNESCO Institute of Statistics 2014). Similarly, Thailand, through its Office of the Higher Education Commission, has invested heavily in research training, with US$370 million spent over 2010–2012 (UNESCO Institute of Statistics 2014). Thailand has given nine of its public universities the responsibility to lead this initiative, based on the belief that Thailand's global and regional competitiveness depends on the success it has in not only transmitting knowledge, but also producing it. The rest of the countries in Southeast Asia have yet to develop any meaningful systems of research and research training, with a very small number of graduate students at their HEIs.

To meet the growing demand for higher education, almost all governments in Southeast Asia have increased public expenditure on higher education, albeit at levels that vary greatly (World Bank 2014). With this funding, Malaysia and Thailand have been able to increase the number of public universities. There has also been some improvement in the employment conditions under which faculty work, and in the ways in which students are supported through resources such as good libraries, technology infrastructure and laboratories. But this has been far from adequate, leaving most public universities grossly underfunded for the rapidly increasing numbers and the ambitious tasks they have been allocated (Bhandari and LeFebure 2015). In addition, many of the new public universities in Southeast Asia have been created as a result of rebadging and rebranding the existing technical schools, polytechnics and teachers colleges, without any substantial shifts in the ways in which they operate, or the type of students they recruit. In Indonesia, the new public universities remain grossly underfunded, and are widely regarded as 'overcrowded factories' (Welch 2011).

Much of the increasing student demand for higher education in Southeast Asia has, however, been met by a relentless march toward privatization. A large number of private institutions have emerged throughout the region, created by philanthropists, corporations or entrepreneurs, with little background in education. Their motivations are mixed, from an interest in making quick profits to more publically-minded altruistic sentiments. They have been helped by the governments throughout Southeast Asia who have steadily relaxed the rules determining the entry of private investment in education, not only to soak up the demand but also to develop a robust and profitable 'higher education industry' (Huang 2015). In Malaysia, for example, the government has encouraged and rewarded private educational entrepreneurs, in an effort to establish Malaysia as a regional 'education hub', attracting fee-paying international students from both the neighboring countries, such as Indonesia and China, as well as the Middle East. Like Singapore, Malaysia has sought to recruit mobile students and integrate cross-border provisions into its fast evolving higher education system (Lee 2015). Southeast Asian countries have also eased conditions under which European, Australian and American universities are able to set up branch campuses, viewing this as a form of internationalization of their systems of higher education. The idea of international trade in higher education services has now become entrenched in the popular imagination of most policy actors in Southeast Asia.

Privatized higher education thus appears to have now become a permanent feature of the higher education landscape in Southeast Asia, with almost 40 percent of higher education students now enrolled in private institutions (UNESCO Institute of Statistics 2014). The Philippines, in particular, has witnessed the most spectacular growth in the number of private institutions of higher education over the past 15 years. Between 2001 and 2010, the number of private higher education institutions increased from 1400 to 1800, growing by an average of 45 new institutions, or 3 percent, each year. In Cambodia, 44 out of 73 of its higher education institutions are private (Asian Development Bank 2011). Under the policy of *doi moi* and the Education Law of 2005, Vietnam now permits private ownership of higher education institutions (Ly *et al.* 2015). Through such liberal investment regimes, national governments have not only been able to meet the growing demand for higher education but also create an industry that employs a large number of its citizens, drawing down unemployment rates.

Knowledge economy, higher education and national development

The role of the state in the rapid expansion of higher education in Southeast Asia has thus been quite significant over the past three decades. Even as most governments have claimed to be largely focused on the schools sector – on improving rates of literacy and participation rates in schools – they have nonetheless circuitously fueled growth in higher education. Their commitment to basic education, in line with global initiatives such as UNESCO's Millennium Development Goals (MDGs), has clearly led to higher progression rates from primary to secondary and through to tertiary levels of education. Success in secondary education has created demand for higher education. At the same time, the idea that higher levels of education contribute simultaneously to personal advancement and national economic prosperity is now taken for granted. Higher education is thus assumed to not only improve life-chances of people, but also assist national economic development.

This claim, however, is not entirely new. What is new is that the importance of higher education is now articulated within a globally converging discourse about the close association between the knowledge economy, higher education and national economic development. For more than three decades, this discourse has been widely promoted by intergovernmental organizations such as the OECD, the World Bank and the Asian Development Bank (ADB) (Mundy *et al.* 2015). At a very general level, it espouses a 'new human capital theory' (Hanusheck 2015), which suggests, just as the old human capital theory (Becker 1964) did, that expenditure on training and education directly correlates with increasing levels of personal income and occupational wage differential, as well as national economic growth. The new human capital theory extends this claim to the requirements of the global economy, suggesting that the competitive advantage of individuals, corporations and nations is linked to the extent to which they are able to participate effectively in it.

The new human capital theory is technically complex and has been the subject of much debate. However, in its popular form, it imagines all human behavior to be based on the economic self-interest of individuals operating within free competitive markets. It assumes economic growth and competitive advantage to be a direct outcome of the levels of investment in developing human capital (Peters 2011). It suggests that in a global economy, performance is increasingly linked to people's knowledge stock, skills level, learning capabilities and cultural adaptability. It therefore demands policy frameworks that enhance labor flexibility not only through the deregulation of the market, but also through reform to systems of education and training, designed to align them to the changing nature of economic activity.

The case for expanding higher education in Southeast Asia is clearly linked to this line of thinking. It is argued that unprecedented rates of growth in Southeast Asian countries have been driven mostly by cheap labor; if they are to sustain this growth and even accelerate it, however, they can no longer rely on the advantage of labor costs alone. They need a different approach to economic activity and progress, especially if they aspire to move from middle-income to high-income levels. More positively, there is a widely held view in Southeast Asia that it is positioned in a unique moment in history with many advantages that can serve as a boost to economic growth, most notably its growing middle class and its active participation in the global consumer market. Furthermore, it is argued by the Asian Development Bank (2014), for example, that as countries in Southeast Asia approach middle-income level, they risk being squeezed between low-wage, low-income competitors that rely on labor-intensive industries and the high-income countries that are undergoing rapid technological change. There is a danger that the comparative labor advantage that the countries of Southeast Asia enjoy is diminishing, as wages rise and productivity levels decline, leading to slower economic growth. So if Southeast Asian countries want to climb the 'development ladder' and catch up with advanced economies they need to make greater investment in higher levels of education, enabling them to transition from a manufacturing economy to an economy based on knowledge and its global exchange.

A knowledge-driven economy, it is argued, is one in which the generation and exploitation of knowledge play a dominant role in driving productivity, and thus the creation of wealth, leading to national growth (Asian Development Bank 2014). In the industrial era, replacing human labor with machines and streamlining production processes would in turn create wealth. In the knowledge economy, in contrast, innovation and entrepreneurialism have become the key drivers of enhanced productivity and economic growth, especially in the services industries such as telecommunications and financial services. The knowledge economy requires higher levels of education to produce a greater proportion of workers who are highly skilled; who not only have the ability to use new technologies, but also display certain cultural attitudes toward change. In a rapidly changing world, education must therefore involve the development of behavioral traits such as adaptability, organizational loyalty and integrity, as well as the ability to work in culturally diverse contexts and provide leadership.

In this way, the idea of a knowledge economy has fundamentally altered the relationship between the creation of knowledge and its commercial application, leading to the development of new models of work and labor relations, and demanding new ways of thinking about education, grounded not only in the formal qualifications individuals possess, but also in the learning attributes they are able to demonstrate, such as dealing effectively and creatively with the unfamiliar and constantly changing conditions of work. It emphasizes the development of broad generic competencies such as communication skills, problem solving, the ability to work independently and under pressure, take responsibility for decisions and quickly and efficiently obtain field-specific knowledge and spot its commercial potential. In the knowledge economy, hence, knowing about facts is less important than an understanding of the world of economic relations and networks through which knowledge is converted into commercially viable products. The principles of flexibility and dynamism are thus stressed – as indeed are the ideas of innovation and knowledge application – as more important than formal, codified, structured and explicit knowledge.

What this analysis suggests is that national economic development is now closely tied to a nation's capacity to take advantage of the globalized knowledge economy, especially within the fast growing services sector, which now generates the bulk of output and employment. It highlights the need to develop new learning cultures, not only within the formal sectors of education but also in various work situations. Such learning involves both the ability to access globally networked knowledge and to use it for commercial exchange. In a knowledge economy, individuals, corporations, and nations are seen to create wealth in proportion to their capacity to learn from a wide variety of sources, both local and global, in ways that are strategic and incessant. As the OECD (2004) has noted, it must not be restricted to formal settings only – it must be 'life-long and life-wide'.

It is the recognition of the increased pace of economic globalization and technological change, the changing nature of work and the labor market, and the forces emphasizing the need for continual upgrading of work and life skills throughout life, that have led most Southeast Asian countries to embrace the idea that investment in education is beneficial to both individuals and nations. According to Jain (2015, p. 39), policy makers throughout Southeast

Asia now accept the contention that 'useful knowledge' is a key mechanism for economic growth, and that knowledge is not in itself useful until it is 'applied, shared and transferred for competitive advantage toward an intended or specific purpose'. In this way, knowledge is a measurable commodity and a key driver of value exchange. This shifts the focus of learning from 'knowing that' to 'knowing how', giving rise to new conceptions of the ways in which learning is defined, arranged, valued, utilized and promoted. Knowledge that facilitates productivity and economic growth is considered more valuable.

Problems of managing expansion

What this account of the knowledge economy and its implications for higher education suggests is that an increase in GER is not sufficient to drive economic growth and prosperity. What is required is a comprehensive program of higher education reform. This involves re-imagining and renewing curriculum and teaching methods, as well as the ways in which higher educational institutions are governed. To what extent then have HEIs in Southeast Asia been able to transform their curriculum and governance? While, in quantitative terms, the success of Southeast Asian systems of higher education in expanding student numbers cannot be denied, it is also clear that this expansion has not accompanied qualitative improvements of the kind that the logic of the global knowledge economy prescribes. Indeed, at the level of management, the success in expanding access has itself triggered a number of organizational problems. To begin with, almost every country in Southeast Asia has lacked qualified instructors, with an understanding of the new requirements of educational reform and the professional traits that the idea of education for the knowledge economy entails. The proliferation of HEIs has meant that under-qualified instructors have often been employed, in both private and public institutions. At the same time, systems have been unable to recruit and train faculty rapidly enough to ensure the maintenance of instructional effectiveness and curriculum revitalization. In Vietnam, for example, 14 percent of university instructors hold a doctorate, with 46 percent holding a Master's degree only. In Indonesia, only 11 percent of the faculty employed in its higher education institutions is considered qualified and competent, let alone innovative and entrepreneurial (Asian Development Bank 2011).

Various international development organizations have pointed to the urgent need to upgrade the competencies of existing teaching staff throughout Southeast Asia (SHARE 2015). The need to prepare instructors to fill new openings and upgrade those already in the system has created a substantial demand for graduate programs; while these programs have proliferated, especially in Malaysia and Thailand, their quality is even more dubious (UNESCO Institute of Statistics 2014). Graduate education has been emphasized in Malaysia and Thailand not only to prepare instructional staff to serve undergraduate programs but also to drive research and innovation in ways that might accelerate national economic development. This expansion has however placed new demands on government funds, potentially competing with funds allocated for undergraduate education. At the same time, the quality of research training has often been either inadequate or irrelevant to meet the needs of the developing economies.

The rapid growth in student enrolments has put considerable financial pressure on university budgets. Throughout Southeast Asia, while enrolments and unit costs have increased, public funding has not kept pace, adding considerable financial strain on institutions. In most countries, public expenditure per higher education student has not matched the rise in gross domestic product (Johnstone 2009, p. 2). This is partly due to the prevalent view among policymakers that higher education yields greater private benefits and should therefore be financed primarily by its direct beneficiaries, instead of public funds. The reduction in public funds for higher education has led to an erosion of faculty salaries and a general decline in the conditions under which they operate. So, for example, in several countries or territories (Brunei Darussalam, Cambodia, Indonesia, Laos and Vietnam), the student–instructor ratios have increased considerably, with unmanageable teaching loads further threatening the quality of education. In Indonesia, for example, each instructor needed to teach on average only 14 students in the late 1990s; the average a decade later had increased to 22 students (Susanti 2011).

While there are some variations across the region, governments in Southeast Asia have employed remarkably similar strategies to accommodate the explosive growth in student numbers. They have encouraged both public and private universities to improve system efficiency, contain public expenditure to higher education and develop new sources of funding for higher education (Asian Development Bank 2011). Increasingly, the cost of instruction in public universities has been shifted to students and their families. Some universities have introduced more fee-based courses, such as special adult education, English, computer training and executive leadership courses, since they are low-cost and demand-absorbing. Smaller private institutions, which represent the largest and the fastest-growing segment of higher education in Southeast Asia, rely on student fees as their major source of income. Many have attempted to forge closer links with the corporate sector, but this has not generated the kind of financial benefits enjoyed, for example, by many American universities.

The attempts to shift the costs of higher education to students and their families have had serious implications for the goal of equity of access. As students are expected to pay more for their education, those from poorer financial backgrounds are increasingly excluded or are forced to attend poor-quality low-cost private institutions. Even this option requires them to seek scholarships, but very few private HEIs in Southeast Asia offer such scholarships. The alternative to scholarships are student loans. A wide variety of student loan schemes have been tried across the region, including those that are income-contingent and those that involve a mortgage (Asian

Development Bank 2011). Income contingent loans do not require repayment until students have graduated, while a mortgage involves students paying the principal, together with an interest at a negotiated rate and over a specified period. The advantages and disadvantages of each type of loan have been widely debated, but what is abundantly clear is that many of these loan schemes involve considerable financial hazards for students and their families. Serious instances of corruption have also been reported. In both Thailand and Indonesia, governments introduced income-contingent loan schemes in the 1990s, only to withdraw funding from them once the demand became too great. Research also showed that a majority of students who took out these loans failed to complete their programs. High drop-out rates have been reported across the region, with the notable exception of Singapore (Asian Development Bank 2011).

In the context of rapidly expanding systems of higher education, issues of policy coordination and oversight by governments in Southeast Asia have also drawn critical attention. It has been noted, for example, that the administrative expertise in government departments in the region in general is limited. As the Asian Development Bank (2011, p. 24) has observed, 'of particular concern are the managerial and analytical capabilities of administrators at both the system and institutional levels. Of particular importance is their ability to assess needs and to design, analyze, manage, and evaluate education programs'. There is considerable variation in governance traditions in Southeast Asia, including the ways in which countries approach issues of state control, funding arrangements and accountability measures. A common pattern in some countries, such as Vietnam, is that the responsibility for higher education is distributed across multiple ministries, pertaining to their portfolio (Ly *et al.* 2015). This makes government-wide coordination very difficult, against the distributed and decentralized locus of authority for policy development and implementation. Furthermore, the autonomy of public universities across the region is severely constrained by political interference in such matters as senior appointments, program design and implementation, as well as student admission and assessment.

Perhaps the most serious effect of the rapid expansion of higher education institutions in Southeast Asia relates to the quality of instruction. Most observers of higher education have noted that the massification of higher education in Southeast Asia has occurred at the cost of quality. According to Bhandari and Lefebure (2015, p. xii), for example, the issue of quality is paramount, especially as many Southeast Asian countries 'are seeing a large growth in the number of private institutions that are not regulated by a government body'. Mahbubani and Chye (2015) have similarly warned that it is a mistake for Asian governments to continue on a steady course of expansion and massive investments in higher education without paying attention to the issues of quality and the changing educational landscape.

One way of expanding access to higher education in Southeast Asia has been through the use of new information and communication technologies.

Throughout the region, online learning has been viewed as having the potential to soak up increasing demand for higher education, especially in the marginalized and remote communities. In Indonesia, for example, in 2010, Univeristas Terbuka Indonesia served more than 645,000 students (Zuhairi 2010). A national Open University was created in 1995 in the Philippines to provide access to higher education to students unable to attend campus (Asian Development Bank 2011). The technology-driven programs have clearly expanded access, but their quality has been at best uneven. The designers of online programs have failed to think seriously about how the use of the new technologies requires curriculum and instruction to be re-envisaged. In the end, both privatization and the use of technologies have not delivered on quality, and on the kind of outcomes that massification promises and the new economy demands.

Regional collaboration

The governments in Southeast Asia are fully aware of the problems with massification. They recognize that the rapid rise in student numbers has given rise to a whole range of administrative and governance issues. They are also aware of the fact that larger classes and poor facilities have inevitably led to the decline in instructional quality. At the same time, while the privatization of higher education has soaked up much of the demand, serious challenges of state oversight and control have emerged. In some Southeast Asian countries the state appears to have lost its capacity to coordinate the system, especially of the low-cost private institutions. On the other hand, in public institutions, coordination has become too onerous and over-regulated, with HEIs losing much of their autonomy, resulting in the erosion of their ability to create new programs, reform governance practices and even make academic appointments. Governments throughout the region have found it difficult to balance the competing requirements of accountability and academic freedom.

At the same time, while expanded access to higher education is widely regarded as a major accomplishment, systematic inequities have intensified, with educational opportunities increasingly becoming a function of people's ability to pay for them. The argument that the growth of private higher education and technology-based instruction will inevitably promote equality of access and outcomes has been shown to be at best misleading, since education provided through these platforms has mostly not led to improved employment opportunities or life chances for the marginalized communities (Welch 2011).

That they face serious challenges in the management and coordination of their systems of higher education is widely acknowledged by governments and HEIs across Southeast Asia. Each government has in its own way attempted to meet these challenges, either by increasingly levels of investment in higher education or by developing policies and programs that address system-wide issues. They have also looked to global development agencies, such as the ADB, UNESCO and EU to assist them in reforming their systems of coordination, accountability and quality assurance. Furthermore, they have recognized that they face many of the same issues of reform and renewal, and have therefore seen the Association of the Southeast Asian Nations (ASEAN) as a forum in which their common concerns can be addressed.

ASEAN now views higher education as a major priority in its mission of 'Community Integration 2015' (ASEAN Secretariat 2016), regarding it as relevant to each of its three pillars – economic, socio-cultural and political-security. It is convinced that despite major differences in culture, social norms, religion, history, natural resources and rates of economic growth, the economic prospects of its ten member countries depend largely on the extent to which they are not only able to trade with each other but also collaborate in developing policy frameworks that steer them toward greater regional integration. In successive declarations, ASEAN's Community Integration agenda has envisioned a region that is deeply conscious of its historical ties and is bound by an aspiration to develop a common identity. According to Mittelman (2000, p. 112), ASEAN represents a new form of regionalism with 'concentrations of political power competing in the global economy with multiple interregional and intraregional flows'. The idea of the ASEAN WAY stresses 'informality, organization minimalism, inclusiveness, intensive consultations leading to consensus…' (Narine 2008, p. 413).

With respect to higher education, ASEAN's regionalization agenda fully embraces the globally circulating discourses around the knowledge economy, and its importance in driving economic growth. The Association insists that its member countries cannot fully take advantage of the global economy unless its HEIs not only recognize the importance of knowledge industries in steering national development, but are also able to rethink the role of higher education in driving national economic development. In this way, ASEAN views the main goal of higher education largely in terms of human capital development. Borrowing heavily from international agencies such as the OECD, the World Bank and EU, it promotes vigorously a policy discourse that assumes global mobility and exchange of capital, ideas and people to be an intrinsically good thing. It encourages national systems of higher education to focus on the quality and adaptability of education within the region. In addition to its calls to increase literacy rates and the provision of technical and vocational education, ASEAN also highlights the importance of a regional approach to higher education reform that consists of university networks, student and staff exchanges and the development of research clusters in order to share intellectual and material resources for addressing common problems and issues, such as sustainable development. In order to achieve these objectives, ASEAN has sponsored or supported various regional initiatives, such as University Mobility in Asia and the Pacific (UMAP), ASEAN University Network (AUN) and the Regional Centre for Higher Education and Development (RIHED). To carry its agenda forward, the Southeast Asian Ministers of Education Organization (SEAMEO) meet regularly to develop policies, compare experiences and benchmark objectives and achievements.

In recent years, much of the work of SEAMEO has been focused on 'harmonizing' the reform efforts across the region. The idea of harmonizing higher education in Southeast Asia has been inspired by the presumed success of the processes of regional cooperation in the European Higher Education Area. Accordingly, while acknowledging the diversity of higher education systems and cultures in Southeast Asia, ASEAN has insisted on the need to create a 'common educational space', which promotes a higher level of understanding, together with a sense of shared purpose and common destiny in a highly globalized world. In terms both discursive and material, the EU has greatly supported ASEAN's regional efforts in higher education. It has established a four-year initiative called SHARE to support harmonization of higher education systems and institutions in Southeast Asia. According to one of SHARE's first policy briefs (SHARE 2016, p. 2),

> building modern higher education systems in the region will be central to states' transition to knowledge economies, as it will allow the young populations of ASEAN to be integrated into the rapidly evolving labour markets. If this transition is managed successfully, it will ensure further economic growth and international economic competitiveness.

SHARE insists that harmonization does not entail a uniform or standardized system of higher education, but represents an attempt to forge general guidelines in areas such as degree comparability through similar degree cycle and qualifications frameworks, quality assurance, lifelong learning, or credit transfer systems and so on.

According to Sirat *et al.* (2015), the ASEAN community has prioritized six major areas of action for harmonizing higher education. First, the community is developing a set of regional accreditation tools designed to help HEIs to evaluate their own educational activities, as well as develop the capacity to offer an independent judgment about the extent to which the objectives of comparable institutions are being met. Second, the community is committed to creating a Unified Education Framework that specifies region-wide standards for learning outcomes, leading eventually to the development of a unified curriculum in the ASEAN region. Third, it is developing programs designed to improve the quality of education systems so that graduates possess the skills that are needed in the rapidly changing workplace in the Asia-Pacific Region and around the world. Fourth, under the policy of harmonization, various programs of student and faculty exchange have been established, so that graduates can more easily circulate within the region, and begin to view ASEAN as an integrated labor market. Fifth, ASEAN has encouraged higher education institutions to participate in skills competitions, in an effort to enhance the competency of workers to achieve certain minimum labor standards. And finally, the harmonization efforts in the region have involved support for greater use of English, as a language that is not only essential for communication within the region, but also for participating more effectively within the globalizing knowledge economy.

Overriding these initiatives to reform systems of higher education is ASEAN's attempt to develop a Quality Assurance Framework. In line with the principles articulated in 2008 by a broader ASEAN Quality Network (AQAN), and with the support of the EU, ASEAN is aiming to strengthen regional cooperation by 'enhancing the quality, competitiveness and internationalisation of ASEAN higher education institutions and students, thus contributing to an ASEAN Community beyond 2015'. On the basis of its experiences with the Bologna Process over the past two decades, the EU believes that a harmonized QA framework is essential for ASEAN if it is to 'enhance regional cooperation and mobility and be a key to an internationally competitive higher education' (Niedermeier and Pohlenz 2016, p. i). Both ASEAN and EU have thus espoused a commitment to cooperation across the two regions, even as they compete within the global economy.

This approach to cooperation, within a context of competition, is based on a range of convictions about the nature of the global knowledge economy. It is argued, for example, that as economies becomes globalized and knowledge-based, their HEIs need to work together, and share their intellectual and material resources. This demands freer movement of knowledge and people, together with policy shifts toward greater flexibility and integration. Furthermore, for cooperation to generate mutually beneficial outcomes, the demands of the knowledge economy puts at center stage the issues of quality and quality assurance across all aspects of the work of HEIs. Without a focus on quality, investment in higher education is unlikely to produce the human resources needed for economic participation on the global stage. To meet this goal, ASEAN has committed itself to a regional quality assurance framework for higher education, which involves collaboration to build capacity, share information and develop principles for the mutual recognition of qualifications throughout the region.

Persistent challenges

It is perhaps too early to make an assessment of the efforts by ASEAN to promote greater harmonization in higher education. ASEAN has certainly been successful in stimulating dialogue and in ensuring that each of its member states is committed to the same understanding of the role of higher education in a global knowledge economy. Its analysis of the challenges facing HEIs in Southeast Asia is now widely shared, as indeed is their commitment to the development of a quality assurance framework within a common educational space. However this commitment is more easily espoused than realized. Harmonization is difficult to achieve because many of the challenges of higher education are grounded in the variations that exist across the region. Higher education systems in the region are at very different levels of development relating to the robustness and integrity of their administrative systems and their financial capacity to invest in improvement. ASEAN countries are characterized by enormous diversity. As Marginson (2015, p. 61) has observed, Southeast Asia is 'a patchwork of distinct cultures and systems with unequal economic and educational resources'. Cambodia, Laos and Myanmar, for example, have weak bureaucratic structures to implement regionally developed harmonization policies.

To expect a high degree of harmonization has therefore always been something a pipe dream in Southeast Asia, not least because of the lack of a common language in the region. Not surprisingly, it is difficult to negotiate commonalities – beyond a most generalized set of values – in English. Furthermore, even when harmonization efforts are based on wide-ranging agreements at SEAMEO, the capacity of governments to steer all of their HEIs toward reform is limited. This has particularly been the case with the fast-growing private institutions, which are often driven by short-term profit motives than a broader commitment to national and regional priorities. At the same time, without the ability to assess needs and to design, analyze, manage, and evaluate education programs, the administrators at both the system and institutional levels often lack the managerial and analytical capabilities to drive reform (Kuroda and Passarelli 2009).

These capabilities are of utmost importance in higher education systems that are growing rapidly, and have to balance the often-competing demands for greater access, more research, cost containment and prestige. A recent report, published for SHARE by Niedermeier and Pohlenz (2016), acknowledges that in the context of rapid growth, quality assurance is inevitably a casualty. Despite the existence of a clear set of principles of quality assurance, actual commitment to these principles can be quite diverse, along with the mechanisms for implementing them. At the institutional level, such mechanisms are often poorly understood or resisted, especially among the casual and poorly trained and paid instructors at small private institutions. Such institutions do not provide incentives for faculty improvement and a culture of professionalism in which quality is intimately linked with integrity, honesty, and merit. As a consequence, quality assurance principles often apply only to the leading universities, where there is a more positive institutional culture, and where incentives exist to improve performance and participate in activities beyond the mandated instruction.

Beyond the issues of implementation, the ASEAN Quality Assurance Framework (AQAF), while in its infancy, has various design concerns – most notably how to work with a system that is supposed to be voluntary and develop capacity but is also used for the purposes of accreditation, accountability and benchmarking. Moreover, the Framework is written in a very general and formal way, and therefore focuses on procedural compliance rather than substantive practices and outcomes. In the end, it is mostly a management tool that is also expected to perform an educative role, with the capacity to bring about genuine reform.

AQAF has very little to say about the curriculum, and how it might need to be reimagined for the requirements of the globalizing knowledge economy. A paradox of higher education in Southeast Asia is that while its HEIs are producing a record number of graduates, employers complain of a shortage of qualified workers. Graduate unemployment rates have continued to creep up, especially in the Philippines and Indonesia (Postiglione 2011). There is, furthermore, a growing concern among employers throughout the region that graduates' knowledge and skills are not aligned to the shifting labor market needs. From a human capital perspective, quality of higher education is indicated when students are prepared for fields in which there is a clear demand, and in which graduate skills and knowledge have a reasonable prospect of being employed. Yet there is much evidence to suggest that, in Southeast Asia, as elsewhere, there is a major misalignment between higher education curriculum and its professional relevance in the labor market. There is, for example, a severe shortage of graduates in science and technology throughout the region, even as it is recognized that these fields of studies are more likely to drive innovation, job creation, and economic development. Vietnam has a shortage of graduates in the areas of health and welfare, humanities and arts, and service industries, while in Cambodia 66 percent of students graduate in social sciences, business, or law (Asian Development Bank 2011). A large proportion of the students in private HEIs are enrolled in management and business studies, not least because they are cheaper for the institutions and students alike.

The relationship between the discourse of the knowledge economy and developments in higher education is a complicated one. On the one hand, throughout the region, higher education is widely viewed as an investment in human capital that can be expected to bring various returns to both individuals and the state. Learning for learning sake is no longer considered sufficient but must always be linked to the instrumental purposes of human capital formation and economic self-maximization. On the other hand, investment in research and development (R&D) remains peripheral. Governments in Southeast Asia widely accept the contentions that economic and social development increasingly depend on innovation; that there are strong links among innovation, technological change and economic growth; and that R&D makes an important contribution to productivity. Yet, apart from Singapore, and to a lesser extent Thailand and Malaysia, most HEIs in the region lack the necessary financial, structural, and human resources to achieve excellence in traditional forms of scholarly research, let alone research that leads to cutting-edge innovation and commercialization.

Many public and most private universities in the region view themselves as teaching institutions only, with their practices seldom matching their rhetoric about the knowledge economy. With some notable exceptions, much of the instruction in Southeast Asian continues to follow traditional didactic methods, with heavy reliance on memorization, rote learning and examinations. In most HEIs, there is little incentive to experiment with new teaching methods that focus on the requirements of the knowledge economy and the changing labor markets. These institutions have neither the resources nor the inclination to conduct research. Of course, research is expensive and requires specialized talent and skills; not everyone employed in a university should be required to do research. However, it is also the case that the lack of research experience and the ability to critically read and interpret research has major consequences for the quality of instruction, making it less scholarly. At the same time, the lack of R&D has profound effects on the international ranking and prestige of universities and systems of higher education in Southeast Asia. The extent to which they are able to grow their international reputation will, in the future, clearly depend on the investment they are able to make in research and research training – as a way of both enhancing their economic growth and improving the quality of instruction.

Conclusion

This chapter has argued that the countries in Southeast Asia have been enormously successful in expanding their systems of higher education, providing access to greater portions of their populations. GERs have increased and are approaching 25 percent. Communities across the region are now convinced that national economic development and prosperity demands higher levels of education, especially in economies that are becoming increasingly global and knowledge-based. To meet the growing demand for higher education, governments across the region have enabled the creation of for-profit private HEIs. They have encouraged the diversification of the curriculum as well as experimentation with new instructional delivery systems. However, these achievements have also created new challenges brought about by explosive growth in student numbers, shortage of qualified teaching staff, various financial constraints, poor systems of governance and quality assurance and improvement. At the same time, while access to higher education has expanded dramatically, equity has not.

The governments in Southeast Asia are deeply aware of these challenges and have taken a number of steps to tackle them, both within their national borders and through regional collaboration. The Association of Southeast Asian Nations (ASEAN) has widely been employed to pursue programs of institutional and cultural reform in higher education. These programs have been focused on efforts to harmonize policies across the region – develop an ASEAN Quality Assurance Framework, encourage student and faculty exchange, outline a Unified Education Framework that specifies region-wide standards for learning outcomes, and encourage research that addresses regionally-based problems. These initiatives have, however, had limited success, due to problems of both design and implementation. The region has yet to develop ways of improving educational quality, especially in the face of serious financial constraints; of increasing the relevance of the curriculum within the context of rapid changes in the labor market; establishing a culture of research and research training, designed to create new knowledge and ensuing applications; and balancing the continued expansion of access to higher education with greater attention to equity.

References

ASEAN Secretariat. 2016. Retrieved January 2017, http://asean.org/asean-to-boost-quality-of-higher-education-in-the-region/.

Asian Development Bank (ADB). 2011. *Higher Education across Asia: An Overview of Issues and Challenges*. Manila: Asia Development Bank.

Asian Development Bank (ADB). 2014. *Innovation Asia: Advancing the Knowledge-Based Economy*. Manila: Asian Development Bank.

Becker, G. 1964. *Human Capital: A Theoretical and Empirical Analysis*. New York: Columbia University Press.

Bhandari, R. and A. Lefebure, eds. 2015. *Asia: The Next Higher Education Superpower?* New York: Institute of International Education.

Hanusheck, E. 2015. Economic growth in developing countries: The role of human capital. In K. Mundy, A. Green, B. Lingard and A. Verger, eds. *The Handbook of Global Education Policy*. Oxford: Wiley.

Huang, F. 2015. Internationalization in Asian higher education in the era of globalization. In R. Bhandari and A. Lefebure, eds. *Asia: The Next Higher Education Superpower?* New York: The Institute of International Education.

Jain, C.R. 2015. The knowledge economy and the transformational dynamics of education in Asia's emergent economic growth. In R. Bhandari and A. Lefebure, eds. *Asia: The Next Higher Education Superpower?* (pp. 39–56). New York: Institute of International Education.

Johnstone, B. 2009. Financing higher education: Who pays and other issues. http://gse.buffalo.edu/org/inthigheredfinance/files/Publications/foundation_papers/.2009._Financing_Higher_Education.pdf (accessed January 2017).

Kuroda, K. and D. Passarelli, eds. 2009. *Higher Education and Asian Regional Integration Symposium Report*. Tokyo: Waseda University.

Lee, J. 2015. Education hubs in Asia: A common façade for uncommon futures. In R. Bhandari and A. Lefebure, eds. *Asia: The Next Higher Education Superpower?* (pp. 93–108). New York: Institute of International Education.

Ly, P., N. Tat and M. Hayden. 2015. Vietnam's higher education in transition: The struggle to achieve potential. In R. Bhandari and A. Lefebure, eds. *Asia: The Next Higher Education Superpower?* (pp. 145–160). New York: Institute of International Education.

Mahbubani, K. and T. Chye. 2015. Is Asia the next higher education superpower? In R. Bhandari and A. Lefebure, eds. *Asia: The Next Higher Education Superpower?* (pp. 1–22). New York: Institute of International Education.

Marginson, S. 2015. Systemic challenges to educational quality and global competitiveness. In R. Bhandari and A. Lefebure, eds. *Asia: The Next Higher Education Superpower?* New York: The Institute of International Education.

Mundy, K., A. Green, B. Lingard and A. Verger, eds. 2015. *The Handbook of Global Education Policy*. Oxford: Wiley.

Mittelman, J. 2000. *The Globalization Syndrome: Transformation and Resistance*. Princeton: Princeton University Press.

Narine, S. 2008. Forty years of ASEAN: A historical review. *The Pacific Review* 21(4): 411–429.

Niedermeier, F. and P. Pohlenz. 2016. *State of Play and Development Needs: Higher Education Quality Assurance in the ASEAN Region*. Jakarta: DAAD.

OECD. 2004. *Lifelong Learning: Policy Brief*. February, Paris: OECD.

Postiglione, G. 2011. Asian higher education: Heightening external efficiency: A background study paper for the Regional Technical Assistance Project on Higher Education in Dynamic Asia. Manila: Asian Development Bank.

Peters, M. 2011. *Neoliberalism and After: Education, Social Policy and the Crisis of Western Capitalism*. New York: Peter Lang Publishers.

Rizvi, F. and B. Lingard. 2010. *Globalizing Education Policy*. London: Routledge.

SHARE. 2016. Towards greater harmonization of higher education in ASEAN. http://share-asean.eu/wp-content/uploads/2016/06/PB1-190516.pdf (accessed January 2017).

Sirat, M., N. Azman and A. Bakar. 2015. Towards harmonization of higher education in Southeast Asia: Malaysia's perspective. www.insidehighered.com/blogs/global highered/towards-harmonization-higher-education-southeast-asia (accessed January 2017).

Susanti, D. 2011. Privatisation and marketisation of higher education in Indonesia: The challenge for equal access and academic values. *Higher Education* 61(2), 209–218.

Trow, M. 2006. Reflections on the transition from elite to mass to universal access: Forms and phases of higher education in modern societies since WWII. In P. Altbach, ed. *International Handbook of Higher Education*. Amsterdam: Kluwer.

UNESCO Institute of Statistics (UIS). 2014. *Higher Education in Asia: Expanding Out. Expanding Up*. Montreal: UNESCO Institute of Statistics.

Welch, A. 2011. *Higher Education in Southeast Asia: Blurring Boundaries, Changing Balance*. London: Routledge.

World Bank. 2014. *Explore. Create. Share: Development Data*. http://databank.worldbank.org/data/home.aspx (accessed January 2017).

Zuhairi, A. 2010. *Access and Equity in Higher Education: Indonesia*. Manila: Asian Development Bank.

4 The rise of Global English and language policies of China, Japan, Thailand and Malaysia

Zawiah Yahya

Introduction

There is no official definition of 'Global English', but experts in language and communication have described its characteristics and functions. Crystal (2003) describes it as a common means of communication across cultures and also as a form of English used in texts intended for an international audience. Graddol (1997) forecasts the global reach of English through the British Council's implementation strategies of the 'English 2000' project while Galloway and Rose (2015 pp. 11–12) have given an impressive list of this 'global reach' in the twenty-first century in all areas of life.

'Global English' in its singular form, though, is not to be confused with its pluralized form 'Global Englishes', the latter of which refers to varieties and sub-varieties of English spoken in different parts of the world. The 'Global Englishes' paradigm would focus discussions on the identification and codification of national varieties of English (Galloway and Rose 2015), on issues of linguistic hybridity (Canagarajah 2013), on notions of standard English versus English as a Native Language (ENL) or on global ownership of English (Pennycook 2007).

This chapter is not about problematizing the linguistic evolution of the English language. Rather, the focus is on the impact of Global English on the state of affairs of non-English-speaking countries and how they respond to the global rise of this language. Specifically, what this chapter sets out to do is to explore how Global English influences the language policies of two Northeast Asian (NEA) countries (China and Japan) and two Southeast Asian (SEA) countries (Thailand and Malaysia). It also intends to compare how, in the planning and implementation of such policies, each country in the region (NEA and SEA) has to negotiate the slippery slopes between planning and implementation, between national and international imperatives, to name but a few vexing problematics caught up in the new global phenomenon. The chapter examines these contextual differences that impact policy planning and implementation differently between, as well as within, NEA and SEA.

The analytical approach chosen for this study is macro in nature and essentially top-down; that is to say, it will examine large-scale socio-political forces, broad historical movements, and mainstream national policy narratives in different geo-political-economic contexts. Johnson (2013, p. 124) calls it 'the historical-textual analysis', an approach that requires a reading of historical narratives and language policy texts in particular contexts.

Although there are newer approaches for research on language planning and policy, for instance, through political and legal theories, media discourse and ethnographic studies (Johnson 2013, pp. 121–166), the older historical-textual method is better suited to the current paper, which focuses on a broad comparative analysis of specific policies in specific contexts. Fishman (1977, p. 33) describes such studies as 'more comparative and substantive, rather than methodological and theoretical'.

The rise of Global English

For clarity in the current discourse, the spread of English and the rise of Global English are to be understood as two different but closely related phenomena. The spread of the English language is the result of British colonization of territories across the world for trade and commerce; the rise of Global English, on the other hand, is a result of the force of globalization powered by the economic strength and technological advance of the USA after the Second World War when the sun finally set on the British Empire. The current paper focuses on the 'rise' but it has to keep looking back at the 'spread' because, historically, they are on the same continuum.

Looking back, the early spread of English under British colonialism seems to be the direct result of two diasporic movements: the first involves large-scale migrations of English native speakers from the British Isles to North America, Australia and New Zealand in the seventeenth and eighteenth centuries (Jenkins 2009) that had ensured the spread of English as a Native Language (ENL) in the settler countries; the second involves the fanning out of British colonizers to trading and colonial outposts in Asia, Africa and the Caribbean 'at various points during the eighteenth and nineteenth centuries' (Jenkins 2009, p. 7) resulting in the emergence of two forms of English, creolized English in the Caribbean plantations and English as a second language (ESL) in British colonies and protectorates across the globe.

The rise of Global English, on the other hand, happens in the era of globalization starting from mid-twentieth century until today, during which period English has risen to be the world lingua franca even in countries that had never been under British rule, such as China, Japan and Thailand. The driving force that has placed Global English there is the process of globalization that demands worldwide interconnectedness, and the leading player of this process is the English native speaking country of the US, the world's leading economy and master of advanced technology.

Due to this historical coincidence of the colonial past and the present reality, the UK–US baton-passing has resulted in unprecedented momentum for the rise of Global English. In both cases, the facts of history have shown us that the spread and rise of English was driven by trade and commerce and that a language dominates only when its native speakers dominate and that a language becomes a global language only when the political and economic power of its native speakers continues to maintain its domination. According to Crystal it has less to do with the number of people who speak it (think China or India) than it has with *who* those speakers are (think UK and USA), there being 'the closest of links between language dominance and economic, technological and cultural power' (Crystal 2003, p. 7).

Globalization has given birth to new communication technologies that create and link massive international corporations, leading to massive international marketing and advertising. The new electronic media can traverse the entire world in a nanosecond and the new mass entertainment industries are defining a common lowest-denomination culture for the world. At the center of the explosion of these international activities is the USA; and, as Crystal drily observes, the language behind the American dollar is English.

It is then not hard to understand why non-English-speaking, underdeveloped and developing countries of Asia have chosen to embrace English as a global language. They see English as 'the language of power and opportunity, free of the limitations that the ambitious attribute to their native languages' (Kachru 2002, p. 218). They see English proficiency as a powerful tool for national development, for countries and corporations to be competitive in global markets, for individuals to get better pay and better jobs in order to be better equipped with the 'basic skill of modern life comparable with the ability to drive a car or use a personal computer' (*The Economist* quoted in Short *et al.* 2001, p. 4) or to be associated with international glamour and an elite lifestyle. In short, for countries, corporations and individuals in pursuit of social and economic mobility, they need English when they want to communicate globalism, modernism and progressivism.

Therefore, the desire to master this global language has become increasingly overpowering because of its international, economic and personal value. Countries across the globe are now trying to establish English language studies in their national curricula, where before there was almost no such studies (China), or to expand the study of the language where it already exists (Japan, Thailand), or to consciously upgrade English language teaching (ELT) where before it was neglected (Malaysia).

A comparative framework: contextualizing English in China, Japan, Thailand and Malaysia

Owing to different historical trajectories, the starting point for the Global English race is not the same nor is the scramble for it conducted on a level playing field for everyone. There exists critical English proficiency gaps between the four countries selected for the present study, which must be taken on board if any comparative analysis is to be done.

As indicators of these differences, Braj Kachru's three concentric circles (Figure 4.1) provide a useful model to explain the use of English around the globe: English as a native language (ENL) in the inner circle, English as a second language (ESL) in the outer circle, and English as a foreign language (EFL) in the expanding circle between the inner and outer ones (Kachru 1992).

This classification has implications for gaps in English proficiency and the choice of content method and evaluation planned for English Language teaching (ELT) in non-native speaking contexts, whether it should be TESL (Teaching of English as a Second Language) or TEFL (Teaching of English as a Foreign Language).

As can be gathered, among the four countries selected for study, Malaysia is the only ESL context located in the outer circle while China, Japan and Thailand are EFL contexts in the expanding circle.

For further clarification, countries that had a history of colonization by Great Britain (such as Malaysia) have had a head start in the management of ELT because English had been the medium of instruction in their education

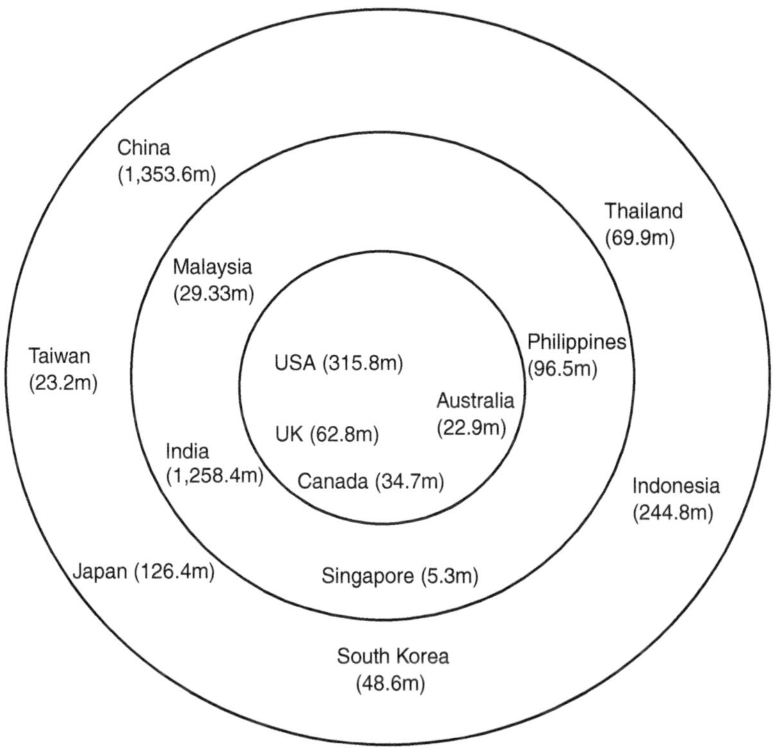

Figure 4.1 An adapted version of Kachru's Three Circle Model (1992) showing selected countries with updated national population figures for 2014 (*The Economist*, 2015).

systems as well as the official language of courts, government and business of the colonial administration. Such ex-colonies now constitute the ESL context in which learners use English relatively regularly in a generally English-speaking environment and have wide exposure to it in the written and electronic media.

On the other hand, in countries that have had no history of colonization by any English-speaking power, English lacks all the characteristics of ESL: the historical link, the media exposure and opportunities for use. As a result, these countries do not have a comparatively long and well established tradition of ELT in their education systems. China, Japan and Thailand fit into this category and constitute the EFL context. In the EFL context, the acquisition of the language may only be a necessary part of the educational system designed primarily to equip students for possible careers in organizations with international links.

Obviously, there are differences in English language policy and planning between the ESL and the EFL contexts, reflective of differences in proficiency levels and learning environments. Any analysis of language policy and planning must not lose sight of the fact that an EFL context, for instance, has to grapple with a different set of problems specific to their situation in which both the function of English and the environment for learning it are extremely limited.

As for the individual trajectory that will now follow, each account will be structured on the following themes:

- a country's history with the English language;
- Global English in the present economic context;
- action plans and policy shifts;
- problems of policy implementation.

English in China

The country's history with the English language

For centuries, English as a foreign language has had a rollercoaster ride in government opinion in China. There is little doubt that in a country such as China with a centralized approach to education, the leadership and its state machinery determine the macro picture of the country's linguistic landscape to this day. What concerned early Chinese leadership about English oscillated between Western 'pollution' and 'cultural imperialism' on the one hand and the Western military-political system being a threat to China's sovereignty on the other. English enjoyed brief support during Mao's early years after China's fall-out with the Soviet Union but suffered during Mao's isolationist Cultural Revolution period of 1966–1976 on account of 'being all things bad – feudal, bourgeois, revisionist … hothouses for cultivating revisionist sprouts and intellectual aristocrats' (Ross 1993, p. 56). China then closed its doors to everything foreign, and English simply ceased to be taught. China finally opened its doors ten years later, only to be shocked by the impact of globalization of the English language that accompanied rapid modernization in other countries (Du Hui 2001). That would explain the rise of English under Deng Xiaoping's reformist policies of the 1980s.

Global English in the current economic context

Now China has embraced English as a necessary instrument for development and commerce as well as a powerful tool for social and economic mobility. The State is convinced that in the business world in the era of globalization, an English-speaking workforce will help its economy to be more competitive in the world market. When there is convergence between the state economic and educational agenda like this, plus an overwhelming desire to catch up with advanced economies, especially among its neighbors Taiwan, South Korea and Japan, one can expect changes and reforms to come fast and furious.

The man in the street seeking upward mobility is also convinced that English would help him escape poverty, that 'people who are good in English are never unemployed … enterprises do not employ graduates without English Certificate CET 4' (Du Hui 2001, p. 131). According to a case study research on China, all interviewees 'cited economic reasons for their decision to study English' and English language fluency seems to be the answer for 'self-sufficiency and success' (Johnson 2009, p. 133). Another popular reason cited in favor of studying English is that the language is associated with all things modern, hip, glamourous and fashionable. Advertising companies, capitalizing on this new fetish, have unapologetically used English to communicate globalism, modernism and progressivism to their receptive audience.

In the twenty-first century, China needs a large English-speaking workforce as it starts a shift from manufacturing to services according to its 10th Five-Year Plan (2001–2005) followed by a focus on trade in services in the 12th Five-Year Plan (2011–2015). New technologies have increased 'the tradability of service' that have facilitated the globalization of financial services and capital markets (Tham 2017). China is exporting its investment-led growth model in loans in Latin America and Africa, in the BRICS New Development Bank, in the Asia Infrastructure Investment Bank (Nederveen Pieterse 2015b), to name a few. China has to train a large English-speaking workforce quickly almost from scratch.

Action plans and policy shifts

Currently, English is the most widely taught foreign language in China and the Ministry of Education (MOE) has speedily reformed its language policies down to micro prescriptions for each language skill both at school and college levels, so that 'the day will come when English becomes a second language in China' (Du Hui 2001, p. 132).

To keep in step with the rest of the world, a modernization program was launched in which ELT became one of the driving forces of development, on the conviction that 'China would need to access scientific knowledge base needed for national revitalization' and that to have access to international know-how was 'predicated on the availability of a large pool of personnel proficient in English, the international medium of scientific and technological information' (Hu 2005, p. 7). That is how English has ended up playing a strategic role in national development and assumed top priority on the national agenda for educational transformation.

Two events at the beginning of the twenty-first century accelerated the expansion of English by leaps and bounds: China's membership of the World Trade Organization (WTO) and the awarding of the 2008 Olympic Games to Beijing. In preparation, the MOE issued a policy initiative in 2001 to introduce English as a compulsory subject from Grade 3 upwards in all elementary schools, signaling 'a lowering of the age of compulsory instruction from 11 to 9' (Nunan 2003, p. 595), although in their enthusiasm, 'many schools start from the first grade' (Galloway and Rose 2015, p. 132).

Further indicators for the impact of Global English on China's language policy and planning are many. Except for the remote and backward interior of China, English is now taught in every junior and senior school at five periods per week and 6–7 periods per week respectively. The MOE compiles the English textbooks used, even in high schools, even stipulating specific targets in the syllabus, such as reading at the speed of 40–50 words per minute or familiarity with 450 words and expressions (Du Hui 2001). English is also now compulsory for two years in colleges and universities and a pass in the College English Test (CET) is even a requirement for graduating in some universities. The China Public English Test (PETS) is also used by Chinese companies to measure English proficiency in the same way that Japan uses the Test of English for International Communication (TOEIC) for the same purpose (Galloway and Rose 2015). Some top schools in large urban centers have started teaching content courses (such as Science and Mathematics) in English and more universities are making it compulsory to do the same in certain disciplines. The impact of Global English is also reflected in how it affects promotional prospects in the workplace, the curricula, published materials and the mushrooming of private English schools (Nunan 2003).

Reforms are introduced by the MOE to improve the effectiveness of ELT by 'updating teaching content, absorbing progressive thinking from abroad and innovating in pedagogy so as to deliver quality education' (Hu 2004, p. 10) which is equated with English proficiency. In 2001, all colleges and universities were instructed by the MOE to use English as the main medium of instruction in information technology, biotechnology, new-material technology, finance, foreign trade, economics and law (Nunan 2003. pp. 595–596). Educational structures have been changed to decentralize decision-making in curricular matters to selected regions to better handle ELT problems associated with the size and diversity of the country. There is also an introduction to bilingual education in certain urban areas such as Shanghai, which uses English as an additional language of instruction for school subjects such as mathematics, physics and computer science. These regions are also allowed to develop their own English syllabuses 'to encourage educational innovation and diversity of English provision in order to cater for varying local needs' (Hu 2004, p. 14). And the age for compulsory education has been lowered from 11 to 9 years since 2001.

Problems of policy implementation

However, despite all the efforts put in, it is not easy to play catch-up in Kachru's expanding circle, especially in a huge country of about 9,560,900 km^2 with a population of 1353.6 million (*The Economist*, 2015). The journey from EFL to ESL is long and arduous. There have been complaints of inadequately trained local English teachers; of the disadvantage of using a foreign language to get information while ENL and ESL speakers have it easy; of the reality that 'China still has a very long way to go' (Du Hui 2001, p. 133). The rush to produce an English-speaking human capital with very limited resources results in unequal access to English by privileging urban students while denying the right of the masses in the rural areas. The wisdom of an early instruction (at the age of 9) in a new language is questioned by Nunan and other linguists. In fact, much research points to the advantages of postponing formal language teaching in specific cases where teachers and resources are inadequate.

English in Japan

The country's history with the English language

The past and present English language policies in Japan are consistently characterized by a series of pendulum swings 'from eager interest to absolute rejection' (Hagerman 2009, p. 47), a tension 'between the desire for useful foreign ideas … and the desire to avoid foreign influence' (Hagerman 2009, p. 48) and keeping foreign influence 'both at a distance and close at hand' (Hagerman 2009, p. 49). This is because for the past 400 years of Japanese history, language policies were always in step with changing political events of the country.

In the worst of times, when Japan isolated itself from the rest of the world in 1683, foreign language study was banned, up until the isolationist policy ended the following century. In the best of times, in the Meiji era (from 1868) when Japan welcomed and embraced western ideas and goods, foreign language policies were reformed to enable Japanese scholars to be sent to Western institutions and Western experts to come in to teach languages. The linguist Harold Palmer was invited in 1922 by the Japanese government to improve ELT and made proposals for an oral approach to replace the traditional grammar-translation method (*yakudoku*). However, the early 1900s witnessed a strong surge of anti-Western and anti-English sentiments and by 1930s the pendulum swung back to nationalism, resulting in the termination of ELT completely. It was not until after Japan's defeat in the Second World War that ELT made a comeback, riding on the wings of globalization and English became a compulsory foreign language subject in secondary schools.

Global English in the present economic context

Japan invested in heavy industry after the Second World War and, after an initial period of Western imitations, had generated, through 'technological upgrading and indigenous innovation' (Nederveen Pieterse 2014), its own internationally accepted brands such as Toyota, Honda, Mitsubishi, Sony, etc. However, following the collapse of the bubble economy in 1989, Japan experienced a recession and felt it was falling behind in information technology, which politicians and corporations blamed on workers' poor English skills. *Harvard Business Review* of May 2012 reported that Hiroshi Mikitani – CEO of Rakuten, Japan's largest online marketplace – had in March 2010 mandated that English be the multibillion-dollar company's official language of the business, which would affect 7100 employees (Neely 2012). This, happening in conservative Japan, is testimony to a willingness to compromise for practical solutions to an economic stagnation.

There currently seems to be in Japan a national recognition of the importance of English proficiency and its links to better employment and internationalism. State preoccupation with it is reflected in projects institutionalized by the Ministry of Education, Home Affairs and Foreign Affairs. English education is now seen as an economic engine to advance national goals, not unlike what is happening in China.

Japanese students are likewise driven to focus on English proficiency for its utilitarian value, as a requirement to get into Japanese universities and enter the workforce in business corporations. Research on the attitudes of Japanese learners toward English as an international language shows that although they are positive about its global role, they prefer ENL teachers to teach them (Matsuda 2003), want to sound like ENL speakers, feel that ENL teachers and ELT materials from the inner circle are more authentic (Galloway and Rose 2015) while acknowledging that Japanese teachers are experienced teachers of grammar with whom they feel more comfortable (Zawiah 2012, 2015). In short, they are as ambivalent as the rest of Japan.

There is evident tension between the new enthusiasm about English and Japan's traditional resistance to all foreign influence. There is always 'a conscious effort by policy-makers to ensure access to foreign ideas without sacrificing Japanese identity' (Ressor 2002, p. 41). This is reflected in the contradictions between policy statements and implementation of the action plan. For instance, while the policy promotes a communicative teaching approach in ELT for learners to obtain a practical communicative command of English to improve Japan's links with the rest of the world, it does not stop the traditional grammar-translation method from flourishing on the ground. 'The tension between developing these contacts on the one hand, and maintaining Japan's 'uniqueness' and identity on the other, has long been a factor in language policy (Carroll 2001, p. 7).

Action plans and policy shifts

There have been attempts at reforming ELT over the past 50 years, although 'admittedly inadequate in scope and only effecting incremental change' (Eades *et al.* 2005, p. 246). But when Japan found itself repeatedly near the bottom of the English standardized TOEFL scores of Japanese test-takers, the unfavorable rankings set the alarm bells ringing. The relevant ministry, the *Monbusho*, in response, outlined a five-year plan called 'Action Plan to Cultivate "Japanese with English Abilities"' in 2003. The plan continues to devise strategies to stimulate the economy and identifies seven areas in ELT where action would be taken to achieve this, including improving the ability of English teachers, upgrading the teaching system and supporting English conversation activities in schools.

The difference between the new action plan of 2003 and previous reforms is that the new plan spells out implementation strategies and specific targets in policy statements. It gives more autonomy to teachers and Boards of Education, promotes the oral communicative approach over the traditional grammar-translation method and retools university entrance examinations to include a listening component by 2006. English was compulsory in the first year of junior high when learners were 12 but became compulsory in primary education in 2011.

English has been a compulsory sub-test of university entrance examinations as well as a required subject at university level. This has forced over ten million 12 to 18-year-olds, and another million or so university students, to study English whether they like it or not (Eades *et al.* 2005, p. 247).

Owing to intense competition for places in preferred universities, entrance examinations are big business in Japan and have spawned private 'mirror institutions' such as the *juku* (cram schools) and *katei kyoshi* (home tuitions) outside the regular school system to help candidates with additional examination preparation, a similar phenomenon, as has been mentioned, as is happening in China. It has also spawned the JET (Japanese Exchange and Teaching) program, which handles the annual invitation to Japan of over 4500 non-Japanese assistant English teachers (AETs) and coordinators of international relations (CIRs) comprising mostly NLS speakers.

Problems of policy implementation

Yet, despite all the perceived need for English, Japanese students seem to have great difficulty in mastering the language. McVeigh (2002) reported a decline in their achievement over the years. According to the TOEFL 1993 statistics, Japanese candidates achieved lower scores than China's 531, South Korea's 504, Taiwan's 503 and Vietnam's 511, ranking 149th in scores. In fact, McVeigh went on to elaborate, a subsequent report published four years later showed scores of Japanese students on the same test had not improved over three decades 'while students in much of the rest of Asia have shown marked improvement' (McVeigh 2002, p. 151). Worse, it is predicted that the ranking will drop further once a new composition section is added to the test (Yoshida 1997) which has always been based, in the past, on the multiple-choice and fill-in-the-blank format. The Test and Score Data summary for TOEFL iBT Tests January–December 2014 on a range of 0–120 show Japan (70) lagging behind China (77), South Korea (84) and Vietnam (79) (www.ets.org/s/toefl/pdf/94227_un/web.pdf). Indeed, *The Asahi Shimbun* reported on 10 September 2014 that Japan was 40th out of 48th in the average TOEIC (Test of English for International Communication) scores for 2013.

Some critics have blamed this on the teaching methodology. In the school system, as is in some universities, the preferred methodology is the Grammar-Translation method (*yakudoku*). Basically, it operates in three stages: first, a sentence or text in English is translated word-by-word into Japanese; then the translated words will then be re-ordered and re-coded according to the Japanese syntax. English taught this way loses its communicative purpose. Furthermore, the medium of instruction is not English but Japanese. Despite the downside of the method, it is deemed by practicing Japanese teachers to be the most appropriate way for dealing with EFL learners of very limited proficiency in English (Zawiah 2012, 2015) despite a policy that promotes a communicative approach instead.

However, growing concern for such lack in communicative skills did prompt some attempts to bring about reforms in ELT at the tertiary level. The result is the oral approach to teaching, which began with what was called the 'Palmer Oral English' approach in the pre-war period, followed by the post-war Fries Oral Approach to language learning, called the 'Michigan Method', implemented in Japan in 1956 by the English Language Exploratory Committee (ELEC) and funded by the Rockefeller Foundation. Although this method was abandoned after 12 years in 1968, the oral input in ELT is still reflected in the oral and public speaking courses in the basic university proficiency programs, while the tradition of *yakudoku* survives in the reading and writing courses (Zawiah 2012, 2015).

Today, Japanese ELT experts are divided in their support between the traditional *yakudoku* approach and the 'new' communicative approach. The pro-*yakudoku* supporters say that cultural enrichment through reading is important; the pro-communicative converts say English is needed for international communication (Zawiah 2012, 2015). But as with all imported teaching methodology that fails to contextualize method with local learning environment, the new communicative method too suffers a gap between theory and practice and has encountered both teacher and student resistance and this is 'especially pronounced in Japan and the rest of Asia' (Eades *et al.* 2005, p. 252) because it brought a sense of sterility into language learning as the simulated dialogues supposed to happen in everyday life became contrived and stagey.

English in Thailand

The country's history with the English language

In the history of Thailand in an era of European colonization of Southeast Asia, the king was the highest authority that decided policies in the running of the country. It was a royal strategy that a spirit of openness to Western influence could act as a bulwark against Western colonization of the country. Hence, Western-friendly policies have prevailed since the reign of King Rama III in the nineteenth century.

In fact, English education began in the reign of King Rama III (1824–1851). English, French, Spanish and Portuguese languages were introduced to Thailand during his reign as part of a defense strategy against colonization by competing European powers. However, it was English that enjoyed a special position as the language that promised security and prosperity. According to Sukamolson (1998, in Methitham 2009, p. 32), to 'counterbalance the influences', Thailand decided to sign trade treaties with both England in 1825 and America in 1832 as it began to realize the importance of English for the safety and prosperity of the country. The fear of being colonized by England was exacerbated by China's defeat by England in the Opium War of 1842.

The other reason for the preference for English was the technological advances brought by Protestant missionaries that greatly impressed King Rama IV (1851–1868) as 'essential and appropriate for modernizing the country' (Sukamolson 1998, in Methitham 2009, p. 33). The mission to modernize the kingdom was intensified by King Rama V (1868–1910) who established even more extensive contact with the West in his reign. This Western-friendly royal tradition was sustained through the reign of Rama VI (1910–1925), who introduced English as a compulsory subject in 1913 which was allocated more hours of instruction than the Thai language.

It is a known historical fact that the kings of Thailand embraced the English language and welcomed English tutors into their court and country so that Thais would get acquainted with the language to interact with the wider world community. During their reigns, Thai officers and students were sent abroad for higher education and English was made compulsory in all government secondary schools and later beyond Grade 4. English language teaching then was supposed to 'produce modern thinkers for the country and to provide children with a sufficient knowledge of English to be able to function in English-speaking classrooms' (Aksornkul 1980, in Methitham 2009, p. 35).

English was then taught based on rote-memorization and grammar-translation, a methodology that was replaced by the audio-lingual approach in the 1960s when there was a greater emphasis on English for international communication in the curriculum, just like what happened in Japan. It was suggested that this shift might have been triggered by the US involvement in Vietnam. However, this method had little success because 'it ran counter to the rote memorization that was long ingrained in the educational traditions of Thai culture' (Methitham 2009, p. 36).

Global English in the current economic context

Thailand's venture into assembly and automotive industries faces competition from China and has floundered. As the industry winds down, Thailand is developing the service sector as a driver of growth, apart from its agricultural sector.

English has become an important part of the daily lives of many Thais, especially those involved in the service sector of the tourism and hospitality industry, which has become a great income-earner for Thailand. Needless to say, English oral fluency is a must-have skill for operators in this business. It has become the de facto working language in other areas as well.

In addition, through its English education, Thailand made preparations to improve its English proficiency because English was to be the official language of the ASEAN Economic Community (AEC), launched in Kuala Lumpur in November 2015. The AEC's intention is to bring together ASEAN member nations into a single market able to compete in the global economy and it aims to transform Southeast Asia into a region with free movement of capital, goods, services and skilled labor. 2012 was declared the 'English Speaking Year' in Thailand to prepare its people for this transformation.

Action plans and policy shifts

A new national curricula introduced in 1977 and 1980, which required students in higher education to take six foreign language credits made English the preferred foreign language in the universities over such languages as French, German and Japanese. During this period, English was taught using a new method called 'the communicative approach', a teaching methodology that the omnipresent ELT agency called the British Council helped to promote by providing ELT specialists for training courses.

English was given another shot in the arm in 1996 when it became a compulsory subject in primary schools, thus making the language mandatory from Grade 1 to the end of secondary school. The English language curriculum was revamped based on a new functional-communicative approach designed to lay the foundation for 'international communication, acquisition of knowledge, use of English in higher education, and career prospects' (Methitham 2009, p. 37). In 2001, English was made compulsory in universities. There was even a proposal to make English an official second language in 2010, but the attempt was aborted. However, in the same year, the Minister of Education announced plans to 'raise the profile of English, particularly in the teaching of Mathematics and Science' (Galloway and Rose 2015, p. 137).

In preparation for the AEC, Thailand made several strategic moves. A target was set for English programs to cover 150 vocational colleges in 2013; emphasis was placed on English language education in the government sector, and the Office of the Civil Service Commission launched an English-language training e-learning project to prepare officials. Branch campuses were also opening in the country and, from 2014, the Office of the Civil Services Commission required applicants to take an English test. From 2014, Chulalongkorn University would open an English program for engineering students and Sukhothani Thammathirat Open University would commence its 'Communication Arts for ASEAN' Master's degree (Galloway and Rose 2015, p. 140).

Problems of policy implementation

However, English proficiency among Thai students is an elusive achievement. Many critics have acknowledged a failure in English education in Thailand (Debyyasuvarn 1981; Broughton 1996; Wiriyachitra 2001; Meteetham 2001; Wongsothorn 2000, 2003, and Wongsothorn *et al.* 2003; all cited in Methitham 2009, p. 200). According to research conducted between June 1999 and February 2000, the proficiency level of university candidates was below average. According to a recent local English newspaper, the TOEFL scores of Thai candidates are among the lowest in the region.

As in other non-English speaking countries in both the outer and expanding circles, ELT in Thailand has come under constant scrutiny, especially on the lack of qualified English staff in the system. In 2010, the Thai government embarked on a native-speaker recruitment project that failed due to the low salary offered (Kirkpatrick 2010, p. 49). In contrast, this English-speaker project is flourishing in Japan and China, though it is not without its own problems.

English in Malaysia

The country's history with the English language

The story of the English language in Malaysia shares more or less the same plot as other ESL countries in Kachru's outer circle. During the long period of British colonization, English was made the official language for administration, education, commerce and law in these colonies while local languages were marginalized, downgraded and, in some cases, driven to extinction to make way for a 'superior' language and civilization.

In the same way, the people of pre-Independent Malaya were made to turn their backs on their own language, the Malay language, whose written tradition was already in place by the seventh century and which had been an international language of commerce in the fifteenth century for spice-traders plying the Straits of Malacca. This alone would explain why such people are left with historical baggage that would complicate their post-Independence management of this killer language in their system of education. Then, further down the post-Independence love-hate journey with the English language, just as they think they have got the better of their schizophrenia through their new language policies, the waves of globalization strike like a tsunami to wash back this 'lingua Frankensteinia' (Wilton 2012), this 'Tyrannosaurus Rex' (Tardy 2004), while they would scramble on dry land to adjust priorities, yet again, to survive the demands of a new landscape.

Such are the chronicles of the English language in the education of Malaysians who, through colonial indentured labor policy, had become multi-racial, multi-lingual, multi-religious and multi-cultural by the time the British left. Is it any wonder then that the prime objective of the national language policy of Malaysia has been the use of Malay as the official and national language as well as the medium of instruction in institutions of learning to replace English? The Education Act of 1961 was passed for this purpose with the hope that it would also forge some form of national identity and unity out of Malaysia's diverse citizenry. Consequently, when it was implemented in 1962, the Education Act made Malay the medium of instruction with the plan to phase out English as a medium of instruction in public schools by 1980 starting from standard 1 in 1970.

Subsequently, the National Language Acts of 1963–1967 downgraded English to the position of second language. The national language was to be used for official purposes and English was to be phased out in Parliament, Legislative Assembly and court of law. Universiti Kebangsaan Malaysia, the National University of Malaysia, the first Malay-medium University was born in 1970 with much passion and pain, amidst much skepticism from prophets of doom.

So, to summarize: in the beginning, Malaysia needed a national language for nation-building because a common language was thought to be a powerful instrument for unifying a diverse population and bringing together individuals and sub-groups into the national system. However, not everyone was in favor of the paradigm shift. During this transition period between policy and implementation, a great number of urban and wealthy citizens began an exodus to settle in Kachrul's inner circle. Others who had more faith or possibly no choice stayed in the national school system, as more Acts were enacted to consolidate changes.

One could say that Malaysians have been divided on the English language issue since Independence in 1957.

Global English in the present economic context

There is one word to describe the Malaysian attitude to Global English: ambivalent.

With the advent of globalization, English once again reigns supreme as the lingua franca of a globalized communication system. Concerned Malaysians watch in exasperation with each passing day the way this new linguistic imperialism is in the process of undoing all the hard work that had gone into the making of their national language which is not English and their national identity which is not American. Yet now, the desire to master this global language has become so overpowering that there is even pressure from urban Malaysian parents to bring back the English-medium school system because they have seen how 'disadvantaged' Asian countries in the expanding circle are falling over one another in the quest for English proficiency and might even overtake them in the near future.

Furthermore, Malaysia is now shifting from the highly competitive sector of manufacturing to 'knowledge-based and technology-intensive intermediate services that can provide a competitive edge to an economy in the globalized information era' (Tham 2017). Economic zones are created. The Multimedia Super Corridor, Iskandar Malaysia; tourism, computer-related businesses, private hospitals, international schools and private universities are part of the unilateral liberalization of services. Needless to say, English is needed in the operation of these services.

Action plans and policy shifts

As time went on, the realities on the ground caught up with national ideals. For example, faced with the pressures of globalization and impatient with the slow transfer of scientific and technological knowledge through translation into Malay, the Malaysian government decided in the 1990s to modify the language policy to allow the use of English as a medium of instruction for teaching certain science and technology courses in public universities. There was a hue and cry. Defenders of the national language saw this as a regressive step and feared that giving in to this global linguistic imperative might undo all the hard work that had gone into making Malay the language for academic and intellectual discourse in the country. Others regarded the move as necessary to keep pace with global advance in information technology and are still convinced to this day that English is a pre-requisite for the country to be fully developed by the year 2020.

Another example of a U-turn in language policy is the Private Higher Educational Institutional Act of 1996. This act allows for English to be the medium of instruction in private institutions, in an effort to liberalize tertiary education. As expected, the nationalists saw it as a betrayal of the spirit of the National Language Act of 1967 that would create a dual system of tertiary education, one using Malay in public universities, the other using English in private university colleges. Today, these English-medium private institutions have become a flourishing business through twinning programs with, and branch campuses of, universities in ENL countries from Australia to the USA.

A more controversial policy change was made in 2002 when the MOE decided to make English the medium of instruction for mathematics and science at all levels of the education system, from the primary upwards, to be implemented in stages. The policy promptly divided the nation into pro-Malay and pro-English factions, screaming their arguments in the old and new media for six years.

Then, in 2012, a new education minister reversed this language policy of 2002 and documented a new blueprint for Malaysian education. The new move involved 11 paradigm shifts. Of the 11 shifts, the second shift is meant to address the vexing issue of an understandable drop in English language proficiency since the time when English-medium schools ceased to exist. There is a clear agenda for bilingualism in the Ministry's promotional slogan: 'To uphold Malay; to strengthen English'. Language policy implementation strategies were also clearly spelled out. Of interest to language teachers are the two deadlines given: by 2016, English will be a compulsory subject to pass for SPM (the local replacement for the Cambridge School Certificate), obviously a compromise move; and by 2025, every student is encouraged to learn an additional language in preparation for a globalized world. As far as language issues are concerned, the Blueprint has taken the middle ground to accommodate the needs of those who want to retain the vernacular school while transforming the national school as an educational system of choice for parents.

Problems of policy implementation

English in Malaysia is not a simple proficiency issue. Among other things, it is an ideological schizophrenia on a national scale. Between the perceived threats of English to the agenda for nation-building and the perceived economic value of English as an international language, the post-Independence nation of Malaysia is caught in an endless ambivalence. The result could be a flip-flop damage-control attempt at worst or a long-term blueprint yet to prove its worth, at best. Such flip-flops and reversals speak of a nation still in a state of becoming, and not yet in a stable state of being. This is a typical narrative in most countries in Kachru's outer circle.

Comparative analysis

This section will compare and contrast the different ways in which each of the four countries has responded, through its language policies, to the rise of Global English, according to its own national needs, while negotiating specific problems created by policy choices it makes in the process.

A similarity shared by China, Japan and Thailand is that they are all in Kachru's expanding circle, a position that indicates an EFL category and, therefore, an expected English language proficiency level that is lower than that associated with an ESL country such as Malaysia. In addition, as their individual historical accounts have shown, their pre-globalization romance with this language was an on-off affair greatly dependent on the unilateral decisions or desires of their Party leaders, emperors or kings. For example, China switched English off during the Cultural Revolution of 1966–1976; Japan banned it in 1683 at the height of its isolationist policy and terminated it altogether in the 1930s at the height of its anti-West and anti-English sentiments. What this means is that any curricular and pedagogical change that these countries decide to make to suit the temper of any particular point of their history can be effected top-down with relative ease and minimum resistance.

The same cannot be said of an ESL country with a colonial history such as Malaysia. The colonial baggage Malaysia has to carry beyond Independence (1957), to re-claim the status of its indigenous language for nation-building, was explained at great length earlier, as is the multi-lingual mix of its citizenry as a result of colonial indentured labor policies. Although the English proficiency level is relatively higher due to an accident in history, the nation is beset with controversies and contestations not only on the role of English vis-à-vis the Malay language but also on the claims of other mediums of instruction (Mandarin, Tamil, Arabic) in vernacular/religious schools, a reality that has more to do with political compromise than with best practices in curriculum and pedagogy.

What this means for Malaysia is that any change involving language policies is a slow process that has to go through countless consultations, debates, reports, and acts of Parliament. It took a decade to replace English with Malay as the medium of instruction in schools. The 2012 new blueprint for education could only be announced after completing a survey of 14,000 respondents from public universities, a collaborative research with local and international experts, and a series of discussions in focus groups, interviews and workshops involving more than 200 school principals, 200 teachers, 300 federal/state/district officials from the Ministry and 100 parents (*New Straits Times*, September 2013, pp. 5–7). Even the latest effort to promote bilingualism in schools through the Dual Language Programme (DLP), starting with a pilot project in 300 schools, needs to take on board feedback from schools and presumably their parent–teacher associations (*New Straits Times*, 28 November 2015, p. 18). Already there has been resistance from 34 Pro-national language NGOs (*Utusan Malaysia*, 28 November 2015, p. 10).

In comparison, China, Japan and Thailand share the same linguistic priority for its own language as the medium of instruction and a single national system of education, a choice made possible by having a largely homogeneous population. Whatever reforms engineered for these three EFL countries to upgrade the unsurprisingly low English scores of their candidates are conducted within the limits of a non-threatening status of English as a foreign language. A homogeneous nation of stakeholders does ensure that there are no spanners in the works to derail a national agenda.

However, as far as perceptions on the usefulness of English is concerned, there is no doubt all four countries are on the same page. When globalization swept the world in the 1990s and reached its highpoint of popularity in Asia in the early twenty-first Century, Asian countries have become increasingly convinced that the rapidly growing emerging Asian markets could also be major winners in this game. Cubs actively dreamed to be tigers. It dawned on them that even 'under-developed' and 'Third World' countries also have the potential to become global hegemons. Thus began the Asian scramble for global connectedness. The connected economy requires a flow of communication across geographies, suppliers, partners and customers; therefore, English as the language of international communication is a must-have commodity.

It is a reality equally understood by China, Japan, Thailand and Malaysia that the global economy has clearly adopted English as the de facto language of business. They accept the fact that global success requires a common language to understand documents, legal contracts, strategic planning, research in product and services, design, operational tactics and sales processes, among myriad other things. The shift from manufacturing to services and from heavy industry to a knowledge economy helps push Asian nations to look West for enlightenment. To citizens on the ground, English becomes a passport to higher education both at home and abroad, to lucrative employment both in the public and the private sectors and to upward mobility both professionally and socially. For the government of the day, action plans need to be put in place to quickly upgrade English proficiency for the masses to fulfil a national ambition which, when transformed into a national agenda, promises the creation of the right human capital in the new globally competitive environment.

In the case of China, once the Chinese leadership recognizes the vital role that English proficiency can play in the modernization and development of China, ELT becomes top priority on the national agenda for education. Huge resources have been invested in it. The basic language policy that ensues as a result is a shift from the old focus on the political and ideological functions of English as merely a part of a foreign language education to a focus on its new and specific role of facilitating economic development and national modernization (Hu 2002). English then becomes a tool for a state agenda and will continue to be useful as long as the political and the linguistic ideologies converge.

Reforms that have been introduced by MOA in China to improve the effectiveness of ELT have come fast and furious, almost as if China is fighting against time to catch up with the rest of the great economies of the world. The early exposure to English at age 9 was implemented without 'a clearly articulated rationale' (Nunan 2003, p. 609). It is not surprising that this new competitiveness that has driven China headlong into accelerated large scale reforms within its vast territory of 9,560,900 square kilometers affecting a population of 1353.6 million (*The Economist* 2015, p. 132) seems to have created more problems than solutions.

China's limited resources and time have forced the government to select only urban areas for ELT access, leaving vast rural areas without the benefit of the new reforms taking place. This seems to be a quick-fix approach to quickly develop the service sector by churning out workers proficient in English to fulfil a rushed plan for adequate human resources. The resulting shift in language policy and the speed of implementation on such a large scale have been derailed by an acute shortage of teachers and a greatly compromised quality of teacher-training. This in turn creates a mushrooming of privately run English tuition outfits and institutes of dubious reputation to fill the gap, the same problem that is bothering the Japanese MOE, as has already been mentioned. Thailand escaped this malady simply because its native-speaker recruitment project of 2010 failed due to the low salary offered.

Like China, Japan recognizes the importance of English for global connectedness and has made reforms in ELT accordingly but, unlike China, Japan is already considered a developed country with a developed economy comparable to the West. This may explain why Japan seems to be more cautious and ambivalent than China about letting English take over its national agenda. This is reflected in the disconnect between what the ministry promotes and what actually happens in practice in teaching institutions, between the official promotion of the communicative approach to ELT and the traditional grammar-translation method that is still practiced. The ensuing debate on this divisive issue has already been explained in the previous section; the only comment to add to the discussion now is that, at the core of the debate, the issue may be more about cultural preservation than it is about best practices in pedagogy.

Similarly, cultural preservation may be at the heart of the Japanese interpretation of globalization (*kokusaika*). The term *Kokusaika* meaning 'internationalization' that appeared in official policy in the 1980s may have similar connotations to globalization used in the West, and can be equated with 'the urgent need for Japan to emerge from cultural isolation and assimilate a set of Western values' (McConnell 1996, p. 447). In fact, certain Western observers think that the Japanese interpretation is 'more focused on communicating Japan's uniqueness abroad rather than taking part in Western cultural imperialism' (Hagerman 2009, p. 52). A Japanese compromise, on the other hand, would claim that *kokusaika* 'embraces both Westernization through learning the communication mode of English *and* the promotion of nationalistic values' (Kubota 1998, p. 300) and 'the promotion of "Japaneseness" in the international communities' (Hashimoto 2009, p. 22).

In the case of Malaysia, its colonial legacy poses a different set of problems. In contrast to the relatively homogeneous nations of China, Japan and Thailand, Malaysia's multi-ethnic, multi-cultural, multi-religious and multi-lingual population that colonialism has left behind poses a challenge from within that involves the otherness of its own people-as-one, a sign of post-Independence clashes between national and communal ideologies. The Malaysian dream is that multilingualism, as a symbol of democracy and freedom, will flourish without the nation breaking up into a linguistically failed state. It can be a perilous road filled with ambushes and landmines but bilingualism is already writ in stone in the constitution of the country. The new language Blueprint of 2012 'to uphold Malay and to strengthen English' tries to promote a kind of controlled bilingualism. The new balance is designed to arrest the falling standards of English so that the country can be an effective player of the international economic scramble that comes with globalization, especially during Malaysia's chairmanship of ASEAN in 2015, when the ASEAN Economic Community was formed at the ASEAN Summit in 2015 in Kuala Lumpur.

While there is a growing post-Independence bilingualism (English and indigenous language) in other former British colonies, EFL countries such as China, Japan and Thailand remain mostly monolingual, although their language policies and implementations may reflect their acknowledgment of the current usefulness of Global English for international communication and economic wealth. China is trying to go multilingual in safe urban areas such as Shanghai (possibly with a view to marginalizing the recalcitrant ex-British colony of Hong Kong).

The last word

It must be said that while geography and politics could be a convenient device for categorizing the four countries into NEA and SEA as a way of drawing broad comparisons between their policy responses to Global English, many country-specific features of one country do not coincide with those of the other fellow country in the same region. For example, although China and Japan are in the same region, they have different political ideologies. Japan is the world's 20th most democratic country while China is the ninth least democratic (*The Economist* 2015, p. 39). In the related matter of top-down unilateral power of the governing bodies, China is a centralized bureaucracy while Japan is more liberal and democratic in its educational approach. While both these NEA countries have had an erratic relationship with the English language as a foreign language, albeit for different reasons, Japan opened up to western pedagogy (Palmer's oral approach) as early as in 1922.

Similarly, while Thailand is in the same SEA region as Malaysia, it had never been colonized by any Western power, as Malaysia was by Britain for three centuries. Consequently, Thailand does not have to contend with competing linguistic issues as Malaysia does. In fact, on this score, Thailand shares the same characteristics not with Malaysia but with the two countries in NEA. Like them, it has a homogeneous population, an uncontested medium of communication in a national system of education; but like them, it is an EFL context in Kachru's Expanding Circle and ELT is a more uphill task than in an ESL context such as Malaysia.

The upshot of all this is that when we talk of differences between these four countries in relation to Global English, we are essentially talking of the gaps between ESL and EFL levels of proficiency that define the language policy and curricular shifts of each country. For example, to cater for the general economic shift from manufacturing or heavy industry to services, the common educational trend for all would be toward developing communicational skills and knowledge for the workforce. But it is the ESL–EFL gap that will draw the different starting points, determine the content and approach of the curriculum and set achievable targets. It is when the targets exceed the capabilities that there will be a breakdown in the system – shortage of trained teachers, compromised quality of teacher training and untold pressures on students due to unrealistic demands and expectations. Similarly, it is the colonized and uncolonized histories that eventually created the ESL-EFL gap that will determine each country's engagement with Global English – to resist it, to accept it with caution or to embrace it with self-abandon. Each country has its own sense of the boon and bane of an imperial language depending on its linguistic heritage.

Official documents cited

The Razak Report of 1956.
The Rahman Talib Report of 1960.
The Education Act of 1961.
The National Language Acts of 1963–67.
The National Language Act of 1967.
The Private Higher Educational Institutional Act of 1996.
The language policy of 2002.
Blueprint for Malaysian education 2012.

References

Canagarajah, A.S. 2013. *Translingual Practice: Global Englishes and Cosmopolitan Relations*. New York: Routledge.
Carroll, T. 2000. *Language Planning and Language Change in Japan*. The Netherlands, Springer.
Carroll, T. 2001. Language Planning and Language Change in Japan. Surrey: Curzon Press.
Crystal, David. 2003. *English as a Global Language*. Cambridge, UK: Cambridge University Press.
Du Hui. 2001. The globalisation of the English language: Reflections on the teaching of English in China. *International Education Journal* 2(4). Educational Research Conference 2001 Special Issue.
Eades, J.S., Roger Goodman and Yumiko Hada, eds. 2005. *The 'Big Bang' in Japanese Higher Education*. Melbourne: Trans Pacific Press.
Fishman, J.A. 1997. Comparative study of language planning: Introducing a survey. In J. Rubin, B.H. Jernudd, J. Das Gupta, J.A. Fishman and C.A. Ferguson, eds. *Language Planning Processes* (pp. 31–40). The Hague: Mouton.
Galloway, Nicola and Heath Rose. 2015. *Introducing Global Englishes*. New York: Routledge.

Graddol, D. 1997. *The Future of English? A Guide to Forecasting the Popularity of the English Language in the 21st. Century*. London: British Council.

Hagerman, Craig. 2009. English language policy and practice in Japan. www.wilmina.ac.jp/ojc/edu/kiyo_06_PDF/2009_04.pdf (accessed 18 August 2015).

Hashimoto, K. 2009. Cultivating Japanese who can use English: Problems and contradictions in government policy. *Asian Studies Review* 33(1): 21–42.

Hu, Guangwei. 2002. Recent important developments in secondary English-language teaching in the People's Republic of China. *Language, Culture and Curriculum*, 15: 30–49.

Hu, Guangwei. 2005. *Lang Policy* 4: 5. DOI: 10. 1007/s10993-004-6561-7.

Hu, Guangwei. 2014. Study on the framework of e-government services capability: An empirical investigation. *Social Science Computer Review*, February 2014.

Jenkins, J. 2009. *World Englishes: A Resource Book for Student*, 2nd ed. London: Routledge.

Johnson, A. 2009. The rise of English: The language of globalization in China and the European Union. *Macalester International*, 22, Article 12, Winter.

Johnson, David Cassels. 2013. *Language Policy*. New York: Palgrave Macmillan.

Hashimoto, K. 2009. Cultivating Japanese who can use English: Problems and contradictions in government policy. *Asian Studies Review* 33(1): 21–42.

Kachru, B.B. 1992. *The Other Tongue: English across Cultures*. Urbana, IL: University of Illinois Press.

Kachru, B.B., quoted in Guo, Zhongshi and Yu Huang. 2002. Hybridized discourse: Social openness and functions of English media in Post-Mao China. *World Englishes* 21 (2002): 218.

Kirkpatrick, A. 2010. *English as a Lingua Franca in ASEAN: A Multilingual Model*. Hong Kong: Hong Kong University Press.

Kubota, R. 1998. Ideologies of English in Japan. *World Englishes* 17(3): 295–306.

McConnell, D. 1996. Education for global integration in Japan: A case study of the JET program. *Human Organization* 55(4): 446–457.

McVeigh, Brian J. 2002. *Japanese Higher Education as Myth*. New York: M.E. Sharpe.

Matsuda, Aya. 2003. The ownership of English in Japanese secondary schools. *World Englishes* 22(4): 483–490.

Methitham, Phongsakorn. 2009. An exploration of culturally-based assumptions guiding ELT practice in Thailand, a non-colonized nation. PhD thesis. Indiana University of Pennsylvania.

Neely, Tsedal. 2012. Global Business speaks English. *Harvard Business Review*. May.

Nederveen Pieterse, J. 2014. Asia rising: Welcome to the multipolar world. In Hyun-Chin, W. Schafer and Suk-Man Hwang, eds. *Global Challenges in Asia: New Developmental Models and Regional Community Building* (pp. 31–62). Seoul: Seoul National University Press.

Nederveen Pieterse, J. 2015a. What happened to the Miracle Eight? Looking East in the twenty-first century. *Canadian Journal of Development Research* 63(3): 263–282.

Nederveen Pieterse, J. 2015b. *Goodbye Miracle Eight*. Bangi: Penerbit UKM.

New Straits Times. 2013. Malaysia Education Blueprint (2013–2025). Saturday 7 September: 5–7.

New Straits Times. 2015. Our children's future rests on right decision. Saturday 28 November: 18.

Nunan, David. 2003. The impact of English as a global language on educational policies and practices in the Asia-Pacific region. *TESOL Quarterly* 37(4): 589–613.

Pennycook, A.D. 2007. *Global Englishes and Transcultural Flows, 1*. London, New York: Routledge.
Ressor, M. 2002. The bear and the honeycomb: A history of Japanese English language policy. *NUCBA Journal of Language, Culture and Communication* 4(1): 41–52.
Ross, H.A. 1993. *China Learns English*. New Haven, CT: Yale University Press.
Short, J.R., A. Boniche, Y. Kim and P. Li. 2001. Cultural globalization, Global English, and geography journals. *The Professional Geographer*, 53(1): n.p.
Tardy, C. 2004. The role of English in scientific communication: lingua franca or Tyrannosaurus rex? *Journal of English for Academic Purposes* 3(3): 247–269.
The Asahi Shimbun. 2014, 10 September.
The Economist. Pocket World in Figures. London, 2015 Edition.
Tham, S.Y. 2017. Examining the shift to services: Malaysia and China compared. *Journal of Contemporary Asia*, published online 20 April. http://dx.doi.org/10.1080/00472336.2017.1310273.
TOEFL iBT Test Data. 2014. www.ets.org/s/toefl/pdf/94227_un/web.pdf.
Wilton, Antje. 2012. The monster and the zombie: English as lingua franca and the Latin analogy. *Journal of English as Lingua Franca* 1(2): 339.
Yoshida, K. 1997. Language gap. *AEN March* 28(5): 1–12.
Zawiah Yahya. 2003. *Resisting Colonialist Discourse*, 2nd ed. Bangi: Universiti Kebangsaan Press.
Zawiah Yahya. 2012. Western texts in uncolonized contexts: English studies in Japan and Thailand. In *Understanding Confluences and Contestations, Continuities and Changes: Towards Transforming Society and Empowering People*. The Nippon Foundation for Asian Public Intellectuals, March 2012: 193–203.
Zawiah Yahya. 2015. Method in madness: Teaching of English literature in Japanese Universities. *3L – The Southeast Asian Journal of Language Studies* 21(3).

Part II

Institutions

5 Diversity of Southeast Asian capitalisms

Evolving state-business relations in Malaysia

Edmund Terence Gomez and
Elsa Lafaye de Micheaux

Institutional framing of Malaysian capitalism

In the prolific and diverse range of research in the New Political Economy literature conducted over the past 15 years, East Asia has only recently been taken into account. For example, when Hall and Soskice (2001) pioneered the varieties of capitalism (VoC) concept, they mentioned Japan while South Korea, Taiwan and China were incorporated into the discussion about a decade later (Huang 2008). Southeast Asian countries, however, remain at the margin of this recent scientific agenda to assess the varieties of capitalism in Asia. The most obvious explanation for this empirical gap is that the VoC framework appears theoretically ill-equipped to deal with the concepts of power and state-business nexuses when the political system is not democratic in nature. This chapter fills this lacuna by dealing with the specific features of capitalism of post-colonial, semi-authoritarian and multi-ethnic Malaysia, using an alternative political economy framework, the French-based *Regulation theory*.

The VoC literature is one part of a broader corpus of the Comparative Capitalism perspective (Ebenau *et al.* 2015), a heterodox approach that offers strong methods in the discipline of political economy to assess and analyze the institutional diversity of capitalism. In this wide, relatively porous and eclectic field of research, some studies have stressed various distinctive socioeconomic contexts, especially those of emerging countries where the mode of capitalist development differs from that of the OECD. This Comparative Capitalism approach includes the institutionalist perspective offered by the *Regulation* school (Amable 2003; Boyer 1990; Boyer *et al.* 2012b). It is a critical approach that has, together with other early European theories of the diversity of capitalism, heavily influenced VoC authors when they introduced their perspective (Hall and Soskice 2001, p. 3). The regulationist viewpoint provides a *longue durée* analysis of capital accumulation, assessing over several decades, the deep institutional embeddedness of capitalist systems of production.

Another distinct component of the Comparative Capitalism literature, *business systems theory*, also focuses on the institutional context as well as the multiple rationales that determine international corporate activities dominated by capitalist enterprises (Whitley 1992, 1999; Redding 2006; Witt and Redding 2014). Business systems are used in reference to institutions that govern economic activity inside and outside companies (Witt and Redding 2014, pp. 4–5). Since these theories devote considerable attention to the issue of power behind the institutional framing that determines macro-economic and business systems trajectories, they appear best suited to capture the diversity of Asian capitalisms, as well as analyze the complexity of the Malaysian case, given its distinct institutional hierarchy.

In Asia, state-business nexuses have been recognized as a core theme by regulationist authors (Lechevalier 2007), by VoC proponents (Carney and Andriesse 2014) and by those who adopt a business systems perspective (Witt and Redding 2013; Carney and Witt 2015). However, Malaysian capitalism and its close and evolving state-business ties have never been examined through the lens of the regulationist theoretical framework, leading to an empirical gap that is filled in this chapter.[1] Malaysian capitalism is embedded in a rich and complex social context characterized by, among others, the unique political continuity of a single dominant party, the United Malays National Organization (UMNO), since 1957 when Independence was attained. This chapter provides an in-depth and renewed political economy analysis of state-business nexuses in Malaysia through a less familiar institutionalist theoretical framework. The regulationist perspective carries a number of heuristic benefits as it provides a sharper understanding of the implications of state-business nexuses on macroeconomic issues by drawing attention to the complementarities that occur between different institutions when such ties are created. It allows for an appraisal of fundamental issues such as the inequitable distribution of power and its shifts under different prime ministers, despite the continuity of the ruling UMNO, which have led to major policy changes. Since this mode of analysis does not assume nor require equilibrium at each point in time, the outcomes of economic crises and political turning points that have marked out Malaysia's development path can be incorporated into the picture. This form of theoretical and epistemological framing is particularly necessary when dealing with an electoral authoritarian developmental state (Case 2009) in rapidly industrializing Southeast Asia.

The relevance of the regulationist framework to assess Malaysia seems obvious given the uncertain nature of the economic 'order'; the importance of history and institutions as well as the developmental role of the state, heterogeneity of firms and need for markets to be well-structured and governed; the persistent occurrence of political and economic crises; and finally the diversity of the institutional settings of the capitalist system across time.

To deal with Malaysian capitalism and its forms of state-business ties under the Comparative Capitalisms literature, specific attention must be drawn to the Diversity of Asian Capitalisms literature initiated by Boyer, Uemura and Isogai (2012b), a body of study that employed a comprehensive set of social science methods to better capture the heterogeneity of local firms, their structural change in history, as well as their deep political component (Alary and Lafaye de Micheaux 2015). As a critical theory characterized by a historical analysis (Boyer 1989, 2016), regulation theory allows for an assessment of the changes in the conduct of business, directed and shaped by an authoritarian state that has persistently intervened in the Malaysian economy. This study analyses the development path of capitalism in Malaysia over time through a detailed assessment of the heavily institutionalized relationship between the state and the corporate sector, with specific focus on its links with heterogeneous firms.

This chapter is constructed in three parts in order to analyze comprehensively state-business nexuses in Malaysia from a comparative capitalism perspective. The first part introduces French regulation theory and discusses its relevance to an analysis of Malaysian capitalism, compared with the VoC perspective. This section stresses the methodological complementarities regulation theory shares with business systems theory, which is crucial to better understand the implications of state-business nexuses in Asia. The second part applies this framework to the Malaysian case. This section indicates how Malaysia's form of capitalism is different from that of contemporary China and the former French 'Fordist' model through the regulation theory's five institutional forms. The third part historically reviews Malaysia's business systems and state policies involving the development of domestic firms since the 1950s, with a specific focus on how government-linked companies (GLCs) and small and medium-scale enterprises (SMEs) function under the administration of Prime Minister Najib Razak.

Comparative capitalism research in Asia: crises, conflicts, institutions and history

Epistemology of diversity of capitalism

Studies within the Comparative Capitalism literature share a common argument about the existence of a variety of models against the normative idea of 'one best way of capitalism' (that is, the US or British form). Its strong interdisciplinary method, derived from sociology, economics, history and political science, is another of this literature's distinctive strengths. These two elements are found in regulation theory within the Diversity of Capitalisms literature as well as in the VoC approach, although there are significant differences between the latter and the French School.

In their seminal *Varieties of Capitalism*, published in 2001, Hall and Soskice's objective was to create a framework to understand institutional similarities and differences among developed economies. They aimed to open academic research agendas, restricted then by the dominant mainstream neoclassical economics based on rational choice theory. Hall and Soskice (2001, pp. 2–4) wanted to go beyond the arguments presented in several heterodox perspectives that dealt with institutional embeddedness within economies; this included the *modernization* approach, the *neo-corporatism* literature and studies quoting Hollingsworth and Boyer (1997) that focused on *social systems of production*. They distanced themselves from these intellectual paradigms, which adequately characterized national differences in the post-war era, because they were 'overstating what government can accomplish' (Hall and Soskice 2001, p. 4). At that time in the 1990s when research leading to the VoC was being undertaken, globalization and market-opening policies advocated by the dominant neoliberal ideology were on the ascendancy; it, therefore, seemed obvious to the authors that economic and institutional adjustments as well as capital accumulation patterns were firm-led. They intended to 'bring back firms into the center of the analysis of comparing capitalisms' (Hall and Soskice 2001, p. 4) and their book was a project to build a 'firm-centered political economy' perspective. Methodologically, they paved the way for new disciplinary linkages between business studies and political economy. Their ideas have since enjoyed broad support. In retrospect, Coates (2015, pp. 18–19) judges that their timing was excellent.

Focusing on coordination, Hall and Soskice (2001) argued that there were not only liberal market economies (LCEs) but also coordinated market economies (CMEs). This perspective opened a distinctive way for the authors to determine the impact of institutions on economic performance. By doing so, they proposed a powerful dichotomy to model the varieties of capitalism. In this theory, coordination is the core mechanism that interlocks the relevant actors of the economy – individuals, firms, producer groups and governments. The main institutions of a political economy frame, condition, constrain and define the strategies and the activities of companies, from which economic performance will be determined.[2] This led them to argue that comparative advantage was primarily institutionally determined and therefore politically constructed. However, their firm-centered political economy approach regards companies, whose activities aggregate into overall levels of economic performance, as the crucial actor in a capitalist system and serves as the key agent of modification or adaptation in the face of technological change or international competition.

Witt and Redding (2014), adopting a business systems approach, make a pertinent point when they argue that VoC's typology was not designed to encompass Asian countries and that 'none of the existing business systems typologies adequately categorizes the institutional variations visible in Asia and the West'. About Asia's own diversity, they contend that 'compared with the differences between the West and the East, the variations inside the West seem to be minor', and conclude that 'when it comes to understanding Asia, however, the VoC framework clearly falls short' (Witt and Redding 2014).

Fifteen years after the VoC's fruitful academic élan, a shift is required from this individualist and firm-centered framework to a more holistic perspective, or a holist-individualist view as Boyer (2016) puts it. Given the VOC's focus on democratic and developed economies, this perspective is necessary as it can deal with the self-sustaining but continuously changing capitalist mode of production seen in a variety of forms in Asia.

Among the political economy perspectives, the French 'Ecole de la Régulation' deserves special attention. Regulationist scholars assume that the dual dichotomy offered by Hall and Soskice (2001) fails to grasp the much deeper diversity of relevant forms in capitalism. Amable (2003), for example, argues that there are five forms of capitalism, instead of two. The French school[3] allows therefore for an exploration of issues that are not covered in the VOC and opens a theoretical space for concepts such as power, conflict, crisis and history to be incorporated in order to understand how capitalism functions (Boyer 1989). Institutions are expressions of a compromise, as they influence and are influenced by the formation of stable socio-political blocs (Amable 2003, p. 10). Power stands at the center as institutions are defined as temporary political-economy accords and the diverse institutional designs shaping national capitalisms reflect a nation's conflicts over local (national) distributional issues.

Our study's institutionalist framework therefore argues that institutions are not designed to solve coordination problems between equal agents with similar interests but to resolve conflicts among unequal actors with divergent interests (Amable 2003, p. 10). By postulating so, our perspective clearly departs from the neo-institutionalist direction that has been adopted by proponents of VoC (Ebenau *et al.* 2015, p. 2) who identify institutions as the rules of the game and mechanisms through which uncertainty is reduced. Meanwhile, our perspective defines institutions as unfinished expressions of political compromises. It conceptualizes power, class struggle and history very differently from the New Institutional Economics (NIE).[4] The concept of power is central to our perspective. For this reason, our mode of analysis departs from the NIE and from mainstream theory of economic equilibrium.[5] Moreover, by grounding its theoretical roots in a less-normative and non-universalizing institutionalist perspective, our approach, mixing the regulationist framework with references to business systems theory, is able to grasp how capitalism functions in less developed countries.

Renewing the political economy of capitalism

The authors of Diversity of Asian Capitalism reject the assumptions of mainstream economics and focus on social and historical compromise, functionality and viability; their primary concern is understanding how a system works – or does not work – rather than on optimal performance. They refuse to put at the center of analysis the normative optimality, derived from the equilibrium formalist agenda. Under this rich framework, an analysis of politics, including its conduct through single dominant party states, as observed in Malaysia, Singapore, Vietnam and China, can be incorporated and comprehended. By staying theoretically out of the normative and functionalist scheme of the NIE, also adopted in a certain way by the VoC,[6] this opens a necessary space to 'bring back the political and the politicized variant' (Streeck, with Labrousse, 2016).

Since Aglietta's (1979) seminal work on American capitalism, the theory of the regulation of capital accumulation has been focusing on capitalism as a specific system of organizing and reproducing social relations, among which wage relations are the cornerstone of capitalist economies. As Boyer (1990, p. 16) notes:

> the study of capitalist regulation therefore, cannot be the investigation of abstract economic laws. It is the study of the transformation of social relations as it creates new forms that are both economic and non-economic, that are organized in structures and themselves reproduce a deterministic structure, 'the mode of production'.

The intellectual project involves dealing with both the structure of the economy and its transformation over time, issues that constitute the development path (Boyer 1990; Boyer and Saillard 2002). In this *longue durée* approach, where politics and distributive conflicts are absolutely central, different institutions have emerged in response to these issues, yielding different trajectories in the economy.

Boyer (2003) makes the case that, in regulation theory, institutions constitute specific expressions of one or more social relations that shape the short run process of economic adjustment (the 'regulation' mode) as well as the growth regime. Since long-term transformations of capitalism are the core concern of this theory, it developed a variety of tools to understand the factors that shaped consistent growth, the nature of emerging inequalities, the significance of social conflicts and subsequent political processes that contributed to alternative 'institutionalized compromises' (Boyer 2003). The coexistence of various types of capitalism could be explained by understanding how institutions evolved as this provided insights into institutional hierarchy or complementarity (Boyer 2003; Vercueil 2016).

The five institutional forms of a capitalist economy are forms of competition, in which publicly-owned companies may play a specific role; the wage–labor nexus, i.e. the nature of labor relations; state–economy relations (or their nexus), a component of which is different modes of state-business relationships; the monetary/financial and credit regime; and integration into the international economy (Boyer *et al.* 2012a: 3–4).[7] Since these institutional forms are shaped primarily by political struggles, several types of capitalisms can emerge in different countries.

The concept of *accumulation regime* is at the heart of the dynamics of the economy. The regime of capital accumulation is characterized by growth rates and volume of investments. This regime expresses how production, circulation, consumption and distribution organize and expand capital in a way that stabilizes the economy. Sustained by a set of institutional forms at each given moment in time, it is itself the result of history, conflicts and policies.

The *mode of regulation* is the institutional and ideological framework that facilitates the reproduction of particular regimes of accumulation and modes of growth. It stabilizes and frames behaviors and expectations in order to support a given growth path. However, this consistent support is, by nature, temporary because social and economic change occurs during the development of the capitalist production process: contradictions arise, creating tensions in the accumulation dynamics (over-investment, under-investment, excess production, bottlenecks, etc.). Tensions occurring between economic dynamics (the accumulation regime) and the socio-political institutional frame (mode of regulation) lead to different types of crises such as the separation between consumption and production norms. Inevitably, crises occur and are part of the process of the capitalism. This non-equilibrium frame is thus able to explain the major crises that have occurred in Asian economies (Boyer *et al.* 2012b).

Malaysian capitalism (1970–2016) under regulation theory

What do we know about Southeast Asian capitalisms?

The developmental states of East Asia, as many have argued,[8] have exhibited a remarkably strong pace of growth over the last 50 years, a pattern of development that cannot properly fit the framework set by VoC. Amable's (2003) regulationist framework, in his *Diversity of Modern Capitalisms*, where he introduced a specific type of 'Asian Capitalism', therefore merits review.

Among Amable's (2003, p. 174) five identified models of modern capitalism, Asian capitalism is characterized as being a 'governed' rather than a regulated market, which shapes product competition, regulates labor markets, has a bank-based financial system, a low level of social protection and a private tertiary education system. But since Amable used OECD data, he took into account only Japan and South Korea; while emerging Asian economies were neglected. Second, his model of power and of political and economic feedback (Amable 2003, p. 48) can be considered as far too democracy-centered, and that differs substantially from the political reality in Southeast Asia. Moreover, the rise of state-led capitalism in China and the geopolitical and normative influence it has over Southeast Asian countries further supports this assertion.

Importantly too, the reality of the national configurations of the so-called 'Asian Capitalism' encompasses great diversity. *Diversity and Transformation of Asian Capitalisms* by Boyer, Uemura and Isogai (2012a), relying on regulationist-based research on China from 1978 to the 1990s, as well as the studies by Chavance (2000), Song (2001), Uni (2007) and Aglietta and Landy (2007), compare extensively China's capitalism with that of Japan and South Korea; but pay little attention to Southeast Asia. Useful concepts from Boyer *et al.* (2012b) are employed here to re-construct an understanding of the political economy of Malaysian capitalism, one method that opens the possibility for further research from a comparative perspective. By doing so, this study indicates the theoretical comparative advantage of the Diversity of Capitalism agenda, from the regulation theory perspective, over the VoC, given the former's focus on the state-business nexus.

Business systems in Asia include the Japanese keiretsu, the Korean chaebols, the Taiwanese SMEs and the Singaporean and Malaysian GLCs. Highly diversified business groups, or conglomerates, thrive in the Thai and Indonesian economies. This diversity of Asian Capitalism was not recognized until a decade later, following the publication of the results of a longstanding French–Japanese research collaboration, a project that extended to China and South Korea (Boyer, Uemura and Isogai 2012b). After Boyer *et al.*'s book was released, a number of special issue journals were published, deliberately aiming to bring Asia into the comparative capitalism perspective, to fill this empirical gap as well as open avenues for further theoretical debates.[9] However, even in this literature, notwithstanding Alary and Lafaye de Micheaux (2014) and Lafaye de Micheaux (2017), Southeast Asia tends to remain very much at the margin. Malaysia, for example, has never been the subject of specific attention from the VoC approach. However, this country appears in comparative exercises after 2012 and in a few articles on regulationist (Delfolie 2013) and business systems (Carney and Andriesse 2014).

According to Harada and Tohyama (2012, pp. 250–254), using cluster analysis combined with a multiple factor analysis (MFA),[10] Malaysia in the 2000s, along with Thailand, had a *Trade-led Industrializing capitalism*. This is because in Malaysia and Thailand 'liberalization and industrialization steadily advanced and the countries are articulated in the network of world trade' (Harada and Tohyama 2012, p. 253). This type of capitalism shares with the insular semi-agrarian capitalism of Indonesia and the Philippines a lower degree of liberalization of markets, compared with other Asian capitalisms. However, Malaysia and Thailand show relatively higher public expenditure on education and a greater dependence on external trade, but less rigidity of employment and hours worked. Indonesia and the Philippines could be considered as less negatively impacted by economic crises. These models are distinctive from other East Asian capitalisms, namely the *City capitalism* of Hong Kong and Singapore, the *Innovation-led capitalism* of Japan, South Korea and Taiwan and the *Continental mixed capitalism* of China. Crucially too, Harada and Tohyama (2012, p. 245) note fundamental differences in the political economic systems of these countries: China, Indonesia and Thailand are 'authoritative'; Malaysia and the Philippines are 'emergent-fragile'; Hong Kong and Singapore are 'key junctions of financial trade'; and Japan, Korea and Taiwan are characterized as 'the pursuit of technological progress coupled with the strict security of employment contract'.

A very important outcome of the analysis by Harada and Tohyama (2012) is that there has been no institutional convergence between these countries during the period from the 1990s to the mid-2000s. The crucial point of their comparative analysis of the direction of institutional change is that there is no common orientation among East Asian countries. There is no 'one best institutional way' to be followed. Harada and Tohyama (2012, p. 252) assert that:

> the economies would not converge for ten years at least. First, Indonesia and the Philippines show peculiar transitions that are very different from the other economies. Second, the position of China does not radically change, contrary to our expectation. This might imply that the institutional configuration of China is comparatively rigid in spite of the embracement of capitalist institutions.

Whitley and Zhang (2013) note a similar point: between the 1980s and the 2000s in Malaysia, Thailand, Taiwan and Japan, there were varying state directions of the economy together with evolving degrees of business coordination of economic activities. The conclusions drawn from Harada and Tohyama's (2012) clustering are in line with the business systems of Indonesia and the Philippines studied by Witt and Redding (2014). Harada and Tohyama's (2012) study suggests some unique features of Malaysia's structures, even if it is encompassed within a larger cluster of Emerging Southeast Asia business systems,[11] an idea that will be further developed in this study.

Institutional configuration of Malaysian capitalism

A regulationist framework is employed in this study to embed consistently an analysis of business activity, business performance and state-business nexuses. As argued, the five institutional forms or meta-institutions codifying social and economic relations are hierarchically structured. In Malaysian capitalism, the state–economy relationship is at the pinnacle of its institutional architecture. Since the historical riots of 1969 and the commencement of strong intervention in the economy, the state has come to dominate all other institutional forms by imposing its own logic and constraints. In this hierarchy, the pecking order below the state–economy relationship is the International Integration regime of Malaysia's very open economy; the Monetary Regime (favoring stability for trade, but even more importantly for constantly supporting and sustaining economic growth); the Competition form (resulting from the interplay between State intervention, the multinational companies (MNCs) and the monetary and credit policy); and, as the less autonomous and most endogenous institutional dimension, the labor nexus (wages, productivity level, labor condition, share of migrant workers, etc.). Despite its important contribution to growth, labor has constantly been subaltern in nature, subjected to exploitation in Malaysian capitalism and required to adjust itself to other institutional forms and to the economic dynamic in order to ensure high profits are registered as well as to facilitate a high inflow of investments from domestic and foreign investors.

The regulation framework helps to consistently establish the hierarchy of the main institutions framing Malaysian capitalism and to characterize its investment-led accumulation regime (Lafaye de Micheaux 2017). Table 5.1 compares Malaysia with the contemporary Chinese (Boyer, 2012, p. 193) and French configuration of the 'Thirty Glorious Years', depicting the golden age of growth based on the Fordist regulation regime (1945–1975) (Fourastié 1979).

Malaysia's configuration is very different from that of China where the implicit compromise is pro-growth and the accumulation regime is driven by the primacy of competition. In this institutional hierarchy in China, as opposed to Malaysia, 'integration into the international economy is the consequence of domestic institutional forms' (Boyer 2012, 193). Malaysia's system is also completely distinct from France's post-War Fordist regulation mode where the social compromise was about redistributing high wages and sustaining revenue and consumption, from which growth and profits ensued. The Wage–Labor nexus has been leading the institutional hierarchy since the introduction of the welfare state. In Malaysia, since 1971 but with forerunners since the 1950s, the State–Economy relationship, specifically State–Business ties, heavily influences the nature of market competition. But other key institutions shape Malaysian capitalism.

A crucial component of Malaysia's regulation framework is the monetary regime, specifically Bank Negara, the central bank, which diligently supports growth, industrialization and exports rather than paying sole attention to maintaining monetarist orthodoxy. The monetary regime is thus closely intertwined with other institutions, although also subservient to the hegemonic UMNO. Bank Negara and regulatory oversight institutions such as the

Table 5.1 Institutional configuration of Malaysian capitalism in comparative perspective

Institutional forms	*Malaysia (since the 1970s)*	*China (since 1989)*	*France (1945–1975)*
1 (top of the institutional hierarchy; supreme)	State/economy nexus	Forms of competition	Wage–labor nexus
2	Integration into the international economy	Wage–labor nexus	State/economy nexus
3	Monetary/credit regime	Monetary/credit regime	Forms of competition
4	Forms of competition	State/economy nexus	Monetary/credit regime
5 (bottom; totally dependent on the others)	Wage–labor nexus	Integration into the international economy	Integration into the international economy

Sources: Malaysia (Lafaye de Micheaux 2017); China (Boyer 2012, p. 193); France (adapted from Boyer 2016, pp. 240–241).

Securities Commission fastidiously monitor speculation and corrupt practices, but selectively prosecute those who violate the law. These oversight institutions serve both political objectives as well as sustain an environment that generates investments, given Malaysia's integration in international trade. Apart from the objective of economic growth, monetary policy is dedicated to sustaining extreme, if not excessive, strong trade openness. Furthermore, Malaysia is highly dependent on foreign direct investments to finance and drive strategic and competitive industrial sectors.

International integration is a core dimension of Malaysia's regulation framework that has evolved with certain constants in place, specifically the country's dependence on foreign direct investments to advance industrialization. Malaysia, a high middle-income country with an impressive literacy rate of about 94 percent, has long been one of the most open economies in the world. This export-oriented economic structure has its roots in colonial history when the country was a lucrative British imperial possession; all government administrations have since welcomed multinational corporations (MNCs) with generous investment incentives. The manufacturing sector, for example, has been dominated over time by British, American and Japanese firms, while China's state-owned enterprises (SOEs) have been acquiring a growing presence in the economy since 2010. These foreign meta-institutions have shaped competition in Malaysia, contributing to its capacity to function as an open economy.

Regarding the wage–labor nexus, while there was fair distribution of power between labor and capital after the Second World War, trade unions have since been persistently suppressed by the Malaysian state to keep wages low to draw foreign investments (Bhopal and Todd 2000). From the 1980s, the government actively proposed in-house unions, ostensibly following the Japanese model, as a means to break the once influential trade unions (Carney and Andriesse 2014, pp. 155–157). Interestingly too, because of structurally low unemployment, a large segment of the workforce is from abroad, allowing for economic activity to continue without serious capital–labor conflicts.

In spite of Malaysia's rapid modernization, a shortage of skilled workers has hampered its endeavor to attain the status of a highly industrialized economy, a major difference with Singapore, Taiwan and South Korea. For this reason, Malaysia is reputedly stuck in a high middle-income trap (Hill *et al.* 2011). The low volume of skilled labor is an outcome of the perceptible decline in the quality of public education, a problem the government has acknowledged by issuing numerous reform plans. The most recent reform proposal, the *Malaysia Education Blueprint 2013–2025*, provides a clear testimony of the parlous state of public education (Malaysia 2013). To deal with this problem, the education sector was significantly liberalized in the early 1990s, allowing the middle class to resort to private schooling, which has ensured a continued supply of well-educated labor. But with public education, which caters to the poor and the lower middle class, in decline and a persistent reluctance by the state to institute reforms that also entail retrenching an ill-equipped teaching force – a key constituency for UMNO in rural areas – a dual class society has emerged.

In Malaysia, following a major political shift in 1970 involving extensive state intervention in the economy, the socio-political consensus regarding the pattern of wealth distribution, which shapes the mode of regulation, has tended to be ethnically-based, rather than class-based, despite the government's stated emphasis on eradicating poverty regardless of race (Malaysia 1971). This merits further investigation as it would be an important distinction within the regulationist view, which argues that 'the founding social relations of capitalism are market competition and the capital/labor relations' (Boyer 2012, p. 190). This study of Malaysia's enterprise development policies indicates that the nature of the relations between the state and businesses is extremely complex, framed primarily around the affirmative action-based New Economic Policy (NEP).

Affirmative action was officially introduced in 1970, although it was applied in a variety of forms from the 1950s. A holistic review of income and wealth distribution and an understanding of the modes of NEP implementation are far more relevant than merely analyzing the conduct of individual firms if one is to describe Malaysian capitalism and understand its macroeconomic trajectory. Decisions taken by the state about social and economic policies that help ruling politicians retain power can have an impact on the mode of enterprise development. The key actor in the economy cannot be reduced to the firm, the reason why we focus on state–business relationships in the Malaysian economy and contest the crucial assumption that the activities of companies aggregate into overall levels of economic performance. Crucially too, Malaysia's policies involving the development of domestic conglomerates and small and medium-scale enterprises (SMEs) are strongly conditioned by the government's longstanding extensive assistance to firms along ethnic lines. This study, therefore, favors a materialist and historical perspective, with a focus on the macro-economic level while also dealing with the heterogeneity of Malaysian businesses.

Malaysia: politics, changing state–business ties and varieties of capital

Primacy of government-linked companies

Among macro-institutions of Malaysian capitalism, the state has a premier position in the institutional hierarchy. UMNO, the hegemonic party in the state, imposes its logic – as well as constraints – on institutions in this structure in order to suit the dictates of party leaders. Although Malaysia is governed by the multi-party *Barisan Nasional* (BN, or National Front), UMNO is recognized as one of the world's few remaining single dominant parties that governs in an electoral authoritarian system (Case 2009). The BN was an outcome of UMNO's near loss of power in the 1969 general election, after which nearly all major opposition parties were incorporated into this coalition.

The nexus between the state and business commenced in a well-structured manner when the New Economic Policy (NEP) was introduced, an endeavor to rectify wealth and income inequities between the *Bumiputera*[12] and other ethnic groups. The NEP justified extensive state intervention in the economy to redistribute corporate equity, alleviate poverty and promote Bumiputera entrepreneurship.[13] Since then, the government has resorted to assorted forms of state-business ties to nurture different types of enterprises: GLCs, SMEs and conglomerates. The nature of the links between political elites and these enterprises and mode of corporate development has varied considerably, most evident in the differences of the Mahathir Mohamad (1981–2003) and Najib Razak (2009–) administrations (see Table 5.2). However, the state has retained a dogged presence in key sectors of the economy through GLCs. Enterprise development plans have not been wholly Bumiputera-centered, while vendor programs involving GLCs are officially open to all companies. Well-formulated policies have shaped structural change (from plantations and mining to industrialization and services) and have contributed to capital accumulation through the monitoring of macroeconomic performance, including frequent budget stimuli and pro-growth monetary policies.

SMEs are regulated primarily through public policies, introduced to nurture domestic enterprises, and are tied to the state through procurement and vendor programs, involving SMEs and MNCs that are merit-based but tending to largely favor the Bumiputeras. A high level of intra-Chinese competition prevails among SMEs because of the NEP, a reason why persistent entrepreneurial activity has been evident at this level (Gomez 2012b). This type of competition is not as pervasive among Bumiputera-owned SMEs because they are recurrently privy to state-generated rents. Rents disbursed through these programs include government contracts that are implemented through subcontracts to non-Bumiputera firms, a reason for the continued growth of Chinese enterprises. This promotion of state-engineered enterprise development programs that have led to different business systems and state-business ties has remained in place in spite of Malaysia's very open economy.

GLCs at all levels, federal, state and municipal, have not been developed in a coherently linear direction; they incorporate hybrid features and are required to fulfill a range of business and social duties (Menon and Ng 2013). At the federal level, GLCs are primarily owned and controlled by five savings- and investment-based institutions: the Employees Provident Fund, the Government Pension Fund, the Islamic Pilgrimage Fund, the Armed Forces Pension Fund and Permodalan Nasional (PNB, or National Trust Fund), as well as Khazanah Nasional, the sovereign wealth,[14] and the Minister of Finance Incorporated (MoF Inc.), this ministry's holding company. These seven institutions, collectively known as government-linked investment companies (GLICs), vary considerably in terms of their size and objectives and are ultimately controlled by the Minister of Finance through complex

Table 5.2 Differences in state–business ties under Mahathir and Najib

	Prime Minister	
	Mahathir Mohamad	*Najib Razak*
State–business ties	Used stock market to develop conglomerates	Uses covert shell companies. No fence posts between government and personal
Business development mode	First diversified conglomerates; later focused approach. Realized with greater diversification, firms more likely to be dependent on political links and rents to develop	Businesses mixed and meandering; emphasis on GLCs. Sold lucrative state assets (e.g. power plants) to private firms in return for political funding
Businesses style	Transactional and market-driven; captured key sectors (plantations, mining, banks); early movers in emerging sectors (health; logistics)	Not market focused; philanthropic (film-making; donations to UN; property speculation abroad)
Policies and politics	State-business and policy strategies tightly linked (NEP; heavy industries and car sector to nurture Malay SMEs; privatization to create conglomerates)	No clear link between state-business and policy strategies constantly subjected to change (market friendly affirmative action; BEE)
Political business links	Heavy control over well-connected Malay firms by politicians in power	No clear links with well-connected firms; more a source of political funding
Ownership and control pattern	Ownership of firms widely held – allowed private firms to emerge. Did not use GLCs to control firms (but used for bailouts when necessary)	Focus on GLCs – ownership tightly held through Ministry of Finance. GLCs abused financially by politicians in power but are also required to expand abroad and emerge as key players in Southeast Asia. Not driven by clear development policy agenda

Source: Gomez (2016).

pyramid-type organizational structures (Gomez 2017). GLICs and GLCs implement interventionist-type policies, including those that drive industrialization, while also actively participating in corporate-type practices such as takeovers and mergers.

By 2015, GLICs had majority ownership of Malaysia's largest publicly-listed firms along with a multitude of private companies in all sectors of the economy. The leading publicly-listed GLCs, known as the G20,[15] had a market capitalization of RM431.1 billion – about 42 percent of total market capitalization – and a presence in 42 countries (*Malay Mail*, 23 April 2015). Seven of the top ten quoted firms are GLCs; so too are half of the top 50 companies, making them the most important enterprises in the country.

The GLICs and GLCs are led by professional managers who report to a board of directors whose members are appointed by the state. Through these directors, the state can shape decision-making within the GLICs and GLCs, determining how the rents they generate are distributed. The state can also inform decision-making within these enterprises through a series of other mechanisms such as legislation, public policies and golden shares. Since the state has a substantial equity stake in the banking sector, it has been able to involve GLCs in capital-intensive sectors such as those in heavy industries and high technology.

Growing presence of GLCs

It was not always that the GLCs had functioned as Malaysia's leading enterprises. In the immediate post-colonial period, the largest publicly listed companies were foreign, primarily British, enterprises. In the 1960s, foreigners owned 62 percent of the share capital of all registered companies that included a majority of the quoted companies. The Chinese owned about 23 percent of this share capital while Bumiputeras owned a mere 1.5 percent, an issue that justified affirmative action to redistribute wealth between ethnic groups. GLC presence in the economy grew rapidly in the 1970s when they were endowed with substantial public funds to acquire corporate assets owned by foreigners. These corporate assets were to be eventually redistributed among poor Bumiputeras, but state elites began abusing their access to this corporate equity to serve vested political interests and accumulate wealth (Wain 2009).

In the 1970s, another major type of state-associated company emerged, serving as an additional mode of capital accumulation for political elites. These companies were owned by BN-based political parties. UMNO, in particular, owned an array of key private and publicly-listed companies. By 1995, about 16,000 companies had been established by UMNO's divisions and branches, owned and managed usually by the party's proxies (Gomez 2012a). Due to the complicated ownership structures of these firms, as well as proxy ownership, the extent of UMNO's business ownership was difficult to estimate but it was reputed to own direct and indirect interests in key companies in media, banking, construction and property development.

A third type of state-linked enterprise emerged in the 1980s when privatization was actively pursued. State-owned companies were privatized through a process of selective patronage to create an entrepreneurial 'new rich' (Searle 1999; Sloane 1999). This new rich were to create profit-generating enterprises that were to be at the heart of Malaysia's industrialization drive. These companies were typically one-person or family enterprises whose owners were active in management and seen as corporate captains. By the early

1990s, well-connected businesspeople owned two-thirds of the top 30 quoted companies. These business figures, although predominantly Bumiputeras such as Halim Saad, Tajudin Ralim, Wan Azmi Wan Hamzah, Azman Hashim and Rashid Hussain, included non-Bumiputeras such as Vincent Tan, T. Ananda Krishnan and the Yeoh and Lim families.

If the 1969 riots was the critical juncture in history that led to greater state intervention in the economy, the 1997 Asian currency crisis had a similar outcome (Pepinsky 2009). During this crisis, GLCs were deployed to take over highly leveraged well-connected firms owned by UMNO and the new rich, concentrating corporate power in the hands of the state. Following demands for corporate governance reforms, three areas were targeted: the regulatory structure, the legislative context and the financial reporting framework. This reform drive unleashed a series of regulatory changes through the main oversight agencies: the Securities Commission, Bursa Malaysia and the Registrar of Companies. The regulatory structure was streamlined to remove ambiguity in terms of jurisdiction and enforcement while the relevant legislation was amended to deal with the limitations exposed during the crisis. These reforms contributed little in terms of reducing selective patronage, rent-seeking and corruption that were again exposed after the 2008 global financial crisis.

Mixing interventionism with neoliberal policies

As in 1997, the 2008 crisis emphasized the repercussions of the mix of interventionist and neoliberal policies, indicating UMNO's unwillingness to change policy direction and institute the requisite institutional and regulatory reforms. By 1998, it was patently clear that because of a preferential system based on ethnic quotas, a once well-functioning bureaucracy had come to be dominated by one ethnic group and was seen to be bloated, inefficient and subservient to UMNO. When the capacity of the bureaucracy to promulgate viable policies was called into question, government leaders began relying heavily on think tanks in the 1990s for policy input. From the early 2000s, the government began turning to foreign consultancies such as Goldman Sachs and McKinsey to prepare policy plans. In terms of bureaucratic capacity to implement policies, the government, by its own admission, voiced the need in 2005 to improve the 'public delivery system' (Malaysia 2006).

Intra-elite feuds have been the primary agent of change in the political system, the corporate sector and the nexus between state and business, most obvious in 1987, 1998, 2009 and 2015. Although political crises have occurred when this strong state was challenged, it has not been replaced, or reformed. On these occasions, prominent leaders have been consigned to the opposition or removed from the political system. In 1987, a number of UMNO members were ousted after a deep factional dispute; although they created an opposition party, many returned to the party fold after faring badly in the 2005 general election. In 1998, then Prime Minister Mahathir sacked his deputy and Finance Minister, Anwar Ibrahim, and GLCs were used to take over companies owned by the latter's business allies. In 2009, UMNO elites used the BN's poor electoral performance in the 2008 general election to justify forcing Abdullah Ahmad Badawi to step down as Prime Minister. In 2015, when a serious feud began between Prime Minister Najib and Mahathir over how GLCs were being abused to channel funds into the political system, this seriously undermined investor confidence. The funds from savings-based GLICs had allegedly been abused to bailout 1MDB, a GLC closely associated with the Prime Minister (*Malaysiakini* 12 May 2015).

In an assessment of Malaysia's regulatory process, how GLICs and GLCs function merits crucial attention because, since 1999, the Prime Minister has concurrently occupied the post of Finance Minister. This issue is of particular significance because Malaysia's leading commercial banks, Malayan Banking, the CIMB Group and RHB Bank, are GLCs. The state also owns development financial institutions (DFIs) such as the SME Bank, the Export-Import (EXIM) Bank and Agro Bank that play a role in channeling funds to SMEs. DFIs reputedly serve as a source of patronage, specifically to channel funds to Bumiputeras to secure political support (Gomez *et al.* 2015). State-led industrial-financial ties involve DFIs and had been productively used by Mahathir to drive industrialization and by Abdullah to create new economic sectors and nurture SMEs.

The internal structure of privately owned publicly listed companies is characterized by interlocking stock ownership, used by their owners to protect themselves from financially well-endowed GLICs that can institute corporate takeovers with ease (Searle 1999). Ex-UMNO leaders and ex-bureaucrats are appointed by these companies as board directors to protect their economic interests. The founders of these firms as well as family-owned companies remain principal corporate decision-makers, evident among the largest firms, Genting, IOI, Public Bank and the Hong Leong, Air Asia, Maxis/Astro, Berjaya and YTL groups.

However, a vital mechanism available to the state to control private firms is public policies, particularly those based on affirmative action. When the NEP ended in 1990, Mahathir championed his Bumiputera Commercial and Industrial Community (BCIC) policy. Najib promulgated the Bumiputera Economic Empowerment (BEE) policy in September 2013, even though he had admitted, following the 2008 economic crisis, that affirmative action in business had to cease (Gomez 2102b). Although privately owned firms are willing to work with the GLCs as a means to secure access to state rents, they are aware that they can be privy to takeovers. Such takeovers have occurred most conspicuously in the construction and property development sector. Gamuda, IJM, Sunrise and SP Setia, all prominent publicly listed Chinese companies that have worked closely with GLCs, have been taken over by GLICs. Two of Malaysia's top three GLC-based banks, Malayan Banking and RHB Bank, were established by Chinese businessmen, while the origins of the second largest bank, state-controlled CIMB, can be traced to a Chinese-based institution, Bian

Chiang Bank. This bank evolved into Bank of Commerce when it came under the control of UMNO and was subsequently merged with the then ailing and scandal-ridden government-owned Bank Bumiputra (Gomez 2017).

Pseudo support of SMEs? The Bumiputera factor

The state is, however, supportive of SMEs, including those traditionally owned by non-Bumiputeras (Lee and Tan 2000). From 2003, the government's focus was on SMEs as they had come to constitute 99 percent of all business establishments.[16] The state has recognized the need to maintain an entrepreneurial SME base as these companies serve as key drivers of employment; SMEs employ about 5.6 million workers. However, the government has not been able to foster the rise of entrepreneurial domestic firms because SMEs hardly invest in research and development (R&D),[17] mainly because they fear expropriation by the state through equity redistribution regulations that will be enforced when they emerge as large companies seeking public listing. How business systems evolved were hugely determined by the practice of selective patronage, although it was conducted in different forms depending on whether it involved GLCs, business groups or SMEs. In all cases, firms privy to state rents were expected to promote industrialization as well as register profits; among large enterprises, a share of the profits had to be channeled back to politicians for political party activities (Gomez 2012a). State leaders have sought to ensure that the conglomerates that emerged remained under their direct or indirect control. State-business ties consequently serve two goals: to industrialize economies and to create a source for funds for politicians to help them retain power. With the institutionalization of selective patronage, state-business nexuses were characterized by an intimate familiarity between elites from UMNO and from business that contributed to the deep monetization of the political system.[18] After the 2008 general elections, when the opposition emerged as a serious threat to BN's stranglehold on power, and following the 2008 financial crisis, the links between the state and business took on a new form under Najib, with his active and unprecedented employment of GLCs to drive economic growth, even as he continued to strongly espouse the privatization of state-owned firms. A second key feature of Najib's administration was his stress on state–state ties, involving links with SOEs from China. Since Malaysia remains heavily dependent on foreign investments to generate growth, a transition has been noted in the mode adopted by the government to attain this goal: the launching of major public infrastructure projects to be implemented through GLC–SOE joint ventures. These state–state joint ventures are similar to those forged between the governments of China and Singapore in the 1990s (Pereira 2003). However, a major difference in these state–state ties is that these joint ventures serve to also secure private investments. Najib incorporates Malaysian Chinese in these ventures, although he targets well-connected businesses.

The most controversial deal where state–state business relations occurred involved 1MDB, an ailing deeply debt-ridden sovereign wealth fund directly controlled by the Minister of Finance. To deal with its massive debts, 1MDB announced in 2015 its plans to sell 60 percent of its equity in the 486-acre Bandar Malaysia project, the single largest remaining tract of development land in Kuala Lumpur. Bandar Malaysia is estimated to have a gross development value of RM150 billion over the next 25 years.[19] 1MDB's majority stake in Bandar Malaysia was sold to China Railway Group, China's largest construction enterprise, and Indah Waterfront Holdings, controlled by a Malaysian businessman who has direct and indirect business links with prominent elites.[20]

However, Malaysia looks not only to China, with its state-led capitalism, as a source of investments, but also actively courts neoliberal regimes of the West, including by endorsing the Trans-Pacific Partnership Agreement (TPPA). Interestingly, the TPPA was created by the United States to check China's growing global economic influence. The TPPA will, presumably, allow Malaysian companies to enter markets in the Pacific, providing them with an opportunity to compete internationally and accumulate wealth.

After the 2013 general election when BN secured less than 50 percent of the national popular vote – the coalition narrowly retained a majority of the seats in parliament to return to power – Najib launched his affirmative-action-based BEE policy (*The Star*, 14 September 2013). The GLCs are to implement the policy through vendor programs for SMEs (*The Sun*, 26 May 2016). The BEE marked a major policy shift as Najib was aware that race-based affirmative action in business had been hampering domestic investments. Najib had publicly admitted after the 2008 economic crisis that affirmative action had to be removed in order to draw local and foreign investments to drive economic growth. However, following protests from UMNO, in his *10th Malaysia Plan, 2011–2015*, which outlined how he planned to develop the economy over those five years, Najib changed his stand: affirmative action was retained, but it would be 'market friendly'. When the *11th Malaysia Plan, 2016–2020* was released in 2015, in its review of policies implemented over the previous five years, there was no mention of the effectiveness of Najib's market-friendly affirmative action. In fact, the *11th Malaysia Plan* did not mention affirmative action at all! But with the need to retain, as well as increase, Bumiputera electoral support, the political implications of the BEE was evident. Given the way the corporate sector had reacted to similar affirmative action-based policies in the past, it was unlikely that the BEE would inspire private investor confidence.

Conclusion

The mode of capital development in Southeast Asia varies far more considerably than literature such as the VoC suggests. French regulation theory has attempted to expand the analysis to fill empirical and methodological gaps in order to emphasize the complexity of capitalism in this region. This perspective stresses the critical value of an institution-based political economy analysis that focuses on power, polity and distributive conflicts, allowing for a deeper understanding of the play between the state and the business system. The regulation perspective situates this state-business nexus within the context of a country's institutional architecture, which provides better insights into the dynamics of capitalism, involving economic performance and accumulation.

In regions where the state actively shapes the form of capitalism, the VoC's dichotomy is obviously problematic. In Southeast Asia, important variations exist in development plans that have resulted in extremely different and complex business systems. The ties created between public and private institutions are persistently subject to change while the policy focus can be profoundly altered depending on the political situation. State-business relations have taken a variety of directions in Southeast Asia, precipitating differing degrees of elite fracture. In the post-authoritarian period, privately owned business groups have become a major political force, bringing to the forefront concerns about accountability politics (Rodan and Hughes 2014).

Witt and Redding (2014) correctly note that the state in Malaysia is simultaneously developmental and predatory. We built on this point using regulation theory as it provides a useful historical perspective to indicate that while transitions within the state have reshaped state-businesses ties, developmental and predatory practices continue to coexist. This historical perspective also traces how business systems are deeply conditioned by development and social policies as well as the politics of the state.

Malaysia is also an interesting case as it has accommodated different business systems, conditioned by hegemonic state institutions and actors. In this context, a heterogeneity of state enterprises and private firms coexist and function in tandem with each other. Malaysia shares two features with most Southeast Asian governments, which the Comparative Capitalism literature should note: first, the desire to develop entrepreneurial domestic firms – originally business groups, and subsequently SMEs – with the state intervening in the economy to achieve this goal. GLCs were used to nurture these privately owned enterprises through joint ventures and vendor programs.

Second, the Malaysian case indicates that firms are nationally specific and embedded and thus more attuned to domestic political developments. Market-oriented forms of coordination by firms are determined by the politics of the nation, while the location of power determines the mode of state patronage. In this context, new norms emerged under different Prime Ministers in terms of how state institutions were to be employed to nurture domestic enterprises as well as create Bumiputera capitalists. The policy choices of these premiers as well as the politics of the state have shaped how economic rents have been distributed to business groups (under Mahathir), to SMEs (under Abdullah) and to GLCs (under Najib). Of related concern is whether non-Bumiputera-owned enterprises, particularly SMEs, will invest adequately to upgrade the quality of their products and services if they fear that their property rights will not be protected in the presence of a state that continues to advocate affirmative action.

This historical analysis of Malaysia's political economy indicates three pertinent points: first, the inequitable distribution of wealth between ethnic groups can be an enduring and compelling political justification and social compromise that shapes a specific and, by and large, operable regulation mode. This ethnic compromise has served to stifle discontent arising from capital's exploitation of labor and appropriation of rents meant for poor Bumiputeras by UMNO elites. Second, all relevant regulatory institutions exist as required of an open economy, but they are not mechanisms through which uncertainty is reduced, as the 1MDB scandal has indicated. Third, business systems involving GLCs, business groups and SMEs and their ties with each other constantly evolve. State-business ties have changed from private-led (1950s and 1960s), to state-led (1970s), to public–private (1980s to 1990s), to state-led (early 2000s) and to state–state (from the late 2000s). New institutions were created on each occasion to complement or support businesses responsible for generating economic development. After the 1997 crisis led to intra-elite feuds, GLCs re-emerged as Malaysia's most powerful business enterprise and political power in the state was further concentrated in the office of the Prime Minister. Conflicts over distributional issues led to reconfigured institutional designs as they served as tools of capital accumulation.

Malaysia has arrived at this point where, because of economic crises and intra-elite feuds, corporate equity wealth is concentrated in the hands of GLCs. About half the equity of publicly listed companies, in terms of market capitalization, is owned by GLCs, under majority ownership of GLICs that also control Malaysia's leading pension and savings funds, trust funds and sovereign wealth funds. GLICs are ultimately controlled by the Minister of Finance. What now prevails is a situation of extreme concentration of political and economic wealth in the hands of the executive who can shape the evolution of GLICs and GLCs.

A defining feature of state-business ties operating in electoral authoritarian regimes of the sort found in Malaysia is that while business owners have the capacity to accumulate wealth, they have little control over their assets that can be appropriated through social policies. As a result, state-business links have been inherently unstable, changing rapidly following power elite disputes or after a change in the premiership. Patronage continues to define UMNO politics, but the flow of rents to the well-connected has become more covert with greater difficulty to trace the implications of this practice on the corporate sector. Concerns about covert corporate concentration have grown as the concealed nature of state-business ties have progressively increased. When the 1MDB debt crisis was exposed in 2015, it indicated that GLCs had emerged as a means of capital accumulation while state-led transnational business ventures serve as a mechanism to channel abroad funds that are re-directed into the bank accounts of political elites (*The Edge Financial Daily*, 20 July 2015).

The functioning of business systems is evidently rooted in the unpredictable terrain of politics, made even more tenuous as by the fact that the Prime Minister concurrently serves as the Finance Minister. The Finance Minister, through the GLICs, oversees a core–periphery structure comprising layers of key publicly listed and private firms, sovereign wealth funds, savings- and pension-based funds and Malaysia's leading banks and DFIs. This concentration of economic power has serious implications on the development of the corporate sector. State-business ties evidently require reform, specifically major structural changes where power is devolved to relevant oversight institutions, to ensure productive and progressive economic and business development.

Notes

1 For an in-depth discussion of the development and transformation of Malaysian capitalism from British rule to the present, see Lafaye de Micheaux (2017).

2 Emphasizing actors, the first of them being the firm, is highly consistent with a view based on strategy and justified when game theory is sometimes employed in the VoC framework.

3 The French Intellectual School of Political Economy has been influential over the last 30 years in the United States, in Latin America and in Japan and South Korea (Aglietta 1979; Hollingsworth and Boyer 1997). Its scientific contribution has relied on studies published in two key academic journals: *L'Année de la Régulation* and *Régulation Review* (see www.cairn.info/l-annee-de-la-regulation-n-6-2002-2003-9782724608925.htm and https://regulation.revues.org/?lang=en).

4 The NIE refers to social relations as contracts and holds the view that exchange is central and intrinsically superior to all other economic activities, as emphasized by North (Maucourant 2012).

5 In neo-classical theory, this equilibrium exists. It is self-regulating and stable. If an external shock occurs, the quantity of goods and/or price will automatically re-adjust themselves back to the point of this equilibrium. In this model, the concept of power is not relevant as it is assumed that the market functions correctly and coordinates exchanges.

6 Streeck, an early partner of this intellectual project, has now distanced himself from 'the functionalist, economistic rational choice version of the VoC' (Streeck, interviewed by Labrousse, 2016).

7 This contention is similar to Amable's (2003, p. 14) argument about fundamental institutions of modern capitalism: product–market competition; wage–labor nexus and labor–market institutions; financial intermediation sector and corporate governance; social protection and welfare state; and education sector.

8 See, for example, Johnson (1982), Amsden (1989), Wade (1990), Haggard (1990) and Evans (1995).

9 See, for example, Storz *et al.* (2013), Alary and Lafaye de Micheaux (2013, 2014).

10 To capture the variance of the East Asian economies, the MFA deals with two factors: the degree of liberalization in different markets and the contrast of trade dependence and domestic social protection (Harada and Tohyama 2012, p. 246).

11 Malaysia remains closer to Thailand than to Indonesia and the Philippines. The bilateral institutional distance between the four of them is smaller than with any other East Asian country. Based on this, Witt and Redding (2014) conclude, from

a business systems perspective, that the four Southeast Asian countries should be included in a common larger cluster.

12 Bumiputera, or sons of the soil, is an epithet used to refer to the Malays, although it includes indigenous communities, including those in the Borneo states of Sabah and Sarawak.

13 The NEP sanctioned the distribution of state-generated contracts and licenses to Bumiputeras to increase their ownership of corporate equity. However, a number of these rents were channeled to Chinese firms. These rents were productively deployed, contributing to economic growth, but it did not contribute to the NEP's inter-ethnic wealth restructuring goal (Gomez 2012b).

14 Khazanah also sees itself as a sovereign development fund given its social obligations.

15 The G20 now comprises 17 firms, following a spate of mergers to create huge enterprises that can compete globally when they invest in foreign countries, a key government agenda.

16 The government classifies a company as small if its sales turnover is between RM250,000 and RM10 million or if it has between five and 50 full-time employees. Companies with a sales turnover of RM10–25 million or between 51 and 150 full-time employees are classified as medium-sized.

17 In the mid-2000s, Malaysia's spending on R&D as a share of GDP was about 0.95 percent, very much behind Japan (3.4 percent), Singapore (2.39 percent) and South Korea (3.23 percent).

18 When Najib took office as Prime Minister in 2009, he pledged to curb money politics and corruption. However, he was aware that he had to devolve power to oversight institutions to ensure they had the autonomy to act without favor. This was not done.

19 The Bandar Malaysia project entails the construction of a mammoth underground city that will accommodate Mass Rapid Transit lines and a commuter and express rail link. Twelve highways are to converge in Bandar Malaysia and will serve as the gateway for the proposed high speed rail-line between Kuala Lumpur and Singapore.

20 This businessman, Lim Kang Hoo, was ranked by *Forbes* in 2015 as Malaysia's 27th richest person with assets worth US$650 million (*Forbes Asia*, 24 February 2016). He has an interest in four publicly-listed companies: Iskandar Waterfront City, Ekovest, Knusford and PLS Plantations. Ekovest's shareholders include Haris Onn Hussein, the brother of the Minister of Defence, Hishamuddin Hussein. The son of the Sultan of Johor, Tunku Ismail Sultan Ibrahim, is the chairman of Knusford whose Managing Director is Ahmad Zaki Zahid, once closely associated with former Prime Minister Abdullah.

References

Aglietta, M. 1979. *A Theory of Capitalist Regulation: The US Experience*. New York: New Left Books.

Aglietta, M. and Y. Landy. 2007. *La Chine vers la superpuissance*. Paris: Economica.

Alary, P. and E. Lafaye de Micheaux, eds. 2013. Economie Politique de l'Asie: 1. Asie du Sud-Est. *Revue de la Régulation* 13: http://regulation.revues.org/10266.

Alary, P. and E. Lafaye de Micheaux, eds. 2014. Political economy of Asia 2. *Revue de la Régulation* 15, Spring: http://regulation.revues.org/10614.

Alary, P. and E. Lafaye de Micheaux, eds. 2015. *Asian Capitalisms and Chinese Power. The Diverse Reconfigurations National Trajectories* (in French). Paris: Presses de Sciences Po.

Amable, B. 2003. *The Diversity of Modern Capitalism*. Oxford: Oxford University Press.

Amsden, A.H. 1989. *Asia's Next Giant: South Korea and Late Industrialisation*. New York: Oxford University Press.

Bhopal, M. and P. Todd. 2000. Multinational corporations and trade union development in Malaysia. *Asia Pacific Business Review* 6(3–4): 193–213.

Boyer, R. 1989. Economie et histoire: vers de nouvelles alliances? *Annales ESC* 6 November-December: 1397–1426.

Boyer, R. 1990. *The Regulation School: A Critical Introduction*. New York: Columbia University Press.

Boyer, R. 2003. Les institutions dans la théorie de la régulation. *Cahiers d'économie Politique/Papers in Political Economy* 1(44): 79–101.

Boyer R. 2012. The Chinese growth regime and the world economy. In R. Boyer, H. Uemura and A. Isogai, eds. *Diversity and Transformations of Asian Capitalisms* (pp. 184–205). London: Routledge.

Boyer, R. 2016. *Economie politique des capitalismes*. Paris: La Découverte.

Boyer, R. and Y. Saillard, eds. 2002. *Regulation Theory: The State of the Art*. London: Routledge.

Boyer, R., H. Uemura and A. Isogai. 2012a. Asia: A social laboratory of contemporary capitalisms? In R. Boyer, H. Uemura and A. Isogai, eds. *Diversity and Transformations of Asian Capitalisms* (pp. 1–11). London: Routledge.

Boyer, R., H. Uemura and A. Isogai, eds. 2012b. *Diversity and Transformations of Asian Capitalisms*. London: Routledge.

Carney, M. and E. Andriesse. 2014. Malaysia: Personal capitalism. In M.A. Witt and G. Redding, eds. *The Oxford Handbook of Asian Business Systems* (pp. 144–168). Oxford: Oxford University Press.

Carney, R. and M.A. Witt. 2014. The role of the state in Asian business systems. In M.A. Witt and G. Redding, eds. *The Oxford Handbook of Asian Business Systems* (pp. 538–560). Oxford: Oxford University Press.

Case, W. 2009. Electoral authoritarianism in Malaysia: Trajectory shift. *The Pacific Review* 22(3): 311–333.

Chavance B. 2000. The evolutionary path away from socialism: The Chinese experience. In E.S. Maskin and A. Simonovits, eds. *Planning, Shortage and Transformation: Essays in Honor of Janos Kornai*. Cambridge, MA: MIT Press.

Coates, D., ed. 2005. *Varieties of Capitalism: Varieties of Approaches*. Basingstoke: Palgrave Macmillan.

Coates, D. 2015. Varieties of capitalism and 'the great moderation'. In M. Ebenau, I. Bruff and C. May, eds. *New Directions in Comparative Capitalisms Research: Critical and Global Perspectives* (pp. 11–27). London: Routledge.

Delfolie, D. 2013. Le développement de la finance islamique en Malaisie: l'histoire d'un volontarisme d'Etat. *La Revue de la régulation* 13. 'Political Economy of Asia 1'. https://regulation.revues.org/10080.

Ebenau, M., I. Bruff and C. May, eds. 2015. *New Directions in Comparative Capitalisms Research: Critical and Global Perspectives*. London: Routledge.

Evans, P. 1995. *Embedded Autonomy, States and Industrial Transformation*. Princeton, NJ: Princeton University Press.

Fourastié, J. 1979. *Les Trente Glorieuses*. Paris: Hachette.

Gomez, E.T. 2012a. Monetizing politics: Financing parties and elections in Malaysia. *Modern Asian Studies* 46(5): 1370–1397.

Gomez, E.T. 2012b. Targeting horizontal inequalities: Ethnicity, equity and entrepreneurship in Malaysia. *Asian Economic Papers* 11(2): 31–57.

Gomez, E.T. 2016. Politics and business: Fundamental differences between Dr M and Najib. *Malaysiakini*, 22 March.

Gomez, E.T. 2017. *Minister of Finance Incorporated: Ownership and Control of Corporate Malaysia*. Basingstoke: Palgrave-Macmillan.

Gomez, E.T., E. Satkunasingham and H.A. Lee. 2015. The state's business: Government-linked companies, the financial sector and socioeconomic development in Malaysia. In E.T. Gomez, F. Bafoil and K.C. Cheong, eds. *Government-linked Companies and Sustainable, Equitable Development* (pp. 39–59). London: Routledge.

Haggard, S. 1990. *Pathways from the Periphery: The Politics of Growth in the Newly Industrializing Countries*. Ithaca: Cornell University Press.

Hall, P.A. and D. Soskice, eds. 2001. *Varieties of Capitalism: The Institutional Foundations of Comparative Advantage*. Oxford: Oxford University Press.

Harada Y. and H. Tohyama. 2012. Asian capitalisms: Institutional configurations and firm heterogeneity. In R. Boyer, H. Uemura and A. Isogai, eds. *Diversity and Transformations of Asian Capitalisms* (pp. 243–263). London: Routledge.

Hill, H., S.Y. Tham and M.Z. Ragayah, eds. 2011. *Malaysia's Development Challenges: Graduating from the Middle*. London: Routledge.

Hollingsworth, J.R. and R. Boyer, eds. 1997. *Contemporary Capitalism: The Embeddedness of Institutions*. Cambridge, UK: Cambridge University Press.

Huang, Y. 2008. *Capitalism with Chinese Characteristics: Entrepreneurship and the State*. Cambridge, UK: Cambridge University Press.

Johnson, C. 1982. *Miti and the Japanese Miracle: The Growth of Industrial Policy, 1925–1975*. Stanford: Stanford University Press.

Lafaye de Micheaux, E. 2017. *The Development of Malaysian Capitalism, From British Rule to the Present Days*. Petaling Jaya: SIRD.

Lechevalier, S. 2007. The diversity of capitalism and heterogeneity of firms: A case study of Japan during the lost decade. *Evolutionary and Institutional Economics Review* 4: 113–142.

Lee K.H. and C.B. Tan, eds. 2000. *The Chinese in Malaysia*. Shah Alam: Oxford University Press.

Malaysia. 1971. *Second Malaysia Plan, 1971–1975*. Kuala Lumpur: Government Printers.

Malaysia. 2006. *Ninth Malaysia Plan, 2006–2010*. Kuala Lumpur: Government Printers.

Malaysia. 2010. *Tenth Malaysia Plan, 2011–2015*. Kuala Lumpur: Percetakan Nasional Malaysia.

Malaysia. 2013. *Malaysia Education Blueprint: 2013–2025*. Putrajaya: Ministry of Education.

Malaysia. 2015. *Eleventh Malaysia Plan, 2016–2020*. Kuala Lumpur: Percetakan Nasional Malaysia.

Maucourant, J. 2012. New institutional economics and history. *Journal of Economic Issues* XLV(1) March: 193–207.

Menon, J. and T.H. Ng. 2013. Are government-linked corporations crowding out private investment in Malaysia? *ADB Economics Working Paper Series No. 345*. Manila: Asian Development Bank.

Pepinsky, T.B. 2009. *Economic Crises and the Breakdown of Authoritarian Regimes: Indonesia and Malaysia in Comparative Perspective*. Cambridge, UK: Cambridge University Press.

Pereira, A.A. 2003. *State Collaboration and Development Strategies: The Case of the China Singapore Suzhou Industrial Park (1992–2002).* London: Routledge.

Redding, G. 2006. The thick description of societal systems of capitalism. *Journal of International Business Studies* 36: 123–155.

Rodan, G. and C. Hughes. 2014. *The Politics of Accountability in Southeast Asia: The Dominance of Moral Ideologies.* New York: Oxford University Press.

Searle, P. 1999. *The Riddle of Malaysian Capitalism: Rent-seekers or Real Capitalists.* Honolulu: University of Hawai'i Press.

Sloane, P. 1999. *Islam, Modernity and Entrepreneurship among the Malays.* Basingstoke: Macmillan.

Song, L. 2001. *The Limit of Gradual Reform without Long Term Perspective. Instability of Institutional Arrangements in Mainland China.* Mimeo: Nagoya University.

Storz, C., B. Amable, S. Casper and S. Lechevalier (2013). Editorial: Bringing Asia into the comparative capitalism perspective. *SocioEconomic Review* 11(2): 1–16.

Streeck, W. (In interview with A. Labrousse). 2016. Order is an exception, not the rule. *Revue de la régulation* 19. http://regulation.revues.org/11925.

Uni, H. 2007. Export biased productivity increase and exchange rate regime in East Asia. *Kyoto Economic Review* 76(2): 117–138.

Vercueil, J. 2016. Régulation theory: From textbook to research agenda. *Revue de la régulation* 19. http://regulation.revues.org/11869.

Wade, R. 1990. *Governing the Market: Economic Theory and the Role of Government in East Asian Industrialization.* Princeton, NJ: Princeton University Press.

Wain, B. 2009. *Malaysian Maverick: Mahathir Mohamad in Turbulent Times.* Basingstoke: Palgrave Macmillan.

Whitley, R. 1992. *Business Systems in East Asia: Firms, Markets and Societies.* London: Sage.

Whitley, R. 1999. *Divergent Capitalisms: The Social Structuring and Change of Business Systems.* Oxford: Oxford University Press.

Whitley R. and X. Zhang. 2013. Changing macro-structural varieties of East Asian capitalism. *Socioeconomic Review* 11(2): 301–336.

Witt, M.A. and G. Redding. 2013. Asian business systems: Institutional comparison, clusters and implications for varieties of capitalism and business systems theory. *Socio-Economic Review* 11: 265–300.

Witt, M.A. and G. Redding, eds. 2014. *The Oxford Handbook of Asian Business Systems.* Oxford: Oxford University Press.

6 How to escape the transformation trap

Building social consensus for sustainable development

Marc Saxer

The race against time

When newly industrializing countries reach middle income level, their economic growth rate often begins to slow down. Squeezed between low wage competitors that make inroads into mature industries and advanced innovator economies, middle income countries face the seminal challenge to quickly and disruptively adapt their growth strategies to a changing environment (Gill and Kharas 2015). Gill and Kharas (2007) have described these challenges as the Middle-Income Trap. Others have expressed doubts that such a general economic pattern exists (Bulman *et al.* 2014). Whatever the empirical evidence, the merit of the Middle-Income Trap concept is to have highlighted some of the challenges policy makers are facing when the first phase of industrialization is losing steam. In order to graduate to the next development level, it is argued, economies have to move up the global skills value chain. Disruptively adapting the growth strategies then, means overhauling the entire business model from labor-intensive manufacturing to innovation-driven growth. Arguing from this narrow economic perspective, policy recommendations tend to be technical and market oriented in nature (Kharas and Kholi 2011; Griffith 2011; Felipe *et al.* 2012; Eichengreen *et al.* 2013).

Development, however, is not a technical challenge, but the outcome of societal struggles. Transformation produces conflict between winners and losers. The foundation for sustainable development therefore needs to be laid amid social, political and cultural conflicts rocking transformation societies. A narrow economic perspective is therefore in danger of misunderstanding the complexity of transformations. Consequently, recommended policies are at risk of provoking political backlash, aggravating social conflict and triggering cultural resistance. Failure to address the political, social and cultural challenges of transformation can make the economic growth engine stutter. The challenges facing middle income countries should therefore be understood as a social and political transformation trap.

This chapter will explore how deeply sustainable economic growth is intertwined with social and political development. Escaping this transformation trap requires more than a new business model, but equally the political stability necessary to implement the disruptive policies required to move up the value chain. This stability can only can only be produced by an inclusive compromise between established and emerging classes. Laying this social foundation for sustainable development is the essential challenge for a progressive transformation project. The Good Society with full capabilities for all can bring together a broad societal coalition to shape the Great Transformations of today.

The global window of opportunity is closing

East Asia's spectacular rise is claimed by rival schools of development economics. The neoclassical school points to the centrality of opening up the economy for trade and foreign investment. In contrast to an inward-looking import substitution model, Japan, Taiwan, South Korea, Thailand, Malaysia and, today, China encouraged exporting as a catalyst for disciplined resource allocation and technological innovation (Solow 1956; Acemoglu 2009). The mercantilist school points to the infant industry promotion straight out of the textbooks of Alexander Hamilton and Friedrich List (Hamilton 1791; List 1841). In contrast to the laissez-faire policies promoted by many development agencies today, the Asian tigers used every instrument at their disposal to nurture infant industries into internationally competitive players (Chang 2003). Both sides would agree, however, on the central role of manufacturing for export. Forced to compete internationally, the export sector is under pressure to constantly increase productivity, thereby becoming the engine of overall development (Studwell 2014). In the early stages of the 'Great Transformation', the sharp increase in productivity is driven by the absorption of millions of underemployed farmhands into urban factories (Polanyi 1944). As long as this excess labor keeps flowing, productivity can be increased without losing the competitive cost advantage of cheap labor. When this pool of excess labor dries up, wages start to rise, driving labor intensive industries on to the next location.

With the comparative advantage of cheap labor cost gone, the challenge for middle-income countries is then to find new sources of growth. However, some countries continue to rely on labor-intensive manufacturing, or nurture industries without economic foundation. Others fail to tackle vulnerability to external shocks with domestic demand, or pursue growth strategies with natural limits, such as natural resource or FDI-driven growth (Ohno 2009a, 2009b; Gill and Kharas 2015). These countries might well find themselves in the squeeze between low cost competitors on the one side, and highly productive innovators on the other. In contrast to concepts of self-reliance or self-sufficiency, the only option for middle income countries is to move up the global skill and value chain to find new markets for new products. To facilitate this shift to a new growth model, conventional literature recommends investing more in education, upgrading the infrastructure, and diversifying exports with high technology manufacturing and high yield services (Kharas and Kohli 2011; Griffith 2011; Eichengreen *et al.* 2013).

What worked so spectacularly well in East Asia over the last decades, however, may no longer work under rapidly shifting global conditions (Yusuf 2010). Higher labor productivity means that fewer jobs are needed to produce the same output (Felipe *et al.* 2014). Dani Rodrik observed that in a globalized market, manufacturing moves on as soon as wages start to rise, leading to premature deindustrialization in newly industrializing economies (Rodrik 2015). Even if emerging manufacturers manage to build up a competitive sector, global overcapacities created by the secular stagnation in the West (Summers 2014; Gordon 2012; Cowen 2013; Foster and McChesney 2012) make it questionable if the markets are deep enough to absorb all of their goods (Rajan 2014). Moreover, energy and resource driven industrialization is bound to bounce against planetary boundaries (United Nations 2012; Steffen *et al.* 2015). Simply put, if giants such as China and India continue to expand at current rates, rising costs for fossil energy and raw materials may price them out of the market (Sharma 2012). To make things worse, manufacturing costs in many emerging economies have almost reached parity with the United States (Sirkin *et al.* 2014; *New York Times* 2015). This trend is further accelerated by a drop of manufacturing cost through digital automation (McAfee and Brynjolfsson 2014). When cost advantages level out, factors such as lack in quality, legal insecurity and local corruption become more important. At the same time, retailers revolve their merchandise in ever faster cycles, turning long supply chains into a competitive disadvantage (Guidry 2014). Consequently, multinational manufacturers have started to re-shore production back to the old industrial centers (Simchi-Levi 2012). All of this means the window of opportunity for export led manufacturing growth is closing, and another route to development has not yet been discovered. Shifting global opportunity structures turn the struggle for development into a gigantic race against time.

Who can win the race against time?

China's recent economic turmoil indicates that its export and investment driven growth model is running out of steam. Cheap labor intensive industries have started to move on to lower cost neighbors (*Wall Street Journal* 2013). Beijing seems determined to offset export dependency with domestic demand and deliberately lets wages increase. Following early East Asian industrializers, Beijing's goal is to take technological destiny into its own hands by aggressively moving up the global skills and value chain. Like Japan, South Korea and Taiwan, China has built international brands strong enough to push toward the technological frontier. The growth slowdown, however, will make it harder to satisfy the hopes and needs of the growing middle classes and urban workers. To generate political stability for development, China needs to compensate waning output legitimacy with higher input legitimacy.

Southeast Asia, by contrast, followed a less effective version of the export-driven industrialization model. For domestic political reasons (Huang 2002;

Lagace 2002), Southeast Asian industrializers chose a foreign investment driven development path, leaving them at the mercy of multinational corporations. The assembly of foreign goods did not lead to technological learning (Studwell 2014). In Thailand, rising production cost, shortages of skilled labor and political instability are driving foreign investors out, leaving behind unproductive services (Sharma 2012). Given its chronic inability to modernize its social and political order, Thailand looks increasingly likely to stagnate and fall behind. Malaysia, mired in ethno-religious strife and patronage sleaze, hopes to revive FDI driven growth by joining the Trans Pacific Partnership Agreement (TPP). Vietnam seems determined to use the external pressure created by the TPP to fuel its internal reform agenda. The protectionist mood that carried Donald Trump to the US Presidency, however, will cast some dark clouds if the TPP ever comes into action. Even if these hopes should materialize, it would not address the main weakness of extractive political economies, the lack of innovation. For Southeast Asia, the main challenge is to build a powerful societal coalition for inclusive and innovation-driven development.

The social and political challenges of transformation

From an economic perspective, transformation countries need to graduate from labor intensive to knowledge driven growth. To escape the squeeze between low wage competitors and advanced innovator economies, middle income countries need to move up the global skills and value chain. On the policy level, this requires heavy investment into infrastructure and the skills of the workforce.

What is desirable from an economic point of view may not be implementable politically. To unleash the full potential of creative destruction, inclusive institutions are needed (Acemoglu and Robinson 2012). In the extractive political economies of most transformation societies, however, innovation is not in the interest of the few who benefit from the status quo.

In order to tackle these challenges, a deeper understanding of the nature of transformation processes is needed. Structurally, transformation crises reflect the gap between political and social orders and the new social and economic realities. It is not a coincidence that these interdependencies make themselves felt more pronouncedly once a country has reached middle income level. After several decades of industrialization, not only have economies become more complex but societies have started to fragment and pluralize (Parsons 1969; Luhmann 1984; Huntington 1991; Boix and Stokes 2003; Inglehart and Welzel 2005; Merkel 2010). The differentiation of lifestyles, interests and identities erodes symbolic orders, especially in those East and Southeast Asian cultures that are rooted in conformity, unity and discipline (Saxer 2014a). Vertical political systems informed by patrimonial cultures find it increasingly challenging to govern complex, dynamic and conflict-ridden transformation societies (Bremmer 2006). Unable to deliver to the growing hopes, demands and needs of rapidly changing societies, the legitimacy of the old order is eroding. Conflicts between winners and losers of transformation paralyze the political process and undermine the ability to implement reforms (Huntington 1968; Fukuyama 2014).

Transformation conflicts around the world

Who are those resisting change, and why? Joshua Kurlantzick sees a common thread connecting the wave of mass protests around the world (Kurlantzick 2013; Mason 2013). Starting from the campaign against the Filipino President Estrada in 2000/01, there have been mass protests in Venezuela (2001–2003), Taiwan (2004 and 2006), Ukraine (2004 and 2013), Kirgizstan (2005), Thailand (2006, 2008, 2013/14), Bangladesh (2006/07), Kenya (2007/08), Bolivia (2008), Georgia (2003 and 2007), Lebanon (2011), Tunisia (2010/11), Russia (2012), Egypt (2011 and 2012/13), Turkey (2013) Brazil (2013 and 2014), Hong Kong (2014), Malaysia (2015) and Ecuador (2015). While the occasions and outcomes of these protests may vary, most (but not all) of them follow a similar script.

With the exception of the Arab Spring, all these mass protests were directed against elected governments. This means despite all the shortcomings of these defective democracies, elections have developed into a central even if not exclusive mechanism to mandate the government (Merkel 2003). Clever politicians have made use of this new avenue to power. There is little these leaders, from the Bolivarian socialist Chavez, the crony capitalist Thaksin, or the Islamic conservative Erdogan, have in common. What they all have understood is how to win electoral victories by catering to the hopes and needs of voters in the provinces. With a policy mix of social welfare, local development and populist handouts, they manage to win election after election. The majority population, until recently excluded from the provision of public goods, shows its gratitude with staunch loyalty at the voting booth. Establishment parties, having failed to update their platforms to cater to the majority population, are losing one election after the other.

Once in power, popular leaders follow the logic of the patronage system by rewarding supporters, protecting clients, favoring kin and distributing the spoils. This is why many popular leaders quickly turn into ‘elected autocrats’, threatening the opposition, silencing media, and undermining democratic institutions. This is why many in the established elite and middle class perceive these ‘elected autocrats’ as a threat. Often, it is not only the ‘elected autocrats’ who are blamed for corruption, incompetence and instability, but the democratic system itself. Amidst a discourse of national crisis and moral decay, militaries, courts or bureaucracies heed the calls for an authoritarian strong hand to remove the government, in effect seizing the moment to defend their status and privileges. However, not all ‘elected autocrats’ are swept away by middle class revolt and authoritarian intervention (Kurlantzick 2013). Some manage to survive or return to power with the help of their popular base. In Egypt and Thailand, the alliance of traditional elites, established middle class and the military responded by cracking down even harder, abolishing electoral democracy altogether. In Turkey, Erdogan used the botched military coup attempt to consolidate his grip on power. As long as the underlying transformation conflict is not resolved, these crises are bound to continue.

The outcome of those power struggles is of course largely determined by the specific balance of power between those who benefit from the status quo and those who want change. The status quo alliance consists not alone of the old elites trying to protect their status and privilege, but all those who fear that a rapid transformation would turn their world upside down. Within less than a generation, fundamental concepts such as family, work, or the role of men and women have undergone a radical change. Some people happily embrace the new opportunities, while others feel that the loss of the world they were born into threatens their identities (Blom 2010). The fear of social decline gives these social struggles a paranoid, aggressive undertone. It is not a coincidence that in times of rapid change, fascist groups are framing scapegoats for the alleged moral decline, and resort to violent tactics to restore an imagined golden past (Schlee 2002; Lyons and Berlet 1996). As Antonio Gramsci gloomily remarked from his prison cell, 'The crisis consists precisely in the fact that the old is dying and the new cannot be born; in this interregnum a great variety of morbid symptoms appear' (Gramsci 1971).

In this transformation conflict between the forces of change and the forces of restoration, the middle classes play a decisive role. As long as the established middle class sticks with the old elites, the status quo may be upheld. If the established middle classes make common cause with emerging classes, change will be the likely outcome. What does motivate the middle classes?

First, the rage of well-off protesters shows that the established middle class is not satisfied with the 'deal' it has been offered. Abuse by elected autocrats strikes fear in the heart of middle classes. To secure their voter base, elected autocrats redistribute wealth and opportunities. For social and political reasons, it is difficult to raise the necessary revenue to finance these programs from either the rich or the poor, leaving the tax burden on the backs of the middle class. As long as the middle class feels unsafe and abused it will resist calls for solidarity with other segments of society (Saxer 2014b, 2015). On the other side, as long as demands for equal opportunities are not met, the majority population will challenge the old social order. This protracted social conflict again scares the middle classes, which in return starts to protest against the demands of the 'undeserving masses'. This conflict over the question of 'solidarity with whom?' gives a working definition of who is considered a full member of the polity, and who is regarded as a subaltern subject without the same rights. In many societies, solidarity is only expected between members of the same group, class, caste or community. It is precisely this question of the inclusion of the former rural laborers into the polity which is at the core of a transformation conflict. Simply put, a transformation crisis occurs when the old social contract has been terminated, and a new one has not yet been concluded (Hewison 2004; Saxer 2011, 2012).

Second, the centrality of corruption, nepotism and populism in middle class protests points to frustration over the patronage system. Patronage practices seem to proliferate in times of transformation (Lovell 2005; Huntington 1968, 2001; Saxer 2014c). This has to do with the lack of effective institutions providing the necessary trust for day-to-day transactions. Small and less-developed societies organize their social life along personal relationships between patron and client. If millions of people interact within a complex economy and a pluralist society, however, the necessary trust can no longer be created on an interpersonal level. What is needed according to Max Weber is a modern nation state based on efficient legalistic-rationalistic institutions and rule of law (Weber 1918). As long as these modern institutions are absent or do not function properly, a phone call to the 'big man' might still be the only way to solve everyday problems. While the elites benefit from the patronage system, the poor rely on it for physical survival. The middle class considers patronage a necessity, wrong if practiced by others, but right if useful for oneself (Varma 2007). The periodic outpourings against corruptions may therefore be less motivated by moral conviction, but reflect a deeper shift toward capitalist contractual culture. When economic matters are governed by contractual relationships between equals, many are asking, why do then the same people have little or no say in public matters? Hence demands for accountability, transparency, participation, and responsiveness are in fact calls for the modernization of the polity. Accordingly, patronage practices are reframed. The rewarding of supporters is now demonized as 'populism', favoring of kin is scourged as nepotism, protecting of clients denounced as cronyism and the distribution of spoils outlawed as corruption. Corruption, in particular, is the new code for the abuse of power by unaccountable elites. Hence, in its essence, the protests of the middle classes are aimed at the patronage system as the main obstacle to modernization.

This explains why good governance discourses are gaining currency with the middle classes. Classical modernization theory would equally expect the middle classes to be the primary drivers of democratization (De Tocqueville 1835; Lipset 1963). But why is it then that the 'young unemployed graduates' (Mason 2013) from Tel Aviv to New York, from Athens to Madrid, from Hong Kong to Kuala Lumpur are demanding a more inclusive and participatory order, while their peers in Bangkok and Cairo march for the disenfranchisement of the 'uneducated' masses, and the abolition of electoral democracy?

The revolt of the Bangkok middle class

To better understand this ambivalent role of the middle classes, it may therefore be fruitful to further explore the motivations, frustrations and fears of the raging middle class in Bangkok over the last decade (Saxer 2014b, 2015).

In its latest round, the People's Committee for Complete Democracy under the Constitutional Monarchy (PDRC) brought public life in Bangkok to a standstill. What puzzled many observers was that the declared aim of the protesters was to 'save democracy' by blocking elections and calling for a military coup to oust an elected government.

The orientation of the Bangkok middle class has not always been anti-democratic. On the contrary, in the 1990s it was the urban civil society that installed a liberal democracy after decades of military authoritarianism. Today, some of the same protagonists believe that democracy does not fit Thai society. How can one explain this change of mind?

Bangkok's middle class was horrified to find itself in a permanent minority in the new electoral democracy (De Tocqueville 1835). The establishment felt trapped by the alliance between the 'elected autocrat' Thaksin Shinawatra and the emerging masses of the Northern and North-eastern provinces. Thaksin's open disregard for the rule of law and checks and balances aggravated this feeling of being left unprotected against the abuse of power. Certainly, it did not help that the prosecuted activists, silenced journalists and transferred bureaucrats were members of the established middle class. Echoing de Tocqueville's famous 'tyranny of the majority', it is fear and anger that drives the Bangkok middle class into opposition of an elected government.

Still, this fear cannot fully explain the open hostility of many protesters against the democratic system. Again, this can only be explained by the interpretations, expectations and explanations dominating middle class discourses. The established Bangkok middle class fears being 'robbed by corrupt politicians who buy the votes of the greedy poor with populist schemes' (Saxer 2015). Looking deeper into the way corruption is defined may therefore offer a clue why the Bangkok middle class, as opposed to its peers around the world, protest not for but against democracy.

The so-called 'yellow' discourse explains corruption as an individual moral failure (Satha-Anand 2006). In the Siamese political discourse, rooted in the Theravada Buddhist cosmology, an immoral ruler will bring suffering into the world. In other words, rule is legitimized by the morality of the ruler. If corruption is moral failure, then corruption of the ruler must lead to social decay. This is why, in Thailand, corruption allegations are the weapon of choice to bring down a government. To save the social order, it is claimed, morality must be restored by replacing immoral 'bad people' with 'good people' of high moral virtue. However, when elections would most likely result in the confirmation of the 'corrupt government', then elections as the very mechanism which seems to bring 'bad people' to the top in the first place must be abandoned altogether. Hence, the yellow battle-cry, which brought together a heterogeneous protest mob of hundreds of thousands, was 'Reform before Elections!'

This means, on the paradigm level, the so-called 'red yellow conflict' is constructed by opposing interpretations of corruption. While one side equates corruption with democracy, consequentially calling for the overthrow of democracy, the other side sees it as a leftover of the feudal system, thus demanding real democracy. On the metaphysical level, the transformation conflict is not defined by materialist class interests, but constructed around rival political, normative and symbolic orders. Accordingly, the status quo and the change alliance are not class alliances, but discourse alliances founded upon a common moral identity. By giving the antagonized middle class of Bangkok a way to interpret and understand the ills of the country, the yellow discourse effectively built a bridge between former pro-democracy activists and the feudal establishment. The red discourse, on the other hand, builds a bridge between the new capitalist class and the emerging classes in the provinces. In effect, the red and yellow discourse alliances bring together social groups with vastly different or even opposing socio-economic interests.

The Thai case must not be generalized, but it does give some insight into how transformation conflicts are formatted. Middle class rage does not flow from some ahistorical or objective class interest, but is fueled by the way the transformation conflict is framed in the discourse. Transformation conflicts cannot be reduced to 'class struggles'. While it is true that extractive political economies systematically exclude the majority population, transformation conflicts are not simply struggles between the rich and the poor. Both the status quo as well as the change alliance cut across all social strata and sectors. The balance of power between those who seek to uphold the status quo and those who want to modernize the political and social order depends on the ability of each side to co-opt social groups into their struggle. This suggests that the outcome of the transformation conflict will not simply be a mirror function of structural changes, but will be also be determined by the way the conflict is constructed in the discourse. Transformation conflicts are rarely framed in socio-economic terms, but often constructed as identity conflicts between different races, religions, gender or ethnicities. By framing the community as threatened by another, those who seek internal socio-economic reform can be reined in to close ranks against the external threat (Varma 2007). This means culturalist communalism and identity politics are the ideal instruments for all those who seek to uphold the social and economic status quo. Contrary to historical determinist expectations, traditional elites can uphold the status quo against the onslaught of capitalist globalization and social emancipation if they can co-opt the middle classes into their alliance by framing the conflict in cultural essentialist terms.

Escaping the transformation trap

What is the transformation trap?

In the race against time, emerging economies need to outpace global headwinds by shifting from labor-intensive to innovation-led growth. What makes this so extremely difficult is the interconnectedness of economic, social, cultural and political challenges. Amidst social and political conflicts, policies designed to move the economy up the global skills and value chain can prove to be difficult to implement politically.

To unleash innovation-led growth, a highly skilled workforce is needed. To finance this investment into human resources, the tax revenue needs to be significantly increased. However, as long as the middle class feels unsafe and abused, it refuses to pick up the bill. In the absence of a social contract that entitles all members of society to solidarity, policies aimed at improving the skills and physical fitness of the workforce may be resisted. Redistributive pro poor policies are even more likely to antagonize the middle classes. The failure to upgrade human capital, however, makes the economy highly vulnerable to competitors who are either cheaper or more productive. Rising inequality, a stuttering economic engine, and spreading unrest may in the long run lead to economic stagnation and decline.

In a differentiated and mobilized society, top down imposition of policies is more likely to be resisted by those affected, making it more difficult to stir development by institutional and social engineering. Innovation cannot be imposed, but can only flourish in a more open and free environment. When slowing growth rates make it more difficult to lift all boats, building consensus for development becomes even more difficult. The transformation trap, in short, is not some economic law that causes a systematic slowdown when a country reaches middle income level. It is the inability to resolve the political, social and economic contradictions typical for transformation societies.

Sustainable development needs a social foundation

Escaping the transformation trap is more than an economic task, it is a seminal political challenge. In the vertigo of change, cultural and social fears can be exploited to stifle disruptive innovations. Building a skilled workforce for innovation-led growth is difficult in the absence of a social contract that constitutes solidarity with millions of former farmhands. Politically speaking, moving up the value chain means building social consensus for creative destruction as well as redistribution. Or, in other words, building a stable social and political foundation for sustainable high growth.

What is needed is a social compromise between all classes to generate the social and political stability needed for the modernization of the economy and the state. Only an inclusive social compromise can square this circle of reassuring the established classes while integrating millions into the polity as citizens with equal rights and opportunities.

Historically, such a social democratic 'New Deal' was concluded to overcome the Great Depression (Meyer 2015). In essence, social democracy promises prosperity for all by lifting all boats. In return for equal opportunities to fully participate in political, social and cultural life, the majority population accepted checks and balances to majority rule. In return for social peace, protection by the rule of law, good governance and quality public goods, the middle classes pay rolled redistributive policies. Finally, in return for social peace and political stability, the elites addressed the crisis of social justice by creating opportunities for all. It was this social democratic compromise that helped to restore social peace after a century of conflicts, thereby laying the social foundation for post-war prosperity.

Of course, the historical New Deal cannot be the blueprint for social compromises under different political, social and cultural conditions. However, it showed that a social compromise needs to be more than the lowest common denominator between opposing interests.

Collective action problems in transformation societies

Amidst transformation conflict, negotiating a social compromise is not an easy task. In fact, it is the very nature of transformation that makes it difficult to conclude a social consensus. Ernst Bloch observed that different people seem to live in different stages of modernization in terms of values, identities and ideologies, making the transformation process uneven and conflict prone (Bloch 1935). This 'non-simultaneity of the simultaneous' means that it would be easier to forge a social consensus for universal rights in a political culture based on egalitarian, pluralistic and democratic norms and values. Such a modern political culture, however, tends to emerge only after political rights and participation, economic equality and social inclusion are already in place. When traditional cultural frames are still dominant, elites and middle classes may refuse to recognize the majority population as equal citizens, even if a social compromise would be in their own long-term interest (Pongsudhirak 2012).

The emergence of a social compromise is further hampered by collective action problems. First, social groups differ in their interests and priorities, making it hard to define a common platform. Second, the fragmentation of societies in silos, and the differentiation of lifestyles, identities and values into different life-worlds hamper inclusive, participatory deliberation processes. Third, change agents often lack a clear understanding of their role in driving political processes as well as the strategies, skills and capacities to do so successfully. Finally, if facilitation, deliberation and funding mechanisms are lacking, it becomes difficult for society to organize itself.

How to build a social consensus for development

Those who want to modernize the economic, social and political order should pursue a dialectical strategy. An enlightened strategy needs to look beyond transactional gains and aim at a sustainable transformation. A successful transformation project, therefore, lays the social foundation for sustainable development with an inclusive social compromise.

What is needed is a development model that can produce the social peace and political stability necessary for the rollercoaster ride of transformation. To provide opportunities for all, high GDP growth is necessary but not sufficient.

A sustainable development model needs to be combine growth with equity, inclusiveness with innovation and preservation with disruptive change. The Economy of Tomorrow project, bringing together more than 200 thinkers from emerging Asian economies, has proposed such a model for socially just, resilient and green dynamic development. Building upon Amartya Sen's capabilities approach,[1] the Economy of Tomorrow model seeks to generate innovation-led growth by unleashing the full creative, entrepreneurial, and cognitive potential of all citizens (Sen 1999; Saxer 2014d).

In order to create the basis for solidarity between all classes, the narrative needs to shift the focus from communalist patronage and identity politics toward social empowerment and economic development (Sharma 2015). The capabilities narrative promises to escape the transformation trap and graduate to the next level of development. Based on this central promise, a broad developmental discourse alliance can be built. The promise to unleash innovation-led growth is attractive to the 'high growth first' discourse community. The focus on empowerment can connect the 'equity', 'inclusiveness' and 'justice' discourse communities. 'Development as freedom' even connects the 'emancipation' and 'liberty' discourse communities. Bringing together the 'growth', 'justice', 'emancipation' and 'stability' discourse communities, a discourse alliance for modernization can emerge.

This transformative discourse alliance can shift the development paradigm from 'high GDP growth' to 'high sustainable growth'. In this frame, progressives can make a powerful case that the best way to achieve sustainable high growth is to lay a stable social foundation with a social democratic compromise.

By constructing the social compromise around the capabilities platform, a broad societal change coalition can be built out of the development discourse alliance. By combining the struggles of those who seek distributional justice with those who want justice of recognition, the capabilities platform can bring together the progressive tribes. By providing opportunities for all to unleash their full potential, the capabilities approach combines the private sector goal of economic innovation with the state sector concern for political stability. The capabilities platform reaches out to the hopes and needs of emerging classes while at the same time offering the middle classes quality public services in return for their tax bills. By combining the middle class ideal of meritocracy with the yearning of the majority population for equal opportunities, the capabilities approach opens the door for a social compromise between the elites, the middle classes and the majority population.

Based on this social compromise over capabilities, a broad societal coalition for modernization and development can be built. The 'Good Society with full capabilities for all' is therefore a good starting point for all those who struggle to shape the Great Transformation of today (Kellerman and Meyer 2013; Meyer and Rutherford 2011).

Note

1 Amartya Sen and Martha Nussbaum name capability clusters that empower individuals to live a Good Life: Bodily Health; Bodily Integrity; Senses, Imagination and Thought; Emotions; Practical Reason; Affiliation; Other Species; Play; Control over One's Environment.

References

Acemoglu, Daron. 2009. The Solow growth model. In *Introduction to Modern Economic Growth* (pp. 26–76). Princeton, NJ: Princeton University Press.

Acemoglu, Daron and James A. Robinson. 2012. *Why Nations Fail, The Origins of Power, Prosperity and Poverty*. New York: Crown.

Bloch, Ernst. 1935. *Heritage of our Times* [*Erbschaft dieser Zeit*]. Trans. Neville Plaice and Stephen Plaice. Cambridge, UK: Polity Press.

Blom, Philipp. 2010. *The Vertigo Years. Europe 1900–1914*. New York: Basic Books.

Boix, Carl and Carol Stokes. 2003. Endogenous democratisation. *World Politics* 55: n.p.

Bremmer, Ian. 2006. *The J Curve. A New Way to Understand Why Nations Rise and fall*. New York: Simon & Schuster.

Bulman, David, Maya Eden, and Ha Nguyen. 2014. Transitioning from low-income growth to high-income growth: Is there a middle income trap? *Policy Research Working Paper Series 7104*. World Bank.

Chang, Ha-Joon. 2003. Kicking away the ladder. In *Development Strategy in Historical Perspective*. London: Anthem Press.

Cowen, Tyler. 2013. *Average Is Over: Powering America beyond the Age of the Great Stagnation*. New York: Dutton.

De Tocqueville, Alexis. 1835. *Democracy in America*.

Eichengreen Barry, Donghyun Park, and Kwanho Shin. 2013. Growth slowdowns redux: New evidence on the middle-income trap. NBER Working Paper No. 18673, www.nber.org/papers/w18673.pdf (accessed 15 August 2015).

Felipe, Jesus, Arnelyn Abdon, and Utsav Kumar. 2012. Tracking the middle-income trap: What is it, who is in it, and why? Levy Economics Institute, Working Paper No. 715. Available at http://ssrn.com/abstract=2049330 (accessed 15 August 2015).

Felipe, Jesus, Aashish Mehta, and Changyong Rhee. 2014. Manufacturing matters … but it's the jobs that count. ABD Economics Working Papers No 420, www.adb.org/sites/default/files/publication/149984/ewp-420.pdf (accessed 16 August 2015).

Foster, John Bellamy and Robert W. McChesney. 2012. The endless crisis: How monopoly-finance capital produces stagnation and upheaval from the USA to China. *Monthly Review Press* (accessed 16 August 2015).

Fukuyama, Francis. 2014. *Political Order and Political Decay. From the Industrial Revolution to the Globalization of Democracy*. New York: Farrar, Straus and Giroux.

Gill, Indermit and Homi Kharas. 2007. *An East Asian Renaissance: Ideas for Economic Growth*. Washington, DC: World Bank.

Gill, Indermit and Homi Kharas. 2015. The middle income trap turns ten. Pacific Trade and Development Working Paper Series, No. YF37–09, May.

Gordon, Robert J. 2012. Is U.S. economic growth over? Faltering innovation confronts the six headwinds. NBER Working Paper No. 18315, www.nber.org/papers/w18315 (accessed 16 August 2015).

Gramsci, Antonio. 1971. *Selections from the Prison Notebooks*. Edited and translated by Quintin Hoare and Geoffrey Nowell-Smith. London: Lawrence & Wishart.

Griffith, Breda. 2011. The middle income trap. In Shahid Yusuf, Breda Griffith, and Rwitwika Bhattacharya, eds. *Frontiers in Development Policy: A Primer on Emerging Issues*, World Bank Publication (accessed 15 August 2015).

Guidry, Brian. 2014. Faster fashion: Digital operations and the fashion supply chain. *Pixelz*, 4 August 2014. http://uk.pixelz.com/blog/faster_fashion_supply_chain/ (accessed 15 August 2015).

Hamilton, Alexander. 1791. *Reports of the Secretary of the Treasury on the Subject of Manufactures*.

Hewison, Kevin. 2004. Crafting Thailand's new social contract. *The Pacific Review* 17(4): 503–522.

Huang, Yasheng. 2002. *Selling China: Foreign Direct Investment during the Reform Era*. Cambridge, UK: Cambridge University Press.

Huntington, Samuel. 1968. *Political Order in Changing Societies*. New Haven, Yale University Press.

Huntington, Samuel. 1991. *The Third Wave: Democratization in the Late Twentieth Century*. Norman, Oklahoma: University of Oklahoma Press.

Huntington, Samuel. 2001. Modernization and corruption. In A.J. Heidenheimer and M.J. Johnston, eds. *Political Corruption*, 3rd edn (p. 254). Oxford: Transaction Publishers.

Inglehart, Ronald and Christian Welzel. 2005. Modernization, cultural change, and democracy. In *The Human Development Sequence*. New York; Cambridge University Press.

Kellermann, Christian and Henning Meyer. 2013. *Die Gute Gesellschaft. Soziale und demokratische Politik im 1. Jahrhundert*. Berlin: Suhrkamp.

Kharas, Homi and Harinder Kohli. 2011. What is the middle income trap, why do countries fall into it, and how can it be avoided? *Global Journal of Emerging Market Economies*, 3(3): 281–289.

Kurlantzick, Joshua. 2013. *Democracy in Retreat: The Revolt of the Middle Class and the Worldwide Decline of Representative Government*. New Haven: Yale University Press.

Lagace, Martha. 2002. Entrepreneurship in Asia and Foreign Direct Investment. *Harvard Business School Working Knowledge*, 17 June 2002. http://hbswk.hbs.edu/item/2948.html (accessed 16 August 2015).

Lipset, Seymour Martin. 1963. *Political Man*. New York: Anchor Books.

List, Friedrich. 1841. *The National System of Political Economy*. London: Longmans, Green, and Co.

Lovell, David W. 2005. Corruption as a transnational phenomenon: Understanding endemic corruption in postcommunist states. In Haller Dieter and Shore Cris, eds. *Corruption: Anthropological Perspectives* (pp. 65–82). London: Pluto Books.

Luhmann, Niklas. 1984. *Ökologische Kommunikation*. Opladen: Westdeutscher Verlag.

Lyons, Matthew N. and Chip Berlet. 1996. *Too Close for Comfort: Right Wing Populism, Scapegoating, and Fascist Potentials in US Politics*. Boston: South End Press.

Mason, Paul. 2013. *Why It's Still Kicking off Everywhere. The New Global Revolutions*, 2nd edn. London: Verso.

McAfee, Andrew and Erik Brynjolfsson. 2014. *The Second Machine Age: Work, Progress, and Prosperity in a Time of Brilliant Technologies*. New York: Norton.

Meyer, Henning and Jonathan Rutherford. 2011. *The Future of European Social Democracy: Building the Good Society*. UK: Palgrave.

Meyer, Thomas. 2015. How to defeat fear-mongering: Take fears seriously. *Social Europe Journal*, 16 July, http://goo.gl/3wgaW9 (accessed 27 September 2015).

Merkel, Wolfgang. 2010. *Systemtransformation: Eine Einführung in die Theorie und Empirie der Transformationsforschung*, 2. Aufl. Wiesbaden: Verlag für Sozialwissenschaften.

Merkel, Wolfgang, Hans-Jürgen Puhle, and Aurel Croissant, eds. 2003. *Defekte Demokratien*. Opladen: Leske + Budrich.

New York Times. 2015. The Rising Cost of Manufacturing. http://goo.gl/UHnCs7 (accessed 16 August 2015).

Ohno, K. 2009a. Avoiding the middle income trap: Renovating industrial policy formulation in Vietnam. *ASEAN Economic Bulletin*, 26(1): 25–43.

Ohno, K. 2009b. The middle income trap: Implications for industrialization strategies in East Asia and Africa. Tokyo, GRIPS Development Forum.

Parsons, Talcott. 1969. Das Problem des Strukturwandels: eine theoretische Skizze. In Wolfgang Zapf, ed. *Theories des sozialen Wandels* (pp. 35–54). Köln/Berlin: Springer.

Polanyi, Karl. 1944. *The Great Transformation*. New York: Farrar & Rinehart.

Pongsudhirak, Thitinan. 2012. Thailand's uneasy passage. *Journal of Democracy* 23(2): 47–61, http://goo.gl/bqZbq4 (accessed 29 September 2015).

Rajan, Raghuram. 2014. Make in India, largely for India. Talk delivered by Dr. Governor Reserve Bank of India at the Bharat Ram Memorial Lecture on 12 December 2014 in New Delhi. www.rbi.org.in/SCRIPTS/BS_SpeechesView.aspx?Id=930 (accessed 4 October 2015).

Rodrik, Dani. 2015. Premature deindustrialization. NBER Working Paper No. 20935. Issued in February, www.nber.org/papers/w20935.pdf (accessed 15 August 2015).

Satha-Anand, Suwanna. 2006. Reconstructing Karma and moral justice in Thai Buddhism. In Inwon/Lee Choue and Pierre Samuel/Sané, eds. *Inter-Regional Philosophical Dialogues: Democracy and Social Justice in Asia and the Arab World*. Korean National Commission for UNESCO.

Saxer, Marc. 2011. In the vertigo of change: How to resolve the political crisis? Friedrich-Ebert-Stiftung, Bangkok. http://library.fes.de/pdf-files/bueros/thailand/08259.pdf (accessed 15 August 2015).

Saxer, Marc. 2012. How can Thailand overcome its transformation crisis? A strategy for democratic change – Friedrich-Ebert-Stiftung, Bangkok. http://library.fes.de/pdf-files/bueros/thailand/09496-20121217.pdf (accessed 15 August 2015).

Saxer, Marc. 2014a. Building the good society in Thailand. Resolving transformation conflict through inclusive compromise. Friedrich-Ebert-Stiftung, Bangkok. http://goo.gl/vn4wo8 (accessed 16 August 2015).

Saxer, Marc. 2014b. Middle class rage threatens democracy. *New Mandala* 21 January 2014. http://goo.gl/CluruL (accessed 15 August 2015).

Saxer, Marc. 2014c. *Fighting Corruption in Transformation Societies*, 2nd ed. Bangkok: Friedrich-Ebert-Stiftung. http://library.fes.de/pdf-files/bueros/thailand/11137.pdf (accessed 15 August 2015).

Saxer, Marc. 2014d. *The Economy of Tomorrow: How to Produce Socially Just, Resilient, and Green Dynamic Growth for a Good Society*. Bangkok: Friedrich-Ebert-Stiftung. http://library.fes.de/pdf-files/bueros/thailand/11020.pdf (accessed 16 August 2015).

Saxer, Marc. 2015. The ambivalent role of middle classes in transformation conflicts. In Michèle Roth, Cornelia Ulbert, and Tobias Debiel, eds. *Global Trends*. Frankfurt am Main: Fischer Taschenbuch Verlag. http://goo.gl/mZqwFi (accessed 15 August 2015).

Schlee, Günther. 2002. *Imagined Differences: Hatred and the Construction of Identity*. New York: Palgrave Macmillan.

Sen, Amartya. 1999. *Development as Freedom*. Oxford: Oxford University Press.

Sharma, Ruchir. 2012. *Breakout Nations: In Pursuit of the Next Economic Miracles*. New York: Norton.

Sharma, Vivek S. 2015. The myth of a liberal India. *The National Interest*, 20 October 2015. http://nationalinterest.org/feature/the-myth-liberal-india-14103 (accessed 25 October 2015).

Simchi-Levi, David. 2012. U.S. re-shoring: A turning point. Annual Re-Shoring Report. http://goo.gl/doKVWL (accessed 4 October 2015).

Sirkin, Harold L., Michael Zinser, and Justin Rose. 2014. The shifting economics of global manufacturing, how cost competitiveness is changing worldwide. *BCG Perspectives*, https://goo.gl/lHTgwA.

Solow, Robert M. 1956. A contribution to the theory of economic growth. *Quarterly Journal of Economics* 70(1): 65–94.

Steffen, W., K. Richardson, J. Rockstrom, S.E. Cornell, I. Fetzer, E.M. Bennett, R. Biggs, S.R. Carpenter, W. De Vries, C.A. De Wit, C. Folke, D. Gerten, J. Heinke, G.M. Mace, L.M. Persson, V. Ramanathan, B. Reyers, and S. Sorlin. 2015. Planetary boundaries: Guiding human development on a changing planet. *Science* 347(6223): 1259855.

Studwell, Joe. 2014. *How Asia Works*. London: Grove Press.

Summers, Lawrence H. 2014. U.S. economic prospects: Secular stagnation, hysteresis, and the zero lower bound. Keynote Address at the NABE Policy Conference, 24 February 2014. *Business Economics* 49(2). http://goo.gl/9Z6s4M (accessed 16 August 2015).

United Nations Secretary-General's High-Level Panel on Global Sustainability. 2012. Resilient people, resilient planet: A future worth choosing (.pdf) (Report). United Nations. p. 24 (retrieved 30 January 2012).

Varma, Pavan K. 2007. *The Great Indian Middle Class*, revised edn. Gurgaon, India: Penguin Books.

Wall Street Journal. 2013. China begins to lose edge as world's factory floor, 16 January 2013. http://goo.gl/jcD56a (accessed 4 October 2015).

Weber, Max. 1918. *Parlament und Regierung im neugeordneten Deutschland: Zur politischen Kritik des Beamtentums und Parteiwesens*. Munich: Duncker and Humblot.

Yusuf, Shahid. 2010. The past and future of export-led growth. World Bank Blog 24 February 2010. http://blogs.worldbank.org/growth/past-and-future-export-led-growth.

7 Thailand

Exception to the rule or rule by exception?

Tim Rackett

A strong case can be made that the 'elephant in the room' (Nederveen Pieterse, Chapter 8, this volume) is responsible for the development gap between Northeast and Southeast Asian nations: forms of power, government, traditions, practices and institutions. How can we understand politics and government rule in Thailand? Is Thailand an exception to the rule? A form of rule that has captured the economy and put it in chains in a post-truth society? This chapter draws upon recent and exemplary accounts of the nature of Thai modernity, power relations, culture and polity, and explores Thailand as a case study of political factors impeding socioeconomic development. First, an overview of the state of Thailand is presented. Second, a critical examination of problems in western theory in understanding Thailand will be adumbrated. Third, three myths of Thailand as unique and exceptional are followed by an in-depth focus on five problem-spaces: (a) the problem of Thai style anti-politics; (b) schizoid splitting and the colonial formation of truth and aesthetic power in Thailand's alternative modernity; (c) subjection and rule through the political development of democratization; (d) 1932 and the common people; (e) King Thaksin, or 1932 redux.

In the current context of military dictatorship, elections and politics are seen as dirty and impure by the military, which acts as a self-appointed guardian to protect the nation-state and people from politics. That is, politics based on popular sovereignty and subalterns. Since the military coup of 2014, by 'good' people to save the country from exceptional circumstances, namely the ousted PM Yingluck's popular electoral mandate, Thailand has been led by a military dictator, General Prayuth Chan-ocha, who promises to hand power back to civilian rule and hold elections when 'the people' are ready. Thailand could be interpreted as being locked into a form of royalist paternalism, a localized version of western colonial despotism, in the name of 'Thai style democracy with the king as head of state'. For the rulers, common Thais' are under-developed gullible dependent 'children' who are not ready for freedom and self-government, government has to be exercised for them on their behalf and in their best interests. Politics are under-developed in Thailand in a historical form of rule that is both anti-democratic and anti-political, generating high levels of inequality, injustice and oppression.

Thailand's polity according the Freedom House scores always been mostly not free under authoritarian and/or military royal rule (Ferrara 2015, p. 8). There exists a vast gap between rural and urban, and intra-urban 'haves and have nots' in Thailand, despite decades of industrialization and five-year national development plans. GDP growth ranges from a value of 6.28 percent in 2004 (southern massacre); 4.18 percent in 2005; 4.96 percent in 2006 (post-coup); 5.4 percent in 2007; 1.72 percent in 2008; 0.73 percent in 2009; 7.5 percent in 2010 (Bangkok massacre); 0.83 percent in 2011; 7.2 percent in 2012; 2.7 percent in 2013; 0.81 percent in 2014 (post-coup); and 2.82 percent in 2015.

Inequality and uneven distribution of wealth and social mobility abound, as Hewison states: 'gains in rapid economic growth have been captured by particular economic interests' and equal access to benefits has been prevented by a pro-authoritarian economic and political elite which shuns welfare and electoral democracy (Hewison 2014, 847). Wealth is concentrated in a Sino-Thai elite. The late king Bhumipol was a quarter Chinese. In the Crown Property Bureau, a bundle of companies, members of the royal family own vast amounts of land (Unaldi 2016). Sino-Thai capitalists ride on the monarchy's coattails (Grey 1986; Unaldi 2016) and economic development is caught in the force-field of Thai power and politics that sets the parameters of equality, growth and income distribution.

The present state of Thailand

Profound inequality is built into modern Thai society and is entrenched in and across multiple institutions, which are failing. Thailand is in a right state: sub-standard education, inadequate health service, corrupt police, serial military coups and massacres, extra-constitutional exercises of Thai power. Institutions do not work and have been captured by ruling royalist and ethnonationalist classes. The law functions as an instrument of rule to censor and control. The law is outside itself in 'states of exception' which it suspends itself (Agamben 1998; Schmitt 1985). The force of law enforces Thai norms of belief, conduct and censors anti-royalist expressions and political dissent (Streckfuss 2011). Hence, it is not a question of judicial coup, as argued by Merieau (2016). The powers of Thai laws are extra-legal and extra-moral and are used to repress and justify state murder of seditious internal enemies of Thainess. There is a permanent war on and against the common people in which particularism and local tyranny triumphs over universalism.

Thailand since 1932 has been ruled, the economy run and business conducted, in the name of the monarchy and democracy by the military and civilians in authoritarian ways against the common people (Thak Chaloemtiarana 2007). Other Asian tiger nations, notably South Korea and Singapore, chose economic development over political and social development, but Thailand did the opposite: its economic development has been politically controlled by the ruling elite (until disrupted when Thaksin Shinawatra became PM) and royal sanctioned capitalism. The most important legacy of king Rama IX Bhumipol, who died in 2016, was not 'his support of dictatorships and military coups' but 'his charismatic support of capitalism and consumerism, and its unintended consequences' (Unaldi 2016, p. 221) The rise of Thaksin represented the subalterns re-asserting their class interests against being oppressed into servile poverty, by royal 'sufficiency economy' ideology and domination, which widened the rich–poor gap dramatically: Gini ratings range from 48 in 1992, 42 in 2006 and 38 in 2013, averaging around 40 over the last 10 years.

Authoritarian power mitigates against a fully functioning market, which presupposes individuals have enough information to make informed rational choices. Thai subjects are not free to maximize and pursue their self-interests. The economy is controlled by a pro-royalist elite who monopolize and proscribe open and fair competition, Sino-Thai businessmen, corrupt police and army mafias who run gambling, sell drugs, are involved in the sex industry, narcotics, logging, and land grabs. Sino-Thai big businesses 'work towards the monarchy' (Unaldi 2016), with the military in an ultra-nationalist version of political development, termed 'Thai style democracy': government using the authority of the king, who rules in the name/place of the people, who are deemed childish, not ready for self-rule, and thus have to be guided and ruled by 'good' people represented by the military, as is the case in 2017.

Thailand is governed by a rightwing state and increasingly a militarized, 'mentality of rule' focused on controlling insecurity and anxiety of a failed Thainess. Ferrara (2015, p. 14) argues that there has been little change over the last 80 years, a political continuity of oscillation between democracy and dictatorship. Nationalism did not lead to civic inclusion of the masses and democracy but to permanent instability (Ferrara 2015, p. 22). Thai democracy centers on: an identity politics in which the moral boundaries of the few exclude anti-establishment ideas and subaltern rural and working class ethno-regional peoples. The royalist domination of Thainess places the monarchy above politics after 1932 (Ferrara 2015, pp. 2, 23, 31). Civilian governments are removed by the military in coups, which attempt to turn the clock back. Mass opposition to dictatorship and authoritarian government is met by political violence, gunning down people in 1973, 1976, 1992 and 2010. Yet the perpetrators of murder, killing with impunity in the name of Thainess, are absolved in a 'ritual purification state' (Streckfuss 2011, pp. 77–79). Amartya Sen (2000) has made a cogent case for freedom, justice, flourishing and human rights as essential means of empowering participatory development. The Thai particularistic form of government mitigates against the formation of practices of freedom and justice in the name of national security and culture. Thai culture, promoting an imagined primordial race and civilization, is imposed with symbolic and deadly force against the people.

Method and truth-telling: same or other?

We need to be able to understand the paradoxical and counter-intuitive ways development and politics work and are used in modern Thailand. Historically, inter-civilizational encounters, western colonialist thought and forms, were translated into Thai aesthetic and authoritarian modes of practice and knowledge. The analyses of Western commentators, notably McCargo and Connors, tend to be marred by Eurocentric rationalist and individualist presuppositions and descriptive empiricism. They make careless overgeneralizations when explaining Thai reality and politics as a 'legitimation crisis of network monarchy' (McCargo 2005, 2009, 2012) and 'political development' which arrests 'democracy' and 'liberalism' (Connors, 2007, 2008, 2009). Their moral relativist attitude, adopting an 'emic' perspective, embraces local myth, the monarchy as sovereign, and ignores Thai racism. They fail by self-censoring (Jackson 2004a, p. 212) which results in tacit support of local Thai fascism using political science as if impartial and value-neutral. The problem is the phenomenon of Thai political violence, which retards development:

> Clashes between progressives, soldiers, and royalists have exposed time and again the immense atrocities of which Thai people are capable and the inability to resolve, under a regime of silence and repression, difference of opinion, peacefully through open discussion and dialogue.
>
> (Unaldi 2016, p. 49)

The key instance is the application of the draconian lèse majesté law to impose a silence of servitude and extra-judicial murder of citizens: fascism, Thai style, with a smile!

There is a crucial need to transculturate western theory into a form capable of making Thai discourses intelligible (Jackson 2004a, p. 185). Weber can be used in a non-Eurocentric way to understand a Southeast Asian country like Thailand. Unaldi argues that Weber saw Asia as an 'enchanted garden' wherein people use, revere, coerce spirits to seek salvation through ritualistic idolatrous or sacramental procedures and magical religiosity; this is in contrast to an instrumental-rational orientation, which is not intentionally driven, nor is there any necessary evolution toward (western-style) rationalization (Weber 1978, p. 630). Thai magic and supernatural belief in the truth of belief endures, but with which consequences and possibilities? Weber understood that affective value-inspired orientation of social action generates charismatic leaders – in Thailand, rightwing ones: Phibun, Sarit, Bhumipol; leftwing: Pridi; and ethno-regional populist: Thaksin, as we explore in the final section.

We need, without slipping into relativism or realism, to attend to other categories and entities, as neither false nor true, traditional or modern, making possible different truth regimes, ontologies and epistemologies as products of power and force relations. Foucault's notion of 'governmentality' (Foucault

2000) entails a 'mentality of rule': ordering things, shaping truth-or-falsehood, conducting conduct of self and other, identities, thoughts, affects. The emphasis is not on what, for instance, the Thai monarchy and democracy are, as if primordial essences, but rather, how these normative concepts are used within practices, institutions, techniques of power, with what unintended consequences? Thai society, culture and politics are the ambiguous and hybrid products of locally translated, qua transformed and transvaluated western signs and norms. What might be termed the 'recoil-effects' of intercultural encounters.

Western commentators on Thai politics, such as Ferrara, Connors and McCargo, problematically presuppose reductionist Eurocentric social science dualisms, doctrines of structure and agency and personalist metaphysics to focus on networks of concrete individual personalities and their subjective intentions (Unaldi 2016, pp. 47, 52). Western analysts tend to presuppose rational autonomous individual actors with pre-given transcultural cognitive capacities (Hindess 1993, 1996; Hirst and Woolley 1982). However, Unaldi (2016, p. 13) uses Weber subtly to show non-subjectivist intentions in a clash of rationalities and charisma, in subjects and objects, urban space and buildings.

West European and North American political concepts and categories, for example of a public and private realm, are used to understand Thailand, but their articulation needs to be addressed. Connors' (2007) sophisticated analysis shows how an ethnocentric and evolutionary model of political development was not just applied by westerners to promote democracy against communism, but was internalized and re-articulated by Thai thinkers and politicians for their particular interests. Yet, commentators such as McCargo ethnocentrically presuppose that legitimacy is key to understanding Thai politics. Understanding Thailand's form of government and politics as a legitimation crisis, turning on individual consent and rights, explains everything and nothing. Given the seemingly permanent, multiple and interminable nature of 'crisis', signified by the number of military coups, extra-judicial killings and arrests of people under lèse majesté, it begs the question of when was rule ever legitimate? The myth of populist royal power guiding Thai democracy plays down the role of a right-wing military using the monarchy to justify killing. In other words, an authoritarian tradition is the enduring and entrenched norm, not the exception.

The monarchy as an institution is used to foreclose electoral politics from being a viable option. Thailand has never been liberal or democratic. There was a republican attempt in 1932 to institute an egalitarian society along the lines of western-style democracy, popular sovereignty and place the monarchy under the constitution and law, notably by Pridi Panomyong, but this was subverted. Liberalism and democracy are alien traditions, were never entrenched in Siam and have always been resisted by the military and monarchy – pace Connors' (2007, 2008, 2009) nonsensical notion of 'royal liberalism'. The Thai polity is of a different complex, hybrid Buddhist Hindu animist ontology and metaphysics. It is not founded upon 'possessive individualism', rights, consent and popular sovereignty. We must embrace 'ontological relativity' to make other forms of life and different styles of reasoning intelligible: modes of individuating entities, judging truth-and-falsehood, domains of subjectivity and objectivity. But the question is, what are the practical, ethical and political consequences of Thai metaphysical doctrines in social relations? For example, appeals are made in Thai politics and policy for Thai self-rule, but how and which category of a Thai self? Is Thai personhood the same as western modes of individualization and individuation? As we shall see below, Thais have no core being or essential Thai identity, only 'insignia': nothing but places/positions in hierarchies of social roles (Hanks 1967, p. 1252). Thus, Connors (2007) is correct, Althusser's theory of humans as subject-effects, without anthropological attributes, perfectly describes Thai's subjectivity.

The Thai monarch exercises the people's sovereignty on their behalf. He incarnates/is the people. The king is above the constitution and the law. Thus, any politics resembling western liberalism and democracy would dethrone him by subjecting the institution of monarchy to legal and political regulations and limits. Thais are subject to 'Thainess' – the three pillars being: Nation, Religion and Monarchy. Thais are free to be free 'Thai style'. Thai freedom, judged by universal and western standards, means subjugated subjects not citizens. If we are relativists this is not a problem. Following Chakrabarty (2010), there is an alternate tradition in Thailand of subaltern resistance and rebellion to royalist Bangkok rule by past and present forms of peasants, rural populations and dissenting groups. Recently, the most notable is the irregular war fought by 'Barisan Revolusi Nasional-Koordinasi' (BRN-C): Malay Muslim freedom fighters in southern Thailand, who wish to liberate their minds, bodies and territory from Thai Buddhism and right-wing royalist security forces (Helbardt 2015).

The power of governing–governed relations, governing in the name of Thai truth is central to understanding recent Thai politics – the overthrowing of Thaksin and his sister and massacres of common people, Tak Bai and Kru Se 2004, Red Shirts 2010, expressing a right not to be governed in a particular way. Massacres, military coups, revolutions, rebellions, popular political unrest, from 1932, 1973, 1976, 1992, 2004, 2006, 2010 to the most recent coup of 2014 and current military dictatorship. In this pantomime, the players have western masks and manners, to fight the big bad British/French colonial wolf, but are all-too Thai, using indigenous forms of extra-moral evil in the name of purification (Rackett 2014a), for the king and nation. Let us now explore the three main myths of Thai exceptionalism and uniqueness and their justification.

The first reason Thailand sees itself as unique in Southeast Asia is that it was never directly colonized, or occupied, by a western power, which has enabled its traditions to endure. The reality is somewhat different and complex. The Thai socio-political and economic landscape has been shaped by how it has responded to and re-configured western knowledge and powers: imperialism, capitalism, colonization, modernity, development and democratic forms of politics and government. Crucial is the historical event of Siam's defeat by the French Imperial forces in 1893, sailing up the Chao-praya River (Thongchai 1994). In addition, Thailand has been profoundly shaped by western theories, socio-political norms, forms, presuppositions, language and concepts.

Thailand has a myth of uniqueness, doing it the Thai way, but it is comparable to others in Southeast Asia, for instance its southern neighbor of Malaysia. Both nations were structured by a British colonial racist form of rule. Siam 'creatively adapted' the latter in an assimilating program of 'inner colonization' of lesser 'Others within' (Thongchai 2000) to govern marginalized ethnic and religious populations. This splitting, argues Loos (2002, p. 21), means we should not 'isolate Siam as exceptional, Siam's split identity as colonizer and colonized makes it eminently comparable to both and simultaneously capable of illuminating the limits of the categories'.

Today, in Thailand and Malaysia, and Burma, post-colonial elites subscribe to and impose ultra-nationalist formations and fantasies of race and religion upon diverse peoples, which foment multi-racist, rather than multicultural, society, politically fixing exclusive particular identities using religion as a marker of ethnicity: Buddhism in Thailand and Islam in Malaysia, to be a true authentic Thai is to be Buddhist, and to be Malay is to be Muslim (Jerryson 2011; Rackett 2014b).

Siamese wolf?

Rama V visited colonies of Singapore, Malaya, Burma, India and Java in 1871–1872 with a vision 'to turn his kingdom into a miniature European colony without the Europeans, making it a modern 'civilized' Asian state' (Jackson 2004b, p 279). King Rama V used colonial forms of government to promote economic development. Development in the twentieth century was carried out by the urban sacred center of rural peripheries taming and domesticating savage areas and peoples. British and Dutch colonial rule's effect on Siam was, according to Kasian (2001, p. 6), an 'authoritarian and centralized modernized auto-colonial state', as if the Siamese did the colonialists work for them. Populations were enslaved by the Siamese elites' self-colonization and self-civilization (Kasian 2001, p. 53), as they felt inferior to the west but superior to local 'savage' primitive ethno-religious subalterns within who they needed to make it civilized. The absolutist monarchy exercised 'internal tyranny' subjugating its own peoples (Kasian 2001, p. 53). As Loos (2002) argues, Siam's rule over 'Malay states became a showcase to demonstrate Siam's ability to modernize/colonize'. Siam wished to compete as an equal with the British colonies, it did this by using law to efficiently rule the native populations displacing Islamic authority in the deep south. Siam's 'civilizing mission' was to domesticate 'semi-barbaric states' in which local rulers were seen as lazy natives "abusive, ineffectual, corrupt, nepotistic and oppressive to the 'people' (Somchat 1978, in Jackson 2004b). The Malay savages needed Thai-ifying by Bangkok civility.

Another myth is that the monarchy is an exceptional institution. However, the king, now Rama X, might reign but does he rule, exercise sovereignty? A sole focus on the monarchy, its network of agents, as the main actor driving Thai politics and power is wrong and misplaced. It colludes with and perpetuates an elite myth. It misrepresents the workings and nature of sovereign powers in Thailand. The past Rama IX and current king Rama X can be seen as weak and reactive, whilst their institutional role has a manufactured sacred aura of barami-(prestige and charismatic power) ascribed to it as the effects of usage in power–truth relations. Monarchy as a historical institution is an 'ideology' and instrument of repression deployed by the military to govern through Thainess: a mentality of rule using culture, nationalism, monarchy and Buddhism.

In the myth that Siam was never colonized it is king Chulalongkorn, with his reforms and 'creative adaptation' of western ways, who is seen as having saved it from Imperial subjection. Siam was 'not directly colonized' 'it was subjected to western Imperial power in an informal Empire' (Jackson 2004b, p. 229) in which its economy and law were forced to conform to western norms resulting in splitting into a global political regime and educational system and local cultural productions (Jackson 2004b, 230). Siam's sovereignty was ceded by unequal trading treaties (Bowring 1855) and extra-territorial legal status of foreign nationals (Streckfuss 2011) who had to be free from inferior and immoral backward un-Christian Siamese laws (Jackson 2004b, pp. 223, 224). Siam became the number 1 rice supplier for the British Empire. Siam had to self-civilize and became 'an indirectly colonized dynastic state' (Kasian 2001, p. 5). The weak king capitulated to the west. By giving in to the British, Chulalongkorn got rich empowering his government to subjugate and colonize his regional populations more efficiently. In this two-faced Siamese strategy, freedom entailed 'a more intense form of state authority while representing this as a form of liberty, from the west, rather than as subjection to the new form of local tyranny' (Jackson 2004b, p. 235). Siam was not a victim of the west but an alternate colonizer of its own people through Bangkok's racist domination. This is hardly mitigated by the royal projection of images of Siamese civilization, through drama – see below. Siamese duplicity was a part of 'intensified power exercised over local populations to orchestrate the national performance of "civilized" behavior for foreign consumption, which in turn enhanced the international status and helped secure the autonomy of Siamese elites from direct western political control' (Jackson 2004b, pp. 236, 237). The message was that there is no need to colonize Siam: 'we can "auto-colonize"' (Kasian 2001). Furthermore, enforced free trade and direct economic penetration of Siam was not by military force as: 'Siam's door opened from the inside' (Chaiyan 1994 cited by Jackson 2004b).

Herzfield (2010, p. 173) interprets Thailand as an instance of 'crypto-colonialism': 'the condition in which the very claim of independence marks a symbolic as well as a material dependence on intrusive colonial power'. Political independence at the price of massive economic dependence. Aggressive nationalist culture fashioned to suit foreign models' 'independent but effective dependence in a zone of what the state represses in response to externally imposed values, yet on what it covertly relies to sustain the continuing loyalty of its citizens' (Herzfield 2010, p. 175). Herzfield's account suffers from what might be termed the 'subaltern agency fallacy': a Eurocentric moralistic championing of canny natives, premised upon intentional actors with rational choice: 'Thais have long been, and still are, adroitly strategic and selective in their adaption and use of western forms' (Herzfield 2010, p. 178). This ignores the unintended consequences of the 'recoil effects' of intercultural translation transforming and setting apart entities and subjects and also the role of non-human actors. The self-image of Thais as 'sorng na', being two-faced and duplicitous, is not, pace Herzfield, an ironic adoption of a western view, it's a product of splitting and an expression of narcissistic indifference.

The second myth of Thailand's attributed uniqueness in Southeast Asia is that, unlike some of its neighbors, Thailand did not succumb to communism; this made it seem free and independent. But Thailand's defeat of/freedom from communism was not exceptional. The rabid anti-communist pogroms supported by the United States, especially in Indonesia and 'counter-insurgency' in Malaya, resulted in authoritarianism and totalitarian societies of control wherein states manufacture consent and attempt to engineer ideal political and social relations in the name of Asian values: harmony, consensus, unity and order. The anti-communist law criminalized dissent, enforcing Thainess; it was a thought crime and act to cause others 'to lose faith in religion or the traditions or customs of the Thai race' (Steckfuss 2011, p. 237). A modernist myth perpetuated by western commentators, following the defeat of communism, is that Thailand has seen a liberalization and democratization of its institutions and policies, in 'network monarchy' (McCargo) and 'royal liberalism' (Connors).

The third myth is that imperial Siam and its kings outsmarted the colonial threat by creatively adapting British colonial discourse to resist colonization to make modern Thailand exceptional. The means of this operation were 'self-colonization' and a self-civilizing program: a selective mimicry of western colonial institutions, norms and values used to rule its diverse populations through race and religion. Siam's feeling of inferiority and being savage in the international society of states drove a particular translation of an image of western civilization. Power and fantasy (Harrison 2010) are central to the Siamese encounter with the colonial other and its strategy of coping with foreign and alien thought, as these shaped future forms, and the limits, of Thai politics and development. Siam's alternate modernity entailed processes of ambiguous identification and splitting in its identity: it, Thainess, emerged as hybrid, both this and that, modern and traditional, neither/nor, as in-between

Siam and the West (Harrison 2010, p. 14). The Bangkok elite in the nineteenth century (Kasian 2001, p. 6) regarded themselves 'subjectively as almost a supra-ethnic or supra-national cosmopolitan ruling caste, they lorded it up over the Siamese nation-people as colonial master with a royal Thai face'. Bangkok was the center of Siamese imperial racist rule. The myth that Siam resisted the West presupposes agency and pragmatism. Rather, Siam dissimulated its own domination and barbarity to subalterns within, pace Herzfield, by 'fending off the wolves by donning their clothes' (Sulak Sivaraksa).

Siam negotiated western civilization through the display of objects, ornaments and symbols of the west – a strategy of appearances and aesthetic mode of power; literally, an appropriation western styles of dress: etiquette not ethics. Putting on the clothes of the other and adopting their manners facilitated stepping out of one's own skin into shoes of the other. Siamese King Rama V Chulalongkorn put on peasant dress 'pak-ar-mah' to pass among his own subjects and wore a three piece English suit. He was almost the same, but not quite/not white. Educated in England, Eton and Oxford he 'returned more Siamese than when he left. More English than the English'. The Siamese aesthetic rendering of western discourse in terms of appearances and images is extra-epistemological: neither just, nor true, but is caught up in the thrall of power relations and violence.

These three myths have shaped an image of Thailand into a regional success story. Thais are made to believe in their nationalist and royalist myths, which suppress and exclude dissent and alternative narratives. They have to unconditionally love the king as the fount and cause of good and virtue. For instance, criticizing royal-sponsored development is prohibited, in spite of the fact that the building of dams, as a sign of modernity, funded by the royal Siam cement company, and changing the crops of 'Hill Tribes', damages the environment, destroys traditions and displaces indigenous peoples. These royal projects are a form of 'internal colonization' which convert ethnic populations to Buddhism, teach them to speak Bangkok Thai and demand they revere the king and queen.

Thailand faces multiple institutional failures: legal, constitutional, parliamentary, the separation of powers, and a history of serial coups and military dictatorships. Thai political culture justifies dictatorship by 'good' moral people in the name of a pure spiritual Buddhist (Rackett 2014a; Streckfuss 2011) non-political government. Carl Schmitt's (1985, 1996) notions of the 'state of exception' and sovereignty and Agamben (1998) are useful to show how Thailand is ruled through manufacturing moral panics, and crises in states of exception. Thailand's authoritarian politics is highly developed in its capability to create existential threats from enemies within – anti-royalists, communists, Muslims, Red Shirts and ex-PM Thaksin – and to rule through exception, with dire consequences for social equality, liberty and justice.

Thai rule thrives on crisis, security threats, ethnic religious and political 'enemy others' within, badged with 'un-Thainess', who dissent from right-wing military supported royalism. The socio-political order needs bad enemy-others and the threat of anarchy, to justify its interventions and rule and enact extra-legal anti-political 'Thai-style democracy'. Practicing a form of democracy entails recognizing individuals, ascribing rights, freedom, the sovereignty of the people electoral politics and autonomous political parties. The rule of law, the constitution, can be suspended and trumped in the name of dangers posed – by impure morally bad people seen as uneducated and gullible – to social order and security and the sacred institution of monarchy. Authoritarian rule syncopates in its forces. Ferrara (2015) makes a very strong case for Thai politics as following a pattern set out in 1932 of illegal military coups and revolutions overthrowing governments, overturning constitutions by self-appointed good people to purify bad forces and people to protect the Thai race, culture and monarchy.

Monarchy is used as an instrument of subjugation. Any attributes of being revered and sacred are effects of the power of using the king as a symbol to control and rule above the law. The law of rule enforces nationalist, racist and royalist myths and illusions. The tyranny of Thai tradition and custom hypostatizes an imaginary nation in which 'things are the way they are because that is the way they are', and 'what is, was, and will be'. Change is prevented by imposing an invented past, that never was, to colonize the future, as a continuation of things, as they have always been, to control the present. Thai coups are a way of not changing anything, the status quo, which is rather surprising for a Buddhist nation in which the only thing permanent is impermanence. This illustrates how much work is expended to keep things the same: a remarkable achievement of the illusion of the suppression of time and history in an eternal moment of myth and imposition of a monolithic master narrative of Thai ultimate Truth and God-King. Thailand is a pre-emptive society in which everything is under the purview of state control. As military dictator Suchinda once boasted, 'The only thing we do not control are the moon and the stars'.

Thai-style politics entails propagating beliefs in cultural myths, and nationalist illusions border on the delusional, demanding the believers' certitude, incredulous incredulity. The people know what they are allowed to know and lack discursive resources to articulate disagreement and dissent from a simulacrum of western democracy, rule of law, elections and party politics. Signs of democracy are translated in practice and function institutionally in ways that totally transforms and transvalues them: subverting their political and ethical valence into their opposite, so they become void of meaning and value, just ornaments. Thaksin and his sister who democratically won elections were removed illegally with manufactured justifications in an instance of Thai socio-legal and political 'ontological gerrymandering'.

Problem: Thai style politics without politics

What is the country's priority under military tutelage and strong leadership? Government governs through development, which as seen as a matter of national security rather than industry, productivity or market growth. National development was sidelined, if not derailed by developing nationalism in the name of the official economy, whilst, at the same time, in the dark underground economy, pursuing self-interest. Corruption as a way of life in the government, army and police force, supporting crony capitalism. Thai history is one of unethical conduct by the king and his men.

Thai politics is anti-politics. Politics is seen as 'bad': venal, selfish, practiced by corrupt politicians, democratic dictatorship and uncontrollable political parties. But Thai power still has 'the political', following Carl Schmitt's definition, deciding and making existential friend and foe distinctions; good kings, people and coups who protect and save the country – from democracy and the interests of the masses, peasants and working classes. Sarit's authoritarianism was government without politics (Ferrara 2015, p. 158) and he gave 'one great freedom, freedom from politics' (Neher 1920, cited in Ferrara 2015). Democracy was seen as the tyranny of the majority as a 'disease of freedom' (Seni Pramoj, cited in Connors 2010, pp. 185–186). The dangerous threat of people's excess liberty and freedom had to be contained and all watched over by the king. Next we turn to the conditions of possibility and problem-spaces of the present in Thailand.

Schizoid truth and reality in Thailand's alternate modernity in the colonial encounter

Jackson (2004a, p. 181) wishes to grasp the nature of the Thai order of things, truth and power as a tyranny of images and representational violence supporting Thainess and punishing un-Thainess. The Thai mode of power is a 'regime of images' which controls and censors statements in the public realm whilst allowing those in the private realm to be freer. An image or statement deemed to be abnormal, or dissenting from the normative idealized form, is judged as disruptive, disturbing the peace and order of a 'smooth calm surface' 'phap-pot haeng-sa-ngop-riap-roy' and legal and cultural powers will be used to expel and censor an unwanted representation from the public realm. (Jackson 2004a, p. 181). Thai society is profoundly superficial; that is, it is presentational. Thai power monitors and polices public appearances, images and conduct but not private ones; this is a legacy of Siam's colonial encounter. The consequences, we argue, are a totalitarian racist society wherein anything goes and is permitted to the rich and those in power. A 'Salo' in the sun.

As Morris (2000) argues, Thai reality, culture and society has no ontological depth. It is ordered through images and an 'overinvestment in appearances' (Morris 2000, p. 5). The genesis of this ontology needs to be understood in the historical formation of Thai alternate modernity and political power, which did not need the 'creation of a national subjectivity or an essential Thai personhood only the performance of appearing to conform to nationalist behavior' (Morris 2000, p. 147). Connors realism, and talk of liberalization and democratization efforts misses the point that they are not positive, but empty rhetoric or forms, as the 'government and state are indifferent to people's desires and inner states of mind' (Morris 2000). Thai alternate modernity rests on a 'fetishism of appearances, on the demand for a signifying surface, and on a representational politics in which the processes of enframement are repressed' (Morris 2000, p. 238).

Schizoid saying and doing

Significantly, many commentators, Loos, Thongchai, Jackson and especially Streckfuss (2011, pp. 222, 306) use the trope of schizophrenia to talk about the nature of Thai reality and truth. All that is important are social appearances not private reality, it is as if there is not any individual subjectivity behind collective performances. Jackson argues that Thai metaphysics and ontology are not structured by dualism appearance/reality and there is no cultural necessity to disclose Truth. This makes for a state resembling a 'postmodern nightmare' of permissiveness: Thailand is authoritarian in shaping normative public presentations but comparatively tolerant of private diversities (Jackson 2004a, p. 182). Thus, one can say and do one thing in public and another in private. Whilst this might be a universal of human conduct, in Thailand this dislocation and splitting is not treated as a serious issue. The schizoid nature of Thai reality, forms of saying and doing, mean there is no problem if you do not ripple the surface calm of presentation of face/self in social relations (Jackson 2004a, p. 183). Does the public–private split of the Thai 'regime of images' constitute a contradiction for Thai culture and society? No, asserts Jackson from a Thai emic point of view. That would be imposing a western ethnocentric standard. Thai logic has multiple contexts of operations of power (Jackson 2004a, p. 187). Why should Thai knowledge and truth, be coherent, consistent and logically relative? For Jackson, Thai cultural logic: saying one thing and doing something different is rational. Such Siamese sophistry is socially organized hypocrisy and duplicity, which makes moral responsibility and ethics impossible.

Thai logic means the significance of an act, or speech, in public or private, is judged as normal and acceptable according to its situational context: the 'time and place' it is said or done 'kala-thesa' (van Esterik 2000), not its truth content or moral content. Thus, it is extra-moral and extra-epistemological. Thai speech and conduct are formal, ritualistic performances in a specific context. It doesn't matter whether what is said and done is true or not! Is Jackson seriously suggesting, a form of ultra-relativism of anything goes: that Thais can tell the truth, or lie, act anyway, as long as conforming to the grooves of socio-cultural norms and beliefs? Jackson says this is not illogical and absurd, but it does preclude a persisting and enduring subject responsible for ethical conduct, synchronizing saying and doing, in making promises and signing contracts, across different times and places and situations.

Thai logic, Jackson (2004a, p. 183) clarifies, entails a 'form of power-knowledge with distinctive epistemological effects'. Jackson is unclear and incoherent here. Does he mean people are allowed to know different realities? Or have different knowledge of the same reality? Truth-or-falsehood of an utterance is insignificant. The Thai 'regime of images' is indifferent: what matters are aesthetics not veracity, and culturally syntonic sentiments and affects. The state/government polices and controls which truths can be uttered in public, if they are disruptive, i.e. anti-royalist, then criminal sanctions and extra-legal force can be applied (Jackson 2004a, p. 184). Duality, two-facedness, lies at the 'very heart of the Thai regime of images [and] constitutes the very form of Thailand's alternate modernity' (Morris 1994, p. 35). The effects of 'translating' and re-configuring western Colonial thought and forms means only good positive images, upholding public face and reputation, must be allowed (Jackson 2004a, p. 185). Image management is a part of Thai political culture, not an effect of globalization and capitalist marketing (Jackson 2004a, p. 187).

A distinctive Thai ontology involves a constitutive disjuncture between representations and practices and surfaces over essences. Thai metaphysics is radically other: it has no logos, 'deep furniture' of cosmos or mind, only shifting flux of surface seeming. No appearance–truth distinction obtains. Thai society-civilization is shallow and superficial. As Niels Mulder (1996, pp. 143–144), perspicaciously noted of Thai culture and society, there is a 'cultural fetishization of surface effects' and a superabundance of rituals and ceremonies. 'Presentation [is] the heart of things, essence of reality' in which the 'outside appearance is taken to be the essence of social life'. It is imperative to 'manipulate signs and symbols of reality as mastery'. Thai cosmetic metaphysics and the self, identity, are appearances not individualized, pace Connors and McCargo's presuppositions about Thai democracy and liberalism. Existential Thai individuals exist but individuated autonomous bounded persons-personalities seem not to in Thai culture and society. Thai human relations are presenting appearances, whatever truth or reality lies behind them, in a 'social cosmetic right time and place and social form' (Jackson 2004a, p. 191). This power of correct performance of appearances has schizoid consequences, permitting 'the formation of multiple identities that easily slip over each other like tectonic plates'. So, multiple conflictual identities, forms of saying and doing, is normal (for western standards pathological) Thai reality. Content or substance are irrelevant as only a correct performance in a 'politicized aesthetic' (Jackson 2004a, p. 191) matters. Aesthetics are supreme, not ethics. The true is beautiful, and the beautiful true; for instance, Thai feminine beauty – including transgendered lady boys – as the national image of Thailand (Jackson 2003). As Van Esterik (2000, p. 129) points out, the Buddhist value of the moral-spiritual power of beauty objectified in/as Thai women is consumed globally.

Topics such as the monarchy, the sex industry, state murder are unspeakable in public, but not in private. Criticism and negative comments concerning the Thai monarchy, living or dead, including their dogs, is a key taboo in a regime of images criminalized and punishable by the 'lèse majesté' law.

Being unable to judge the truth or moral value of the contents of statements about the king, 'devalues "truth" while fetishizing positive images' (Jackson 2004a, p. 194). Prostitution and polygyny, for instance, in the eyes of the international community, the global gaze, are prohibited, whilst, for Thai-eyes-only, the local gaze, they are permissible.

Splitting

Thongchai (2010, p. 136) argues that Siam coped with the west by an intellectual strategy of bifurcation as a coping strategy to deal with western otherness and enmity. Thailand has Buddhism whilst the west had science. Thai Buddhism was modernized and rationalized as a superior spiritual science, an 'essence of inner selfhood' by king Monkut. Western culture and science is superficial, dealing with senses, and is instrumental, whilst Thai culture deals with ultimate goals and truth. This splitting helps construct a schizoid Thai Self, wherein bifurcation is 'normative rationality fixed as the Thai mentality' (Thongchai 2010, p. 139). Democracy is not a Thai concept (Thongchai 2010, p. 141), yet the rebellions of 1973, 1976, 1992, 2010 show that Thais care and want it. Thongchai (2010: 148–149) argues that in the parochial closed Thai mind, western elements are Thai-ized. Buddhism is transculturated 'as the heart and soul of modern Thai identity'. Thais are ignorant of this: a (hybrid) product of a locally transformation induced by western influences. And 'Thais experience Buddhism as Buddhism, not westernized Thai-ized Buddhism'. Likewise, national borders, demarcated boundaries are western techno-scientific invented and induced geo-political phenomena.

The effect of Thailand's alternate modernity (Jackson) is to de-rail the course of capitalism and economic development, as it is re-configured by magic and supernatural beliefs and practices, to form enchanting Thai capitalism (Jackson 1999a,b, 2010a). The complexity of the imperial legacy for Thailand is a 'double colonization' by foreign Euro-American discourses and local royal-centric forms of hegemony (Jackson 2010b, p. 191). British colonial power upset and destabilized the politico-religious-cultural ideology of Siam's rulers, forcing them to re-make their symbolic capita with goods and thought from the west instead of India and China in the mid-1850s. The rulers assimilated, swallowed 'kleun-klai' foreign elements to change ambivalently into themselves/others (Jackson 2010b: 197). They protected political autonomy by hybridity, re-fashioning Siamese institutions and practice along western lines of civilization, modernity, development and democracy. The hybrid term 'siwilai' was more a 'project of constructing Occidentalized images of Siamese prestige than a program of materially transforming the country into a western styled polity' (Jackson 2010, p. 198). Siwilai is like a cosmetic 'make over' and cross-dressing in the 'clothes': foreign forms and alien ways of the other in aesthetic performance of 'oriental' erotic and exotic beauty and dancing to enhance local magico-religious power relations with the 'cachet of foreign prestige as well as the authenticity of the local'

(Reynolds 1998 in Jackson 2010b 124). Re-invented Siamese traditions as enacting a local-foreign split have important unintended consequences: profound transformations fomenting the Thai middle classes' republican desires (Barme 2002; Copeland 1993; Jackson 2010b, p. 201). Jackson argues that a class struggle against the royals was fueled by hybridity: 'subaltern assimilation of the foreign as resistance to internal colonization' in assertions of ethno-regional diversity, division and dissent, threatening a national civil war against enforced sameness and unity.

On truth and Thais in a non-moral sense

The relativist cul-de-sac and nihilist truth of Jackson's emic gaze is disclosed when he claims that 'a discursive and representational system based on epistemological multiplicity should not be equated with duplicity' (Jackson 2004a, p. 201). Why not? Thais can lie and deceive as it is their culture and tradition, which is normal relative to multiple contextual performances and demands. What if a statement is judged as false and unjust? This is not Foucauldian as Jackson claims, but 'post-modern' relativist nonsense. It is not just an issue of 'just being Thai, performing Thainess, in speech and acts, correctly'. This is a schizophrenic 'Thai episteme' of multiple representations of reality and forms of truth. One truth for foreigners, another for the royalist elite, and yet a different one for the common masses? Anything goes in Thailand, foreclosing moral and socio-economic development possibilities: permissiveness by some royals, military and rich, who can sell and use drugs, rape and murder with impunity in Thailand, some in public, but mostly in private with or without consent. For Jackson, official discourse denies 'facts' and 'truth' permitting lies and subjectivism, but, he adds the caveat, 'Such denials should not be interpreted in epistemological terms [this contradicts what he said earlier about epistemological effects] in relation to a notion of truth but rather in performative terms as an effect of power' (Jackson 2004a, pp. 202–203). So, in Thai cultural logic, spoiling or damaging a false nationalist positive Thai image is a crime. What matters is the prestige of Thai schizoid truths.

In fact, we could advance a Baudrillardian analysis of Thailand as totally made up, a make-believe land. A nation woven out of nothing but images, an image-nation, which dissimulates it is an aesthetic simulacrum (Jackson 2004a, p. 204). In Jackson's terms, a 'dominance of image or representation over reality or truth' (lies are true, myth is reality). 'Truth is abandoned as a structuring principle in the Thai symbolic domain', states Jackson. Thus, it is not a question of judging or finding the truth of a statement, only an instance of working 'to construct and uphold the relationally determined prestige or barami of representations and statements' whose 'significance does not depend on an anchoring relationship with truth and reality'. Does this mean Thai social relations are built on lies as a social norm?

Thai culture, in Jackson's interpretation, turns on performative power in a system of power/prestige not as in Foucault power/knowledge: power is mobilized not in the name of truth (knowledge) but 'to enhance the prestige of images, not truth-value, but association with high status symbols'. From a western point of view this is 'cultural ritualism' an 'over-identification with appearances, to the mistaking of form for reality, and even more, to the attribution of reality to form' (Morris 2000, p. 146). This is why Connors' analysis of Thai politics is wrong and unfounded. Thai use of models, of democracy, liberalism, rule of law and a constitution, are aesthetic-forms, without content and substance. Prestige and truth value are split and independent of one another (Jackson 2004a, pp. 205–206). So, the Red Shirt graffiti: 'King Bhumipol is a monitor lizard (aii hia)' is true but received and judged as dangerous, damaging the positive image and unimpeachable reputation of the revered sacred institution of monarchy.

Jackson's claim that the Thai split between public–private, sayings and doings, is not contradictory, but with pre-moral hypocritical consequences is giving into a relativist blackmail: 'We, westerners, are just other Thais and cannot judge them' (Jackson 2004a, p. 212). But, Jackson's acute insights show very well how a Thai culture of extreme violence flows from extra-moral and extra-epistemological forms of Thai Truth that can permit everything and incite pre-Kantian imperatives of 'You may!', 'Enjoy', in Thai fascism. Tyranny Thai style works via images in a performative state (Jackson 2004b, p. 219). Thus, 'The contemporary Thai political system remains authoritarian'. The 'recoil-effects' of translating western forms and norms: Siam responded to the western colonial demand for civilized conduct in law and morality by splitting and enacting a disjuncture: conforming in public whilst doing something else in private: a bifurcation of restriction and prohibition and more open circulation of images and knowledge. Not all social relations were transformed, only those, argues Jackson (2004b: 220), necessary to maintain national autonomy. Siamese rulers just projected and performed an image to the British colonizers.

Siam, if we follow Hegel's master–slave trope gave up its human freedom and became a slave by refusing to fight to the death. Siam dressed up, put on a face mask to cope with western colonialism dissimulating its subjective thoughts and values. Buddhism was transformed by Thais, for westerners into a rational master science, for themselves into a technique of magic, sacred power and enchantment: not 'moral self-reliance' but auspiciousness, luck, 'merit making for money' (Mulder 1996, p. 19). In Thai Buddhist aesthetics 'ontology is disavowed as there are only appearances' (Morris 2002 in Jackson 2004b). The aim of the Thai 'regime of images' in Jackson's analysis is the 'maintenance of public shows of harmony at its core, valuing conformity to displays of orderliness (khwarm-riap-roi) above epistemological concern with truth' (Jackson 2004b, p. 223); thus making intelligible, toleration and indifference to inequality, injustice, political violence and murder.

Siam as a dance drama

The theatrical modality of Thai polity and society is in the tradition of Geertz's 'theater state': the king as (master) sign among signs incarnating power of representations and the representation of power flowing through the social body. Royalty is driven by ritual pageantry and ceremonies, staging the king and his power as in drama: a song and dance. Dance-dramas were central to the Siamese royal court, were performed to western embassies, not for entertainment, but as 'carefully staged displays intended to impress foreign visitors with symbolic representations of the authority, legitimacy and power of the Siamese court' (Jackson 2004b, p. 225). An aesthetic mise-en-scène, which rather than being a resistance as argued by Jackson, may be just entertainment for the guests with its exotic and erotic arts of beautiful bodies in motion and otherness: how Thailand is globally consumed today. Western technology, especially mass media and ICT, have been transforming and have resulted not in secularization, rationalization, but super-charging enchantment in a Thai society of the simulacrum (Jackson 2004b, p. 227), proliferating magic, ghosts, mediums and spirit cults in the late twentieth and early twenty-first centuries (Jackson 1999a, 1999b, 2008, 2010; Morris 2000; Thongchai 2006), especially the sacred aura personality cult of king Bhumipol with authoritarian effects (Jackson 2004b, p. 229).

Siam as a transvestite?

Siam fashioned and staged itself to the colonial Other through cross-dressing: putting on the clothes of the west. Western style clothes were worn, compulsory under Phibun's fascist government, in a hybrid ensemble unique style, signifying a 'civilized', but not quite western, authentic Siamese style, 'different modes of self-presentation – one for the colonial stage, one for the domestic stage, one for the private realm' (Peleggi 2002, cited by Jackson 2004b) to negotiate external western expectations and personal taste. The elite rulers, thus, re-fashioned themselves, by splitting Thai culture, form of government, administration, law, marriage customs, sexual, erotic displays, conduct and religion (Jackson 2004b, 238–241) into puritan and permissive aspects, in the Colonial Mirror; this centralized their power and the rule of absolute monarchy (Thongchai 2000) as a re-invented hybrid alternate modern tradition. The latter mentality of rule persisted even under a republican form of government in 1932 which saw a more intense regime of civilized puritan respectability at the core of nation building. Phibun's fascist 'cultural mandates' performed Thai racial civilization for local rule in a regime of the constitutional right to rule in place of absolute monarchy, a common peoples' dictatorship (Jackson 2004b, pp. 243–244).

Subjugation and rule through political development of democratization

Connors (2007) addresses the question of whether Thailand has ever been democratic: is it just all talk in a 'statist development moral project of rational citizenship' in which national security comes first? For Connors, democracy is used in Thailand as an ideology of 'democrasubjection: the imaginary forms of self and collective rule', which is 'politically unequal, exploitative and interest driven power' and works via 'tying national-peoples to myths of self and nation, as subjects in the process of self-realization and agency' (Connors 2007, p. 4). Thai national identity formation is a 'euphemism for the untold symbolic and real violence that is done in the name of sameness' (Connors 2007, p. 6).

Political development discourse (Connors 2007, pp. 7–9) aimed to produce a 'modern rational man capable of change and choice to break out of cultural constraints to implant a capitalist regime in 3rd world countries like Thailand' (Connors 2007, pp. 10–12). The paradox of political development discourse is that it presupposes what it seeks to create: a sovereign people capable of self-rule 'as mute-rational objects' who have to change into sovereign subject-citizens. Connors sees democracy as a hegemonic ideology turning on the consent of individuals, but 'consent in Thai politics is manufactured and serves particular interests', so ideology only partially interpellates subjects, as a governmental objective, to be modern political citizens 'held to be autonomous agents and capable of consent to participate in a political community' (Connors 2007, p. 23). Connors use of Althusser, is contradictory, as Marxian epistemological realism conflicts with Foucault's post-epistemology. In a Marxian analysis of power as negative, an ideology and domination: democratic freedom is false and subjecting. For Foucault (2000), governmental power is positive, producing: a truth and forming personhood as effects of power and discourses neither true nor false. Connors is judging Thai reality and politics as false, and posits political liberation, a subject free from its ideological blinkers and power relation via his privileged 'objective' scientific truth; this is Marxian essentialism.

Democracy 'Thai-style' 'prachapatipitai bep thai' with dictatorial father figures Sarit and king Bumipol, forced order, unity and discipline in a government appropriate to the special characteristics and realities of the Thai (Connors 2007, p. 58): the idea that the people are not capable of self-rule (Connors 2007, pp. 78–79). Development under 'Thai style democracy' was 'not capitalist individualization of the subject but a concern to construct citizens as the "eyes" and "ears" of the security state' (Connors 2007, p. 87). Economic development was caught in a bounded rationality of loyalty to the king, nation and religion, not economic equality. After the 1976 massacre of socialist and democratic student forces, PM Thanin advocated 'democracy with the king as head of state': positioning of king as above politics and as the symbol of Thai identity and 'military coups as instruments of democratic development' (Ferrara 2015, p. 161). The military did the people's duty and represented their collective desires and interests (Connors 2007, p. 108) – for Connors, a 'social contract of the military and monarchy embodying the general will'. Connors does not grasp the Schmittian paradox: military coups exercise sovereignty, on behalf of the sovereign, who exercises sovereignty on behalf of sovereignty of people. It is the military who are sovereign not the monarch using the language of democracy. The king was used by politicians to rule (Connors 2007, p. 131) and promote a 'conservative capitalist state' (Hewison 1977). Thainess, concludes Connors, is a 'control strategy by 'elite subjects over subaltern object' and rendering the problem of governing a people as a 'problem self-motivation and development'. In this way, elites blocked and controlled development of Thai capitalism (Connors 2007, p. 159).

Thai representations are imposed by violence not liberal democracy, pace Connors (2007), in Thai aesthetic and authoritarian practices. Despite his acute insights into the reflexive nature of Thai rule re-articulating liberal and democratic normative ideals and forms, these are non-substantive without content. Signs of democracy are displayed in rituals as if this institutes democracy in practices and ways of life.

1932 and common people

1932 marked the end of absolute monarchy, not the beginning of a lasting republic or democracy. Pridi Panomyong's republican egalitarianism criticized aristocrats and royals as dishonest, corrupt, indifferent to the people's suffering: 'The king's government held people as slaves … animals, and did not consider them as human beings … instead of helping them, it contrived to plant rice on the back of the people' and 'the country belongs to the people not the king' (cited in Connors 2007). But this was not the end of monarchy or absolutism. The constitution was received as if written by and a gift from the king, and not the people, as sovereign, wresting themselves free from masters and aristocracy. The institution of monarchy was heavily criticized and under attack in the 1920s and 1930s, leading to the abdication of the king under Phibun, monarchy faded until 1957.

The pattern of Thai politics until the present day started when the 1933 military coup removed Pridi's government as corrupt. Eighty years later, the military removed the government of Thaksin's sister, Yingluck, on 22 May 2014 with its championing of a fully elected senate (Ferrara 2015, p. xi, xii). A call was made for a 'peoples' revolution' by 'good' people against a democratically elected PM's government to defend the constitution and to block an amnesty bill to pardon Thaksin – removed in the last 2006 coup. At stake was Thaksin as a rival to the royalist order and its authoritative mono-truth. Ferrara phrases this constitutive contradiction and non-resolution of peoples sovereignty manifest in elections versus an unelected military whose support of authoritarian royalist rule is spiritually and morally good (Ferrara 2015, p. xiii); and we can also add, to justify a 'state of exception' suspending the constitution. The coup against Thaksin in 2006 was named a 'good coup' in the name of monarchy: military might making 'right' by illegally overturning the 1997 constitution, acting above the law. This event goes back to the republican struggle of the 1932 revolution which aimed to put the king and his powers both under the constitution and the law of the land (Ferrara 2015, p. 2). This unsuccessful attempt ignited a 'slow-burn civil war' (Montesano 2012).

Thailand is presently a military dictatorship. Thailand is not constrained by the legality of its government, it has no entrenched and instituted tradition of liberalism or democracy-aspirations as articulated and mobilized in and by subaltern struggles and popular politics such as Thaksin. Ferrara ignores what Jackson points out: the aesthetic and cosmetic nature of Thai power–truth–prestige relations which make the rule of law and constitutions into ornaments and signs easily dismissed and overturned in interminable crises, as Streckfuss (2011) puts it, in permanent 'abnormal times'. In 1957–1958, Sarit set the pattern of anti-constitutional validity and veracity of royalist ultra-nationalist rule termed the 'politics of despotic paternalism' by Thak Chaleomtiarana (2007); it was anti: popular sovereignty, individual equality, the constitution, and electoral substantive democracy. Rightwing royalists like Prem and Abhisit dissolved Thaksin's Peoples Power Party after Yellow Shirt demonstrations and violence against its electoral success in 2008, in a judicial coup outside the law, leading to Red Shirt protests in 2010 in which soldiers massacred 96 unarmed people to save the country. In 2011, the people voted in Yingluck (her party is Pheu Thai), as PM only to see her removed over alleged corruption.

Thai Fascism started under Phibun's racist and militarized republican nationalism. Dissent was not tolerated and progressive politicians were murdered. Phibun imposed a cultural mentality of rule conduct, manners, speech habits and clothes (Ferrara 2015, p. 114) with a strong leader with 'spiritualized personal authority' (Ferrara 2015, p. 119). A pattern reaching its zenith in Sarit's good dictatorship, and attempted by the feeble buffoonery of Prayuth today. Those at the top were there because of karma. Bhumipol replaced Sarit as a pure force and virtuous leader, a guiding light (Ferrara 2015, pp. 159–166) in the right place in the hierarchy of inferior and superior beings. Connors' notion of 'royal liberalism' is a nonsense as the monarchy has always been right-wing and pro-military. Sarit resurrected and re-sacralized the monarchy as anti-common people, individual rights and liberties (Morell and Chai-anan 1981, cited by Ferrara 2015).

King Bhumipol was implicated in the Thai fascism massacres of un-Thai communist enemies in 1973 and 1976. Bhumipol was not sorry about the massacres, he saw vigilantes and militia as protecting the nation against communism – or his wealth and position. He saw the need for a 'good Thai style dictatorship' (Bumipol 1977, 14 December 1976, p. 275). Post-1976, Thailand was a 'virtual theocracy' (Streckfuss 2011, p. 213), a zone of freedom from politics which silenced dissent and created a rise in inequalities of income and opportunity. Capitalism for the masses was condemned by royalists in a military led society (Ferrara 2015, pp. 191–193). The military functioned as conduit and amplifier for wealth concentration in a few Sino-Thai families.

Commercial military interests were attacked by Chatichai, the PM in 1986, leading to the growth of the business sector and political control of the military. His government was overthrown by a coup led by Suchinda, supported by Bumipol, in 1991, deemed to be impure and a 'parliamentary dictatorship'. In the Black May massacre of anti-dictatorship protestors, 52 or more were murdered. Bhumipol forgave the perpetrators (Ferrara 2015, p. 207). After this regression to Thai fascism, the trends of peasants of middle income and lower middle class status struggling for rights, social mobility and inclusion were advanced against a monarch who condemned self-advancement and mobility as selfish greed (Ferrara 2015, p. 219), which led to the rise of Thaksin. Finally, we turn to the meaning of significance of Thaksin.

King T(h)aksin or 1932 redux?

Thaksin's exceptional politics and exemplary charisma

Thaksin, as Ferrara astutely observes, was in some ways a Sarit style leader (Ferrara 2015, p. 221) using personal charisma and Thainess (Ferrara 2015, p. 222) against his critics and enemies of the nation who questioned his authority (Ferrara 2015, p. 229). Thaksin's charismatic and strong paternal leadership had illiberal aspects: the war on drugs, extra-judicial killings, the massacre of Malay Muslims in 2004, but were approved by the king and queen. But his support was from below, the common masses, ethno-regional subalterns, loyal to him as he offered equality, respect and opportunities (Hewison 2004, cited by Ferrara 2015). Whilst not overtly anti-royalist, he gave millions to the CPB (Ferrara 2015, p. 232), and his support of the then prince to gain influence and subvert the royal powers monopoly, and exercise political control over the army and police, led him to be hated by royalists because he was elected by popular mandate: a democratic enthronement by people power displacing the powers exclusive to the military and monarchy.

Thaksin threatened royalist business families and the elite's monopoly capitalism (Ferrara 2015, pp. 235, 236). Selling his Shin Corporation to Temasek Singapore was seen as a security threat, and made for personal gain and greed as if he was more corrupt than the CPB and the monarchy. He dissolved the House of Representatives and called for an election in 2006 which was construed as 'undemocratic' and he was ousted by a coup 19 September 2006 and replaced by the military Council for National Security led by General Surayuth Chulaanont as PM. The king and queen showed their support for the Yellow Shirts and the People's Alliance for Democracy, which damaged the already severely damaged economy (Ferrara 2015, p. 245). Thaksin's party and policies raised political and social awareness to those self-identifying as 'phrai', subalterns, who wished to exercise popular sovereignty. Thaksin's power appealed to ethno-regional poor areas of racist exclusion as morally and spiritually inferior (Ferrara 2015, p. 255).

Unaldi understands Thaksin as a populist, egalitarian, charismatic rival to king Bhumipol, for not only the king has sacred charisma. Business people, Sino-Thai, latch onto the king's charisma (Unaldi 2016, p. 27) and use it for their own ends, prestige and power. The king's charisma is an effect of propaganda. Thaksin as a charismatic leader enacted a 'royal sanctification of economic success'. Both Thaksin and king Bhumipol are two demi-gods (Unaldi 2016, p. 23). Thaksin and the king are exceptional humans attributed with supernatural and super human powers as exemplary leaders (Unaldi 2016, p. 36).

The charisma of the king can falter and fail, its sacred authority and aura will be tainted if too economic, material and mundane. The Thai polity, stemming from the colonial encounter and alternate modernity is rational-instrumental and magico-religious using 'saksit' supernatural forces, Hindu-Brahmin notions of jati (Unaldi 2016, pp. 40–42). Thais are incredulous, believing in the truth of belief. They are subject to enchantment, not secular modernity but enchanting Thai capitalism. Thongchai 'magic will never go away' (Unaldi 2016). Charisma entails prestige-virtue-magico-divine barami-sakit aspects, Hinduism melded with Buddhism in the king as a damma-raja and deva-raja (Unaldi 2016, p. 43). Charisma can be contested by others, even if inherited karmically by birth and, as Tambiah argues, charisma dwells in objects not just human subjects (Unaldi 2016, p. 46).

There is a reciprocal relation between Thai society and king Bhumipol as a charismatic leader who is the object of a 'personality cult' as in Nazi Germany, where 'people worked towards Hitler' (Unaldi 2016, pp. 48, 49). Subjects show complete abject loyalty to the king for the sake of charisma. Charismatic conflict and competition are thus more important than the nation's economic development and wellbeing. Unaldi's hypothesis is that

> working towards the monarchy's aim is to protect and/or expand the sacred charisma of the monarchy. In turn, the monarchy's sacred charisma serves as the most potent source of symbolic capital in Thailand. It legitimizes the accumulation of other forms … economic capital for the benefit of the person or the group performing the actions.
>
> (Unaldi 2016, p. 50)

The Thai monarchy's sacred charisma is spatially centered in Bangkok's Rachaprasong-Siam area, which is why it was targeted by Red Shirt demonstrators; this area and its use of space and buildings, was an effect of royal involvement in capitalist development (Unaldi 2016, p. 117). Urban Bangkok is supported by royal capitalism while the rural provinces have to be moderate and sufficient, showing the king as a rich hypocrite.

Anti-royalist red shirts (Unaldi 2016, pp. 53–55) see Thaksin as a charismatic leader and use images of past 'King Taksin', standing in for Thaksin, as a figure to challenge king Bhumipol. The charisma of Bhumipol is manufactured as an anti-dictator and yet he was empowered by anti-communist dictator Sarit – who re-invented royal traditions and military manipulated images to enhance the charisma of the king. Military and monarchy reciprocally determined their sacred powers to decide whose lives were worthy and unworthy of living in the massacre of students, as un-Thai communists, on 6 October 1976, raping, lynching, burning alive and desecrating corpses as if sub-human.

The CPB masks monarchy as capitalist (Unaldi 2016, pp. 61, 62). The king acts and is enacted in a royal capitalist boom as a dialectic driving development for the few, whilst common mases have 'sethiakit pho peng' 'sufficiency': endure inequality, injustice in their karmically allotted place of inferiority as if by divine command to suffer 'an austere life but still consume' (1998 Birthday speech). Such was the right-wing mendacity of a king with a charismatic aura and the 'nation's biggest capitalist'. A Buddhist 'sufficiency economy' serves Sino-Thai capitalist classes, it arrests development. The rich use and promote the king's sufficiency ideals, which 'stops rural people participating in the national economy' (Walker 2012). The king's charisma disenfranchises and disempowers. The king is not all powerful but a sign whose value is fixed by those claiming charisma, who chase it and use it (Unaldi 2016, p. 66).

Thaksin criticized royal power as being above the law, like Pridi in 1932, stating 'an extra constitutional charismatic person was behind efforts to topple him' (Unaldi 2016, p. 68). Thaksin provided an alternative to the king's 'magic circle of merit' by rich royally recognized Sino-Thai capitalists in 'khatin' ceremonies (Gray 1986). Royals support big business and they latch onto, or borrow (Grey 1986, p. 431) the barami-charisma of the king; this 'celestial economy' led to a rise of Sino-Thai billionaires – like Thaksin. Royals use money and capitalists use royals as symbolic capital, argues Unaldi (2016, p. 70). They both exploit and expropriate from one another in a race for virtue in 'royally sponsored capitalist development', which shows the tainted truth and impure charisma of the king touched by capitalism all his businesses (Grey 1986, pp. 732, 771). It explodes the myth of the CPB, ownership and use of land and Royal Projects to help poor people. King Bhumipol was selfish, non-altruistic with restricted charisma. In contrast, Thaksin circulated his wealth Buddhist style to help the welfare of the masses: the pro-poor 30 baht health scheme, debt relief and rural policies, which increased his political charisma (Unaldi 2016, p. 73) along with his affective appeal post 1997 crash as a national savior.

Thaksin implemented powerful development policies coupled with his power as a charismatic leader: success in the marketplace was seen as a result of his merit (Unaldi 2016, p. 74). He thus presented a free market challenge to the royal monopoly (Unaldi 2016, p. 75). Unaldi terms his leadership style 'Fuhrerdemokratie' like the king in his use of speeches, popular cleansing war on drugs in 2003. Thaksin copied his visits and imagery from the king. In this way, capitalists could access sacred royal sources of charisma, supernatural power and prestige without the king. Thaksin, argues Unaldi, was working around and against, not toward, the king. Thaksin was seen as an impure immoral, corrupt, greedy capitalist by reformist royal Buddhist conservatives such as Sulak Sivaraksa and Prawet Wasi. But, for the Red Shirts, Thaksin was like an alternate king, sacred; he used black magic forces and spells. Bhumipol was mundane and venal. Thaksin took the place of the king in the royal temple thus was thought to symbolically topple the monarchy (Unaldi 2016, pp. 80–81). Thaksin was associated with royal signs and symbols, and king Taksin (Unaldi 2016, pp. 83–85). This, coupled with the fact that Bhumipol was too far removed from the people, like a god, made Thaksin powerful and charismatic.

Thaksin's rural policies decentered the king, with a new deal. His Thai Rak Thai party was neo-Keynesian not neo-liberal (Unaldi 2016, pp. 91–93). Thaksin liberated the 'serfs' from Bhumipol's sufficiency economy, politicized and socially empowered them. Villagers grew cash crops and became more capitalist and migrated to work in cities and abroad, and sent cash back (Keyes 2012). As Walker's study of rural Northern Thailand shows, where Thaksin is from, 'middle class peasants' have emerged as a new group, engaging in 'contract farming, off-farm employment' having a consumerist lifestyle and more mobility not tied to the land (Walker 2012, p. 330). The king's royal capitalism was radically out of touch with reality, the economy had changed.

Thaksin's worldliness was not a problem for his charisma, unlike the King's other worldly Buddhist-Hindu aura and charisma. A blood sacrifice for Brahmin cursing rite by Thaksin's followers showed his sacred politics and magical powers displacing the King's ascribed sacred charisma. The Red Shirts from the ethno-regional periphery, celestial outer limits of the Buddhist royal cosmos, would become space invaders of the center space of the King's power, Rachaprasong-Siam.

In the 'Thai spirit of capitalism' Buddhist religion is used to sanction economic conduct: 'private accumulation of capital for one's self interest sanctified by the charismatic authority of the Thai monarchy' (Grey 1986, p. 147). Thai royal schizophrenia meant worldly, hence impure, economic actions for the king were permitted and, at the same time, rural subalterns had to practice other worldly renunciation and austerity – what the king should be doing – to accept their lot and inferior place in the order of things (Unaldi 2016, pp. 101–102). The king is allowed to be fabulously rich, along with the Sino-Thais attached to his charisma, as if capitalism Thai-style is a religious experience and the achievement, sacred and enchanted. The king's charisma was transferred to capitalists, whilst capitalist Thaksin was linked to the royal charisma of King Taksin (Unaldi 2016, p. 104). The Red Shirts in the alternative national-political imaginary are sacred freedom fighters for the development of Thai freedom and justice. They attacked the Siam-Rachaprasong area because it is owned by the monarchy (Unaldi 2016, p. 137). Bangkok became a symbolic battlefield for Thainess, competing forms of sovereignty and charisma. Socio-political changes shaped architecture and space which, embody moral, political and spiritual power. Sacralized space (Unaldi 2016, p. 140) embodies royal sanctioned capitalism: shopping malls are a symbol and signify 'ammat'-aristocratic versus 'phrai'-serf/commoner unequal relations of exclusion.

Red Shirts occupying streets and attacking malls signifies commoners taking over space as emancipation. Siam Paragon mall is a royal business owned by princess Sirinthorn, like the Siam Kempinski hotel, numerous retail chains (Unaldi 2016, pp. 156–160,186), and a royal capitalist and life-style temple. Royal space, buildings and wealth were the target of Red Shirt graffiti, subaltern rebellion and resistance. Examples are: 'Ai hia sang kha', which translated reads: 'The king a monitor lizard [cunt] ordered the soldiers to shoot and kill'. Other translated writings on the wall(s) are: 'You [the king] have millions but preach sufficiency to me. Have you killed sufficient Red Shirts?' (Unaldi 2016, p. 216); 'You [the king] ordered the killings' and 'This country is mine you stole from king Taksin' (Unaldi 2016, p. 218). Unaldi likens the Red Shirt protest and occupation to the storming of the Bastille: a symbolic overthrow of the old regime in the French revolution. Or, we can argue, the 1932 redux.

Conclusion

The Red Shirts massacred in Rachaprasong, 2010 were not terrorists but freedom fighters against a failed Thainess. As Red Shirt leader Jatuporn commented, upon Thailand being exceptional 'the only country in the world whose family's children were murdered "for" or on behalf of the nation's mother and father' (cited by Ferrara 2015, 262). King Bhumipol was a right-wing capitalist despot elevated by myth as a Father and superior spiritual being, while in reality he was base and venal. The Red Shirts were the inheritors of Pridi (Unaldi 2016, p. 266). Ferrara is wrong, Thailand is not unexceptional, it is all too exceptional. For it is set apart from the rest of the world by a 'theology of Thai exceptionalism' (Thongchai: Paisarn 16 July 2011) and Thais' ignorant and narcissistic attitude toward others so they cannot understand themselves (Prachathai 22 July 2013). Thailand has failed to develop fully because of Thai authoritarian rule, making it a post-truth society. Thais are put in chains by Thainess and its exceptional form of enslavement by its mind-forged manacles but, paraphrasing Thongchai (2010, p. 151), a future democracy-to-come in a nation without nationalism, neither authentic Siam nor localized elements of the West, awaits 'to be announced'.

References

Agamben, G. 1998. *Homo Sacer: Sovereign Power and Bare Life*. Translated by Daniel Heller-Roazen. Stanford: Stanford University Press.

Barme, S. 2002. *Woman Man Bangkok: Love Sex and Popular Culture in Thailand*. New York: Rowan and Littlefield

Bumipol Adulyadej. 1977 [1976]. Pra Ratcha Damrat Phraratchathan Nai phithi Pradap Yot Nai Thahan Chan Nai Phon Na Phra Thi Nang Boromphiman Wan Angkhan Thi 14 Thanwakhom 2519. Cited in F. Ferrara. 2015. *The Political Development of Modern Thailand* (p. 300). Cambridge: Cambridge University Press.

Chakrabarty, D. 2010. Foreword: The names and repetitions of postcolonial history. In R.V. Harrison and P.A. Jackson, eds. *The Ambiguous Allure of the West: Traces of the Colonial in Thailand.* Hong Kong: Hong Kong University Press.

Connors, M.K. 2007. *Democracy and National Identity in Thailand.* London New York: Routledge Curzon NIAS.

Connors, M.K. 2008. Article of faith: The failure of royal liberalism in Thailand. *Journal of Contemporary Asia* 38(1): 143–165.

Connors, M.K. 2009. Liberalism, authoritarianism and the politics of decisionalism in Thailand. *The Pacific Review* 22(3): 355–373.

Ferrara, F. 2015. *The Political Development of Modern Thailand.* Cambridge: Cambridge University Press.

Foucault, M. 2000. On governmentality. In James D. Faubion, ed. *Power.* Translated by R. Hurley. London: Penguin.

Grey, C. 1986. *Thailand: The Soteriological State in the 1970's.* PhD Dissertation unpublished, Chicago, Illinois

Hanks, L.M. 1962. Merit and power in the Thai social order. *American Anthropologist* 64(6): 1247–1261.

Harrison, R.V. 2010. The allure of ambiguity: The west and the making of Thai identities. In R.V. Harrison and P.A. Jackson, eds. *The Ambiguous Allure of the West: Traces of the Colonial in Thailand.* Hong Kong: Hong Kong University Press.

Helbardt, S. 2015. *Deciphering Southern Thailand's Violence. Organization and Insurgent Practices of BRN-Coordinate.* Singapore: ISEAS.

Herzfield, M. The conceptual allure of the west: Dilemmas and ambiguities of crypto-colonialism in Thailand. In R.V. Harrison and P.A. Jackson, eds. *The Ambiguous Allure of the West: Traces of the Colonial in Thailand.* Hong Kong: Hong Kong University Press.

Hewison, K. 1997. The monarchy and democratization. In Kevin Hewison, ed. *Political Change in Thailand: Democracy and Participation.* London: Routledge

Hewison, K. 2014. Considerations on inequality and politics in Thailand. *Democratization* 21(5): 846–866.

Hindess, B. 1993. Liberalism, socialism and democracy: Variations on a governmental theme. *Economy and Society* 22(3): n.p.

Hindess, B. 1996. *Discourses of Power.* Oxford: Blackwell.

Hirst, P.Q. and P. Woolley. 1982. *Social Relations and Human Attributes.* London: Tavistock.

Jackson, P.A. 1999a. The enchanting spirit of Thai capitalism: Luang Phor Khun and the postmodernization of Thai Buddhism. *South East Asia Research* 7(1): 1–44.

Jackson, P.A. 1999b. Royal spirits, Chinese Gods and magic monks: Thailand's boom time religions of prosperity. *South East Asia Research* 7(3): 245–320.

Jackson, P.A. 2003. Performative genders, perverse desires: A biohistory of Thailand's same-sex and transgender cultures. *Intersections: Gender, History and Culture in the Asian Context*, 9. E-journal – URL http://intersections.anu.edu.au/issue9/jackson.html.

Jackson, P.A. 2004a The Thai regime of images. *Sojourn: Social Issues in Southeast Asia* 19(2): 181–218.

Jackson, P.A. 2004b. The performative state. *Sojourn* 19(2): 219–253.

Jackson, P.A. 2010a. The ambiguities of semicolonial power in Thailand. In R.V. Harrison and P.A. Jackson, eds. *The Ambiguous Allure of the West: Traces of the Colonial in Thailand.* Hong Kong: Hong Kong University Press.

Jackson, P.A. 2010b. Afterword: Postcolonial theories and Thai semicolonial hybridities. In R.V. Harrison and P.A. Jackson, eds. *The Ambiguous Allure of the West: Traces of the Colonial in Thailand.* Hong Kong: Hong Kong University Press.

Jackson, P.A. 2010c. Virtual divinity: A 21st century discourse of royal Thai Influence. In I. Ivarsson and I. Isager, eds. *Saying the Unsayable: Monarchy and Democracy in Thailand.* Copenhagen: NIAS.

Jerryson, M.K. 2011. *Buddhist Fury: Religion and Violence in Southern Thailand.* New York: Oxford University Press.

Kasian, T. 2001. *Commodifying Marxism: The Formation of Modern Radical Thai Culture 1927–58.* Kyoto: Kyoto University Press.

Keyes, C. 2012. 'Cosmopolitan' villagers and popular democracy in Thailand. *South East Asia Research* 20: 343–360.

Loos, T. 2002. *Subject Siam: Family Law and Colonial Modernity in Thailand.* Chiang Mai: Silkworm Books, Cornell University.

McCargo, D. 2005. Network monarchy and legitimacy crises in Thailand. *The Pacific Review* 18.

McCargo, D. 2009. *Tearing Apart the Land.* Singapore: NUS Press.

McCargo, D. 2012. *Mapping National Anxieties.* Denmark: NIAS.

Merieau, E. 2016. Thailand's deep state, royal power and the Constitutional Court (1997–2015). *Journal of Contemporary Asia* 46(3) DOI: 10.1080/00472336.2016, 1151917 (accessed 6 April 2016).

Montesano, M.J. 2012. Introduction: Seeking perspective on a slow-burn civil war. In Michael J. Montesano, Pavin Chachavalpongpun and Aekapol Chonvilaivan, eds. *Bangkok, May 2010: Perspectives on a Divided Thailand.* Singapore, ISEAS.

Morris, R. 1994. Three sexes and four sexualities: Redressing the discourse on gender and sexuality in contemporary Thailand. *Positions* 2(1): 15–43.

Morris, R. 2000. *In Place of Origins Modernity and Mediums in Northern Thailand* Durham: Duke University Press.

Mulder, N. 1996. *Inside Thai Society Interpretation of Everyday Life.* Amsterdam and Kuala Lumpur: Pepin Press.

Rackett, T. 2014a. States of mind and exception: Enactments of Buddhist ontological truth and purification in Thai religious nationalism in the mid-20th and early 21st Centuries. *Journal of Religion and Violence* 2(1): n.p.

Rackett, T. 2014b. Review of *Buddhist Fury. Journal of Religion and Violence* 2(3).

Rackett, T. 2016. Who do you think you are? Imagined ethnic and religious identities: Thai racism and violence in Southern Thailand. Southeast Asian Human Rights Network.

Schmitt, C. 1985. *Political Theology: Four Chapters on the Concept of Sovereignty.* Translated by George Swab. Chicago: University of Chicago Press.

Schmitt, C. 1996. *The Concept of the Political.* Translated by George Swab. Chicago: University of Chicago Press.

Sen, A. 2000. *Development as Freedom.* USA: Random House.

Streckfuss, D. 2011. *Truth on Trial in Thailand.* London: Routledge.

Thak Chaloemtiarana. 2007. *Thailand: The Politics of Despotic Paternalism.* Cornell Southeast Asia Program. Chiang Mai: Silkworm Books.

Thongchai Winichaikul. 1994. *Siam Mapped*. Chiang Mai: Silkworm Books.

Thongchai Winichaikul. 2000. The others within: Travel and ethno-spatial differentiation of siamese subjects 1885–1910. In A. Turton, ed. *Civility and Savagery: Social Identity in Tai States*. Surrey: Curzon.

Thongchai Winichaikul. 2010. Coming to terms with the west: Intellectual strategies of bifurcation and post-westernism in Siam. In R.V. Harrison and P.A. Jackson, eds. *The Ambiguous Allure of the West: Traces of the Colonial in Thailand*. Hong Kong: Hong Kong University Press.

Thongchai Winichaikul. 2016. Thailand's hyper-royalism: Its past success and present predicament. *Trends in Southeast Asia*. Singapore: ISEAS Yusof Ishak Institute.

Unaldi, S. 2016. *Working Towards the Monarchy: The Politics of Space in Downtown Bangkok*. Honolulu: University of Hawaii Press.

Van Esterik, P. 2000. *Materializing Thailand*. Oxford: Berg.

Walker, A. 2012. *Thailand's Political Peasants Power in the Modern Rural Economy*. Madison, WI: University of Wisconsin Press.

Weber, M. 1978. *Economy and Society*. Berkeley: University of California Press.

Part III

Southeast Asia and China

8 Changing constellations of Southeast Asia

Jan Nederveen Pieterse

Introduction

Countries do not simply develop by themselves but as part of wider constellations that may help or hinder development. At each regional or global conjuncture there are centers and zones of influence that shape relations of cooperation and competition. Shifting economic complementarities generate fields that imprint epochs of development, which also involve domestic institutions. Given path dependence, institutions that are in sync with one constellation may linger during another and either foster or block development. Thus, with the Cold War era came national security states. Next, when Japan and later the Asian tiger economies led Asia's flying geese formation, authoritarian developmental states became an institutional model.

This presents us with several considerations, (a) wider constellations are the context for development and may help or hinder; (b) there are elective affinities and osmosis between transnational constellations and national institutions; (c) because of path dependence and because institutions change slowly, institutions that go together with one type of constellation may become a bottleneck in a subsequent constellation; (d) institutions are layered and relations between constellations and institutions are not functionalist and linear but complex.

This chapter (and indeed this volume) focuses on two constellations in the setting of which Southeast Asia has been developing – the constellation with Northeast Asia in the lead and the contemporary constellation that is increasingly shaped by China-centric value chains. This research follows the twin tracks of global and regional political economy and how domestic institutions interact with shifting ecosystems.

In the second half of the twentieth century South Korea and Taiwan achieved developed country status with relatively egalitarian societies and also consolidated their democracies. Their achievements were threefold: advanced industrialization, with low Gini indices, and democratization. Southeast Asian countries, in particular Malaysia, Thailand, Indonesia and the Philippines, were slated for similar achievements. The World Bank coined the term the 'Miracle Eight' as part of the 'East Asian Miracle'. Business media classified them among high-growth emerging markets (EM). Sources such as Freedom House observed ongoing 'reformasi' and viewed countries in the region as poised for achieving democratic reforms (Diamond 2012).

Given growth rates over 5 percent, business and media still often portray them this way. Vietnam and Myanmar have emerged as runners-up in growth. Myanmar is slated to grow by 10 percent in 2015. Chapter 1 asked,

> In Northeast Asia per capita GDP is high and inequality is low while in Southeast Asia per capita GDP is low and inequality is high. Is this a temporary deviation, just a time lag, or is there a pattern of differences between Northeast and Southeast Asia? … Can would-be tigers become tigers?

In SEA, realities over time have not borne out expectations. Yes, there has been steady growth, but in quantity rather than quality and arguably leading to a cul-de-sac. Inequality has not come down, or has increased over time. Democratization and consolidation of democracy have not occurred.

Why is this question important? The question where SEA is headed is part of rising Asia and of emerging economies that play an increasingly important role as drivers of the world economy. The GDP of ASEAN is $5.6 trillion with a population of 600 million. ASEAN plus Three (with Korea, Japan and China) ranks as the world's major economic power house. The China–ASEAN Free Trade Area is the third largest in the world.

The next two sections of this chapter resume the discussion in Chapter 1. The first of these sections argues that the era of the Miracle Eight has passed because manufacturing has become increasingly competitive worldwide and options for manufacturing export-led growth and industrial upgrading have narrowed. The next section, 'The elephant in the room', asks why the opportunities that existed were not utilized effectively and focuses on the nature of political institutions.

The section after, on shifting economic complementarities, examines how changing geoeconomic constellations have influenced developments in Southeast Asia. Section five argues that economic complementarities increasingly include China-centric value networks in East Asia as part of 'globalization with Chinese characteristics'. Section six asks what would be the implications of this development for different tiers of SEAs. The closing section looks at the bright side of SEA and under which conditions it may deliver. Thus, sections 2 and 4 and recent trends in sections 5 and 6 concern dynamics of global political economy that are largely external to Southeast Asia, and section 3 focuses on dynamics internal to SEA, which comes back in the closing section.

Methodological considerations that apply include taking into account temporal disjunctures. Options that were available to NEA countries at an earlier stage are now no longer open to SEA because dynamics of globalization have moved on. To avoid one-dimensionality the analysis takes into account developments across agriculture, industry, services and institutions.

A common distinction runs between three tiers of SEA, the top tier of high-income Singapore and Brunei, the middle tier of Malaysia, Thailand, Indonesia and the Philippines, and the third tier of Vietnam, Myanmar, Cambodia and Laos. The focus is on the middle-income countries that aspire to achieve developed country status, such as Malaysia hopes to do by 2020. With the highest per capita income, the highest rate of urbanization and excellent infrastructure Malaysia is at the highest level of mid-tier SEA. Part of the discussion focuses on Malaysia – if Malaysia cannot rise to the high-income level, which Southeast Asian country can?

The Miracle Eight have gone

In manufacturing, the window of opportunity for technological upgrading that existed in the 1980s and 1990s has narrowed. The manufacturing sector has become more competitive worldwide. Technological changes have increased productivity and facilitate the further splicing of production chains. Global value chains (GVC) of growing complexity now increasingly dominate manufacturing. In addition, the rise of China has crowded out industry in advanced economies such as Europe and triggered deindustrialization in Latin America and African countries (Fernández Jilberto and Hogenboom 2012; Cheru and Obi 2010).

The era when basic industries from the west relocated in low-cost developing countries, the 1970s and 1980s (Gereffi and Korzeniewicz 1994; Dicken 2011) is no more. Technological changes have ushered in different dynamics. Digital communication, containerization, widening GVC, lower production cost, lower end product prices (the 'China price'), new entrants in manufacturing in low-wage developing countries and emerging economies, ample supply (and overproduction in several sectors) means tighter margins across the board (Matsuyama 2009). These trends have reversed the classic terms of trade of low commodities prices/high manufactured goods prices to cheap manufactured goods/high commodities prices (until commodities prices dropped in 2011 as a result of general slowdown). The upshot is that at this juncture the industrial export-led growth model is passé (Palley 2011).

The Asian tiger economies advanced by gradually upgrading industrial production to original equipment manufacturing (OEM), original design manufacturing (ODM) and original brand manufacturing (OBM); but now with industry as part of GVC, competitive and dynamic, with high tech and small margins, this avenue has narrowed. Much tech learning has shifted from domestic firms to MNCs and to large, complex firms such as Korea's chaebol. MNCs have become complex learning units. Deindustrialization is an ongoing trend not just in mature industrialized countries but also in developing countries (Felipe at al. 2014), a trend that is termed 'premature deindustrialization', i.e. at a lower per capita income level than in the past (Rodrik 2015). This also applies to Malaysia.

> While developing countries are often encouraged to process agricultural or mineral outputs before exporting to increase their value, Malaysia appears a rare example of an upper-middle-income country – aspiring to high-income status – that is stunting or even reversing its previous successes in manufacturing. This manufacturing retrenchment has been demonstrated by the overall contraction of this sector's share of GDP, which fell gradually to 24 per cent in 2008 to remain roughly at that level ever since. Malaysia may be experiencing 'premature deindustrialisation', having transitioned to a service led economy before it has fully reaped the benefits of industrialisation.
>
> (Menon and Ng 2015)

In SEA, Malaysia and Indonesia came closest to building domestic industries. Malaysia developed an automobile industry (Proton) and Indonesia manufactured automobiles and aircraft. Both have failed to build internationally competitive industries.

> After 30 years, where's Proton? After 30 years and RM18 billion in R&D, where does Proton stand as an automaker compared with the likes of South Korea's Hyundai and Kia? Both have a longer history than Proton, but they are now among the world's top carmakers. By comparison, Proton is still in its infancy.
>
> (*The Edge Malaysia*, 5 October 2015, p. 9)

As late as 2002, Proton cars held 60 percent of Malaysia's vehicle market. Tariffs on the import of foreign cars helped Proton and technically it survived thanks to joint ventures with Mitsubishi (engines) and more recently Suzuki (models, engines). By 2015 its domestic market share dwindled to 17 percent while its domestic competitor Perodua (an offshoot of Japanese automakers Toyota and Daihatsu) holds a 31 percent market share (Barrock and Shari 2015). If we compare this experience with that of automakers in South Korea, it is similar in long-term state support (loans, tariffs), but different in the absence of simultaneous support for competitors, the absence of 'export discipline' (making government support conditional on success in foreign markets), the absence of a sunset clause to government support and management marred by cronyism (Studwell 2007, 2013). It does matter that projects such as Proton also serve non-economic objectives of building Malay entrepreneurship, but should it matter to the extent of undermining the project?

Industry in SEA is largely owned by foreign investors and MNCs, is part of GVC and operates on the basis of low wages, increasingly with foreign labor. In Malaysia the recorded number of foreign workers is 6 million, 4 million of which work in manufacturing (unrecorded workers are estimated at 3.5 million). The matrix of FDI and low wages holds implications also beyond industry: it implies low taxes, short circuits industrial upgrading and research and development, limits working class organization, and poses limits on what kind of service sector develops alongside industry.

Changing this would require an overhaul of the industrial model. It would entail reducing the reliance on FDI, negotiating better terms with MNCs including tech transfer and joint ventures, providing incentives for domestic capital to invest in domestic industries and establishing science and industrial parks to setup niche industries and start-ups. However, with the profitability of manufacturing declining, limited prospects for industrial exports and ongoing deindustrialization, such an overhaul is not a likely option. It could conceivably be taken up by the ASEAN Economic Community, but Asean is not equipped to undertake this (discussed below).

A growing discussion now concerns whether services are a way forward (Rodrik 2014; Tham, Chapter 10, this volume). A distinction runs between postindustrialism after mature industrialization and postindustrialism without advanced industrialism (i.e. significant domestic firms with international standing). In the 1990s, Korea experienced a cultural turn, a phase that was called 'enjoy capitalism' with an emphasis on wellbeing, urban beautification, design and aesthetics (Jang 2015). With it came a turn to English language skills, also in chaebol hiring.

In NEA, services build on the organizational depth of industry; chaebol conglomerates branched out into services such as hotels and entertainment. Textile companies retooled as fashion companies, such as Cheil, which became Samsung Cheil, which launched a menswear line in 1989, branched out in ladies and casual wear and started Korea's first fast fashion brand (8 Seconds). This background comes through in how the Korean Fashion Week of October 2015 was organized:

> Seoul Fashion Week appointed Jung Ku-ho, the former creative director of Korea's largest fashion power house, Samsung Cheil, as executive director in May to draw global attention to the Korean fashion event. Jung invited over 44,000 foreign and media personalities and some of the best known names in the fashion industry worldwide, including International Vogue Editor Suzy Menkes, fashion critic Diane Pernet and established British fashion blogger Susanna Lau, also known as Susie Bubble, to promote the Seoul fashion show. He also brought a thousand buyers from the world's best luxury malls like Saks Fifth Avenue, Selfridges, Bergdorf and 10 Corso Como Shanghai.
>
> (Kim 2015)

Dongdaemun is Seoul's fashion district. A major share of Dongdaemun's garment production is offshored to low-cost Dalian, China's fashion center, and via Dalian to North Korea.[1] The Dongdaemun model ('the Dongdaemun-style, one-stop apparel service' of combined 'purchasing, producing and selling of apparel') has become influential in Argentina and Brazil (Kang 2015). Thus, Korea's service sector involves organizational capabilities from industry retooled for services, financial depth, high skill levels and adjustments in education policies. It is sustained by deep domestic demand while Hallyu, K pop and Seoul as the capital of design and fashion are also growing as tradable services. A full page advertisement in the *Financial Times* boasts, 'Seoul basks in the glow of cultural success': 'From China to Malaysia and from Indonesia to Hong Kong, Korean clothes, hairstyles, music and soap operas are defining the region in the 21st century' (*Financial Times* 20–21 November 2010, p. 7).

By comparison, in SEA services are limited because of shallow domestic demand, which follows from the low-wage, low-tax policy in industry. In Malaysia the share of wages in GDP is particularly low (33 percent) and has been on a downward trend (Lim 2014). Malaysia has the highest ratio of household debt to GDP in the developing world. (In 2013 the ratio of household debt to GDP was 77 percent; in 2015 it was 89.1 percent, at the same high level as in the US, or higher; McKinsey Global Institute 2015 and IMF estimate for 2016. The US household debt to GDP ratio was 79.75 percent in the first quarter of 2016).

Most services are in retail, food and beverages and the informal sector. Tourism comprises about 20 percent of the GDP of several SEA economies. In most countries the FIRE sector (finance, insurance, real estate) is large and is mostly captured by well-connected elites and GLCs. The 1997 baht crisis in Thailand was triggered by overinvestment in commercial property that was backed by short-term loans.

When services become tradable (which is where the money is, besides high-end services such as finance) they also become footloose, like manufacturing (for instance, call centers now are not just in Gurgaon, Bangalore and Manilla but also in Argentina, Poland and in rural Illinois, as wages have sunk low enough to be competitive). Services in SEA are mostly derivative, approximations of foreign styles and brands (e.g. designer franchises), rather than innovative.

The elephant in the room – institutions

It is often noted that Malaysia and Indonesia are rich in agro-mineral resources and occupy geo-strategic locations. Yet NEA countries have forged ahead without such assets. The key variable in their rise has been, in short, organization, or institutions, which are known in the literature as the East Asian developmental state (EADS; Weiss 1998). Institutions have long been central to development studies, business studies and in new institutional economics (Rodrik 2001; Ezrow *et al.* 2016; Nederveen Pieterse 2017). Acemoglu and Robinson's (2012) book *Why Nations Fail* devotes a chapter to 'Institutions, institutions, institutions'. Elite capture is a keynote of their work.

Resource wealth is an asset in an elementary economic sense and a liability in an institutional and political sense because, due to their often concentrated nature, resources are amenable to elite capture, which is a big part of the 'resource curse' argument. This suggests two lines of inquiry into development paths of SEA. First, focus on institutions. Second, among the institutions to examine is the control of resources, including land.

The absence of land reform on a significant scale in SEA implies fundamental differences with NEA in social and power structures. Reform to curb large landholdings is welcome not just for economic reasons (intensive agriculture is generally more productive than extensive agriculture) but also with a view to power relations, which hold political and electoral implications (e.g. Maaruf 2014; Studwell 2013). No land reform means that rural inequality is built into the social structure. Old elites dating back to precolonial times are still in place, such as priyayi in Indonesia and sultans in Malaysia, or dating back to colonial times, such as large landlords in the Philippines. When the colonizers left, the state – i.e. elites running the state apparatus – took over custody of the land and the plantations. In Malaysia, rubber and palm oil plantations run by British companies were taken over by Government Linked Corporations (GLCs), often keeping the same name such as Guthrie and Sime Darby.

In the Philippines, land reform has been on the agenda for decades but has not been implemented on a significant scale and is now practically off the agenda (Bello 2015). In Thailand, where the uprising of 'red shirts' from the rice-growing Northeast has been countered by military rule aligned with the monarchy, it is not likely to be adopted (short of further major political transformation, which the balance of forces rules out). In Malaysia, the sultans are significant political and economic forces also in relation to land (Lhériteau 2014, p. 322). The GLC FELDA was viewed as a progressive agency that would distribute land to, mostly Malay, smallholders, but after many years it turns out that no land titles have been given out. In addition, the agency has been subject to 'political infiltration' (Lhériteau 2014). In Indonesia and Myanmar the military exercises major control over land. Thus, agricultural reform has been blocked by holdovers of feudalism (Indonesia, Malaysia), colonialism (Philippines), conservative Cold War modernization (Indonesia, Myanmar), or combinations of these. In addition, issues of different legal systems, multiple jurisdictions and lack of technical resources of land registration play a part throughout the region (Jones 2010; Srinivas *et al.* 2014).

In SEA, agro-mineral resources (timber, rubber, tin and, more recently, oil, gas and palm oil) have taken the place of agricultural surplus to serve as capital inputs for industrial development. This was the case for British Malaya[2] and also for Malaysia. However, 'The main concern about petroleum refining and palm oil processing is that they are capital-intensive and generate few jobs' (Menon and Ng 2015). Besides, such resources are more amenable to elite capture than smallholder agriculture.

Political formations in mid-tier SEA are a bricolage of precolonial feudal holdovers, colonial plantation economies (plantations are now run by GLCs or privately owned) and Cold War national security states. Variables in the making of regimes include anti-communism, American counterinsurgency and support for regimes (in some respects similar to the postwar role of the US in Mediterranean countries such as Greece and Italy). While Cold War frontiers affected both NEA and SEA, experiences and emphases were different. Due to geographical proximity to Japan, Japanese colonization and investments, NEA countries were in several respects influenced by the Japanese model (which in turn was influenced by the German model). SEA shared the Cold War experience but its take-off took place later and the Philippines, Indonesia and Thailand followed the American model rather than that of Japan.

In SEA, democracy has stalled or regressed: 'Many of the so-called new or emerging democracies have been plagued by ethno-nationalist and communal conflicts, low levels of socio-economic development and a weak rule of law'. The region hosts 'a variety of political regimes below the democratic threshold: a military government in Myanmar, communist one-party rule in Vietnam and Laos, absolute monarchy in Brunei and 'electoral authoritarianism' in Cambodia, Singapore and Malaysia' (Croissant and Bünte 2011, p. 20). Indonesia might be an exception but the influence of established elites endures in leading political parties.

Although several SEA countries have been well above the economic thresholds for stable democracy in terms of GDP and human development index (Merkel 2011), SEA is a neighborhood with the world's longest ruling parties and the greatest staying power of ruling elites. The PRI in Mexico and the LDP in Japan no longer rule (or have not ruled uninterruptedly) but UMNO in Malaysia, PAP in Singapore and ruling parties in China, Vietnam, Laos and North Korea remain in power.

Military governments tend to be short lived while one-party rule has staying power: 'In the second half of the twentieth century, military regimes had the shortest duration (nine years), followed by "personalized autocratic regimes" (15 years), and finally one-party regimes (23 years)' (Merkel 2011, p. 16). One-party regimes have staying power because they control the bureaucracy, judiciary, army and police, and public media. Because of their longevity, the ruling parties do not merely control the institutions; they *are* the institutions (cf. Chin 2011). In addition, the 'Lampedusa rule' applies – for things to stay the same, everything must change. One-party regimes are often adept at managing change and adept at conservative modernization, i.e. adopting technical or ideological trappings of modernity while keeping political institutions intact. (The extensive lineage of conservative modernization includes the Habsburg Empire and Bismarck Germany.)

The issue, however, is not authoritarianism per se but also whether authoritarianism is developmental or predatory and whether governance is capable or inept. Korea and Taiwan were authoritarian developmental states when they achieved their major spurts of industrialization. China and Singapore achieved major growth with authoritarian political systems.

Regimes endure on condition of (a degree of) economic performance and (a modicum of) legitimacy. Corruption should not be so blatant that it reveals the machinery of the deep state. The deep state in Thailand includes the army and monarchy; in Indonesia it involves the collaboration of the army and priyayi; in the Philippines, landlords and the army; in Myanmar, the army. In Malaysia, UMNO has ruled since the inception of the country, for over 50 years.

These configurations are increasingly out of sync with civil society capabilities. With economic performance limited or weak and legitimacy questionable, there is growing restiveness across a wide bandwidth in civil society throughout the region. Urbanization, education, rising skill levels, professionalization, social media, international savvy and experience exist side-by-side with old elites and tattered institutions, which produces a growing sense of malaise in the region. Wave upon wave of people's movements – such as People Power in the Philippines, the People's Constitution in Thailand, bersih rallies and majority votes for opposition parties in Malaysian elections, doi moi in Vietnam – have, so far, not yielded structural change (Diamond 2015). Decentralization in Indonesia has been an exception in terms of structural change. In Thailand, dismay has become routine (Chachavalpongpun 2011). In Malaysia, cynicism is pervasive (Diamond 2012, p. 9). In Myanmar, democracy is characterized as a 'malnourished child'. According to Filipino scholars, 'The only lists in which the Philippines ranks among the top is the list of countries perceived to be the most corrupt and the list of countries most hit by disasters' (Carlos and Lalata 2011, p. 91). In recent years, the Philippines has experienced an uptick in economic growth but structural limitations remain.

While development studies, political science, institutional economics and business studies have long emphasized the role of institutions, at times institutions emerge on the stage as *deus ex machina*. It would make sense to combine these concerns with a sociological query – how do institutions come about? How do institutions emerge from social structures and social forces?

In SEA we must consider the composition of social forces. Rural conditions have been discussed above. Working classes in SEA are weak (industry is mostly foreign owned and labor organization has been discouraged or repressed), middle classes tend to be insecure (Abdul Rahman 2002), in fear of falling and self-seeking, and all social forces are kept off-balance because of ethnic cleavages and ethnic or religious chauvinism in nearly every country (Kurlantzik 2013). In each SEA country there are different reasons why authoritarian constellations endure. Regimes declare 'states of emergency' that come with 'states of exception' that last for decades. They become functionally autonomous and come with secondary benefits that contribute to their longevity.

In view of its geographically central location, as a portal of Asia, SEA may be the world's most ethnically mixed region. The Caribbean is a typically mixed region but ethnic mixture only goes back to the plantation economies; the ethnic mélange of SEA is much older. SEA is a profoundly mixed, high-connectivity world, the outcome of migratory flows that go back to ancient times, as linguistic analyses and maps indicate (Haspelmath *et al.* 2005). In addition, whenever SEA played a key role in the world economy it attracted waves of immigrants who helped SEA play its key role. A brief overview (limited in time and scope) is given in Table 8.1. As elsewhere, multi-ethnicity in SEA is a function of economic dynamics. Multi-ethnicity has been crucial to civilizational flourishing and economic development, in history as well as in contemporary globalization. This is at odds with conventional assumptions according to which cultural heterogeneity (ethnic divisions, conflict) hampers development, which is not wrong but is a short-term view.

The way mixture has been organized over time, in Southeast as well as in South Asia, is through domination by ethnic majorities, i.e. majority ethnocracies. This applies to Thai Buddhists in Thailand, Javanese Muslims in Indonesia, Malay Muslims in Malaysia, Chinese in Singapore, Buddhists in Myanmar, Sinhala Buddhists in Sri Lanka, Hindus in India, Bengali Muslims in Bangladesh, etc. In each case this involves frictions with minorities, indigenous peoples and hill peoples that verge on internal colonialism (e.g. Myanmar includes 135 ethnicities). It often involves ethnonationalism of a strident bent, such as Islam in Indonesia and Bangladesh, Sinhala Buddhist chauvinism in Sri Lanka and Hindutva nationalism in India.

Throughout the region, ethnicity is a sensitive and contentious issue, a fault line of conflicts, such as Rohingya in Myanmar, Muslims in south Thailand and India and Tamils in Sri Lanka (Hefner 2001). The literature is extensive but is often descriptive and historical, rather than analytical. Research of a critical bent is often written by foreigners or émigrés. Literature rarely takes into account the dynamics of ethnicity, i.e. the conditions under which one form of ethnicity changes into another and the modalities of ethnicity (such as domination, enclosure, competition and optional ethnicity; Nederveen Pieterse 2007). Hence, perspectives on multiculturalism remain static as well. Ethnocracy is sheltered by institutions that serve as tools of elite control, such as the blasphemy law in Indonesia, the Sedition Act in Malaysia and the *lèse majesté* law in Thailand.

Table 8.1 Southeast Asia and the world economy

Time	*Economy*	*Cultural inflows*
1400–1700	Spice trade	Arabs, Hadrahmi (Islam) Chinese, Hakka, Peranakan (Zheng He, maritime Silk Road)
1500		Portuguese, Dutch, British and French colonizers
19C	Tin mining	Chinese workers and entrepreneurs
20C	Rubber Oil, palm oil, industry	Tamil Indians Workers from neighboring countries

In Malaysia, ethnicity is deeply controversial and is the subject of a large literature.[3] Ethnicity ties in with the ruling party. Malay rule, Islam and the monarchy are keynotes of the UMNO platform. Clustered around this are economic policies of NEP and its successors, the concentration of institutional power and GLCs. This theme is large and complex and the following are only sparse observations. The preferential treatment of Malays (bumiputra or 'sons of the soil') has contributed to a formidable uplift of Malays in education, urbanization, social mobility and the development of a Malay middle class (Muhammed 2014). In view of past social unrest, inter-ethnic settlement also contributed to political stability. The upside of policies of Malay emancipation is generally visible, particularly to Malays, while much of the downside is not visible, or visible mainly to non-Malays. Among the hidden cost and side-effects of Malay majority rule in Malaysia is that it has institutionalized race thinking of an early-twentieth century cast in Malaysian discourse and institutions. Ethnic pillarization ('consociational society') has been an organizing force in politics, the economy, civil society and culture. The downside includes questions that are now referred to as 'the elephant in the room' (Nazir Razak 2015).

Malaysian governments have chosen for FDI in industry to avoid that Chinese capital would dominate not just business but also industry (Henderson *et al.* 2007). This set the course of Malaysia's development and decades later Malaysia finds itself locked in the FDI trap. The flipside of bumiputra uplift in economic policies (in government contracts, quotas, business participation rules, government jobs, landownership) has been a cap on the growth of Chinese and other non-Malay businesses. The SME sector in Malaysia represents 31 percent of GDP. Like SMEs in China, they are mostly family-owned and managed. With institutions sparse or weak, trust limited, political conditions and property rights uncertain, SMEs cannot grow large. In Malaysia, SMEs avoid going public because then the 'Bumi rule' kicks in of required Bumiputra participation in management and a 30 percent share in ownership. Thus, they can grow in size only up to a point. Since they cannot grow in size they cannot grow in complexity either, so they cannot manufacture complex products, and research and development is weak. With this comes a trend of outward rather than inward investment of Malaysian wealth and capital (a notable feature of Malaysia's political economy) and brain drain to Singapore, Australia and beyond. Malaysia has 'the fifth largest investment outflow among East and Southeast Asian nations' (Foo 2015).[4]

Over time, institutions of Malay emancipation have increasingly served Malay elites rather than Malays (Muhammed 2014, p. 158). It has contributed to 'party capitalism' (Saravanamuttu 2009). The Gini index *within* ethnic groups is 0.80 (Muhammed 2014, p. 122) so *class* rather than ethnicity is the crucial variable. Government data gathering and reports have replaced 'race' with numerical class categories such as B40 (the bottom 40 percent of the population in income), however discourse and policies sustain the 'plural society' structure, a legacy of colonialism.

Although they are a sizable majority (68 percent of the population), Malays in Malaysia view their position as insecure. The dominant ethnic group controls government and uses the institutions of the state to sustain competition with other ethnic groups, in a word, ethnocracy, or monocultural governance in a multicultural society (Nederveen Pieterse 2007; Wade 2009), and yet remains insecure. Thus, Malaysia is a place 'where politics must be ethnically inclusive and exclusive at the same time' (Ooi Kee Beng 2015).

> There is growing recognition that many of the country's problems – including the slump in private investment – are rooted in the distortions resulting from the design and implementation of the NEP and its subsequent incarnations. The government-linked corporations spawned to serve racial economic redistribution now crowd-out private investment in most sectors of the economy, including manufacturing.
>
> (Menon and Ng 2015)

When ethnic competition prevails over development, results are counterproductive. The policies of preferential treatment of Bumiputra are increasingly out of sync with contemporary dynamics (Gomez and Saravanamuttu 2013; Navaratnam 2015; Gomez 2017). Affirmative action should come with a sunset clause. The case of Malaysia shows that enduring hierarchical ethnic rule in a multiethnic society generates structural malfunction, economic bottlenecks, cultural friction and public institutions that do not mesh with twenty-first century political economics.

A related feature of Malaysian politics is the concentration of power in the Office of the PM, which dates back to the era of Mahathir (who was prime minister for 22 years, 1981–2003). The prime minister heads the ruling party and the Office of the PM wields vast power. It controls the bureaucracy, judiciary, police and army, the functioning of parliament as well as public institutions such as universities. The Sedition Act polices dissidents and media. In effect, there is no separation of powers and little room for independent media. The lack of accountability becomes glaring when it comes to scandals such as 1MDB. The key problem is that regulatory and ownership and control functions are not separated (Gomez 2017).

Are the problems that Malaysia faces atypical or do they represent wider problems in the region? Problems of weak institutions are common in the region and have long been researched under headings such as rent seeking, strategic groups, state capture and crony capitalism.[5] In lower income societies such as Cambodia (see Ear 2016) institutions tend to be weaker still than in the middle-income countries. The institutional bottlenecks of ethnocracy are common as well. It is possible for an ethnic state to function as a developmental state, but it requires deft management of multi-ethnicity. Daphne Lee's book *Managing Chineseness* 'examines the political economy of state-led ethnic and identity management for developmentalist intents' in Singapore and 'the soft balancing of the macropolitics of capitalist industrialization through ethnic and identity management for the purpose of the sustained growth of the economy' (Lee 2017, pp. 11, 14). This is in several respects successful, or at least effective, but what is possible with a capacious and capable state in a city-state without a rural hinterland, other societies in SEA have not been able to deliver.

Shifting economic complementarities

A long time series of the role of Asia in the world economy includes oriental globalization as a precursor of occidental globalization (Frank 1998; Hobson 2004). The resurgence of Asia from the late-nineteenth century onward occurred in several waves, each with distinct characteristics (Arrighi *et al.* 2003). The comeback of Asia, after 200 years of occidental globalization, is part of oriental globalization phase 2 (Nederveen Pieterse 2017). Table 8.2 places the comeback of Asia in a historical context.

The postwar development of SEA has unfolded in the context of several major geoeconomic settings, in short, (a) the Cold War, (b) East Asia led by Japan, (c) the rise of the Asian tigers and emerging economies and (d) 'globalization with Chinese characteristics'.

The initial postwar industrialization of East Asia took place in the context of the Cold War and wars in Korea and Vietnam. It involved American support for national security states, FDI by American multinational corporations and foreign aid (discussed above).

The rise of Japan occurred as part of a series of wars of hegemonic rivalry (1870–1945) with Germany, Russia and the United States as contenders to succeed the British Empire. The era of Asia led by Japan tapered off after the Plaza Accord of 1985 that appreciated the yen and contributed to Japan's bubble bursting. In protest, Shintaro Ishihara, then governor of Tokyo, wrote *The Japan That Can Say No* (1991). With Ishihara, Mahathir co-authored *The Voice of Asia* (1995), a critique of western policies and values.

The World Bank (1993) cast the rise of the Asian tigers as the 'East Asian miracle'. Growth in SEA prompted the idea of the 'Miracle Eight'

Table 8.2 Oriental globalization 2

Time	*Place*	*Keynotes*
1868	Rise of Japan	Meiji restoration
1970–1985	The 'Japanese challenge'	Flexible accumulation, Toyotism
1980>	Rise of Asian tigers, tiger cubs Rise of China	Chaebol, GLC, FDI SOEs, FDI
1990–2008	Asian drivers, emerging economies	BRICS, EMDC, growth in developing countries
2003–2009		Commodities supercycle
2013>	One Belt, One Road	Silk Road Fund, AIIB

(Ohno 1996). Part of this epoch was a contention between the Washington consensus and East Asian perspectives. While the World Bank interpreted the East Asian miracle through the lens of export-led growth and liberalization, in Japan and Asia it was interpreted as the achievement of developmental states, the polar opposite of the doctrine of neoliberalism (Wade 1996; Chang 2003).

In Malaysia, Mahathir was on both sides of this equation and embraced the key role of state policy as well as business entrepreneurialism (Teik 1996). Mahathir's Look East policy looked toward Japan (and to Korea at a later stage). In effect, he adopted the authoritarian developmental state model, the early version of the EADS. His 'new Malay' was entrepreneurial, helped along by government policies of bumiputra uplift (Abdul Rahman 2002).

The successor to the *East Asian Miracle* was another World Bank narrative, *An East Asian Renaissance* (Gill and Kharas 2007), in praise of East Asian countries' rapid recovery from the Asian crisis. Yet, the renaissance does not apply to the entire region. To SEA, a new category of the *middle-income trap* applies, which denotes middle-income countries that remain below the level of per capita income of $10,000, the threshold of high-income status, for longer than 14 years. In later work the authors (Gill and Kharas 2015) point out that it is it not actually a trap but just a diagnosis. Marc Saxer (Chapter 6, this volume) calls it a 'transformation trap' on the argument that the challenges are essentially political, rather than economic.

With the rise of Asia and Latin America came widening ripples of growth and development in emerging market developing countries (EMDC). This is the era of emerging markets and the BRICS. It involves a lengthening and widening of GVC that had begun to take shape in the 1970s with the relocation of industries in low-wage countries, now with the participation of MNCs from EMDC ('new champions') and a 'new geography of trade' of East–South and South–South economic corridors (Nederveen Pieterse 2017). As advanced economies shifted gear to post-industrialism, EMDC industrialized and supplied cheap consumer goods to post-industrial countries. Combined with infrastructure development and growing urbanization in Asia and other emerging economies this required increasing commodities and energy inputs from developing countries, which culminated in the commodities supercycle of 2003–2009.

Since the 2008 downturn in the US and Europe, China slowed down. Commodities prices as well as energy prices bottomed, which triggered adjustments in EMDC across the world. The new normal of slower growth in Asia and China took hold. Growth in SEA slowed down for the same reasons as in most emerging economies – China's new normal, falling commodity prices, quantitative easing in the US tapering off and foreign funds heading for the exit (Akyüz 2015). A climb back of EMDC is occurring but at a lower level than before. To make up for slow demand and rising protectionism in the west, Asian economies seek to adjust by substituting regional and domestic demand. Growing regional cooperation in East Asia (ASEAN plus Three, East Asian Economic Caucus, AEC, etc.) anticipates this momentum. This readjustment is increasingly taking the form of China-centric regional value networks. China's new Silk Road initiatives and the Asian Infrastructure Investment Bank are part of this reorientation (see Chapter 90, this volume). A new constellation has taken shape.

Regionalism with Chinese characteristics

China's share of global GDP was 5 percent in 2004 and rose to 13.3 percent in 2014. According to many assessments (Henderson 2008; Nolan 2012; Henderson *et al.* 2013), this is an epoch of China-centric value networks.

China's lead in Asia differs from that of Japan. Japan's lead has been characterized as the flying geese model; a vertical relationship in which as the lead goose moves up the ladder of upgrading it sheds basic industries to following geese. The Chinese case differs in several ways (Li 2007). Because of China's vast size and uneven development among its regions, China's relationships with firms and producers in other countries are horizontal as well as vertical. Second, because of the large role of FDI in China, cooperation often involves FDI-led regional supply chains. Third, ethnic Chinese diasporas play a role in interconnecting SMEs across the region, especially in SEA (which goes back a long time; Wang and Lin 2008). Thus, this constellation includes cooperation as well as competition with regional producers and parallel development as well as a vertical lead.

China is embedded in East Asia and shares learning curves with the region. Singapore's example influenced China opening up its economy and letting in FDI in the coastal south. China's resistance to American pressure to appreciate the RMB learned from Japan's mistake in allowing the yen to appreciate. China's SOEs seek to emulate Korean chaebol in going global. China seeks to learn from the way Taiwanese companies have achieved industry platform leadership in flat screens and laptops. Singapore's sovereign wealth fund Temasek may serve as a model for the privatization of China's state-owned zombie firms.[6] Chinese smartphone producers Xaomi and Huawei now outcompete Samsung Electronics in China and India.

China contributes to institutions such as the Chiang Mai buffer fund and the Asian Bond Fund. The ASEAN-China Free Trade Area (ACFTA, signed in 2002, went into effect 2010) is the largest FTA in terms of population and the third largest in terms of nominal GDP and trade volume (after the EU and NAFTA). China built institutions such as the Shanghai Cooperation Organization and the Boao Forum and is part of the BRICS' New Development Bank and Contingency Reserve Arrangement (2014). A recent initiative is the Asian Infrastructure Investment Bank (AIIB, 2015 with 57 member countries). Table 8.3 gives a précis of 'globalization with Chinese characteristics'.

China's One Belt One Road (OBOR) is a major initiative that includes a Maritime Silk Road and is backed by the Silk Road Fund. OBOR projects include high-speed rail (HSR) links from Yunnan to Singapore, from Xinjiang to Gwadar port in Pakistan, from Chongqing to Duisburg, from

Table 8.3 Globalization with Chinese characteristics

Time	*Development*	*Keynotes*
21C	'New Silk Roads' 'Chime' – China, India, Middle East China-centric networks	Oil, fiber-optic cables, economic corridors, finance, ports, HSR Regional value networks
2008	Financial economic crisis	Slowdown US, EU, developing countries
2014	OBOR, MSR	SRF, Shanghai FTZ, AIIB, NDB

Xian to Rotterdam, and so forth. Maritime Silk Road (MSR) projects sprawl from ports in China to ports in Thailand, Malaysia, Indonesia, Myanmar to Sri Lanka, Pakistan (Zhao 2015) and beyond to Africa (Tanzania, Djibouti), the Mediterranean (Piraeus, Malta), Europe (Newcastle, Belarus, Lithuania) (CMHI 2015). Along with these initiatives comes the development of Information Silk Roads and regional finance hubs.

OBOR is reminiscent of the American Marshall Plan and the Alliance for Progress in terms of outreach and historical momentum. The differences are also glaring. The American programs were part of postwar reconstruction in Europe and the Cold War. OBOR's reach and financial commitments are far larger in scale and scope and come without ideological trappings. These projects add up to what Varoufakis (2015) calls a Global Surplus Recycling Mechanism (GSRM) and it is in this sense that China's program calls to mind the United States' past initiatives. These were signal parts of the US's 'rise to globalism'. OBOR carries a similar momentous significance for China.

This GSRM represents both an externalization of China's investment-led growth and a regional turn in China's economic relations – westward and south. Within China it represents a 'westward march' to incorporate Xinjiang, China's largest and poorest province, in China's overall development (Yunling 2015). In addition, it externalizes China's investment-led model abroad and thus makes up for China's oversupply. By redeploying construction firms, train companies, iron, steel, cement factories, the China Construction Bank and other investment companies, OBOR projects lessen the resistance of powerful groups to cutting investment growth within China. China Merchants Holdings International in Hong Kong is a major coordinating company of MSR projects: 'The network of CMHI covers 27 ports in 14 countries and regions on 4 continents'. Its recorded investments in ports – ranging from SEA to Djibouti, Malta, Piraeus, Newcastle, Belarus – add up to approximately $100 billion.[7]

Further, add Chinese investments in and loans to developing countries in Latin America, Africa, to the Middle East and Europe over the past decades and together they represent a vast investment in regional and global development, in short, globalization with Chinese characteristics (Henderson *et al.* 2013; Nolan 2012; Table 8.3 above).

Table 8.4 lists China's financial disbursements and commitments in OBOR, regional and international initiatives, which add up to over $1 trillion. Add to this investments, loans and aid to developing countries across the world and China's contribution is much higher still, in the order of half a trillion dollars (estimate). Further, add China's holdings in US Treasuries of over $1 trillion. In sum, this means that China has invested over $2 trillion in the regional and global economy.

Compare this with other major current account surplus economies (Germany and oil-exporters Norway and the Gulf Emirates) and it is clear that China's surplus recycling belongs to a category by itself. Next, compare the United States with (since the 1980s) a structural trade deficit, vast current account deficit and massive borrowing from across the world (notably from China). Then, whether or not China is becoming a 'new hegemon' is not as significant a question as how China is reshaping hegemony and gives it new meaning and content. OBOR projects are succeeding where the US failed, succeeding in entering the Eurasian heartland (which was the tacit strategic objective of the American wars in Afghanistan and Iraq). China is succeeding in establishing port access close to the Persian Gulf (Gwadar in Pakistan), the Indian Ocean (Myanmar, Sri Lanka, Tanzania) and well beyond. China's economic radius, demand, investments and loans have been reshaping the global South and the landscape of international development.

OBOR correlates in various ways with China's transforming its development model from export- and investment- to consumption-led growth, from a production to a consumption economy, from price competition to quality competition and from a labor abundant to an aging society.

What 'China' are the China-centric value networks centered on? China usually refers, besides geographical China, to China's government and SOEs but, of course, it includes 'many Chinas'. First, there is major regional differentiation in a country that comprises a fifth of humanity, coastal and inland,

Table 8.4 China, OBOR, regional and international institutions – financial commitments (US$, 2015)[8]

Institutions		*China*	*Others*	*Total*
OBOR	Silk Road Fund	40b		
	OBOR	890b		
	Ports	100b		
Regional	AIIB	30b	20b (will rise to 70b)	100b
	Chiang Mai IM	77b	163b	240b (2012)
	Asian Bond Fund	250m	2.75b	3b
International	NDB	10b	10b each of BRICS	50b
	CRA	41b	Brazil Russia India each 18b, South Africa 5b	100b
Total		108.9b		493b

east and west and urban–rural differences. Second, multiple capitalist formations coexist in China: state-capitalist SOEs; family-owned and managed SMEs – nicknamed 'guanxi capitalism' because informal networks play a key role; and public–private local state corporates, nicknamed 'clan capitalism' – all of which compete with one another (Redding and Witt 2010). Third, foreign companies operating in China represent a significant share of China's exports:

> the share of domestic content in exports by the PRC … has risen to over 60% … Those sectors that are likely labeled as relatively sophisticated such as electronic devices have particularly low domestic content (about 30% or less).
>
> (Koopman *et al.* 2012, p. 1)

Is ASEAN becoming a manufacturing workshop of the world?

How does China's growing role in East Asia affect the equations? Does it add to the gap in East Asia, the gap between the advanced, highly industrialized North and sputtering SEA, or does it mitigate the gap by generating new economic complementarities? Does it offer SEA regimes a way out and thus deepen the cul-de-sac? Do China's initiatives light up SEA economic horizons? Can the China Dream become a SEA dream? Or, alternatively, does the gap also run within China in terms of quality of growth, wealth and income disparities, capability and legitimacy of rule?

A front page spread of *China Daily* is headlined 'The next world factory: ASEAN poised to become manufacturing hub for companies seeking low wages and strong growth':

> Although China is still perceived as the world's factory, much of the low-end, labor-intensive manufacturing has moved offshore, with much of it within the Association of Southeast Asian Nations (ASEAN).… Wages are a key driver.… the average cost of factory labor is about $7 a day in Vietnam and $9 in Indonesia – far lower than the $28 average in China.
>
> (Wilson 2015)

This trend builds on the existing specialization of SEA economies in low-wage manufacturing in garments (Indonesia, Vietnam, Cambodia, Laos), electronics (Malaysia, Thailand, Vietnam), automobiles (Thailand) with FDI from Japan, the US, South Korea, Taiwan and European countries. For mid-tier SEA – Malaysia, Thailand, Indonesia, the Philippines – this continues a long existing trend. Besides agro-mineral exports, industrialization based on FDI has been their growth path for decades so this extends what they are already doing. For third-tier SEA this development is a leg up while for mid-tier SEA it is the same old.

This overall course of development is plausible and raises several questions. First, an entirely different regional constellation emerges. Instead of SEA being paired with and compared to NEA, it is paired with China. Goodbye Miracle Eight turns into Hello China. Second, SEA as an offshore production network of China depends on China's development and market dynamics, so there may be offshoring as well as onshoring in different sectors and firms. Third, at this stage this locks SEA for the foreseeable time into a low wage, low tax pattern. For third-tier SEA this is a way up and for mid-tier SEA it is a cul-de-sac.

If firms such as Toyota reduce investment in Thailand and instead opt for Indonesia and Vietnam because of lower wages and incentives, this divides countries' interests and 10, 15 years from now Indonesia and Vietnam may find themselves in the same quandary as Thailand and Malaysia are now, stuck with low-value assembly industries and investors shopping for the next low-wage destination. Factor in Chinese companies and the equation barely changes, except for logistical proximity to China and China's infrastructure investments.

Relations with China have become increasingly complex. There are twists and turns to China–SEA relations and they cannot be captured under a single heading. The question is not simply whether relations are of mutual benefit or asymmetric. The relations are multiplex, are both of mutual benefit and asymmetric and their character depends on the extent to which SEA governments, institutions and firms are able to rise to China's challenges. The relations don't have fixed intrinsic meanings but are relations of articulation that take shape as relations develop.

Ups and downs are part of the emerging constellation. Multilevel relations between China and the Asean Economic Community (AEC) mean that they can go up at one level and down at another. A report notes, 'Ringgit rout fails to revive Malaysia exports':

> ... given that 12 per cent of Malaysia's exports are destined for China ... the latter's economic slowdown, combined with its trend towards onshoring, represents another headwind. The latter point could prove particularly problematic for a host of manufacturers across Southeast Asia. 'A recent IMF study shows that China is onshoring and capturing a greater part of the Asian tech supply chain' ... Malaysia, as well as peers such as Thailand, 'are suffering because the Chinese are moving down the supply chain', stealing its neighbours' lunch.
>
> (Johnson 2015)

A conference organized by the *Financial Times* in Kuala Lumpur in 2015 was headed 'Can ASEAN nations adjust to China's "new normal"?'

> Could China's downturn present opportunities for Southeast Asia's growth markets? Given the ongoing implementation of economic policy

> and financial reforms, are ASEAN's economies resilient enough to withstand China's slowdown?
>
> (FT ASEAN Economic Summit, KL 22 October 2015)

Cooperation with China comes with economic and political asymmetries (Beeson 2010; Holslag 2017). In bilateral relations, China has overwhelming leverage. China coupling regional investments with maritime expansion in the South China Sea puts SEA governments off-balance and also costs China in soft power. It is not often mentioned that China's expansion is also a response to the American 'pivot to Asia' (initiated in 2012).

If you are a developing country and your main trading partner is China – which is now the case for most developing countries – will your growth strategy be industrial exports? Can you outcompete the world's best organized and often cheapest industrial exporter? Your main exports are agro-mineral (as in most of Latin America, Africa and SEA, and also Australia), which in effect means deindustrialization and dependence on Chinese and Asian commodities demand, which has also been in evidence in SEA (Coxhead 2007).

Meeting Chinese challenges involves upgrading to a higher efficiency level (as garment producers in Kenya, South Africa and Tunisia have done). A challenge for SEA producers is to bring sectors such as electronics and parts and components to higher levels of quality and efficiency while keeping costs down (which Mexico has done). Another alternative is specializing in a sector that is competitive with China's production (such as garments in Bangladesh). Producing with comparable efficiency and lower wages than China is the key option for low-income SEA economies such as Cambodia, Myanmar, Vietnam, Laos, mostly through FDI from China.

Operating at the level of OEM and OBM production (such as Korea and Taiwan) was a course set during a different economic constellation. Early industrializers such as Germany, France, Japan and the US also function at a higher level, mostly in niches (such as capital goods and automobiles in Germany, Silicon Valley in the US, aerospace in France) for basic industries have mostly been offshored.

How do institutions enter into the equation? A general principle is where institutions are strong, China follows; where there are no norms China goes its own way (Reilly 2012; Gu 2014). Asean coordination would be necessary to negotiate terms of cooperation with China, but this is unlikely to materialize for similar reasons as cooperation in Asean for combined industrial policies is not likely. Thus, SEA leverage is weak and norms remain ad hoc. Yet, China is undertaking new initiatives toward trade governance and economic diplomacy also in relation to OBOR as part of its global turn (Wong 2015, Johnson 2016).

A question that pops up in Malaysian media is that maintaining increasingly important economic relations with China may not sit well with domestic ethno-nationalist rhetoric and policies that discriminate against ethnic Chinese minorities and businesses, from Indonesia to Malaysia (Foon 2015; Bland 2017; Gomez 2017) if such business are to serve as liaisons and bridging social capital with SMEs in China.

Look at the bright side

Looking forward, what are the bright sides for SEA? A major asset of the region is that populations are young (in contrast to aging NEA and China). Proximity to rising China is an advantage (just as in the past proximity to Japan was important to NEA), which is enhanced by China's regional infrastructure investments. Tourism is a growth sector throughout the region.

Growing regional cooperation is an asset but also comes with limitations. It is not likely that better terms with MNCs can be achieved on a bilateral basis so this would require cooperation in Asean, however, countries have different interests and Asean is not equipped for this. Asean is an uneven ensemble of different capitalisms, in some respects like the European Union. Asean combines coordinated market economies (most countries) and state-led market economies (Singapore, Brunei, Vietnam, Laos and Myanmar). A difference between the EU and Asean is that most EU trade is within the EU while most Asean trade is outside Asean; second, Asean cooperation is shallow by design, limited by the principle of non-interference in domestic affairs. Thus, Asean has not been able to intervene in the haze problem caused by forest burning in Sumatra and Kalimantan that has affected SEA for over a decade. Asean may not be able to achieve agreement on regional infrastructure of rail, roads and ports (Karim 2015). If SEA countries cannot deliver transformation, it may fall to external actors to act.

The US abandoning the Trans-Pacific Trade Partnership (TPP) opens greater room for China on the regional and the global stage. China is already the de facto leader of global trade. Already, from a Chinese point of view, 'for every Trans-Pacific Partnership Agreement that is said to hurt China's long-term competitiveness, there will be a corresponding Belt and Road Initiative that promises to boost trade and investment growth' (Hung 2015). The US retreat boosts the AIIB (slated to expand with 25 more members from across the world, 2017) and the Regional Comprehensive Economic Partnership (RCEP) initiated by China. Asean swiftly decided for closer cooperation with China. Headlines observe the transformation right away:

> China readies to take trade mantle.
> (*Wall Street Journal* 12–13 November 2016)

> US change of guard offers Beijing whip hand on trade.
> (*Financial Times* 18 November 2016)

> China's influence grows in ashes of the Trans-Pacific Trade Pact.
> (*New York Times* 20 November 2016)

Malaysia's assets include excellent infrastructure and multiculturalism. GLCs and their major holdings now crowd out private investment (Menon and Ng 2013) but can be significant assets if privatized smartly. Higher education in private institutions offering degrees to students from the region may be a growth sector. Malaysia's major asset is its multi-ethnic makeup arising from the historical confluence of peoples due to trade and resources. Because of multiculturalism Malaysia has stronger and more diverse connections to other regions than other SEA countries. Links to the Middle East and West Asia because of Islam, links to China and to Chinese diasporas in the region and links to India and Indonesia. Such cultural affinities and social capital give Malaysia a wider radius and greater economic potential and appeal than most SEA countries, which matters in relation to tourism, markets, SMEs, finance, investment (and recruitment for higher education).

The upshot of this discussion is that political economic constellations that affect SEA have been changing over time. Each conjuncture offers different opportunities and challenges. To make use of opportunities and rise to challenges internal conditions must also adjust. The keynote is institutions. SEA must reorganize institutions. This does not necessarily mean adopting western-style multiparty democracies; applying such a standard would be ethnocentric. It does mean that SEA countries must, each in their fashion, find ways to reduce elite capture. Elite capture is the major economic and institutional bottleneck throughout the region and has been a drain on capital and resources.

This runs deeply. Changing institutions is not a matter of simple 'social engineering' because institutions are grounded in social structures and change in tandem with other institutions (Amable 2003). The political reasons why industrial policy in SEA has not delivered (such as the deep state) have not changed. Yet, to seize the opportunities of the twenty-first century and to achieve sustainable development, institutions need to adjust. For instance, for Malaysia to unleash the economic and cultural potential of its multi-ethnic makeup, a multi-ethnic form of governance would be productive. Power sharing with Chinese, Indians and Dayaks may produce reforms that enhance social trust and political stability and contribute to wider external relations.

Notes

1 Seoul National University Asia Center unpublished research, with thanks to Jong-Cheol Kim.
2 'By 1929, British Malaya had attained the highest per capita GDP of any country (or territory) in Asia … the rubber industry, combined with the expansion of the tin mining industry, made Malaya one of the most prosperous economies in the colonial world' (Baharumshah 2007).
3 For example, Wade (2009), Yeoh (2010), Lian Kwen Fee (2013), Ting (2014), Gabriel (2015), Olmedo *et al.* (2015); Chapter 1, this volume.
4 'The United Nations World Investment Report put the number [of investment outflow] at US$16.4 billion in 2014, a 16.6% growth year-on-year.' Also, 'The ringgit has been the worst performing currency in the region against the US dollar' (Foo 2015). For a wider analysis cf. Tham (2007).

5 For example, Hewison *et al.* (1993), Searle (1999), Studwell (2007), Jomo (2013), Jomo *et al.* (2014), Gomez (2017).
6 'Beijing hopes to learn from Temasek. Good role model: China wants to boost private ownership while avoiding mass privatization pitfall that cripples Russia' (*New Straits Times*, 5 October 2015, p. B11).
7 This includes Colombo Port City, Sri Lanka ($1.4 billion), Piraeus Port, Greece (€4.3 billion), Tanzania-Bagamoyo Project ($11 billion), Port of Newcastle ($1.75 billion), China–Belarus industrial park ($30 billion) (CMHI 2015) and Gwadar Port, Pakistan ($1.62 billion).
8 Adjusted from Nederveen Pieterse (2017). The entry for ports is probably a double count because MSR is included in OBOR figures. Sources: SRF www.telegraph.co.uk/finance/personalfinance/investing/gold/11630690/Chinas-new-16bn-gold-fund-at-centre-of-new-Silk-Road.html. NDB www.ibtimes.co.uk/brics-promoted-new-development-bank-opens-shanghai-1511764. CMIM http://asiancenturyinstitute.com/economy/248-chiang-mai-initiative-an-asian-imf; www.bsp.gov.ph/downloads/publications/faqs/cmim.pdf.

References

Abdul Rahman Embong. 2002. *State-led Modernization and the New Middle Class in Malaysia*. London: Palgrave Macmillan.

Acemoglu, Daron and James Robinson. 2012. *Why Nations Fail: The Origins of Power, Prosperity, and Poverty*. Cambridge: Cambridge University Press.

Akyüz, Yılmaz. 2015. Internationalization of finance and changing vulnerabilities in emerging and developing economies: The case of Malaysia. Geneva, South Centre, Policy Brief 20.

Amable, Bruno. 2003. *The Diversity of Modern Capitalism*. Oxford: Oxford University Press.

Arrighi, G., T. Hamashita, and M. Selden, eds. 2003. *The Resurgence of East Asia: 500, 150 and 50 Year Perspectives*. New York: Routledge.

Baharumshah, A.Z. 2007. Malaysia. In A. Chowdhury and I. Islam, eds. *Handbook on the Northeast and Southeast Asian Economies* (Chapter 6). London: Edward Elgar.

Barrock, Jose and Izatun Shari. 2015. Auto sector in a state of flux. *The Edge Malaysia*, 28 September: 70–72.

Beeson, Mark. 2010. Asymmetrical regionalism: China, Southeast Asia and uneven development. *East Asia* 27: 329–343.

Bello, Walden. 2015. The left in power. *The Nation*, April: 112–115.

Bland, B. 2017. A nation's tolerance on trial, *Financial Times* 27 January: 9.

Carlos, Clarita R. and Dennis M. Lalata. 2011. Democratic deficits in the Philippines. In *A Future for Democracy* (pp. 91–104). Singapore: Konrad Adenauer Stiftung, Panorama.

Chachavalpongpun, Pavin. 2011. Thai democracy: Recessed, regressed, repressed? In *A Future for Democracy* (pp. 41–50). Singapore: Konrad Adenauer Stiftung, Panorama.

Chang, Ha-Joon. 2003. *Globalisation, Economic Development and the Role of the State*. London: Zed Books.

Cheru, Fantu and Cyril Obi, eds. 2010. *The Rise of China and India in Africa*. London: Zed Books.

Chin, James. 2011. The future of democracy in Malaysia. In *A Future for Democracy* (pp. 81–90). Singapore: Konrad Adenauer Stiftung, Panorama.

CMHI. 2015. *Investment and Cooperation of CMHI at the Ports along the Maritime Silk Road*. Hong Kong: China Merchants Holdings (International).
Croissant, Aurel and Marco Bünte. 2011. Democracy in Southeast Asia – an assessment of practices, problems and prospects. In *A Future for Democracy* (pp. 19–40). Singapore: Konrad Adenauer Stiftung, Panorama.
Coxhead, Ian. 2007. A new resource curse? Impacts of China's boom on comparative advantage and resource dependence in Southeast Asia. *World Development* 35(7): 1099–1119.
Diamond, Larry. 2012. China and East Asian democracy. *Journal of Democracy* 23(1): 5–13.
Diamond, Larry. 2015. Facing up to the democratic recession. *Journal of Democracy* 26(1): 141–155.
Dicken, P. 2011. *Global Shift: Mapping the Changing Contours of the World Economy*, 7th edn. New York: Guilford Press.
Ear, Sophal 2016. Combating corruption in Cambodia. *Asian Education and Development Studies* 5(2): 159–174.
Edge Malaysia. 2015. After 30 years, where's Proton? 5 October: 9.
Ezrow, Natasha, Erica Frantz, and Andrea Kendall-Taylor. 2016. *Development and the State in the 21st Century*. London: Palgrave Macmillan.
Felipe, Jesus, Aashish Mehta, and Changyong Rhee. 2014. Manufacturing matters… but it's the jobs that count. ABD Economics Working Papers No 420, www.adb.org/sites/default/files/publication/149984/ewp-420.pdf (accessed 16 August 2015).
Fernández Jilberto, A.E. and B. Hogenboom, eds. 2012. *Latin America Facing China: South-South Relations beyond the Washington Consensus*. Oxford: Berghahn.
Foo Yen Ne. 2015. Private investment shies away. *The Edge Malaysia*, 28 September: 12.
Foon, Ho Wah. 2015. Too costly to hurt KL-Beijing ties. *Sunday Star* [Kuala Lumpur], 4 October: 23.
Frank, A.G. 1998. *ReOrient: Global Economy in the Asian Age*. Berkeley: University of California Press.
Gabriel, Sharmani P. 2015. The meaning of race in Malaysia: Colonial, post-colonial and possible new conjunctures. *Ethnicities* 15(6): 782–809.
Gereffi, G. and M. Korzeniewicz, eds. 1994. *Commodity Chains and Global Capitalism*. Westport, CN: Praeger.
Gill, Indermit and Homi Kharas. 2007. *An East Asian Renaissance: Ideas for Economic Growth*. Washington, DC: World Bank.
Gill, Indermit and Homi Kharas. 2015. The middle income trap turns ten. Pacific Trade and Development Working Paper Series YF37–09.
Gomez, E. Terence. 2014. Malaysia's political economy: Ownership and control of the corporate sector. In Sophie Lemière, ed. *Misplaced Democracy: Malaysian Politics and People* (pp. 245–282). Petaling Jaya: Strategic Information and Research Development Centre.
Gomez, E. Terence. 2017. *Minister of Finance Inc.: Ownership and Control of Corporate Malaysia*. London: Palgrave Macmillan.
Gomez, E. Terence and Wee Chong Hui. 2014. *Malaysia@50: Economic Development, Distribution, Disparities*. Petaling Jaya: Strategic Information and Research Development Centre.
Gomez, E.T. and J. Saravanamuttu, eds. 2013. *The New Economic Policy in Malaysia: Affirmative action, ethnic inequalities and social justice*. Petaling Jaya: Strategic Information and Research Development Centre.

Gu, Jing. 2014. Understanding China's approaches to international development. IDS Policy Briefing Issue 75.

Haspelmath, M., M.S. Dryer, D. Gil, and B. Comrie, eds. 2005. *The World Atlas of Language Structures (WALS)*. Oxford: Oxford University Press.

Hefner, R.W., ed. 2001. *The Politics of Multiculturalism: Pluralism and Citizenship in Malaysia, Singapore, and Indonesia*. Honolulu: Hawaii University Press.

Henderson, J. 2008. China and global development: Towards a global-Asian era? *Contemporary Politics* 14(4): n.p.

Henderson J. and R. Phillips. 2007. Unintended consequences: Social policy, state institutions and the 'stalling' of the Malaysian industrialization project. *Economy and Society* 36(1): 78–102.

Henderson, J., R. Appelbaum, and Suet Ying Ho. 2013. Globalisation with Chinese characteristics: Externalisation, dynamics and transformation. *Development and Change* 44(6): 1221–1253.

Hewison, K., R. Robison, and G. Rodan, eds. 1993. *Southeast Asia in the 1990s: Authoritarianism, Democracy and Capitalism*. St Leonards, NSW Australia: Allen and Unwin.

Hobson, John. 2004. *The Eastern Origins of Western Civilisation*. Cambridge: Cambridge University Press.

Hofmann, Norbert von. 2009. *Social Democratic Parties in Southeast Asia – Chances and Limits*. Jakarta: Friedrich Ebert Stiftung.

Holslag, Jonathan. 2017. Unequal partnerships and open doors: Probing China's economic ambitions in Asia. In Changgang Guo, Debin Liu, and J. Nederveen Pieterse, eds. *China's Contingencies and Globalization*. London: Routledge.

Hung, Benjamin. 2015. China: Slowing economy far from fragile. *China Daily/Asia Weekly* 23–29 October: 11.

Ishihara, Shintaro. 1991. *The Japan That Can Say No*. New York: Simon & Schuster.

Jang, Jin-Ho. 2015. Imagining the future for Korean capitalism: Analyses and debates. Seoul National University Asia Center conference on Capitalisms in Asia, 22–23 October, paper.

Johnson, C.K. 2016. *President Xi Jinping's 'Belt and Road' Initiative*. Washington, DC: Center for Strategic and International Studies.

Johnson, S. 2015. Ringgit rout fails to revive Malaysia exports. *Financial Times* 1 October.

Jomo, K.S., ed. 2003. *Southeast Asia's Paper Tigers: From Miracle to Debacle and Beyond*. London: Routledge.

Jomo, K.S. and Wee Chong Hui. 2014. *Malaysia@50: Economic Development, Distribution, Disparities*. Petaling Jaya: Strategic Information and Research Development Centre.

Jones, David. 2010. Land registration and administrative reform in Southeast Asian states: Progress and constraints. *International Public Management Review* 11(1): 67–89.

Kang, Hyun-kyung. 2015. Koreans dominate Argentinian textile industry. *The Korea Times* 24–25 October: 5.

Karim, Azhari. 2015. Discordant notes over ASEAN rail network. *New Straits Times* 12 October: 17.

Kim Jae-heun. 2015. Seoul Hera Fashion Week presents trendy and wearable designs. *The Korea Times* 24–25 October: 16.

Koopman, R., Zhi Wang, and Shang-Jin Wei. 2012. Estimating domestic content in exports when processing trade is pervasive. *Journal of Development Economics*, DOI: 10.1016/j.jdeveco.2011.12.004.

Kurlantzick, Joshua. 2013. *Democracy in Retreat: The Revolt of the Middle Class and the Worldwide Decline of Representative Government*. New Haven: Yale University Press.
Lee, Daphne. 2017. *Managing Chineseness: Identity and Ethnic Management in Singapore*. London: Palgrave Macmillan.
Lemière, Sophie, ed. 2014. *Misplaced Democracy: Malaysian Politics and People*. Petaling Jaya: Strategic Information and Research Development Centre.
Lhériteau, Claire. 2014. Felda and the manipulation of land policy in Malaysia. In Sophie Lemière, ed. *Misplaced Democracy: Malaysian Politics and People* (pp. 313–331). Petaling Jaya: Strategic Information and Research Development Centre.
Li, Xing. 2007. East Asian regional integration: From Japan-led 'Flying-geese' to China-centred 'Bamboo capitalism'. Aalborg University: Center for Comparative Integration Studies No. 3.
Lian Kwen Fee. 2013. Citizenship regimes and the politics of difference in Southeast Asia. Universiti Brunei Darussalam, Institute of Asian Studies, Working Paper 8.
Lim, M-H. 2014. Globalization, export-led growth and inequality: the East Asian story. Geneva, South Centre Research Paper 57.
Maaruf, Shaharuddin. 2014. *Malay Ideas on Development: From Feudal Lord to Capitalist*. Petaling Jaya: Strategic Information and Research Development Centre (original 1988).
Mahathir Mohamad and S. Ishihara. 1995. *The Voice of Asia*. Tokyo: Kodansha International.
Matsuyama, Kiminori. 2009. Structural change in an interdependent world: A global view of manufacturing decline. *Journal of the European Economic Association* 7(2–3): 478–486.
McKinsey Global Institute. 2015. Debt and (not much) deleveraging. McKinsey Debt Report, February.
Menon, Jayant and Thiam Hee Ng. 2013. Are Government-Linked Corporations crowding out private investment in Malaysia? Asian Development Bank Economics Working Paper Series No 345.
Menon, Jayant and Thiam Hee Ng. 2015. Malaysian manufacturing's structural regression. Asian Development Bank, Economic Research and Regional Cooperation Department.
Merkel, Wolfgang. 2011. Return of the dictatorships? In *A Future for Democracy* (pp. 13–18). Singapore: Konrad Adenauer Stiftung, Panorama.
Muhammed Abdul Khalid. 2014. *The Colour of Inequality: Ethnicity, Class, Income and Wealth in Malaysia*. Petaling Jaya: MPH Publishing.
Navaratnam, Tan Sri Ramon. 2015. Strong fundamentals are weakening. *The Sun* [Malaysia], 25 August: 11.
Nazir Razak, Datuk Seri. 2015. Addressing the elephant in the room. *New Straits Times*, 6 October: 16–17.
Nederveen Pieterse, J. 2007. *Ethnicities and Global Multiculture: Pants for an Octopus*. Lanham, MD: Rowman and Littlefield.
Nederveen Pieterse, J. 2017. *Multipolar Globalization: Emerging Economies and Development*. London: Routledge.
Nolan, Peter. 2012. *Is China Buying the World?* Cambridge: Polity Press.
Ohno, I. 1996. *Beyond the 'East Asian Miracle': An Asian View*. New York: UNDP, Office of Development Studies.
Olmedo, E., W. Smith and M.M. Noor. 2015. Ethnic groupism: Understanding ethnicisation of work in Malaysia. *Ethnicities* 15(6): 810–828.

Ooi Kee Beng. 2015. Malaysia – where politics must be ethnically inclusive and exclusive at the same time. *The Edge Malaysia* 26 October: 52–53.

Palley, Thomas. 2011. The end of export-led growth: Implications for emerging markets and the global economy. Shanghai: Friedrich Ebert Stiftung Shanghai Briefing Paper 6.

Redding, Gordon and Michael A. Witt. 2010. *The Future of Chinese Capitalism: Choices and Chances*. Oxford: Oxford University Press.

Reilly, James. 2012. A norm-taker or a norm-maker? Chinese aid in Southeast Asia. *Journal of Contemporary China* 21(73): 71–91.

Rodrik, Dani. 2001. Institutions for high-quality growth: What they are and how to acquire them. *Studies in Comparative International Development* 35(3): 3–31.

Rodrik, Dani. 2014. Are services the new manufactures? Project syndicate. 13 October, www.project-syndicate.org/commentary/are-services-the-new-manufactures-by-dani-rodrik-2014-10.

Rodrik, Dani. 2015. Premature deindustrialization. NBER Working Paper No. 20935, www.nber.org/papers/w20935.pdf.

Saravanamuttu, Johan. 2009. *Party Capitalism in Southeast Asia, Democracy's Bane?* Bangi, Selangor: IKMAS, UKM.

Searle, Peter. 1999. *The Riddle of Malaysian Capitalism: Rent-seekers or Real Capitalists?* Honolulu: Allen & Unwin and University of Hawai'i Press.

Srinivas, S. and K.C. Bell *et al.* 2014. *Towards Indonesian Land Reforms: Challenges and Opportunities*. Washington, DC: World Bank.

Studwell, Joe. 2007. *Asian Godfathers: Money and Power in Hong Kong and Southeast Asia*. London: Profile Books.

Studwell, Joe. 2013. *How Asia Works*. London: Profile Books.

Teik, Koo Boo. 1996. *Paradoxes of Mahathirism: An Intellectual Biography of Mahathir Mohamad*. Kuala Lumpur: Oxford University Press.

Tham, Siew Yean. 2007. Outward direct foreign investment from Malaysia: An exploratory study. *Südostasien aktuell* May: 44–72.

Ting, Helen. 2014. Race paradigm and nation-building in Malaysia. In Anthony Milner, Abdul Rahman Embong and Tham Siew Yean, eds. *Transforming Malaysia: Dominant and Competing Paradigms* (pp. 82–110). Singapore: ISEAS Publishing.

Varoufakis, Yanis. 2015. *The Global Minotaur: America, Europe and the Future of the Global Economy*. London: Zed Books.

Wade, Geoff. 2009. The origins and evolution of ethnocracy in Malaysia. National University of Singapore, Asia Research Institute.

Wade, R. 1996. Japan, the World Bank and the art of paradigm maintenance: The East Asian Miracle in political perspective. *New Left Review* 217: 3–36.

Wang, Wangbo and Zhiqing Lin. 2008. Investment in China: The role of Southeast Asian Chinese businessmen. In Emile Yeoh, Kok-Keng, and Joanne Hoi-Lee Loh, eds. *China in the World: Contemporary Issues and Perspectives* (pp. 147–160). Kuala Lumpur: University of Malaya, Institute of China Studies.

Weiss, Linda. 1998. *The Myth of the Powerless State*. Ithaca, NY: Cornell University Press.

Wilson, Karl. 2015. The next world factory. *China Daily/Asia Weekly* 25 September–1 October: 1, 5.

Wong, John. 2015. China's 'One Belt, One Road' initiative: Economic diplomacy with Chinese characteristics. *Silk Road Forum*.

World Bank. 1993. *The East Asian Miracle: Economic Growth and Public Policy*. New York: Oxford University Press.

Yeoh, Emile Kok-Keng. 2010. Beyond reductionism: State, ethnicity and public policy in plural societies. In N. Tarling and E.T. Gomez, eds. *The State, Development and Identity in Multi-ethnic Societies* (pp. 57–96). London: Routledge.

Yunling, Zhang. 2015. One Belt, One Road: A Chinese view. *Global Asia* 10(3): 8–12.

Zhao, Hong. 2015. *China's New Maritime Silk Road: Implications and Opportunities for Southeast Asia*. Singapore: Institute of Southeast Asian Studies (TRS 3/15).

9 The charms of China's New Silk Road

Connecting the dots in Southeast Asia

Abdul Rahman Embong

Analysts have noted that ancient China's Silk Roads may represent civilizational romance but that now they are gathering dust. Yet, in China and beyond, the Silk Roads have been in the news, especially since President Xi Jinping gave a speech in Astana, Kazakhstan in the fall of 2013 about establishing a Silk Road Economic Belt to Europe, and a speech in Jakarta, Indonesia in October 2013 about reviving the ancient route that linked the Pacific and Indian Oceans in a 'Maritime Silk Road of the 21st Century'. When implemented, this new Mega Project, which has been named as 'One Belt One Road' (OBOR), is envisaged to connect more than 60 countries in three continents and 4.4 billion people. China's proposal has been regarded as 'a vision with world-changing implications, an unfolding plan that would weave much of Asia, Europe, Africa, Oceania and the Middle East much more closely together through a patchwork of diplomacy, new infrastructure and free trade zones' (Catanzaro *et al.* 2015).

Using the *longue durée* perspective advocated by renowned French historian Fernand Braudel (see Armitage 2012) in studying China's New Silk Road, we can detect the powerful appeal of China's history in terms of her relations with her neighbors, namely how China's proposal of the twenty-first century New Silk Roads resonates with the past, and very importantly, how the past can be made to serve China's present and her future. A brief look at history tells us that as early as the fourth-century BC, there were already established both land and maritime Silk Roads connecting China and the outside world. The famous overland Silk Road, stretching from China's Chang-an in the east to as far as the capital of the eastern Roman Empire, Istanbul in Turkey in the west (where it linked up with the trade routes from Central Asia, South Asia and West Asia to Europe and North Africa), flourished for almost 2000 years, with China's silk being the most precious commodity. China's maritime trade route was also very important when China's imperial court missions were sent to maritime Southeast Asia, and they also helped establish trade between China and Arab traders, leading to a period of boom from the tenth to fourteenth centuries. The most significant episode along the maritime Silk Road occurred in the fifteenth century, when Admiral Zheng He undertook historic expeditions to Southeast Asia and the Indian Ocean during the reign of Emperor Yongle, which made China the greatest maritime power in the world. Zheng He led an armada of more than 300 ships and 27,000 sailors in voyages from China through Southeast Asia and South Asia to the Persian Gulf, stopping in Melaka on seven occasions, leaving behind lasting impacts. The significance of Zheng He's voyages was that they 'opened up a Maritime Silk Route with a criss-cross networking pattern which was a historical achievement … entering an unprecedentedly splendid historic period' (Sun Guangqi 2000: 298).[1] This could be regarded as the heyday of oriental globalization before the advent of Western colonialism and imperialism in Asia that began in the early sixteenth century.

Melaka in the Malay Peninsula (today's Malaysia) at that time was a center of trade and commerce, with influence spreading all over the eastern part of the world. Before the arrival of Zheng He, Emperor Yongle of China's Ming Dynasty (*c.*1402–1424) sent his envoy Yin Qing to Melaka in 1405, thus opening the way for the establishment of friendly relations between Melaka and China. More Chinese merchants continued calling at the port and pioneering foreign trading bases in Melaka. Other foreign traders, notably the Arabs, Indians and Persians, came to establish their trading bases and settle there as well. Zheng He sailed at various times between 1405 and 1433 through the Straits of Melaka into the Indian Ocean, reaching the Persian Gulf, and the coast of Africa. In 1407, he made his first of seven visits to Melaka. As well as stopping in Melaka, Zheng He also stopped over in the Indonesian archipelago in each of his voyages and toured Java, Sumatra and Kalimantan, thus making China's presence felt in the Nusantara region.

Melaka's relations with China flourished greatly following Zheng He's visit. In 1411, Sultan Iskandar Shah of Melaka headed a royal party of 540 people accompanied by Zheng He to visit Ming's court. Friendly China–Melaka relations were very visible during the reign of Sultan Mansur Shah (1456–1477) who sent his mission, headed by Tun Perpatih Putih, to China, carrying a diplomatic letter from the Sultan to the Emperor. The marriage of Sultan Mansur Shah with Princess Hang Li Po of China was hailed as the highlight of the friendly relations, for which a senior minister of state and five-hundred ladies in waiting accompanied the princess to Melaka, and the Sultan built a palace for his new consort on a hill called Bukit China in Melaka, contributing to the civilizational romance of the classical maritime Silk Road.

These long-established historical connections provide the backdrop for President Xi Jinping's announcement of the revival of the old Silk Roads in the form of the OBOR initiative. As indicated in the Chinese daily, *Xinhua*, the realization of China's new Silk Roads is predicated upon the launching of China's vision of building what it calls 'an open world economy and open international relations', building an 'economic cooperation area' where there will be 'more capital convergence and currency integration', serving as a new model of 'mutual respect and mutual trust'. It is a part of 'China's Dream for national rejuvenation'.

The twenty-first century Maritime Silk Road begins in Quanzhou in Fujian province, and covers Guangzhou (Guangdong province), Beihai (Guangxi), and Haikou (Hainan) through the South China Sea, the Straits of Melaka, and then Lombok and Sunda in Indonesia. From Kuala Lumpur, the Maritime Silk Road heads to Kolkata, India, then crosses the Indian Ocean to the Persian Gulf, the Red Sea and the Gulf of Aden; and also to Nairobi, Kenya. From Nairobi, the Maritime Silk Road goes north around the Horn of Africa and moves through the Red Sea into the Mediterranean, with a stop in Athens before meeting the land-based Silk Road in Venice, Italy. The Maritime Silk Road covers more than 20 countries and several regions that 'share a broad consensus on enhancing exchanges, friendship, promoting development, safety and stability within the region and beyond' (Liu Cigui 2014). The Chinese planners recognize the strategic significance of ASEAN within the Maritime Silk Route framework as the ten ASEAN countries – nine of which are maritime countries themselves – will help connect 'China's ports with other countries through maritime connectivity, intercity cooperation and economic cooperation' (Li Gui 2014).

For Southeast Asia, which had a long history of relations with China as shown above, the rise of the latter has a special meaning and significance. China, the second largest world economy after the US and the most significant economic powerhouse in the region, is ASEAN's largest trading partner. ASEAN, with a population of 630 million and a combined GDP of US$5.6 trillion, officially established the ASEAN Economic Community (AEC) in January 2016, and is of special significance to facilitate China's OBOR. Based on the data released by the China Ministry of Commerce, ASEAN was China's third largest trading partner in 2013 after the US and European Union. China–ASEAN trade contributed 10.7 percent of the total China trade, an increase from 9.0 percent in 2008. (China's largest trading partner in 2013 was the European Union, whose trade contributed 13.4 percent, followed by the US as the second largest with 12.5 percent in 2013). However, China's rise and the OBOR mega project is making waves throughout the world, especially in Southeast Asia and Europe, as well as concerns of a 'hidden political agenda' (Zhang Yunling 2015) and concerns about China's assertiveness. In this regard, the OBOR initiative has received positive responses by some ASEAN countries, particularly Malaysia and Indonesia. However, doubts persist as to whether the 'dots' in Southeast Asia can be connected given the suspicion and skepticism by a number of other countries in the region toward the rise of China, and her OBOR initiative, and the strategic contests between China and the traditional big powers, the US and Japan.

In light of the above, this chapter will first briefly examine the concept of OBOR, the financial costs involved, and evaluate the reasons behind China's new initiative. This will be followed with a discussion of the development gaps in ASEAN, which forms the backdrop as to why some of the ASEAN countries urgently need investment and other financial assistance from friendly countries including China to close the gaps. It will then focus on Malaysia, the first ASEAN country to forge diplomatic relations with China. After showing the evolution of Malaysia–China relations, including investment and trade over the decades, it focuses attention to how Malaysia has lately turned further toward China in a big way by sealing an agreement involving a huge economic, defense and security package. The chapter ends with a discussion on some of the challenges China and ASEAN have to address in order to advance their cooperation and 'connect the dots', especially in light of the suspicion and skepticism by a number of countries in the region toward the rise of China. This chapter argues that the rise of China as a global economic power, which is lush with capital and hungry for markets, serves as a huge source of capital and also as a market for products from various countries including ASEAN. Given ASEAN's economic, political and strategic importance to China, it provides the former a golden opportunity to take advantage of China's global rise for the development of the region. However, in securing China's economic, diplomatic and other supports, these countries should ensure that this is done in keeping with ASEAN's policy of maintaining a Zone of Peace, Freedom and Neutrality (ZOPFAN), the sovereignty of its member states, and the cohesiveness of ASEAN as a whole, and more so with the establishment of the ASEAN Economic Community.

What is behind China's New Silk Road?

Although the Silk Road had existed 2000 years ago, the term 'the Silk Road' is of recent vintage, having been in existence for just over 130 years. It was first used in 1877 by renowned German geographer Ferdinand Freiherr von Richthofen who coined the term die *Seidenstrasse*, meaning the Silk Road (Waugh 2007, Mark 2014). There is in fact a journal called *The Silk Road*, a semi-annual publication of the Silk Road Foundation based in California, US, that was started in the early 2000s. Its tagline 'The Bridge between Eastern and Western Cultures' suggests the Silk Road as a conduit in bridging cultures between different world civilizations.

Analysts have asked the question why the New Silk Roads or OBOR? Is it something well thought out or is it a reaction to the US pivot to Asia, including the now aborted Trans-Pacific Partnership? Is there a 'hidden political agenda' behind China's OBOR? Concerns about such an agenda on the part of China, and that it is meant to counter the US pivot to Asia have been bandied about in various circles. Obviously China's policy circles, including their think tanks, are sensitive about such a view, and a number of China's opinion leaders have spoken on such matters. Zhang Yunling, the Director of International Studies at the Chinese Academy of Social Sciences (CASS), for example, suggests that while OBOR is China's grand strategy, it should also be considered as China's 'pivot to the West – not the US or Europe as commonly understood by "the West", but to China's own landlocked western regions'. His argument is that China's reform since 1978 has focused on the country's eastern coastal region, making it the most dynamic 'due to their geographical advantage and ease of access to imports and exports'. Dismissing concerns of a hidden political agenda, he argues that it is now imperative for China to address the imbalances and inequalities between China's thriving and prosperous eastern provinces and the relatively backward western provinces (Zhang Yunling 2015, pp. 8–12).

Of course, opinions and analyses on the intentions and motivations of China's OBOR vary. Taking a somewhat different position, Zhao Hong (2015), a researcher from China based at Singapore's Institute of Southeast Asian Studies (ISEAS), argues that China's proposal for the New Silk Roads has been propelled by both economic and political considerations. He maintains that the proposal was made at a time when China's 'domestic economy is experiencing structural changes reflecting a new normal of slower but better quality growth' after more than three decades of high double-digit growth. China's high growth rates of more than 10 percent over the decades since the opening up in 1978 have produced huge surpluses for the country, so much so that China has been able to accumulate huge foreign reserves of US$3.9 trillion (by end of 2014), which has enabled her to invest heavily in the US Treasury bonds in the last decade. Given the slowing growth China has been experiencing of late, there is a need to re-strategize, especially in terms of what to do with the reserves. It is argued that through the OBOR initiative, China 'intends to make better use of its foreign exchange reserves to increase its economic returns and to serve critical geopolitical interests' (Zhao Hong 2015, p. 9).

Indeed, analysts have noted that China's outbound direct investment (ODI) has increased by 19 percent between 2009 and 2014, and is expected to increase by 20 percent in the near future, and that China would be able to overtake the US as the world's largest direct investor in the next few years. The amount of China's ODI totaled US$116 billion in 2014 (almost the same amount as the FDI into China at US$120 billion), and is set to increase with the OBOR initiative. The pattern of ODI has also undergone 'Three Waves', with the first wave being focused on acquiring natural resources such as coal, oil and metals; followed by the second wave which was focused on infrastructure (rail, shipping and ports); and, lately, the third wave with a distinct difference, focusing on agri-business, technologies, high-end manufacturing, consumer goods, real estate, services, and brands. Although the shift to the third wave is at an early stage, it is accelerating, with private investors becoming the main driving force of the ODI (HSBC 2015). The increase in China's ODI is driven by the central government's strong encouragement for domestic companies to invest overseas to increase their international competitiveness, and it enables China to utilize 'its surplus domestic capacity and helps to slow the rapid build-up of the country's foreign exchange reserves' (HSBC 2015). The extent of China's manufacturing excess capacity is huge, about 60 percent in September 2012, according to an estimate by the International Monetary Fund (IMF).

Coupled with the need for better quality growth and to utilize surplus domestic capacity, it is clear that China also has political considerations, namely the need to strengthen ties with her neighbors. This neighborhood focus signals an important shift in China's foreign policy. Chinese leaders have often quoted an old Chinese proverb that 'close neighbors are better than distant relatives' to justify their strategic shift and promote the close neighbor policy (see the collected speeches by Xi Jinping 2014). Among China's academics, think tanks and policy circles, there have been vigorous debates over the last several years regarding the need of a strategic shift and what new policies to follow. According to Zhao Hong (2015, p. 9), three schools of thought have prevailed in China regarding the latter's policies toward her neighbors: (1) the 'go west' approach, that is, to develop closer relations with countries on China's western front for economic and political cooperation, especially in the fight against terrorism, separatism and extremism; (2) the 'go south' approach, which is considered to be more desirable compared with the 'go west' approach as it might lead to conflicts with Russia; and (3) the 'great peripheral' approach, which covers Northeast Asia, Southeast Asia, South Asia, West Asia and the Pacific Region and which coordinates both 'maritime' and the western land routes. President Xi Jin Ping's announcement of OBOR seems to reflect the views of the third school of thought, that is, the 'great peripheral' approach. Given the above, it can be concluded that the OBOR initiative is not something sudden or reactive, but a strategic move by China in repositioning itself economically, politically, socially and culturally, leveraging not only on its present strengths, but also tapping on the historical and civilizational assets it had assiduously built through the classical Silk Roads.

The OBOR and related initiatives by China such as the Asian Infrastructure Investment Bank (AIIB), and the Silk Road Fund (established in December 2014) involve massive financial outlays whose scale and scope have been unprecedented in history. Some writers estimate China's investment in all these mega projects to be something not less than US$900 billion 'to establish new, or strengthen existing financial institutions that will form the financial pillars of the initiative' (Guidetti 2015, p. 45). The AIIB, for example, involves US$100 billion, with China's contribution amounting to US$30 billion; while the Silk Road Fund established in December 2014 is funded solely by China involving a sum of US$40 billion (for details, see Nederveen Pieterse 2015, p. 31, Table 4; Yale 2015).

The establishment of these financial institutions armed with massive funds may be described as a Global Surplus Recycling Mechanism – a term used by the former Greek finance minister Yanis Varoufakis (2015) – but they cannot have been regarded as comparable with the American Marshall Plan (for post-war recovery) and the Alliance for Progress whereby the US was the sole provider, imposing demands for economic concessions and also for left-wing containment. China's projects, such as the AIIB, are inclusive in nature, although its transparency can be improved. While China holds 25 percent of

AIIB shares and the bank is headquartered in Beijing, more than 50 countries such as Russia, Germany and Britain in Europe, as well as Malaysia and Indonesia in ASEAN, have joined the institution, with the European partners contributing a significant stake in AIIB's shares. Based on available data, besides China, other shareholders of AIIB are India (second largest with a holding of 7.5 percent shares); Russia (less than 6 percent); and Germany being the fourth biggest shareholder with 4 percent share. And to ensure the Asian character of the institution, non-Asian countries are allowed to hold a maximum of only 30 percent stake in AIIB. Some commentators such as Hewitt (2015) argue that the bank

> will play a major role in speeding up development, in a region where some US$8 trillion in investment is expected to be required in the next five years alone. It is seen as providing an alternative to U.S.-dominated institutions such as the World Bank and Asian Development Bank, which some in Asia consider slow to respond to the needs of the region – and as imposing too many conditions on development.

Indeed, after a year of its formation, misgivings about AIIB seem to be receding. US ally Canada is joining the AIIB, and the US may be considering it too (Hsu 2017), with Trump's advisors reportedly saying it was a mistake for the US not to join AIIB in the first place (Wu 2016). While it has its own aims, the AIIB partially serves as an instrument of OBOR by helping China to bolster its OBOR policy to improve connectivity among the various OBOR-related countries. For example, the AIIB-financed highway project in Pakistan is part of the China–Pakistan Economic Corridor, a major component of China's OBOR initiative, allowing it access to the Pakistan port of Gwadar to 'shorten transit time from inland Chinese cities to the Arabian Sea' (Hsu 2017). AIIB also provides loans to Azerbaijan, Tajikistan, Bangladesh and Myanmar for OBOR related projects.

ASEAN development gaps and the need for China's support

How have China–ASEAN relations developed over the years? In what way can ASEAN address its development gaps through China's support and what is China's position regarding ASEAN Economic Community?

As indicated earlier, China is very interested in its southern neighborhood, especially ASEAN, which is seen as strategic in realizing the objectives of the Maritime Silk Road. China–ASEAN relations have evolved steadily since the establishment of formal relations more than a decade ago, beginning in 1991, although individual countries of ASEAN had established bilateral relations much earlier. After establishing the China–ASEAN dialogue relations in 1991, China became ASEAN's full dialogue partner in 1996, enabling China to participate in the first informal China–ASEAN Summit held in 1997.

In 2003, China and ASEAN decided to enter into a strategic partnership. The significance of the strategic partnership was underscored by China in the speech made by Premier Li Keqiang at the 16th ASEAN + China Summit in Brunei on 9 October 2013. Emphasizing that China–ASEAN relations have entered a 'mature period' and 'cooperation has entered a fast track', he proposed that China and ASEAN should further deepen 'strategic trust and exploring good-neighborly friendship' and deepen 'cooperation by focusing on economic development and to expand mutual benefit and win-win outcomes' (MOFA 2013). To China obviously, politics and economics should go hand in hand.

What Premier Le Keqiang stated at the ASEAN + China Summit was an extension of the announcement made earlier on 2 October 2013 by President Xi Jinping about the Maritime Silk Road. In his speech delivered at the Indonesian Parliament, the Chinese president made no reservation in invoking history and echoing the Chinese plan to turn the centuries-old maritime passageways (the Straits of Melaka and the South China Sea) into one that would spur maritime connectivity in the twenty-first century. In order to support his proposal, Xi reiterated the Chinese government's readiness to fund ASEAN's maritime-related projects through its new state investment arm, the China–ASEAN Maritime Cooperation Fund. Emphasis has been placed on stronger economic cooperation, including financial aspects, close cooperation on joint infrastructure projects (e.g. building roads and railways), the enhancement of security cooperation, and the idea of a twenty-first century maritime Silk Route through strengthened maritime economy, environment, technical and scientific cooperation. China's announcement on utilizing the fund is not new. However, today, in the face of ASEAN's development gaps and the nervousness of China's assertiveness (Cai 2014), China needs to take a much more proactive approach in its financial support and show its sincerity by being more inclusive.

It should be noted that ASEAN is a diverse region with serious development gaps between and within member countries. ASEAN's GDP per capita is about US$3852 which is half that of China's US$6569, but there are wide variations between countries in the region. While Singapore and Brunei, being developed nations, belong to the first tier with a per capita GDP of over US$48,000, the other members of ASEAN 6, namely Malaysia, Indonesia, Thailand and the Philippines, are in the second tier, each with less than half the level of either Singapore or Brunei's per capita GDP, and have been struggling to overcome 'the middle income trap'. Among the remaining ASEAN members, collectively known as the CLMV countries, Cambodia, Laos and Vietnam have become emerging market economies, while Myanmar has just opened up politically and economically, with huge development challenges. All these countries have very much smaller GDP per capita level than their other ASEAN counterparts.

However, while GDP per capita can serve as a rough indicator of income disparities between countries, the issue of development gaps is broader and should be looked at from a more comprehensive perspective. A report published in 2013 by the OECD Development Centre and the ASEAN Secretariat, which focuses on narrowing development gaps in ASEAN, highlights what is called the ASEAN–OECD Narrowing Development Gaps Indicators (NDGIs) that they have developed to measure such gaps in six policy areas. Not surprisingly, the first development gap they have identified concerns the availability and provision of infrastructure, a key issue in many of the member states especially Indonesia, the Philippines, Thailand, and the CLMV countries, and parts of Malaysia especially in East Malaysia (Sabah and Sarawak). This is followed by other gaps in areas of human capital development, information and communication technology (ICT), trade and investment, tourism, and poverty, some of which have been addressed to some extent in these various countries.

With the official establishment of the ASEAN Economic Community (AEC) on 1 January 2016, the need to address such gaps and the mechanism for its implementation become all the more urgent to contribute toward ASEAN's economic integration. The ASEAN Economic Community (AEC) is designed to make the 10 ASEAN member states a single market and production base with free movement of goods and services, as well as one opening up a market with a population of 630 million in the region. ASEAN GDP is expected to reach US$4.7 trillion by 2020 and ASEAN has the potential to be the fourth-largest economy in the world (after the US, China and the European Union) as early as 2030. This means, to achieve the target, the agenda for ASEAN economic integration is fast and furious. This requires improved connectivity within ASEAN and beyond, as indicated in the Master Plan on ASEAN Connectivity adopted in 2010. The Master Plan prioritizes such projects as the completion of the ASEAN Highway Network (AHN) and the upgrading of Transit Transport Routes (TTRs); the completion of the Singapore Kunming Rail Link (SKRL); the establishment of an ASEAN Broadband Corridor (ABC); the study on the Roll-on/roll-off (RoRo) network and short-sea shipping; etc. According to the ASEAN Investment Report 2015 on Infrastructure Investment and Connectivity, at least US$110 billion will be needed in the region through to 2025, which covers transport, power, ICT, as well as water and sanitation developments.

The biggest challenge is sufficient financial resources, technology and technical expertise to ensure the successful implementation of the various projects,[2] and this must be addressed urgently. In this regard, what ASEAN requires and what the Maritime Silk Road initiative promises seems to match in terms of both demand of ASEAN and what China can and is willing to offer.

From ASEAN's perspective, China has the capital, experience as well as the necessary technology and expertise in infrastructure construction including ports and other infrastructure projects. It is noted that China has been involved in the construction of a string of ports along the Maritime Silk Road countries in ASEAN, namely the port in Kuantan (Malaysia – US$2 billion); Batam

(Indonesia – US$2 billion); and Kyaukpyu (Myanmar – US$2.4 billion). Beyond ASEAN into the Indian Ocean, similar ports have been built in Chittagong (Bangladesh – US$8.7 billion), Colombo (Sri Lanka – US$1.3 billion) and Hanbantota (also Sri Lanka – US$1.0 billion); and Gwadar port in Pakistan (US$1.6 billion). Beyond ASEAN and South Asia, China has been involved in the construction of several ports in East Africa such as the port in Djibouti (Ethiopia – US$0.185 billion); Port Bashir (Sudan – US$0.215 billion); Lamu (Kenya – US$0.48 billion); and Bagamoyo (Tanzania – US$10 billion). To connect with the land-based Silk Road through Europe or the One Belt project, China has also been involved in the construction of the Suez Canal Corridor in Egypt with a capital outlay of US$1.8 billion and also the port in Piraeus, Greece (US$0.88 billion) (Arase 2015).

What interests ASEAN is the effort through the Maritime Silk Road initiative to integrate the earlier China's initiatives such as the China–ASEAN Maritime Cooperation Fund (CAMCF) and the China–ASEAN Maritime Partnership, which focuses on the maritime economy, connectivity, scientific research and environmental protection, navigation safety, and search and rescue. The subsequent pledge by Chinese prime minister Li Keqiang, at the Seventh ASEAN Summit in Kuala Lumpur in November 2015, of infrastructure loans totaling US$10 billion to boost the region's connectivity and logistical efficiency has been very much welcome by ASEAN leaders. The Maritime Silk Road initiative is regarded as a timely stimulus to spur the economic development and integration of ASEAN, promote capital and labor mobility, as well as people-to-people contact within and between ASEAN and China and the surrounding countries, and address various development gaps. From China's perspective, ASEAN economic integration through the AEC would serve 'as a huge economic entity that could provide profound development opportunities and deepens economic and trade relations, especially regarding cooperation in production capacity between ASEAN and China' (Zhao Yanrong 2015). In fact, China had already issued, in March 2015, the principles, framework, and cooperation priorities and mechanism of the OBOR initiative to enhance regional connectivity, and it places strong emphasis in orienting trade routes toward ASEAN countries, to help the region upgrade its infrastructure and promote its connectivity.

Within ASEAN there are countries such as Indonesia that used to have a bumpy relationship with China. Indonesia is mentioned specifically here because it is not only the largest country in the region and the third largest in Asia but it is also a pivotal state for China that the latter seeks to win over. The need for such an approach is obvious, as China–Indonesia relations have been 'characterized traditionally by high political drama and a history of enmity',[3] but since the Reformasi era, there has been 'closer economic and foreign policy convergence boosted by the positive effects of democratization on Indonesia's perceptions of the Chinese' (Nabbs-Keller 2011, pp. 23–41). The strategic value of Indonesia for China can clearly be seen in the move by President Xi Jinping who made Indonesia his first stop on his first visit to

Southeast Asia. Indonesia welcomed the opportunity with both sides elevating the bilateral relationship to a comprehensive strategic partnership continuing from the Joint Declaration on Strategic Partnership signed in 2005. The then President Yudhoyono and Xi Jinping signed the Future Direction of Indonesia–China Comprehensive Strategic Partnership in October 2013, and this is being pursued by Indonesia's current President Jokowi. Xi Jinping's vision of maritime cooperation between China and countries in Southeast Asia seemed to jive well with Indonesia and with President Jokowi's goal to restore Indonesia's maritime sector. Jokowi's vision is to make Indonesia as *Poros Maritim Dunia* (the global maritime axis). Strategists in Indonesia felt that this shared vision definitely could be the starting point for discussion on how Indonesia–China relations should be further developed, and put Indonesia–China bilateral relations on the right track.

However, while the close rapport between China and Indonesia is welcome for regional cooperation, there are issues that need to be addressed. On the maritime axis, critics argue that Indonesia is only an archipelagic nation, not a maritime one; it is not yet a nation that knows how to develop, tap and control its maritime resources (Retraubun 2015, p. 8). Further, while the Jokowi-led government is positive toward China's New Maritime Silk Road initiative (Zuraidah 2015), the same cannot be said of the people and businesses. This is indicative in various media reports in Indonesia which stress that China has a lot of things to do if it wants to convince the Indonesian public and the private sector to be supportive of its new and ambitious Silk Road project. It is reported that among Indonesian businesses, especially the small and medium-scale businesses, many perceive China as a threat. Many of these businesses have had to close down because they could not compete with the cheap Chinese products that have been flooding the Indonesian markets for the past decade or so.

However, whatever the criticisms and reservations, analysts are of the view that Indonesia should not lose sight of the longer-term strategic objectives of Indonesia–China relations. Writing several years before the Maritime Silk Road initiative, Chandra and Lontoh (2011) made an insightful comment that although China has made mistakes in its efforts to become a developed country, it is willing to learn from them. They thus argue that Indonesia as well as ASEAN should be able to exploit Beijing's willingness to adjust its position, so that mutual economic benefits can be attained.

Malaysia–China 'special relations': is China connecting the dots with the New Maritime Silk Road?

One of the ASEAN countries that has forged not only close political and diplomatic relations, but also economic relations with China is Malaysia, a country which in the last several years seems to have been at the forefront in terms of aligning itself closer with China and obtaining massive investments and loans from the latter, especially since the launching of the New Maritime

Silk Road. Diplomatic relations between Malaysia and China was established more than four decades ago – in May 1974 – when Prime Minister Abdul Razak Hussein visited Beijing. Despite the Cold War at the time, Malaysia took the bold step to be the first country in ASEAN-6 to establish diplomatic ties with China, followed successively by the Philippines in June 1975 and Thailand in November 1975). (The remaining three ASEAN members established official links much later – Indonesia in August 1990 followed by Singapore in October the same year and Brunei in September the following year.) Malaysia–China relations have evolved steadily and had become more cordial especially since the 1990s with the official ending of the Cold War, with some analysts hailing it as a 'model relationship for the region' (Bower and Phuong Nguyen 2015).

The 'special relationship' mentioned above can be seen in some trade figures. In terms of trade, China has been Malaysia's largest trading partner since 2009, and Malaysia is China's largest trading partner among ASEAN states and the third largest trading partner in Asia after Japan and South Korea. Based on official figures, Malaysia's trade as a whole with China grew by 1.2 percent since 2009 to RM1.466 trillion (US$353 billion) in 2015, compared to RM1.448 trillion (US$349 billion) in 2014. In 2015, Malaysia's trade with China expanded by 11.1 percent to RM230.89 billion (US$55.67 billion), with Malaysia's export to China recording a double-digit growth of 10 percent to RM101.53 billion (US$24.48 billion). To ensure continuing growth in trade, both nations have pledged to increase bilateral trade to US$160 billion by 2017 after Malaysian Prime Minister Najib Razak's official visit to China in May 2014, and further discussions on expanding trade relations took place during Najib's most recent visit in October 2016. Based on official figures, Malaysia's trade as a whole with China grew by 1.2 percent since 2009 to RM1.466 trillion (US$353 billion) in 2015, compared with RM1.448 trillion (US$349 billion) in 2014. In 2015, Malaysia's trade with China expanded by 11.1 percent to RM230.89 billion (US$55.67 billion), with Malaysia's exports to China recording a double-digit growth of 10 percent to RM101.53 billion (US$24.48 billion). To ensure continuing growth in trade, both nations have pledged to increase bilateral trade to US$160 billion by 2017 after Malaysian Prime Minister Najib Razak's official visit to China in May 2014, and further discussions on expanding trade relations took place during Najib's most recent visit in October 2016.

Besides bilateral trade, both countries have been involved in investments in each other's economy. Increasingly, more Chinese investors have been tapping into the Malaysian market. Malaysia is at the center of Southeast Asia and has developed infrastructure and transport links with the region. Chinese entrepreneurs can use Malaysia as the gateway to the AEC and explore business opportunities that can benefit both sides. China began to invest more aggressively in Malaysia in 2010 and, by the end of 2014, 182 manufacturing projects with China's investment of US$2.83 billion had been implemented in the country. However, in keeping with the 'three waves of Chinese investment' mentioned earlier, its focus has begun to shift. While earlier the focus had been on rubber products, metal products, plastic products and food manufacturing, today Chinese investors go for real estate, manufacturing, oil and gas and resource-based industries. The latest development is an increased interest of Chinese investors in using mergers and acquisitions (M&A) to tap foreign markets and move higher up in the value chain. With the Ringgit depreciation against the Renminbi, it provided a favorable environment for China's M&A activities. China's M&A into Malaysia have been the busiest on record, both in terms of volume and number of big deals, with the most active deals being in real estate, consumer products and retail. According to HSBC (2015), in the first seven months of 2015 alone, the total value of Chinese M&A in Malaysia stood at US$830 million (RM3.35 billion), nearly four times the figure for all of 2014. The landmark deals include Greenland Holding Group's purchase of Southern Crest Development Sdn Bhd, at US$658 million (RM2.66 billion), Longcheer Holdings' purchase of Pearl Discovery Development Sdn Bhd at US$89 million (RM359.7 million), and Parkson Retail Group buying YeeHaw Best Practice Sdn Bhd in the dining and lodging industry.

Malaysia has consistently supported China's twenty-first century Maritime Silk Road; in fact, the support was already incorporated into the Joint Communiqué between Malaysia and China in conjunction with the 40th anniversary of diplomatic relations in May 2014. As indicated by the Malaysian Transport Minister, Liow Tiong Lai (2015), Malaysia has repeatedly expressed its support for the Maritime Silk Road on different occasions. When President Xi Jinping met Prime Minister Najib in Manila on 17 November 2015, both of them noted that Malaysia–China relations were at the best period in history with both sides maintaining a high-level mutual trust, and both sides agreed to elevate the bilateral relations to a comprehensive strategic partnership. This agreement calls for the integration of the region into a cohesive economic area through building infrastructure, increasing cultural exchange and broadening trade. The Malaysian and Chinese governments signed a five-year plan to strive for US$160 billion by 2017, by expanding trade, investment, tourism, education, financial and infrastructure projects.

Malaysia's positive response to China's initiative is due to several reasons. First, Malaysia is on its journey to attain the developed nation status by 2020 and beyond. Chinese investment and other forms of cooperation are a big contribution to achieve this goal. However, Malaysia's positive stance is more than for economic or instrumentalist reasons. If history helps us explain anything, we have seen that, in modern history, Malaysia was the first to establish diplomatic relations with China at the height of the Cold War. Obviously, Malaysia would like to benefit from this 'first mover' advantage and leverage on it. Malaysia also feels that history is on its side, given the fact that Malaysia and China have a long history of friendly relations, with the latter never behaving like a colonial power, unlike the West. In an interview with former

Prime Minister Mahathir in November 2014, he articulated such confidence and trust this way: 'We had 2000 years of history of relations. China never conquered Malaysia (unlike Western powers).... The Portuguese came in 1509 to Melaka; in 1511, they attacked and conquered Melaka.'

China has also been quite careful in its approach, and has ensured it is non-intrusive and inclusive. Besides the use of economic incentives to smooth over worries in Kuala Lumpur that the 'special relationship' between China and Malaysia has hit a snag (Tiezzi 2015), visiting Chinese premier Le Keqiang also made a symbolic visit to Melaka, which was regarded by China's media as 'an explicit gesture of China's commitment to peaceful development and common prosperity in East Asia'. As indicated in the introduction, Melaka has served as an important international port for centuries – including playing host to the armada led by Admiral Zheng He, which was a symbol of friendship and peaceful intentions toward China's neighbors, as historical proof that relations with China are to be welcomed, not feared.[4]

Public attitudes toward China's investment in Malaysia in various sectors such as property and infrastructure have generally been favorable, but they underwent a marked change from end of 2015 onwards when the scandal-ridden 1MDB (One Malaysia Development Berhad), a government-owned company chaired by prime minister Najib Razak, sold its power plants and land assets at bargain prices to China. Through such sale, China General Nuclear Power Corp (CGN Group) took over all the Edra energy assets under 1MDB – which consisted of 13 power plants across five countries from Malaysia to Bangladesh and far away Egypt – for RM9.83 billion (US$2.4 billion), and assumed all the relevant gross debt and cash. This was soon followed by the sale in December 2015 of a 60 percent stake of Bandar Malaysia to a China-led consortium, involving 486-acres (about 197 hectares) of prime land, previously an air force base located at the heart the Malaysian capital, Kuala Lumpur, for RM7.41 billion (US$1.722 billion). The consortium consists of two companies – Iskandar Waterfront Holdings Sdn Bhd (IWH) and China Railway Engineering Corporation Sdn Bhd (CREC). These were perceived as attempts by China to 'bail out' 1MDB at the request of Prime Minister Najib and the Malaysian government.

According to plan, the China Railway Group would build the world's biggest underground city in Bandar Malaysia at the cost of US$36 billion (RM160 billion) which will be completed in 25 years, and will serve as the centerpiece for its China Pan Asia rail network. The underground city will be part of the massive Bandar Malaysia project that will include the Kuala Lumpur terminal of the Malaysia–Singapore high-speed rail. It will also house the US$2 billion regional headquarters of the China Railway Group.

One needs to add to this list the Forest City in the Iskandar Malaysia Region in Johor and the Melaka Gateway Project in Melaka. The Forest City is a property development project of mega proportion costing some US$100 billion (RM440 billion) – the biggest among the 60 odd projects in the Iskandar Malaysia Region – 60 percent of which is owned by China. The latter is seen as aggressively turning the Forest City project, which started in February 2016, into the new 'Shenzhen', the modern city in southern China, to house some 700,000 population, the majority of whom are expected to be Chinese citizens. Forest City, built on reclaimed land, is supposed to be a smart eco-city, which has been granted duty-free area status and can enjoy preferential policies with an approval for the establishment of new CIQS (Customs, Immigration, Quarantine and Security) (www.forestcitycgpv.com/en/garden.aspx accessed on 10 January 2017; Whang 2016).

The Melaka Gateway project, on the other hand, also involves China through the joint venture between KAJ Developments with PowerChina International JV at the cost of less than US$10 billion (about RM30 billion) to reclaim three islands off Malacca's coast. The first phase is the construction of the deep sea port and is scheduled to be completed by 2019, while the greater Melaka Gateway development is expected to be completed by 2025.

Can all these be regarded as evidence of a Malaysia–China 'special relationship', which makes it easy for China to successfully 'connect the dots' through Malaysia into ASEAN and of Malaysia taking advantage of China's rise? In many ways, it is true that the 'special relationship' Malaysia has with China has enabled the former to leverage well to attract China's investment, while China too has put the 'special relationship' to good use.

However, the same cannot be said when prime minister Najib Razak undertook another state visit to Beijing in November 2016, and signed 14 economic deals worth some US$34 billion. Among the deals was a directly-negotiated contract with China for the latter to build and finance the 620 km East Coast Rail Line (ECRL), which is to run from Kuala Lumpur through Selangor, and the three east coast states of the Peninsular Malaysia. The loan, amounting to RM55 billion (US$13.1 billion), is said to be competitive, given at a 'low rate with a repayment period of 20 years', but critics allege that the ECRL cost as 'inflated' (Chew 2016a). At the same time, Malaysia also made a purchase of ten China-made patrol boats, making it Malaysia's first military purchase from Beijing. The latest move has been criticized within Malaysia as tantamount to compromising the country's sovereignty and its non-aligned foreign policy, and can be interpreted as evidence of a new unfolding story, an implicit signal to the US. This is quite obvious as the move was taken after the US Department of Justice (DoJ) announced, a few months earlier (in July 2016), its seizure of assets in the US worth more than US$1 billion which the DoJ claimed were 'associated with an international conspiracy to launder funds misappropriated from a Malaysian sovereign wealth fund', 1MDB. This was the largest single action ever brought under the US Kleptocracy Asset Recovery Initiative. The DoJ named Najib's step-son, Riza Mansor, and the prime minister's close associate Jho Low as owners of the ill-gotten assets, but Najib was not mentioned by name except as 'Malaysian Official One' (MO1), a reference made many times in the document (US Department of Justice 2016). While there is no conclusion to the ongoing debate about whether Malaysia under Najib is having a change of heart and distancing itself from its old ally, the US, thus tilting toward China – a situation triggered by domestic political considerations especially the scandals associated with 1MDB (Chew 2016b) – or whether it is 'hedging' between the two big powers as claimed by some analysts (Yang Razali Kassim 2016), the dynamics of the situation show things are relatively fluid and full of uncertainty in the coming years, especially under Donald Trump, the new US president who assumed office on 20 January 2017. (For a brief discussion on this, see Parameswaran 2016; Yang Razali Kassim 2016; Sipalan 2016.)

Conclusion

In the Asian Barometer Survey III, which among others asked the question 'which country has the most influence in Asia' (see Liu Kang 2015), the responses from the respondents surveyed are indicative of the trend of China's rise and dominance in Asia. Respondents from the Northeast Asian countries such as Japan and South Korea view China as playing the most important role today and in the future compared with the US, while those from Southeast Asia view the US as currently more important than China but, in the coming 10 years, the situation would be reversed: with the exception of those in the Philippines and Indonesia, the respondents feel that China would be more important than the US for Southeast Asia in the coming years. Such a view of the changing geopolitics in the region is worth noting. Should the survey be conducted today, after the launching of China's OBOR, namely the New Maritime Silk Road and the setting up of the various financial institutions to support it, the perception toward China's strategic importance would certainly be more enhanced. Traditional or long-held views about the geopolitics of the region have changed or are changing. This implies that the people of East and Southeast Asia – the people of the ASEAN states in particular – have come to terms with and are prepared to accept China playing a bigger role than the US in the region, more so now that the US under Donald Trump has cancelled the Trans-Pacific Partnership Agreement (TPPA).

However, such an acceptance comes with the expectation that the era of big power domination, hegemony or bullying is over. While China's inclusive vision of shared destiny underlined by principles of mutual respect and mutual trust is welcome, such ideals need to be translated into reality, only then can trust be built on a sustained basis. While China's initiative and vision are full of charms, and the post-Obama US is now becoming protectionist under Trump's 'America First' policy, ASEAN as an institution that can define the regional order, needs to speak as one, and to set an inclusive agenda for the region to ensure the big powers respect it as an equal partner in the global community of nations and regions.

Malaysia individually and ASEAN collectively are very keen to work together with China to address the development gaps and 'connect the dots', that is, to make the relations work on the basis of mutual benefit as promised in the Maritime Silk Road initiative. However, there are several pressing issues or challenges that require attention, especially on the part of China as the big power in the region and also by ASEAN member states. These include the asymmetry in the economic relations – both in terms of trade and more so investment. In terms of China–ASEAN trade, the asymmetry or imbalance in favor of China is quite obvious, with China enjoying 56.6 percent, and ASEAN 43.4 percent of the value of trade. In terms of China's investments, they are concentrated in certain member-states which are already more developed, and there are instances of investments that have caused or have triggered political and social problems, controversies and conflicts in the recipient country, as in the case of Myanmar and now Malaysia.

Maintaining the unity and cohesiveness of ASEAN, as well as its neutrality, consistent with the Declaration of the Zone of Peace, Freedom and Neutrality (ZOPFAN) which ASEAN adopted in 1971 is crucial for the region. Southeast Asia is a zone that the big powers, such as the US, Japan and China, have been competing to seek influence in and build alliances with. Currently, besides the China's OBOR, namely the Maritime Silk Road initiative, ASEAN needs to study what strategy the new US President will take toward Asia and ASEAN following the demise of the TPPA. Whatever position the US president decides to take, ASEAN has to avoid the hegemony of any major power, or being involved in the rivalries between them (Shahriman 2015). China and other powers need to respect ASEAN's neutrality and support its unity and cohesiveness, thereby contributing toward ASEAN's third pillar, the formation of the ASEAN Socio-cultural Community.

As a final note, the statement by the Sultan of Perak, Malaysia, Sultan Nazrin, who spoke in 2015 on the significance of China's New Silk Road as 'history in the re-making',[5] is worth pondering. Taking a broad historical sweep, he said the half century of American primacy is now giving way to a more diffused economic order where China is set to resume its position as the world's largest economy after a lapse of five centuries. Clanton (2015) quotes Raja Nazrin thus: 'We are perhaps on the threshold of another grand design, this time emanating from a country that centuries ago also gave us silk, paper and the chemical explosive that goes into fireworks and gunpowder.' But what is left unanswered is: under the 'grand design', will China as the new global power behave the way western imperialist powers behaved in the nineteenth and twentieth centuries, or will China behave differently under conditions of twenty-first century oriental globalization? China's history of over 2000 years has shown that it chose not to colonize other countries but traded and established friendly ties with them. The world is watching if China will follow the same historical trajectory in the twenty-first century, or, on the contrary, betray the trust it has earned among other peoples and nations. The OBOR initiative is a step, a promise, in the right direction, and it should be translated into deeds.

Notes

1 In fact, Zheng He's fleet voyages

> opened the longest navigation line in the history of China's Maritime Silk Route. According to the document describing Zheng He's voyages, his fleet left the east coast of China and either went northwest to the Persian Gulf via the Arabian Sea or crossed the equator into the southern hemisphere, and arrived at Ma Lin Di … (now KIlwa Kisiwani in Tanzania)'
>
> (Sun Guangqi 2000: 300)

2 In fact, as stated by the President of the Asian Development Bank, Takehiko Nakao, at the 19th ASEAN Finance Ministers' Meeting 'Infrastructure Connectivity: Financing Needs, Risks and Challenges', held in Kuala Lumpur on 21 March 2015, ASEAN's physical infrastructure is critical to the AEC's first pillar of establishing a single market and production base. In addition to national projects, he argues that cross-border roads, power lines, railways and maritime development are necessary to help boost existing and new value chains or production networks within ASEAN and beyond, thus contributing to strengthening the AEC.

3 Indonesia established diplomatic relations with China in 1950, but due to political tension, Indonesia severed the relations in 1967, and only resumed them in 1990.

4 China frequently uses Zheng's voyages a symbol of China's friendship and benign intentions toward its neighbors. Li Keqiang in fact visited Zheng He's museum in Melaka. 'Commanding the largest and most advanced fleets in his time, Zheng did not bring hostility and conflicts. That embodies the very essence of the traditional Chinese philosophy, where peace and good-neighborliness always come first', *Xinhua* paraphrased Li as saying during his tour of the museum. Tiezzi (2015) argues that by invoking this history, Li hoped to assuage modern-day fears about China's behavior and intentions, as well as promoting the twenty-first century version of the Maritime Silk Road.

5 The keynote address was delivered at the Seventh World Chinese Economic Summit organized jointly by Asia House and the Asian Strategy and Leadership Institute (ASLI), held in London on 20 November 2015.

References

Arase, D. 2015. China's two Silk Roads initiative: What it means for Southeast Asia. In Daljit Singh, ed. *Southeast Asian Affairs 2015*. Singapore: Institute of Southeast Asian Studies.

Armitage, D. 2012. What is the big idea? Intellectual history and the *longue durée*. *History of European Ideas* 38(4): 493–507.

ASEAN–China Relations. 2015. www.asean-china-center.org/english/2015-04/13/c_13365143.htm (accessed 10 October 2015).

Association of Southeast Asian Nations (ASEAN). 2010. *Master Plan on ASEAN Connectivity*. www.mfa.go.th/asean/contents/files/asean-media-center-20121203-182010-779067.pdf (accessed 20 September 2015).

Bower, E.Z. and Phuong Nguyen. 2015. Will China–Malaysia relations remain a model for Asia? *cogitASIA*. Centre for Strategic and International Studies (CSIS). http://cogitasia.com/will-china-malaysia-relations-remain-a-model-for-asia/ (accessed 26 August 2015).

Cai, Peter. 2014. China's charm offensive in Southeast Asia. *China Spectator* 19 September.

Catanzaro, J., Ren Qi, Chen Jia, and Bu Han. 2015. Silk Road initiative connects countries on path of prosperity. *Daily Telegraph* 3 July. www.telegraph.co.uk/sponsored/china-watch/business/11706380/silk-road-initiative-china.html (accessed 15 November 2015).

Chandra, A.C. and L.A. Lontoh. 2011. *Indonesia-China Trade Relations: The Deepening of Economic Integration amid Uncertainty?* Trade Knowledge Network: International Institute of Sustainable Development.

Chew, Amy. 2016a. Do Malaysia and Singapore really need a high-speed rail link? (11 December). www.scmp.com/week-asia/business/article/2053393/do-malaysia-and-singapore-really-need-high-speed-rail-link (accessed 10 January 2017).

Chew, Amy. 2016b. What has Malaysian leader Najib Razak's China Trip got to do with 1MDB? (29 October). www.scmp.com/week-asia/geopolitics/article/2040709/what-has-malaysian-leader-najib-razaks-china-trip-got-do-1mdb (accessed 10 January 2017).

Clanton, Naomi. 2015. The Belt and Road: what are the opportunities and challenges? *Asia House* 20 November. Source: http://asiahouse.org/belt-road-opportunities-challenges/ (accessed 25 November 2015).

Guidetti, A. 2015. The Silk Road, sand castles and the US–China rivalry. Geneva Centre for Security Policy: *Strategic Security Analysis* 7: 1–7.

Hewitt, Duncan. 2015. Fifty countries sign up to China-led Asian Infrastructure Investment Bank, in diplomatic victory for Beijing. *International Business Times* 30 June.

HSBC. 2015. Malaysia set to benefit from Chinese investors' flurry of overseas investment. *News Release by HSBC Bank Malaysia Berhad* 15 August.

Hsu, Sara. 2017. How China's Asian Infrastructure Investment Bank fared its first year. www.forbes.com/sites/sarahsu/2017/01/14/how-chinas-asian-infrastructure-investment-bank-fared-its-first-year/#41557528f4d1 (accessed 20 January 2017).

Liow Tiong Lai. 2015. Enhancing the 21st century Maritime Silk Road through Malaysia. Text of the speech by Malaysian Minister for Transport opening The Forum on Enhancing the 21st Century Maritime Silk Road through Malaysia. *Xinhuanet* 9 December.

Liu Cigui. 2014. Reflections on maritime partnership: Building the 21st century Maritime Silk Road. China Institute of International Studies. www.ciis.org.cn/english/2014-09/15/content_7231376.htm (accessed 22 August 2017).

Liu Kang. 2015. Interests, values, and geopolitics: The global public opinion on China. *European Review* 23(2): 242–260.

Mark, Joshua. 2014. Silk Road: Definition. *Ancient History Encyclopedia*. www.ancient.eu/Silk_Road/ (accessed 20 October 2015).

Ministry of Foreign Affairs (MOFA) of the People's Republic of China. 2013. Premier Li Keqiang attends the 16th ASEAN-China Summit, stressing to push for wide-ranging, in-depth, high-level, all-dimensional cooperation between China and ASEAN and continue to write new chapter of bilateral relations. (MOFA Statement issued on 10 October 2013).

Nabbs-Keller, Greta. 2011. Growing convergence, greater consequence: The strategic implications of closer Indonesia-China relations. *Security Challenges*, 7(3) (Spring): 23–41.

Nederveen Pieterse. J. 2015. *Goodbye Miracle Eight*. Bangi: Penerbit Universiti Kebangsaan Malaysia.

OECD Development Centre & the ASEAN Secretariat. 2013. *Southeast Asia Economic Outlook 2013 with Perspectives on China and India: Narrowing Development Gaps*. Paris: OECD. Available online from the OECD iLibrary at: http://dx.doi.org/10.1787/saeo-2013-en (accessed 15 February 2014).

Parameswaran, Prashanth. 2016. Malaysia is not pivoting to China with Najib's visit. *The Diplomat* 3 November. http://thediplomat.com.

Retraubun, Alex. 2015. Perlu Leadership yang Kuat untuk Membumikan Poros Maritim [Strong leadership is necessary to anchor the maritime axis]. *Save Indonesia: The Politic*. Edisi 20-Thn IV: 4–17 September: 4–6.

Shahriman, Lockman. 2015. The 21st century Maritime Silk Road and China–Malaysia relations. Paper delivered at 'The Dialogue on China-Malaysia Relations: Strengthening Partnership, Deepening Regional Cooperation', held on 14 April 2015 at the International Conference Hall of the Chinese People's Institute of Foreign Affairs (CPIFA).

Sipalan, Joseph. 2016. Malaysia's Najib risks backlash at home after deals with China. Monday 7 November. www.reuters.com/article/us-malaysia-china-idUSKBN1320EY.

Sun, Guangqi. 2000. The development of China's navigation technology and of the maritime Silk Route. In Vadine Elisseeff, ed. *The Silk Roads: Highways of Culture and Commerce* (Chapter 16). New York, Oxford: Berghan Books & UNESCO Publishing.

Tiezzi, Shannon. 2015. China promotes trade, Maritime Silk Road in Malaysia. *The Diplomat* 24 November 2015. http://thediplomat.com/2015/11/china-promotes-trade-maritime-silk-road-in-malaysia/ (accessed 30 November 2015).

US Department of Justice. 2016. United States seeks to recover more than $1 billion obtained from corruption involving Malaysian sovereign wealth fund. Media release 20 July. www.justice.gov/opa/pr/united-states-seeks-recover-more-1-billion-obtained-corruption-involving-malaysian-sovereign (accessed 10 January 2017).

Varoufakis, Yanis. 2015. *The Global Minotaur: America, Europe and the Future of the Global Economy*, 2nd edn. London: Zed Books.

Waugh, Daniel C. 2007. Richthofen's 'Silk Roads': Toward the archaeology of a concept. *The Silk Road* 5(1) (Summer): 1–8.

Whang, Rennie. 2016. Forest City developer presses ahead amid reclamation issues. *Straits Times (Business Section)*, Singapore, 8 March. www.straitstimes.com/business/property/forest-city-developer-presses-ahead-amid-reclamation-issues.

Wu, Wendy. 2016. US could join China-backed AIIB in wake of Trump win, bank chief says. *South China Morning Post* (14 November). www.scmp.com/news/china/diplomacy-defence/article/2045816/us-could-join-china-backed-aiib-wake-trump-win-bank (accessed 20 January 2017).

Xi Jinping. 2014. *The Governance of China*. Beijing: Foreign Language Press.

Yale, William. 2015. China's Maritime Silk Road gamble, *The Diplomat* 22 April.

Yang Razali Kassim. 2016. Is Malaysia tilting towards China? *RSIS Commentary*, No. 318, 30 December, Rajaratnam School of International Studies, Singapore.

Zhang Yunling. 2015. One Belt, One Road: A Chinese view. *Global Asia* 10(3) (Fall): 8–12.

Zhao Hong. 2015. *China's New Maritime Silk Road: Implications and Opportunities for Southeast Asia*. Institute of Southeast Asian Studies, Trends in Southeast Asia Series.

Zhao Yanrong. 2015. Bloc 'primed to expand' as community. *China Daily* (E-paper) 23 November.

Zuraidah, Ibrahim. 2015. Indonesia to throw open doors to Chinese investment; seeks details on Maritime Silk road. *South China Morning Post* (25 March, updated 21 April).

10 Examining the shift to services

Malaysia and China compared

Siew Yean Tham

Introduction

The nature of the services sector has changed significantly since the 1980s when it was viewed primarily as a non-tradable sector due to the need for consumers and producers to be located in close proximity to each other. Services then were mainly labor-intensive consumer services. However, the emergence of new technologies has transformed this sector as they reduce the need for physical presence, thereby increasing the tradability of services. These new services are knowledge-based and technology-intensive intermediate services that can provide a competitive edge to an economy in a globalized information era. Fragmentation of the production process has further enhanced the demand for intermediate services such as logistic services that can facilitate the movement of goods and services across borders. Inclusion of the services sector in trade liberalization under the World Trade Organization (WTO) and subsequent free trade agreements (FTAs) that have emerged since the stalling of the Doha Round reflects the rapid increase in the tradability of services over time.

Deregulation of the telecommunication industry, and new communication technologies have also facilitated the globalization of financial services and capital markets. This has, in turn, changed the availability and sources of finance for supporting economic activities as well as heightening the risks of financial contagion and crises.

The new services economy is therefore not the same as the traditional tertiary sector in the conventional theory of structural change. Instead it is critical for economic growth as it provides new inputs that are sources of dynamic economies of scale that can increase the labor productivity of final goods. This is especially important when economies undergo structural transformations such as a sectoral shift from manufacturing to services in terms of employment or output or both. The services sector in this case can help to provide new sources of growth for an economy that was previously dependent on manufacturing for growth.

A sectoral shift to the services sector can be motivated by several factors. First, it can be driven by demand. As income grows, the demand for services such as health and education also increases, thereby increasing employment and its share in services (Schettkat and Yocarini 2003). Second, the shift may be due to the existence of a productivity gap between the two sectors, rather than a shift in final demand (Schettkat and Yocarini 2003). Higher productivity in manufacturing occurs with the 'rise of the robots' or the replacement of assembly workers with robots, as manifested by increasing capital-labor intensity in manufacturing. In this case, more labor input is needed in services due to its lower productivity, even if the share of services in real value added is unchanged. Third, the shift may be triggered by a structural change in the economy whereby service activities that used to be produced within a manufacturing firm are now outsourced to external service specialist providers (Rowthorn and Coutts 2004). This effectively shifts some service activities that used to be produced and consumed within a manufacturing firm into marketable services, thereby increasing the share of producer services such as finance or business services in an economy. Fourth, globalization and production fragmentation increases the mobility of firms and the emergence of footloose firms that relocate their production based on changing costs dynamics in countries that are drawn into global value chains (GVCs). International trade facilitates the process of displacing some manufacturing jobs in advanced economies by shifting low value added activities to developing economies and leaving the advanced economies to specialize in the production of knowledge-intensive goods that are less labor intensive (Rowthorn and Coutts 2004). Fifth, decreases in the rate of investment can lead to a decrease in the share of manufacturing in both employment and gross domestic product (GDP), since a disproportionately large share of investment expenditure is accounted for by manufactures (Rowthorn and Coutts 2004). Finally, the 'Dutch-disease' may negatively impact manufacturing employment by shifting resources from the non-mineral to the mineral sector with the discovery of mineral resources in a country (Palma 2014).

For economies that have focused on manufacturing development for growth, does a sectoral shift to the services sector indicate deindustrialization? There are many different definitions for deindustrialization. Bluestone and Harrison (1982, p. 6) define deindustrialization as a 'widespread, systematic disinvestment in the nation's basic productive capacity'. Kutshcer and Personik (1986) views deindustrialization as an erosion of the industrial base of a country. Rowthorn and Ramaswamy (1997), on the other hand, define deindustrialization as a fall in the share of employment in manufacturing and a converse shift in employment to the services sector, thereby using employment as a variable to measure the deterioration in the manufacturing sector relative to the rest of the economy. This is the definition adopted in this chapter as it is commonly used and measurable.

Deindustrialization in turn, is contentious because it can be the outcome of successful manufacturing and economic development and, by implication, rising living standards or a symptom of the failure of a country's manufacturing sector and its economy (Rowthorn and Ramaswamy 1997). More importantly, although deindustrialization occurred mostly in upper income countries in the past, it is increasingly emerging as a middle income phenomenon (Tregenna 2011). In fact, deindustrialization is emerging earlier and earlier in the development process and, conversely, services are rising in importance sooner (Dasgupta and Singh, 2006; Felipe *et al.*, 2014; Rodrik 2015). The per capita income at which the share of manufacturing in GDP peaked for the US, Britain and Germany was around US$9000 to US$11,000 but these manufacturing peaks are now occurring between US$2000 to US$5000. This early onset of deindustrialization is called premature deindustrialization by Rodrik (2015).

Why do countries that pursue manufacturing development shift to the production of services? In particular, what is the role of policies in this shift? Understanding this shift is crucial due to the changing nature and role of services in development and its association with deindustrialization. This chapter seeks to examine the nature of a sectoral shift from manufacturing production to services in two East Asian developing countries. It does so by comparing Malaysia and China's shift from manufacturing to the production of services, with the objective of identifying similarities and differences, including the challenges and prospects of this shift. In particular, it seeks to examine the role of policies in driving this shift. There is no literature that compares Malaysia's sectoral shift to services and its development with China while there are several reasons that support this comparison. Both are upper middle income countries, with Malaysia joining this group of countries in 1996 while China joined much later in 2012. Both utilized foreign direct investment (FDI) to connect with GVCs to develop their respective manufacturing sector, especially in electronics. Both also share the same aspiration to move up the GVC through deepening their manufacturing development. Concurrently, there is also increasing policy emphasis on developing their respective services sector. State-owned enterprises (SOEs) are an important feature in both economies. Given the important role played by the state in their respective manufacturing development, it is pertinent to explore whether the sectoral shift from manufacturing to services is policy driven and the rationales behind their respective policies. Developing countries that have also used a FDI-led development strategy to join GVCs may find it useful to learn from the experiences of Malaysia and China for engineering the shift from manufacturing to services as the next stage in their development.

The chapter is divided into the following sections. The second section traces when the shift to services occurred in Malaysia and China based on output and employment while the third section compares the policies used to promote this sectoral shift[1] and the rationales for the policies in each country. The prospects and challenges in the development of the services sector in the two countries are discussed in the fourth section while the conclusion summarizes the key findings of this chapter and their implications for the development of services in other emerging economies.

Services development in Malaysia and China

In the literature, services are often defined in terms of its salient features, namely intangibility, heterogeneity, simultaneity of production and consumption, and perishability.[2]

The sectoral shift to the services sector in terms of output and employment are explored in this section. In Figure 10.1, the share of services[3] in the Gross Domestic Product (GDP) of Malaysia is clearly larger than manufacturing for the period shown. The services sector was in fact the largest economic sector in 1960, contributing to 42 percent of the GDP of Peninsular Malaysia, followed by agriculture at 31 percent while manufacturing contributed only 9 percent of the GDP (Hirschman and Aghajanian 1980). The increase in the share of manufacturing in GDP is accompanied by a decline in the share of agriculture. Manufacturing's share in GDP peaked in 2000, with a clear decline since 2004.

Likewise, the share of employment in services to total employment is higher than the share of employment in manufacturing for the period shown in Figure 10.2. The relatively higher share of employment in services is attributed to the labor-intensive nature of this sector in Malaysia.[4] As in the case of the share of GDP, the increase in the share of employment in manufacturing is accompanied by a fall in agriculture's share. The share of employment in manufacturing peaked at 22.8 percent in 1997 and then fell slightly over 1998–1999 due to the Asian Financial Crisis (AFC) before reaching the same share in 2000, after which the share fell progressively while the share of services increased continuously.

Since the share of services in GDP and employment is larger than that of manufacturing for the entire time period shown, it is not possible to use

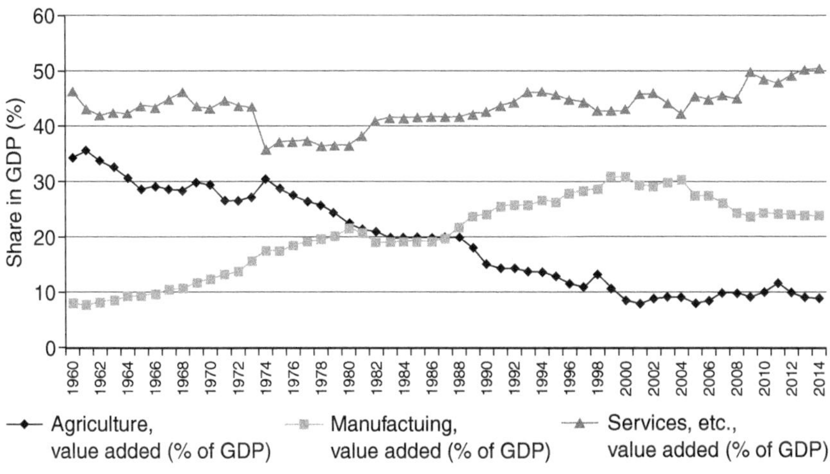

Figure 10.1 Share of agriculture, manufacturing and services, Malaysia, 1960–2014.

Source: World Development Indicators, World Bank.

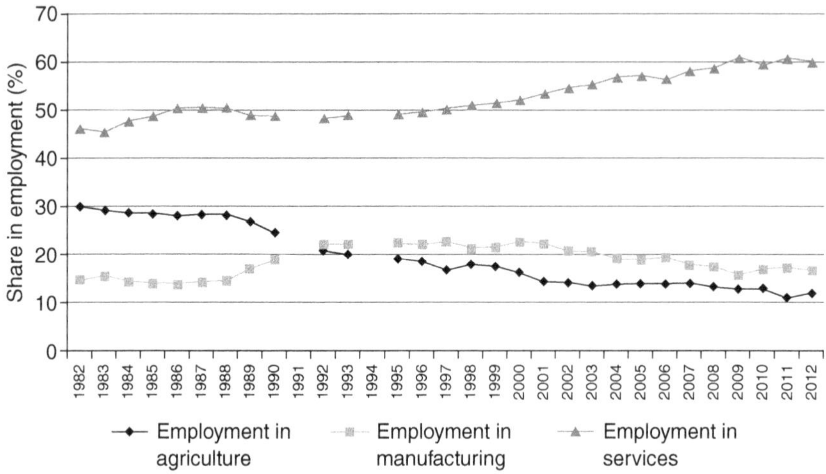

Figure 10.2 Share of employment in agriculture, manufacturing and services, Malaysia, 1982–2012.

Source: Department of Statistics of Malaysia.

changes in the relative shares of output and employment in manufacturing and services, as suggested by Rowthorn and Ramaswamy (1997) to identify a sectoral shift. Instead, it can be seen that there is a downward trend in the share of manufacturing output and employment since 2000, indicating a sectoral shift to services and the onset of a relative decline in the manufacturing sector.[5] The nature of this decline will be explored in the next section of this chapter.

For China, the increasing share of industry in GDP and employment is followed by a declining share in agriculture. The share of industry in GDP exceeded that of services until 2012 (Figure 10.3). The share of employment in services exceeded that of industry in 1994 (Figure 10.4). Using the share of industry and services in GDP, Perkins (2015) suggests that China is beginning to shift to services.[6] However, according to Rodrik (2015), the share of manufacturing employment in China peaked in 1996, but it may not make sense to conclude that China deindustrialized at that time, based on the definition given by Rowthorn and Ramaswamy (1997), due to the difficulties in China's employment data[7] in manufacturing and the lack of reliable data on its manufacturing's share in GDP. The increase in the share of employment in services after 1994 does not necessarily indicate that employment has shifted from industry to services. Rather, it reflects the mass layoff by state-owned enterprises from 1995–2002, after the SOE reform in 1995 as new estimates of the unemployment rate of China differ substantially from the official rate (see Feng *et al.* 2015).[8] There is no other discussion in the literature that is in English, on deindustrialization in China based on changes in the relative share of manufacturing rather than industry due perhaps to the

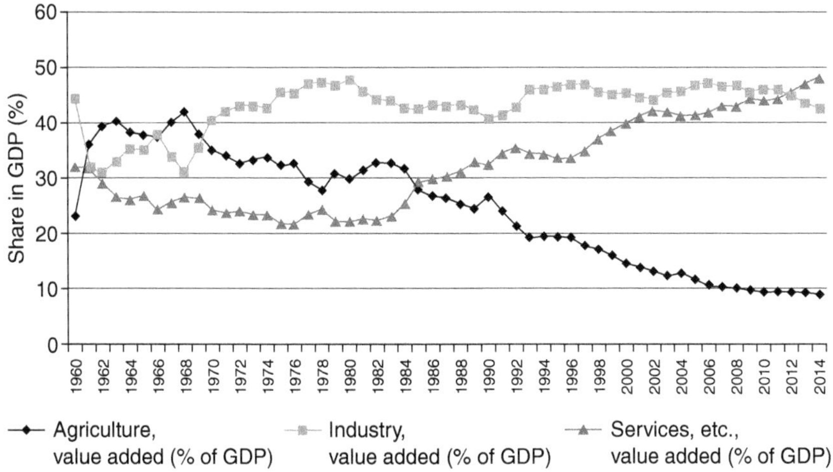

Figure 10.3 Share of agriculture, industry and services, China, 1960–2014.

Source: World Development Indicators, World Bank.

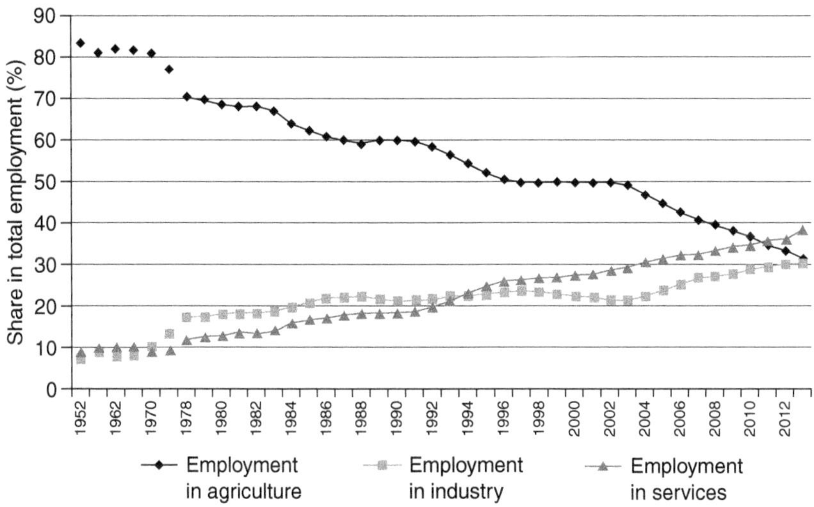

Figure 10.4 Share of agriculture, industry and services in total employment, China, 1952–2013.

Source: National Bureau of Statistics of China.

problematic nature of manufacturing data in China. It therefore appears, based on Figure 10.3, that China shows some evidence of a sectoral shift to services, starting in 2012.

The role of policies in promoting services

Policies in Malaysia and China

There are policy calls in both countries to shift toward services. These include policy directions as stated in the main policy documents, the use of tax and non-tax incentives to promote the development of services, promotion of FDI in selected services, including the use of special zones, and trade liberalization in services in their respective trade agreements with partner countries.

Policy makers in Malaysia have identified the important role of services since the Second Industrial Master Plan (IMP2: 1996–2005), which was launched in 1995, and in which the development of services plays a critical role in industrial upgrading and the development of industrial clusters was intended to deepen industrial development. This policy focus is continued in subsequent policy documents such as the Third Industrial Master Plan (IMP3: 2006–2020), New Economic Model, Economic Transformation Plan, Tenth and Eleventh Malaysia Plan and the Services Sector Blueprint launched in March 2015. While the IMP2 emphasized the development and use of manufacturing-related services to support industrial upgrading, subsequent plans focused on targeting selected services such as Islamic finance, education and medical tourism as new sources of growth. The Services Sector Blueprint, however, chose to emphasize the underlying drivers of service sector development rather than focusing on selected sectors. Tax and non-tax incentives are provided for the development of services.[9]

In the case of China, the focus on services started in the Tenth Five-Year Plan[10] (2001–2005), when the government announced plans to develop the services sector in conjunction with its liberalization commitments as it acceded to the WTO in December 2001. The Chinese government included an acceleration in the development of services in the 12th Five Year Plan (2011–2015) with a strong focus on next-generation information technology (IT) and a shift from production to service-oriented manufacturing (Tong 2013). Service industries that are aimed to be deregulated include education, financial, healthcare and logistics, while reforms are targeted at real estate and commercial banking, given their importance for the country's economic and societal well-being.[11] China aims to improve the contribution of the service industry to the economy in the 13th Five Year Plan (2016–2020), launched in November 2015. The plan emphasizes the need to develop a modern service industry that can provide high value producer services and high quality consumer services (KPMG 2016).

The use of FDI as a tool of industrial policy is common to both countries. Malaysia for example, promoted targeted services subsectors for inbound

FDI,[12] including liberalization of the former Foreign Investment Committee (FIC) investment Guidelines in 2009 so that FIC approval is no longer needed for acquisitions of interests, mergers, and takeovers of local companies by domestic or foreign parties.[13] China has published a Catalogue for the Guidance of Foreign Investment since 1995 that divides industries into encouraged, restricted and prohibited industries for FDI. This catalogue is amended regularly to reflect changes in the thrust of government policies. Modern services were included in the 2011 FDI Catalogue while the 2015 catalogue has an expanded encouraged category that includes selected services that includes among others, the supply of electricity, water, transportation, telecommunications and banking.[14]

In Malaysia, the share of manufacturing in inbound investment was the largest from 1990–1999 (Table 10.1). Subsequently, the share in manufacturing dropped to 41 percent from 2000–2009 while the share in services increased significantly to 27 percent due to the loss in comparative advantage in labor-advantage manufacturing activities and unilateral liberalization of services. From 2010 to 2013, the share of manufacturing and services increased marginally while the share of oil and gas increased significantly.

For China, the share of services in FDI inflows increased progressively from 2010 to 2014 (Table 10.2). While China initially opened up FDI in manufacturing, it also opened up its services sector as part of its commitments in its accession to the WTO in 2001, thereby shifting FDI into its services sector.

Table 10.1 Net FDI inflows by sectors, Malaysia, 1990–2013 (percentage)

Sector	*1990–1999*	*2000–2009*	*2010–2013*
Manufacturing	63	41	45
Services	15	27	29
Oil and gas	17	17	24
Others	5	5	2

Source: Mohamed Rizwan *et al.* (2014).

Note
'Others' consists mainly of the agriculture and construction sectors.

Table 10.2 FDI in China by sectoral breakdown, 1993–2014 (percentage)

Sector	*1998*	*2010*	*2014*
Manufacturing	59.6	46.9	33.4
Services	31.8	46.1	55.4
Real Estate	24.4	43.6	n.a.
Others	8.6	7.0	11.2

Sources: 1998 extracted from OECD (2000), 2010–2014 extracted from KPMG (2015).

Note
'Others' includes agriculture, forestry, animal husbandry, fishery etc.

Special economic zones have been used in the development of services for both countries. In the case of Malaysia, the Multimedia Super Corridor (MSC) is a government initiative to push the country toward high technology activities in the information, technology and communications (ICT) sector. Foreign investors granted MSC status are offered fiscal and non-fiscal incentives but they have to agree to provide technology transfer in exchange.[15] The Multimedia Development Corporation (MDeC) was established for processing applications for MSC status. Iskandar Malaysia (IM), one of the five recent economic corridors,[16] was launched in 2006 and it is currently in the second phase of its four-phased 20 year development plan. IM is important as it is strategically located in the southernmost tip of Malaysia to catch economic spillovers from Singapore. Moreover, services and manufacturing are targeted to be the two main pillars of its development.

Newer SEZs, such as pilot free trade zones in Shanghai, Guangdong, Tianjin and Fujian, are important policy tools used for attracting FDI in China. They were established based on a negative list approach whereby specific sectors that are not permitted for foreign investment are listed, while joint ventures are allowed in some sectors such as oil and natural gas exploration, airplane design manufacture and maintenance and rare earths smelting (Out-law.com, undated). One-hundred percent foreign ownership in e-commerce is allowed in the Shanghai Free Trade Zone (SHFTZ), which was officially launched in September 2013. Qianhai in the western part of Nanshan Peninsula of the Shenzhen Economic Zone, is currently being developed to be an international financial center as part of the overall development plan of Qianhai-Hong Kong Modern Service Industry Cooperative Zone (Chen 2015). It is unique in that it is a special zone within a special economic zone, besides being strategically located along the modern Maritime Silk Road, proposed by China in 2013 under its 'One Belt, One Road' (OBOR) initiative.

Trade liberalization, both unilateral, bilateral and regional initiatives are also used in both countries to promote the development of services. The General Agreement on Trade in Services (GATS) in the WTO is the first multilateral agreement focusing on the liberalization of services and both Malaysia and China are parties of that agreement as WTO members. Malaysia has to date also included services liberalization in bilateral agreements with Pakistan, Japan, New Zealand and India and also with ASEAN including the ASEAN-Plus agreements with China, Japan, Korea and India, as well as Australia and New Zealand. Services liberalization is also included in the recently concluded Trans-Pacific Partnership Agreement (TPPA), of which Malaysia is a partner, and the ongoing negotiations for the Regional Comprehensive Economic Partnership (RCEP), which includes Malaysia and China. China has also included services liberalization in its trade agreements with ASEAN, and separate agreements with Singapore, Chile, Costa Rica, Pakistan, Taiwan, New Zealand and Australia.

Reasons for increasing policy focus on services

The shift in policy focus is due to both external and internal factors. The biggest external challenge for Malaysia is the rise of China and its rapid progression in manufacturing development to become the factory of the world. China affected Malaysia's manufacturing development through three key dimensions, namely competing for FDI, contributing to the commodity price boom in the last decade and competing to move up the GVCs for electronics.

China made a major policy shift in 2000 to reduce the role of SOEs and instead to encourage FDI with tax incentives as compared with the previous period when FDI was heavily restricted (Ernst 2014). This, together with its WTO accession in 2001, caused a significant increase in inflows of FDI into China, spurring the development of its manufacturing sector, especially in electronics where it became part of the GVCs spanning Southeast Asia (SEA) and Northeast Asia (NEA). The relocation of manufacturing firms from Malaysia to China helped the multinationals operating in Asia to keep costs down while China grew rapidly, first in low-tech manufacturing and later in high-tech manufacturing. As China grew, its demand for resources also grew in tandem, contributing significantly to the rise in commodity prices and a progressive shift in Malaysia from electronics to palm oil production and exports to China. In fact, China is Malaysia's largest export destination for palm oil products, accounting for 20.4 percent of Malaysia's global palm oil exports (Tham and Kam 2015a). Both the production and exports of manufactured goods shifted from electronics to resource-based industries, such as palm oil, from 2002 to 2012 and the latter became the largest growth driver from 2002 to 2012 compared with the pre-AFC period (Mohamed Rizwan *et al.*, 2014). As for the competition to shift up the GVCs for electronics, China's ambitions and capabilities coupled with the slow development of indigenous capacity in Malaysia led to a worsening of the relative comparative advantage of Malaysia in its bilateral trade in electronics with China (Tham and Kam 2015a) and a progressive decline in the global position of Malaysia's electronics exports.

Domestically, the shift to services in Malaysia was triggered by the loss of comparative advantage in labor-intensive manufacturing that emerged in the early 1990s when its low labor-cost advantage dissipated with the rapid expansion of the manufacturing sector. The subsequent rise in wages forced Malaysia to consider upgrading and moving up the GVC, as proposed in the IMP2. However, the onset of the Asian Financial Crisis (AFC) derailed the implementation of the cluster development strategies as envisaged in the IMP2 and instead policy attention was directed toward rescuing the ailing economy, especially the financial sector, from the crisis (Tham 2015). Rapid technological changes led to the emergence of mobile electronic devices such as tablets and smart phones that progressively replaced the importance of personal computers globally. Malaysia unfortunately missed the boat to shift to this new wave of development in the semiconductor sector as upgrading plans in the IMP2 were not implemented. Parts and components (P&C) manufacturing instead continues to dominate the semiconductor industry instead of the newer mobile electronic devices. After recovering from the AFC, Malaysia continued to lose its attractiveness as a host economy for FDI as it suffered from shortages of the talent that is needed for upgrading while labor-intensive operations continued to relocate out of the country to more cost competitive locations such as Vietnam and China.

Technology spillovers from the presence of FDI in the country is limited with the affiliated companies of MNCs accounting for over 60 percent of Malaysia's manufacturing output and over 80 percent of manufacturing exports or 65 percent of total exports (Athukorala and Wagle 2011). In the crucial electronics sector, there are some local firms that have spun off from MNC employment to become suppliers, such as LKT Engineering, Shinca, Unico and Globetronics. A few wafer fabrication and chip design companies have also emerged as a result of investment grants offered, first to local firms and later to foreign firms after 2005 (see Table 10.3). This indicates some functional upgrading in this sector but as Tham and Kam (2015a) pointed out; a critical mass of local firms in the electronics sector has yet to be achieved. Instead, the use of passive absorption strategies or where technology transfer is absorbed organically rather than through coordinated, proactive and intense policy effort to deepen the technological capabilities of a country (UNCTAD 2014), has led to limited backward linkages and only a small number of homegrown firms in Malaysia (Yusuf and Nabeshima, 2009).

Therefore, despite its early mover advantage in opening up to FDI in the 1970s, much of the electronics sector still remains in the assembly and packaging and testing segments, while China, a late comer in this FDI-led sector, is moving ahead and Vietnam, another late comer, is also catching up (Table 10.3). Malaysia has yet to produce domestic electronics firms of international

Table 10.3 Number of integrated circuit (IC) firms facing upgrading in Malaysia, China and Vietnam, 2011

Countries	*National*					*Foreign*					
	RD	*CD*	*SRD*	*WF*	*AT*	*RD*	*CD*	*SRD*	*WF*	*AT*	
China	1	3[a]	2[b]	25	34	0	11	8	6	58	148[ab]
Malaysia	0	0	0	2	6	0	4	1	5	25	43
Vietnam	0	1	0	1	0	0	3	1	0	2	8

Source: Yap and Rasiah (2015).

Notes:
RD, CD, SRD, WF, AT refer respectively to R&D, Chip Design, Support R&D, Wafer Fabrication and Assembly and Test operations.
Firms are defined by the registration status, and hence, some subsidiaries of the same firm are counted more than once;
a denotes firms having both R&D and chip design in the same registration premises;
b denotes firms having both R&D and other supportive R&D in the same premises.

standing, as observed in Taiwan and South Korea. Instead, its electronics and manufacturing sector continues to shrink, dogged by a shortage of talents that is exacerbated by brain drain and inflows of less skilled workers (Tham and Kam 2015b). Weak industry–university linkages and inadequate R&D spending of 1.13 percent of its GDP, compared with China's 1.98 percent of its GDP, in 2012, are other contributory factors to the slow deepening of this sector.

The shift to services as new sources of growth in IMP3 and subsequent plan documents merely reflect the government's recognition that the manufacturing sector can no longer be a major source of growth for the country. The government instead chose to focus on selected services as new growth sectors unlike the use of services to complement manufacturing development for the purpose of industrial upgrading as targeted in IMP2. In the 11th Malaysia Plan (2015), the manufacturing sector is expected to grow at 5.1 percent per annum over the plan period and to contribute 22.1 percent to GDP and 18.2 percent of total employment in 2020. In contrast, the services sector is expected to grow at 6.9 percent per annum over the plan period and to contribute to 56.5 percent of GDP and 62.5 percent of total employment by 2020. Selected services such as financial services, wholesale and retail, tourism, information and communication technology (ICT), education, business and private healthcare, are targeted in the 11th Malaysia Plan. The global financial crisis (GFC) and the current growth challenges of China continue to add pressure for Malaysia to seek alternatives to manufacturing development. In the case of the GFC, its impact was transmitted to the country through its trade channels due to the relative openness of Malaysia's small economy. This led to the economic downturn in 2009. Growth slowdown after the GFC in China, especially after 2010, is expected to negatively affect economic growth as China is Malaysia's largest trading partner for the last four years.

Likewise, the policy shift to services in China reflects the underlying changing dynamics in the development of its manufacturing sector. China's reforms in 1978 prioritized the development of the manufacturing sector to the neglect of the services sector, due in part to the ideology at that time, when services were deemed to be non-material products that were not included in national income accounts (Perkins 2015). Hence, investments in services were not deemed to contribute to economic growth. Wholesale and retail trade in 1978 was dominated by a few SOEs and there were few restaurants, while banking services for the public were minimal. Public and foreign direct investments were directed toward manufacturing development, making China a factory of manufactured goods not just for itself but also for the world.

Inbound FDI has played an important role in China's economic development and export success (World Bank 2010; Xing 2013). Foreign invested enterprises account for over half of China's exports and imports; they provide for 30 percent of Chinese industrial output, and generate 22 percent of industrial profits while employing only 10 percent of labor; all because of their high productivity (World Bank 2010). In particular, there is a huge jump in China's high tech exports[17] after 2001 (or the WTO effect), with its share in total manufacturing exports increasing from 6.8 percent in 1995 to 31 percent in 2010 (Xing 2013). In 2002, foreign invested firms contributed toward 79 percent of high-tech exports, while wholly foreign owned firms accounted for 55 percent (Xing 2013). As more FDI flowed into the country since 2002, the share of these two types of firms increased further to a peak of 86 percent and 69 percent, respectively. It has since dropped slightly to 82 percent and 67 percent respectively in 2010 (Xing 2013).

Similar to Malaysia's experience, the increase in demand for labor led to a progressive rise in wages, causing China to also lose its comparative advantage in low labor costs production. By 2005, production costs in China had risen in line with rising wage costs as well as land costs forcing industries to relocate out of China to other countries in SEA such as Vietnam or to the hinterland provinces (Yue and Evenett 2010). Moreover, the deepening of China's integration with the world by joining GVCs, especially in the electronics sector, which is the dominant sector for FDI, intensified competition as all countries linked in the GVCs jostled to move up the chain. This amplified the need to upgrade its manufacturing sector as in the case of Malaysia.

A significant difference between Malaysia and China is the upgrading process in the latter country. In the electronics sector, not only is China located at the low end, but it is also making rapid progress into the high end, that is, from assembly, packaging and testing to wafer fabrication and design. China has become the largest semiconductor producer in the world since 2005 (Yue and Evenett 2010; Ernst 2014). The number of integrated circuit design enterprises in China escalated from a mere 15 in 1990 to 200 in 2001 and more than doubled to 583 in 2013, reportedly as a consequence of the tax incentives given by the government since the implementation of its 12th Five Year Plan in 2011, making it the 'fastest growing segment in China's semiconductor industry' (PWC 2014, p. 2). PWC (2014) also makes two other important observations: first, the number of wafer fabrication in production in China has increased by 186 percent from 2003 to 2013 with a total number of 160 in 2013 while their capacity increased by 314 percent. Second, packaging assembly and testing nevertheless remains the largest segment in terms of value added, production revenue, employees and floor space. Since China is huge in size, the rise in wages has triggered a shift to other regions in China as well as to other countries such as Vietnam.

Significantly, an expanding domestic segment has emerged over the last decade. The number of top Chinese semiconductor companies listed in PWC's updates have increased from 26 to 50 from 2005 to 2013, with the average revenue increasing from US$39 million to US$226 million over this period. These are the 'largest indigenous companies that design, manufacture, market and sell semiconductor devices' (PWC 2014, p. 8). Some of these companies were started by China's diaspora, who were trained in the US and who returned as entrepreneurs to take advantage of the growing market in China.

China's large domestic market also helped to shape the rapid changes in the development of smart phone operating systems. Using Google's open source smart phone operating systems, Android, Xiaomi, a Chinese smart phone company, has emerged as the third largest smart phone vendor in China (Ernst 2014). Its large domestic market further facilitated the development of a local ecosystem for budget smartphones that links IC designers with original equipment manufacturers (OEMs). This is enabling Chinese smart phones to expand beyond domestic shores to other emerging economies in Asia.

Despite these rapid changes and catch up, China is still not yet at the technology frontier since the centers of gravity for chip design are still in the US, Taiwan or Japan, while Chinese foundries manufacturing wafers are still lagging two generations behind in process technology and wafer design (Ernst 2014). As this sector is deemed to be a strategic emerging industry in China, there are plans to promote indigenous innovation to shift the country beyond mere catching up to forging ahead. China aims to make a leap from a mere global electronics factory to a global industry leader across key sectors in the integrated circuit industry supply chain and to create disruptive technological breakthroughs by 2030 (Ernst 2014). But there are several challenges ahead including, among others, navigating the shift from global production networks to global innovation networks; adapting its traditional policy planning cycles to the changing market dynamics of this sector, such as shorter production cycles leading to rapid obsolescence; and duopolistic or oligopolistic global market structures.

Importantly, the old model of development premised on export-oriented manufacturing based on low labor-cost advantages has generated excess capacity, high consumption of resources and a negative environmental impact, making it an unsustainable model of development for the long-term as the resource gap has narrowed and environmental costs escalated (Yue and Evenett 2010). Subsequent onset of the GFC further magnified the imbalances in China's old development model. The new development model is therefore premised on rebalancing the Chinese economy away from its currently unsustainable development path by focusing on domestic consumption rather than just exports, promoting added value and also by promoting services development rather than just manufacturing.

The development of services is critical for rebalancing an economy toward domestic consumption in both China and Malaysia as it includes within it the development of consumption services that cater to the needs of urbanization, which are escalating in both countries. It is also crucial for upgrading as high technology industries are more business service intensive than other sectors and higher business service content is associated with higher export prices obtained in major markets (Nordas and Kim 2013). In other words, services such as, for example, garment design rather than garment production, are a source of competitive advantage for a high-cost country that wants design new products for consumers who are willing to pay a premium. Manufacturers distinguish themselves from competitors through branding and other forms of intellectual property rights protection. The evolving nature of services and its importance to urbanization and upgrading is a common external driver for a change in the direction of the economy in both countries.

Another critical difference between Malaysia and China's policies is the continued focus on the manufacturing sector for China as opposed to Malaysia. For example, the State Council issued a new plan in 2015 called 'Made in China 2025' (MIC2025) that aims to transform China into a manufacturing power by 2049, which will then be the 100th anniversary of the founding of the People's Republic of China (The State Council of The People's Republic of China undated). The plan aims to shift China from low value added to high value added manufacturing through automation and innovation, which will require China to increase knowledge-intensive workers for both manufacturing and services. Malaysia, on the other hand, seems set to switch its focus from manufacturing to selected services as there is only one targeted manufacturing subsector (namely electronics) in the 12 targeted areas[18] in the Economic Transformation Plan (ETP) launched in 2010 to address the needed economic transformation in the country.

Prospects and challenges

Since the shift to services is to facilitate growth in Malaysia and China, this section will examine the prospects and challenges facing the development of services in each country.

Prospects

In Malaysia, measured by output, the top four largest subsectors within services as at 2013 are distributive, financial, real estate and other services (Figure 10.5). By employment, the four largest subsectors are distributive, other services, accommodation and food; and transport and storage (Figure 10.6). In terms of relative contributions to GDP, the top four are distributive, financial, real estate and other services (Figure 10.7). Notably, the contributions of the knowledge-intensive services such as ICT and finance are significantly smaller than the labor-intensive segments such as distributive services.

While it should be noted that the classification of services in China is not directly comparable with Malaysia, some broad comparisons can nevertheless be made. In China, other services – which includes government services, wholesale and retail trades, financial intermediation and real estate – are the key subsectors with services (Figure 10.8). For employment, data excluding private enterprises show that employment is mainly in other services (Figure 10.9), while data for private enterprises indicate that such enterprises are predominantly in wholesale and retail trades (Figure 10.10). The main contributors to GDP are other services, followed by wholesale and retail trade, financial intermediation and real estate (Figure 10.11). It can be concluded that wholesale and retail, financial intermediation and real estate dominates,

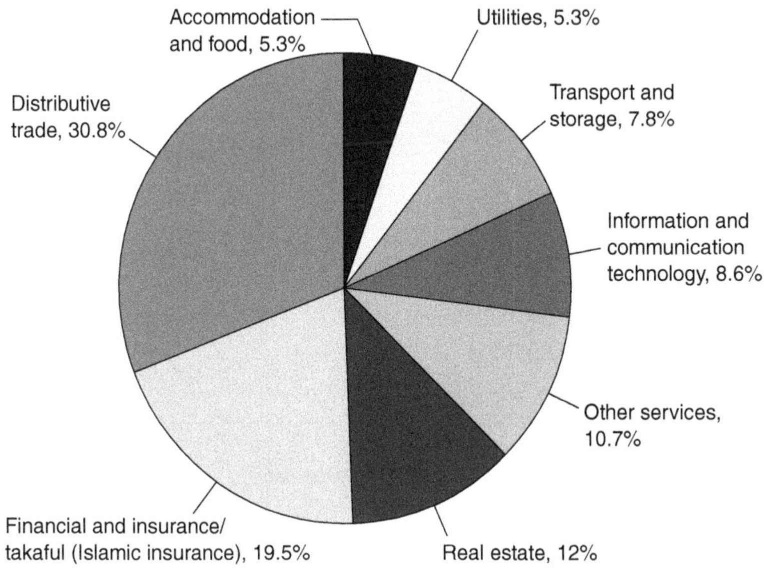

Figure 10.5 Output contribution of subsectors to the services sector, Malaysia, 2013.
Source: Malaysia Productivity Corporation (MPC).

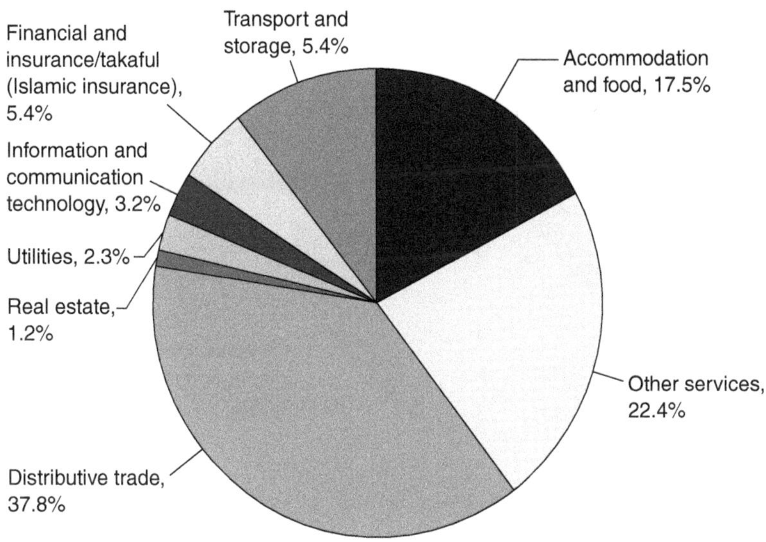

Figure 10.6 Distribution of employment within the services sector, Malaysia, 2013.
Source: Malaysia Productivity Corporation (MPC).

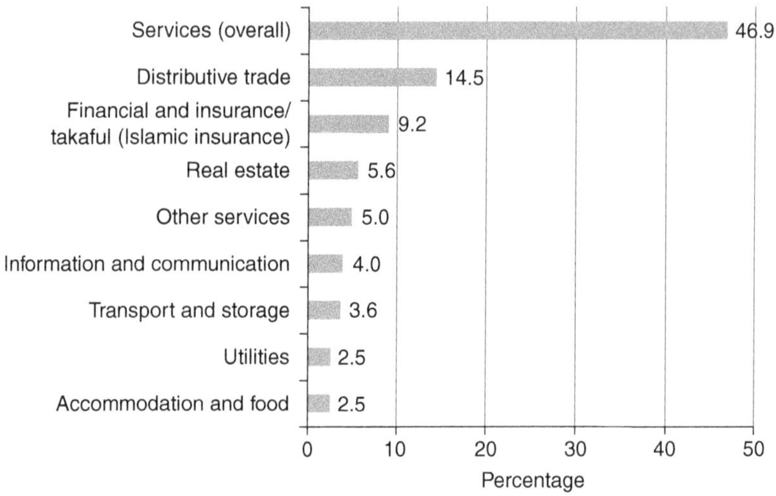

Figure 10.7 Contribution of the services sector to GDP, Malaysia, 2013.
Source: Malaysia Productivity Corporation (MPC).

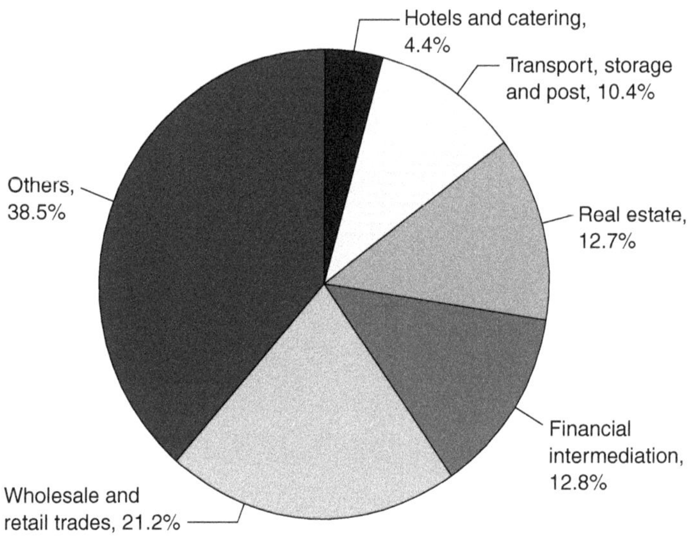

Figure 10.8 Output contribution of subsectors to the services sector, China, 2013.
Source: National Bureau of Statistics of China.

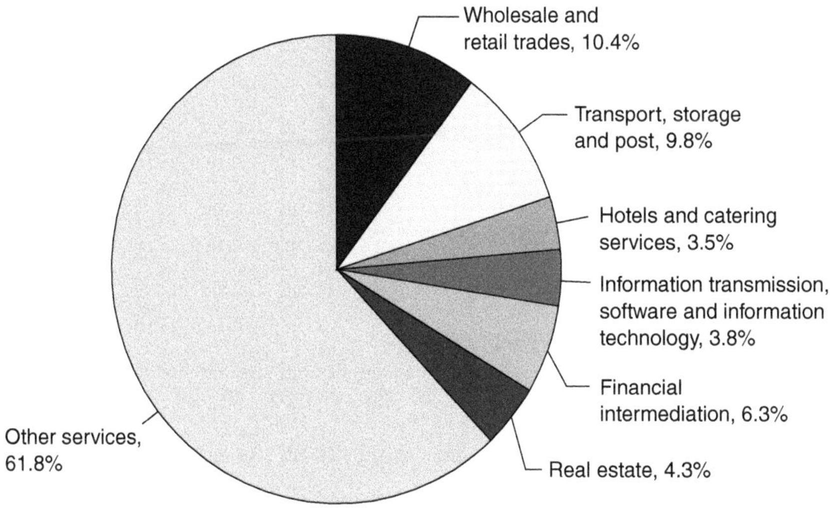

Figure 10.9 Distribution of employment within the services sector in urban units at year-end, China, 2013.

Source: National Bureau of Statistics of China.

Note

Data of employed persons in urban units do not include those of private enterprises.

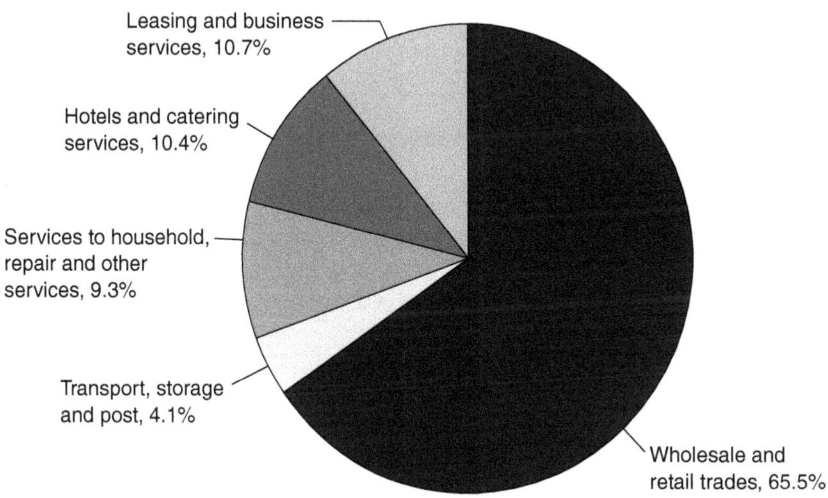

Figure 10.10 Distribution of engaged persons within the services sector in urban private enterprises and self-employed individuals at year-end, China, 2013.

Source: National Bureau of Statistics of China.

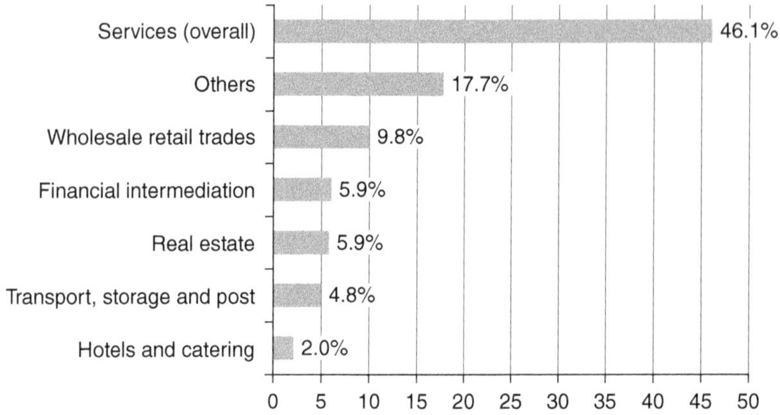

Figure 10.11 Contribution of the services sector to GDP, China, 2013.

Source: National Bureau of Statistics of China.

apart from other services in China's services sector. Importantly, there is no explicit category for ICT but, in e-commerce, China has produced e-commerce giants such as Alibaba, JD com. etc.

The exports of both countries are still dominated by the exports of goods rather than services, as shown by Figures 10.12 and 10.13. The widening gap

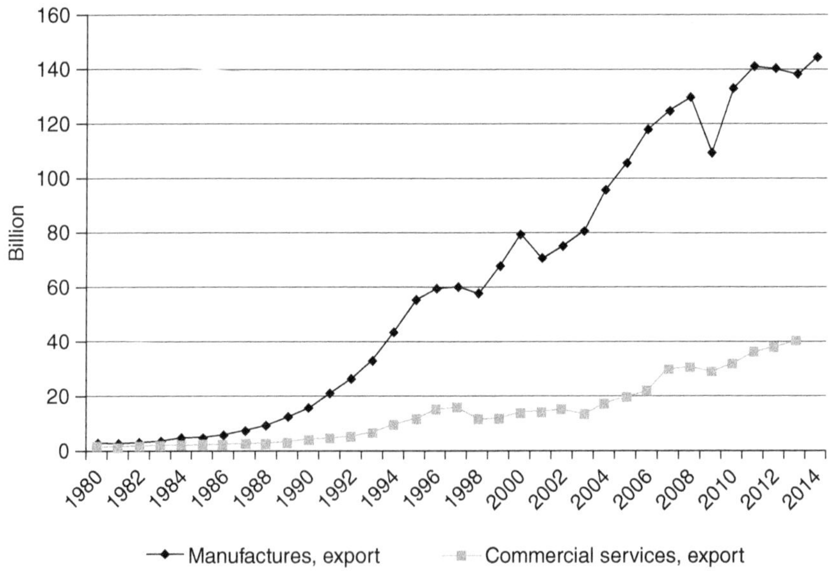

Figure 10.12 Exports of Malaysia, 1980–2014.

Source: The World Trade Organization (WTO).

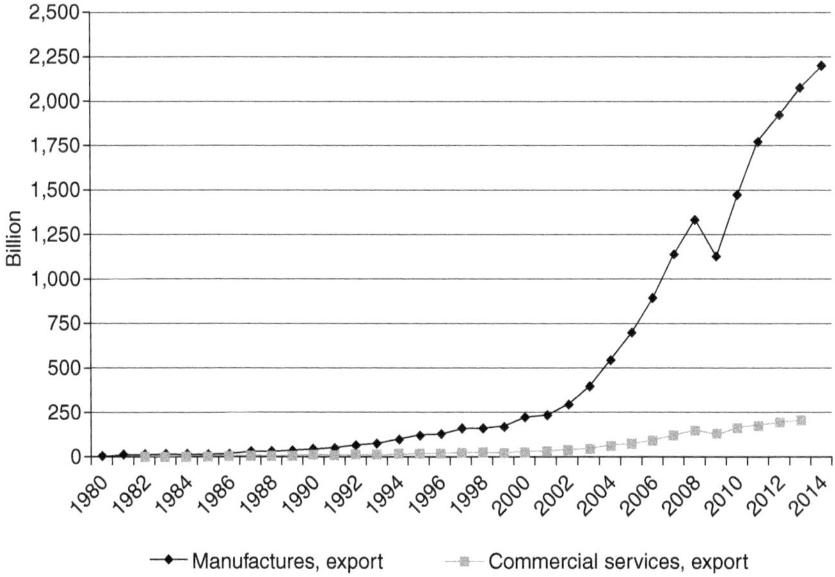

Figure 10.13 Exports of China, 1980–2014.

Source: The World Trade Organization (WTO).

between exports of goods and services indicates services exports are growing much slower than the growth in manufacturing exports and the relative inward-orientation of the services sector in both countries. The services trade restrictiveness index (STRI) of the World Bank (undated (b)) shows Malaysia and China's STRI are higher than the average STRI of the European Union (EU)-20,[19] implying that the services sectors in both countries are relatively more protected than their EU-20 counterparts. Malaysia's STRI is higher than China's, indicating higher barriers to trade in services in the former compared with the latter.

Challenges

Both Malaysia and China face similar challenges of growth slowdowns in 2015, and managing structural change and transformation amidst a backdrop of global uncertainties as well as heightened geopolitical and security concerns. Malaysia, in addition, faces a political stalemate and financial scandals that are yet to be resolved. However, two key issues that can affect the future development of their respective services sector are the substantial presence of SOEs in this sector and talent shortages in each country.

The role of State-Owned Enterprises (SOEs)

A recent OECD study (Büge *et al.* 2013) found China and Malaysia to be among the top five countries with the highest presence of state-owned enterprises (SOEs) among their top firms in terms of sales, assets and market value. For example, the share of SOEs in the respective country's top ten firms as a weighted average of sales, assets and market value is found to be 96 percent in China and 68 percent in Malaysia.

When reforms were started in 1978, China inherited a huge number of SOEs as part of its legacy from the use of central planning prior to reforms. Progressive reforms since mid-1900s have substantially reduced the number of SOEs, from 118,000 in 1995 to a mere 25,000 in 2006 (Cheong *et al.* 2015). But as noted by Cheong *et al.* (2015), this understates the size and reach of the state sector for three reasons: first, there are 'strategic' enterprises that may be completely or partly owned by the government but which do not appear in government statistics; second, there are also sub-national enterprises that belong to provincial and local governments that do not toe the policies of the central government and, third, there are complex ownership structures that render the ownership ambiguous and beyond definition. More importantly, there has been an active re-enlargement of the state sector since 2008 because the state has formally set aside several key sectors, including machinery, automobiles, construction, iron and steel and non-ferrous metals which the state should solely own or have majority share in (Scissors 2011).

In terms of ownership, SOE accounted for 2.8 percent of all firms in China in 2009 while SOEs account for 29.2 percent of the service sector (Wang 2013). In 2010, the share of employment in urban SOEs amounted to 73.8 percent in services, compared with the 12.5 percent in SOEs in manufacturing for the same year. There are, however, sectoral differences. While the share of employment in SOEs in education, healthcare, social security and social welfare, water conservation, environment and public administration, culture, and sports and recreation industries is well above 85 percent, SOEs' share in telecommunication, infrastructure and finance services is about 50 percent. Their share in real estate catering and accommodation, and wholesale and retail trade is below 30 percent (Wang 2013, p. 11).

The root of SOEs in Malaysia can be traced back to Post-independence when the Constitution empowered state governments to establish state economic development corporations (SEDCs) to manage their respective land and water resources (Wan Khatina Nawawi and Saovanee Chan Somchit, 2014). Following the 13 May 1969 politicized racial riots in 1970, the 'New Economic Policy' (NEP) was introduced as the national policy for poverty alleviation and socio-economic objectives including affirmative actions to increase the Bumiputeras'[20] participation in the economy. The NEP set targeted equity ownership levels for foreigners (30 percent), Bumiputeras (30 percent) and other Malaysians (40 percent) to be reached by 1990. SOEs were established in vast numbers to achieve these NEP targets. Malaysia's subsequent privatization program in the 1980s led to the privatization of key enterprises owned by the government to make profits, promote industrialization and nurture Bumiputera entrepreneurs, at the federal and state level.

There are no published data on SOEs in Malaysia. The unpublished data are scattered over the Government-linked investment companies (GLICs), such as Khazanah, different ministries, states and statutory bodies. In the banking sector, Chin (2015) analyzes how internal factors such as the affirmative action and consolidations of local banks by the state, as well as pressures from globalization have changed Malaysia's local banks from mainly Chinese-owned to state-owned (otherwise known as government linked companies (GLCs)) and from medium-size domestically-based to large-scale regionally-based banking groups. By 2010, out of the eight banks left after the merger of the commercial banks, four are GLCs, and the other four are in private hands (Gomez *et al.* 2015). Overall, Menon and Ng's (2013) study shows an extensive presence of GLCs, especially in utilities (93 percent market share) and transportation and warehousing (80 percent market share), while GLCs' market share is greater than 50 percent in agriculture, banking, information communications, and retail trade. Out of the 20 largest companies on the national stock exchange, eight are GLCs (Cheng 2015). Out of the 20 large GLCs (or the G20) earmarked as proxy for GLC performance by the government, 13 are found in the services sector. According to Raj (2012), estimates by the government indicate that GLCs employ about 5 percent of the nation's workforce, account for approximately 36 percent and 54 percent, respectively of market capitalization of Bursa Malaysia and the benchmark Kuala Lumpur Composite Index and a domestic investment of 5 percent, as well as contributing to 10 percent of Malaysia's GDP. This, however, excludes state-level GLCs, GLICs and statutory bodies.

The extensive presence of SOEs has led to a debate on their crowding in or crowding out of private enterprises. Xu and Yang (2014) found that, in China, this depends on the type of goods produced by the SOEs, as production of public goods 'crowd in' private investment significantly while, conversely, production of private goods 'crowds out' private investment significantly. Menon and Ng's 2013 study on Malaysia also shows that GLCs can crowd out private investment. The crowding out effect is linked to the assertion of preferential treatment for SOEs in both countries, including monopolistic or oligopolistic powers that can deter entry for other firms. Their anti-competitive impact can in turn exert a distortionary impact on prices, quality and demand. In China, it is also linked with the phenomenon of over-investment of SOEs in their provision of public goods or complementary products for other-types of ownership, thereby generating inefficiencies that have negative spillover effects on growth and other investments (Lin and Zhu 2007). Liberalization attempts are also jeopardized as, often times, the owners of SOEs are part of government and can therefore exert substantial influence over regulatory bodies and ministries that are in charge of the offers for liberalization. SOEs have a vested interest in keeping the domestic market for themselves and resisting market-opening measures that can threaten their share in the domestic market.

Despite the crowding out effect in both countries, a crucial difference in China is the emergence of a few privately owned enterprises that have global presence and branding. These include among others, Alibaba, Tencent, Baidu, Xiaomi and Huawei. In contrast, there is no significant global presence of Malaysian privately owned companies in the services sector, outside of the hotel and related services. Both countries however, have stated that engaging the private sector is critical for future development and this will require SOE reform in each country.

Talent shortages

The shift to knowledge intensive services can only be possible if the right type of human capital is available in each country. In Malaysia, the Services Sector Blueprint (EPU 2015) notes an old yet-to-be-resolved problem, namely the critical need to increase in the quantity and quality of human capital as there is both a shortage of skilled labor and a mismatch between the supply and demand for skills. This mismatch is manifested in the coexistence of job vacancies and graduate unemployment in Tham (2015). Similarly, China has encountered a shortage of talents since 2005, especially for graduates who can work in multinationals (Farrell and Grant 2005), which are also facing increasing competition from domestic firms in terms of recruiting and keeping talents.

The shortage of talents has led each country to draw up specific initiatives to address this problem. In Malaysia, TalentCorp was established in 2011 to address the overall skills gap by enhancing graduate employability, promoting talent diversity, engaging Malaysians abroad and facilitating foreign talent to work in Malaysia (see www.talentcorp.com.my/ (accessed 20 November 2015)).

Similarly, China has devised a blueprint called the National Talent Development Plan 2010–2020 to increase its share of highly skilled employees and its share of college graduates, and attract overseas talent (Wang 2010). It has also initiated the 'Recruitment Program of Global Experts' (or the 'Thousand Talents Plan) since 2008 to tap overseas top talents for the next ten years (see www.1000plan.org/en/plan.html (accessed 20 November 2015)). Although this scheme has brought back academic talents, businessmen and entrepreneurs to boost China's innovation capacity and international competitiveness, the program is under review for failing to bring back these talents permanently and its ability to really lure back the very best (Sharma 2013).

Although these are general strategies to increase talent shortages in each country, these can also assist in meeting the talent demands of their respective services sectors. It would appear that China is improving in its drive to increase talent shortages despite its demographic disadvantages. The Economist Intelligence Unit's (EIU) Global Talent Index (GTI)[21] shows an overall improvement in China's GTI from 33rd in 2011 to 31st in 2015, out of 60 countries, due its increasing openness to hire foreigners. Malaysia, however, deteriorated from the 36th position to the 39th position over the same period (EIU 2015).

Conclusion

While there is still a significant development gap between NEA and SEA as pointed out in Nederveen Pieterse (Chapter 1, this volume), there is another emerging gap between developing countries in NEA and SEA, as shown in the comparative shift to the services sector in Malaysia and China.

Malaysia's early mover advantage in using FDI for its manufacturing development has not translated into indigenous capabilities of the same stripe, scale and caliber of the earlier industrializers in NEA such as South Korea and Taiwan. There are neither global Malaysian brands nor Malaysian multinationals that have emerged in the electronics sector after four and half decades of manufacturing development in this sector. Instead, the electronics sector is shrinking rapidly and with it the manufacturing sector, due in part to the rise of China and internal upgrading problems in its manufacturing development. In other words, post-industrialism has arrived without significant industrialism (Nederveen Pieterse, Chapter 1, this volume). This has led to an increasing shift toward the services sector and the dire need for selected services to be the next engine of growth for the country. Policy makers in recognition of this need have formulated numerous policies that promote services development over the last two decades.

In contrast, the shift to services in China is more recent while the use of a similar FDI-led model of manufacturing development has led to China becoming a center in global production networks in electronics, increasing the deepening of indigenous capabilities and progressive upgrading of its electronics sector. Nonetheless, it also remains to be seen whether China can develop into another innovation giant in manufacturing as in the developed NEA countries. Policy-makers aim to continue developing both manufacturing capabilities as well as services.

The services sector in both countries are more focused on the labor-intensive segments, and knowledge-intensive services that are export competitive have yet to be nurtured. Exports in both countries remain dependent on manufacturing and commodities. While numerous challenges prevail in both countries, especially in terms of their respective growth dilemmas, the two key challenges for moving ahead in services development lie in SOE reform in terms of improving their efficiency and productivity, breaking up state monopolies and removing barriers to entry for non-state players for a more effective engagement of the private sector; and grooming talents that can meet the needs of export competitive, knowledge-intensive services.

Although manufacturing and services can serve as independent drivers of growth, there are synergies between the two sectors. Indeed, as Nederveen

Pieterse (Chapter 1) has pointed out, the development of services in NEA is built on the organizational depth of industry. It is the chaebol conglomerates in South Korea that branched out into services such as hotels and entertainment after successful manufacturing development. Malaysia's post-industrialism without significant industrialism does not bode well for its development of services as an independent driver of growth, while China's manufacturing development is still unfolding even as it shifts toward services development. China's dual strategy of manufacturing and services development will enable it to harness the synergies between the two to boost its current growth problems, although there are also other obstacles to overcome for it to succeed in this transition. Developing countries need to take heed that using services to complement manufacturing development is a better strategy for enhancing manufacturing value added activities for industrial upgrading than targeting selected services for growth, as shown in Malaysia's development strategy. Malaysia, on the other hand, can strive to use its services sector development to link with the rest of SEA and China to increase the growth potential of this sector.

Notes

1 It should be noted that it is only the formal sectors that are explored in this chapter as there are no official data on the informal sectors, be it in manufacturing or services.
2 In international economic statistics, services correspond to International Standard Industrial Classification divisions 50–99, which include value added in wholesale and retail trade (including hotels and restaurants), transport, and government, financial, professional, and personal services such as education, healthcare, and real estate services (The World Bank undated (a)).
3 Whether services include construction and public utilities is controversial (Ochel and Wegner 1987). This chapter follows Malaysia and China's definition by excluding construction from services. Construction is instead included in the definition for industry.
4 It is important to note the higher share of employment in services rather than manufacturing. Moreover, the importance of service employment is likely to be understated as the employment of informal services are not captured. The services sector can therefore be an important source of employment and a shift to services can help to absorb workers released from manufacturing due to this shift, although retooling of skills will be needed.
5 Rasiah (2011) also uses the trend in the fall of share of industry and manufacturing in GDP to indicate the onset of deindustrialization.
6 Ideally, the data used should be the share of manufacturing in GDP and the share of manufacturing employment in total employment. Although the World Bank does provide data on the former, Szirmai *et al.* (2005) and Banister (2005) demonstrate the difficulties in constructing reliable time series data on the manufacturing sector in China due to changes in concepts, coverage and consistency in the published data over time. The literature on China that is written in English uses the term industry rather than manufacturing. But it is important to note that the definition of industry in China includes mining and quarrying, manufacturing, production and supply of electricity, water and gas, and construction while deindustrialization refers to changes in the manufacturing sector alone.

7 The problems with employment data in manufacturing in China are also acknowledged in Rodrik (2015).
8 According to Feng *et al.* (2015, p. ii), the unemployment rate

> averaged 3.9% in 1988–1995, when the labour market was highly regulated and dominated by state-owned enterprises, but rose sharply during the period of mass layoff from 1995–2002, reaching an average of 10.9% in the subperiod from 2002 to 2009.

9 See MIDA undated (a) for further details of these incentives.
10 The Five Year Plans in Malaysia and China are the social and economic blueprints for the development of the respective countries.
11 See Li and Woetzel (2011), www.mckinsey.com/insights/economic_studies/what_chinas_five-year_plan_means_for_business (accessed 18 November 2015).
12 See US Department of State (2014).
13 Details on Malaysia's FDI liberalization policies are extracted from US Department of State (2014).
14 See Minter Ellison (2015).
15 For further details on incentives, see www.mdec.my.
16 See the list of economic corridors of Malaysia in MIDA (undated (b)).
17 This comprised mainly computers and telecommunications equipment and electronics.
18 The 12 areas are oil, gas and energy; palm oil and rubber; financial services; tourism; business services; electronics and electrical; wholesale and retail; education; healthcare; communications content and infrastructure; agriculture; and Greater Kuala Lumpur and the Klang Valley (Malaysia 2010).
19 For more information, please see World Bank's Services Trade Restrictions Database at http://iresearch.worldbank.org/servicetrade/.
20 Refers to the Malays and indigenous people in the country.
21 This is a weighted index of quantitative and qualitative indicators of seven key variables as measured by demographic trends; compulsory education; university education; quality of labour force; talent environment; openness; and proclivity to attracting talents.

References

Athukorala, Prema-chandra and S. Wagle. 2011. Foreign direct investment in Southeast Asia: Is Malaysia falling behind, *ASEAN Economic Bulletin* 28(2): 115–133.

Banister, Judith. 2005. Manufacturing employment in China. 2005. *Monthly Labor Review* July: 12–29.

Bluestone, Barry and Bennett Harrison. 1982. *The Deindustrialization of America: Plant Closings, Community Abandonment, and the Dismantling of Basic Industry*. New York: Basic Books.

Büge, Max, Matias Egeland, Przemyslaw Kowalski, and Monika Sztajerowska. 2013. State-owned enterprises in the global economy: Reason for concern? *OECD Trade Policy Paper, No. 147*, OECD Publishing. www.voxeu.org/article/state-owned-enterprises-global-economy-reason-concern (accessed 2 May 2013).

Chen, Edward. 2015. Financial development in Qianhai: Opportunities and challenges: A position paper for Qianhai Conference 2014. Unpublished paper.

Cheng, Thomas, K. 2015. *Roundtable on Competition Neutrality*. Paris: OECD. www.oecd.org/officialdocuments/publicdisplaydocumentpdf/?cote=DAF/COMP/WD(2015)49&docLanguage=En (accessed 21 February 2016).

Cheong, Kee Cheok, Li Ran, and Zhang Miao. 2015. The Chinese state, state enterprises and the global crisis, (Chapter 2). In Terence E. Gomez, Francois Bafoil, and Kee-cheok Cheong, eds. *Government-linked Companies and Sustainable Equitable Development*. Abingdon: Routledge.

Chin, Yee Whah. 2015. Changes of ownership and identities of Malaysian banks: Ethnicity, state and globalization, *Copenhagen Discussion Papers 51*, August 2015. Asia Research Center: Copenhagen Business School.

Dasgupta, Sukti and Ajit Singh. 2006. Manufacturing, services and premature deindustrialization in developing countries: A Kaldorian analysis. UNU-WIDER Research Paper No. 2006/49. United Nations University-World Institute for Development Economics Research.

Department of Statistics, Malaysia. Undated. ttps://www.statistics.gov.my/index.php?r=column/ctimeseries&menu_id=NHJlaGc2Rlg4ZXlGTjh1SU1kaWY5UT09 (accessed 20 November 2015).

Economic Planning Unit (EPU). 2015. *The Services Sector Blueprint*. Putrajaya: EPU. www.epu.gov.my/sites/default/files/2blueprint.pdf (accessed 12 July 2017).

Economist Intelligence Unit (EIU). 2015. *The Global Talent Index Report: The Outlook to 2015*. Chicago: Heidrick & Struggles.

Ernst, Dieter. 2014. *From Catching Up to Forging Ahead? China's Prospects in Semiconductors*. Honolulu: East-West Center.

Farrell, Diana and Andrew Grant. 2005. Addressing China's looming shortage talent. www.mckinsey.com/insights/china/addressing_chinas_looming_talent_shortage (accessed 20 November 2015).

Felipe, Jesus, Aashish Mehta, and Changyong Rhee. 2014. Manufacturing matters … but it's the jobs that count, *ADB Working Papers No. 420*. Manila: ADB.

Feng, Shuaizhang, Yingyao Hu, and Robert Moffitt. 2015. Long run trends in unemployment and labor trends in China. *NBER Working Paper No. 21460*. www.nber.org/papers/w21460.pdf (accessed 20 November 2015).

Gomez, T.E., Elsa Satkunasingnam, and Lee Hwok Aun. 2015. The state's business, government-linked companies, the financial sector and socioeconomic development in Malaysia (Chapter 5). In Terence E. Gomez, Francois Bafoil, and Kee-cheok Cheong, eds. *Government-linked Companies and Sustainable Equitable Development*. Abingdon: Routledge.

Hirschman, Charles and Akbar Aghajanian. 1980. Women's labor force participation and socio-economic development: The case of peninsular Malaysia, 1957–1970. *Journal of Southeast Asian Studies* XI(1): 30–49.

KPMG. 2015. *China Outlook 2015*. www.kpmg.com/ES/es/Internacionalizacion-KPMG/Documents/China-Outlook-2015.pdf (accessed 20 November 2015).

KPMG. 2016. *The 13th Five Year Plan – China's Transformation and Integration with the World Economy: Opportunities for Chinese and Foreign Businesses*. KPMG International Cooperative. https://assets.kpmg.com/content/dam/kpmg/cn/pdf/en/2016/10/13fyp-opportunities-analysis-for-chinese-and-foreign-businesses.pdf (accessed 21 February 2017).

Kutscher, Ronald, E. and Valerie E. Personik. 1986. Deindustrialization and the shift to services. *Monthly Labor Review* 109: 3.

Li, Guanyu and Jonathan Woetzel. 2011. What China's Five Year Plan means for business. www.mckinsey.com/insights/economic_studies/what_chinas_five-year_plan_means_for_business (accessed 18 November 2015).

Lin, Shuanglin and Zhu Xiaodong. 2007. *Private Enterprises and Chinese Economic Development*. Abingdon: Routledge.

Malaysia. 2010. *Economic Transformation Plan*. Putrajaya: PEMANDU.

Malaysian Investment Development Authority (MIDA). Undated (a). Incentives in services sector. www.mida.gov.my/home/incentives-in-services-sector/posts/ (accessed 18 November 2015).

Malaysian Investment Development Authority (MIDA). Undated (b). Malaysia economic corridors. www.mida.gov.my/home/malaysia-economic-corridors/posts/ (accessed 19 November 2015).

Malaysia Productivity Corporation. Undated. Productivity Report 2013/14. www.mpc.gov.my/home/?kod1=k&kod2=announcement&item=000165&sstr_lang=en (accessed 20 November 2015).

Menon, Jayant and Thiam Hee Ng. 2013. Are government-linked companies crowding out private investment in Malaysia? ADB Working Economics Paper Series No. 345, April. Manila: ADB.

Minter Ellison. 2015. China's foreign investment industries guidance catalogue. 2015 Version. www.minterellison.com/alerts/Alert-China-releases-new-Foreign-Investment-Industries-Guidance-Catalogue/ (accessed 18 November 2015).

National Bureau of Statistics, China. Undated. *China Statistical Yearbook 2015*. www.stats.gov.cn/english/ (accessed 20 November 2015).

Nordas, H.K. and Y. Kim. 2013. The role of services for competitiveness in manufacturing. OECD Trade Policy Papers, No. 148, OECD Publishing.

Ochel, Wolfgang and Manfred Wegner. 1987. *Service Economies in Europe: Opportunities for Growth*. Boulder, Colorado: Pinter Publishers, London and Westview Press.

OECD. 2000. Main determinants and impacts of FDI on China's economy. OECD Working Papers on International Investment, 2000/04. Paris: PECD Publishing.

Out-law.com. Undated. China announces pilot free trade zones. www.out-law.com/en/articles/2015/april/china-announces-pilot-free-trade-zones/ (accessed 21 February 2016).

Palma, Jose Gabriel. 2014. De-industrialization, 'premature' de-industrialization and the Dutch-Disease. incubadora.periodicos.ufsc.br/index.php/necat/article/download/.../4060 (accessed 26 September 2015).

Perkins, D.H. 2015. Understanding the slow growth rate of the People's Republic of China. *Asian Development Review* 32(1): 1–30.

PWC. 2014. A decade of unprecedented growth: China's impact on the semiconductor industry 2014 update. www.pwc.com/gx/en/industries/technology/chinas-impact-on-semiconductor-industry/2014-full-report.html (accessed 29 January 2014).

Raj, Shila Dorai. 2012. State owned enterprises and competitive neutrality. PowerPoint presentation at the OECD Global Forum on Competition, Paris, 16–17 February.

Rasiah, Rajah. 2011. 'Is Malaysia facing negative deindustrialization? *Pacific Affairs* 84(4): 715–736.

Recruitment Program of Global Experts. Undated. www.1000plan.org/en/plan.html (accessed 20 November 2015).

Rizwan, Mohamed, Habeeb Rahuman, Kevin Wong Tho Foo, and Rachel Cho Suet Li. 2014. Agglomeration in practice: The Malaysian experience in diversifying manufacturing. www.bnm.gov.my/documents/conference_vol/2014_Econs_Research/Paper_6_The_Diversification_of_Manufacturing_in_Malaysia.pdf (accessed 19 November 2015).

Rodrik, Dani 2015. Premature deindustrialization. *NBER Working Paper Series 20935*. www.nber.org/papers/w20935 (accessed 10 September 2015).

Rowthorn, Robert and Ramana Ramaswamy. 1997. *Deindustrialization: Causes and Implications*. IMF Working Paper 97/42. Washington, DC: IMF. www.imf.org/external/pubs/ft/wp/wp9742.pdf (accessed 28 September 2015).

Rowthorn, R. and K. Coutts. 2004. De-industrialization and the balance of payments in advanced economies. *UNCTAD Discussion Papers, No. 170*. UNCTAD/OSG/DP/2004/4. http://unctad.org/en/Docs/osgdp20044_en.pdf (accessed 23 May 2016).

Schettkat, Ronald and Lara Yocarini. 2003. The shift to services: A review of the literature. Discussion Paper No. 964, Institute for the Study of Labor (IZA), Bonn.

Scissors, Derek. 2011. Chinese state-owned enterprises and US–China economic relations. Testimony before the U.S.–China Economic and Security Review Commission. 30 March. www.heritage.org/research/testimony/2011/04/chinese-state-owned-enterprises-and-us-china-economic-relations (accessed 2 October 2015).

Sharma, Yojana. 2013. 'Thousand Talents' academic return scheme under review. www.universityworldnews.com/article.php?story=20130524153852829 (accessed 20 November 2015).

State Council of the People's Republic of China. Undated. Made-in China 2025 Plan issued. http://english.gov.cn/policies/latest_releases/2015/05/19/content_281475110703534.htm (accessed 20 November 2015).

Szirmai, Adam, Ruoen Ren, and Manyin Bai. 2005. Chinese manufacturing performance in comparative perspective. Yale University, Economic Growth Center Discussion Paper No. 920. http://aida.econ.yale.edu/growth_pdf/cdp920.pdf (accessed 20 October 2015).

TalentCorp Malaysia. Undated. www.talentcorp.com.my/ (accessed 20 November 2015).

Tham, Siew Yean. 2015. Diversification and industrial policies in Malaysia. In Jesus Felipe, ed. *Development and Modern Industrial Policy in Practice: Issues and Country Experiences* (Chapter 12). Cheltenham: ADB and Edward Elgar.

Tham, Siew Yean and A.J.Y. Kam. 2015a. Malaysia–China trade: Old and new routes. *The Philippine Review of Economics* LII(2): 100–117.

Tham, Siew Yean and A.J.Y. Kam. 2015b. Trade in value added: Case of Malaysia. Economic Research Institute for ASEAN and East Asia (ERIA) Discussion Paper No. 2015-58. Jakarta: ERIA. www.eria.org/ERIA-DP-2015-58.pdf (accessed 15 October 2015).

Tregenna, Fiona. 2011. Manufacturing productivity, deindustrialization, and reindustrialization. UNU-WIDER Working Paper No. 2011/57. United Nations University-World Institute for Development Economics Research.

Tong, Sarah. 2013. Evolving industrial policies in China. In Wang Gangwu and Zheng Yongnian, eds. *China: Development and Governance* (Chapter 14). Singapore: World Scientific.

United Nations Conference on Trade and Development (UNCTAD). 2014. Transfer of technology and knowledge sharing for development: Science, technology and innovation issues for developing countries. *UNCTAD Current Studies on Science, Technology and Innovation, No. 8*. Geneva: UNCTAD.

US Department of State. 2014. Investment climate. www.state.gov/documents/organization/228922.pdf (accessed 18 November 2015).

Wan Khatina Nawawi and Saovanee Chan Somchit. 2014. SOE regulation in Malaysia and the competitive neutrality principle. In *UNCTAD Research Partnership*

Platform: Competitive Neutrality and its Application in Selected Developing Countries. Geneva: UNCTAD.

Wang Huiyao. 2010. China's national talent plan: Key measures and objectives. www.brookings.edu/research/papers/2010/11/23-china-talent-wang (accessed 20 November 2015).

Wang Wei. 2013. Features, restrictions, and policy recommendations in the services sector of the People's Republic of China. *ADB Economics Working Paper Series*, No. 357, July. Manila: ADB.

World Bank. Undated (a). Services, etc. valued added (% of GDP). http://data.worldbank.org/indicator/NV.SRV.TETC.ZS (accessed 21 February 2016).

World Bank. Undated (b). Services trade restrictions database. http://iresearch.worldbank.org/servicetrade/ (accessed 2 June 2016).

World Bank. 2005. *World Development Indicators 2005.* Washington, DC: The World Bank.

World Bank. 2010. Foreign direct investment – the China story. www.worldbank.org/en/news/feature/2010/07/16/foreign-direct-investment-china-story (accessed 20 November 2015).

World Trade Organization (WTO). Undated. www.wto.org/english/res_e/statis_e/statis_e.htm (accessed 20 November 2015).

Xing, Yuqing. 2013. Rethinking the success of China's high-tech exports. In Wang Gangwu and Zheng Yongnian, eds. *China: Development and Governance* (Chapter 23). Singapore: World Scientific.

Xu, Xiaoming and Yanyang Yan. 2014. Does government investment crowd out private investment in China? *Journal of Economic Policy Reform* 17(1): 1–12.

Yap, Xiao Shan and Rajah Rasiah. 2015. Sticky spots on slippery slopes: The development of the integrated circuits industry in emerging East Asia. Globelics Working Paper Series, No. 2015–05. www.globelics.org/publication/sticky-spots-on-slippery-slopes-the-development-of-the-integrated-circuits-industry-in-emerging-east-asia/ (accessed 15 October 2015).

Yue, Pan and Simon Evenett. 2010. Moving up the value chain: Upgrading China's manufacturing sector. International Institute for Sustainable Development (IISD). www.iisd.org (accessed 20 October 2015).

Yusuf, S. and K. Nabeshima. 2009. *Tigers under Threat: The Search for a New Growth Strategy by Malaysia and its Southeast Asian Neighbors.* Washington, DC, World Bank.

11 Economic diplomacy in ASEAN

The case of Myanmar and China investment relations

Sufian Jusoh

Introduction

Within the context of the economic diplomacy between ASEAN and China, examining Myanmar's changing relationship with China is important as the two countries are long-standing trade and investment partners, while Myanmar is an important partner in ASEAN. Myanmar is an important country for China, as the latter is resource-seeking. China is also seeking access to the Andaman Sea and the Indian Ocean so that it can bypass the busy sea route of the Straits of Malacca and South China Sea. Myanmar is therefore an important part of the China's road and belt policy. Myanmar views China as an important source of capital, investment and trade. China provided the much needed investment to Myanmar during the years of economic sanctions by the western powers. However, political reforms in Myanmar has led to the withdrawal of much of the economic sanctions and increasing changes in the domestic economy. Myanmar's new approach toward trade and investment is beginning to draw new trade and investment partners from other parts of the world, including directly from the West or from third country ties with the West, and it is starting to distance itself from China's interests. Western powers see Myanmar as an important buffer in Southeast Asia to check China's political and economic expansion into the Indian Ocean region.

The chapter examines the changing investment relationship between China and Myanmar due to changes in Myanmar's investment policies. These changes are part of Myanmar's economic reforms after the opening up of the country. The chapter also discusses Myanmar's investment policy reforms and how these affect its economic diplomacy practices with China. Myanmar's economic diplomacy practice through the reform process is also seen from the overall perspective of ASEAN's economic diplomacy practices. The reform process in Myanmar is compared with the reform process undertaken by China, which also shares the same policy objective, which is to attract more foreign direct investment into the country. However, the investment policy reform process in Myanmar has taken place after the political reform process, unlike the situation in China. China's investment policy reform is not driven by the country's political reform process but rather it is based on the need to attract higher quality investments into the country. Consequently, Chinese investors may have to change the way they conduct and implement their investments in Myanmar, as Myanmar has alternative sources of investment due to the ongoing reforms.

ASEAN economic diplomacy

Economic diplomacy has gained increasing attention from major economies at the end the Cold War as a means for enhancing economic prosperity (Bayne and Woolcock 2007). Economic diplomacy may involve several pillars: a free trade system; securing long-term and stable supply of resources, energy and food; international promotion of infrastructure system and promotion of one's country as a tourism-oriented nation (Maehara 2011). Economic diplomacy however is broad and elastic (Bayne and Woolcock 2007), depending on the economic needs and the demands of the country practicing it, in advancing the home country's external economic interests (Rana and Chatterjee 2011).

The Association of Southeast Asian Nations (ASEAN), formed on 8 August 1967, originally comprised Indonesia, Malaysia, the Philippines, Singapore and Thailand, and later expanded to include Brunei, Cambodia, Lao PDR, Myanmar and Vietnam. Compared with the European Union, for example, ASEAN started as a political organization whereas the EU started as the European Economic Community under the Treaty of Rome 1957.

When ASEAN embarked on the ASEAN Vision 2020 in 1997, ASEAN's GDP was US$694 billion. Based on a compound annual growth rate (CAGR) of 5 percent, ASEAN's economy should reach US$1 trillion by 2005 and US$2 trillion in 2020 (IMF 2014). According to the Asian Development Bank, if ASEAN were one economy, it would be the seventh largest in the world with a combined GDP of US$2.4 trillion in 2013 and it could be fourth largest by 2050, if the current growth trend continues.

ASEAN is a large market, with about 625 million people, larger than North America or the European Union, of whom 60 percent of them are youths. ASEAN is situated between two major economies, China and India, which are collaborators and competitors to the region. It is also strategically located within the old and new international trade routes, namely the old Maritime Silk Road, which covered trade between the Middle East, and North-east Asia. The maritime sea route covers the South China Sea, the Straits of Malacca and the Straits of Singapore, three of the busiest shipping lanes in the world.

Although started for geo-political reasons, ASEAN soon developed into an important economic region, especially through the ASEAN Declaration and various initiatives including the Bali Accords I, II and III and the ASEAN Charter. As stated in the ASEAN Declaration, among the aims and objectives of ASEAN are to accelerate economic growth, social progress and cultural development in the region in order to strengthen the foundation for a prosperous and peaceful community of Southeast Asian nations. ASEAN economic cooperation started in earnest with the creation of the ASEAN Free Trade Area (AFTA) through the Agreement on a Common Effective Preferential Tariff of the ASEAN Free Trade Area (CEPT-AFTA) in 1992, which was replaced by the ASEAN Agreement in Trade in Goods (ATIGA), followed by the ASEAN Framework Agreement on Trade in Services (AFAS) and the various agreements relating to investment.

The ASEAN Economic Community (AEC), as part of the larger ASEAN Community, was launched at the end of 2015. The regional grouping adopts the practice of economic diplomacy, in its engagement with the global economic community through the concept of 'Global ASEAN'. This engagement can be traced back to the Bali Concord III, where ASEAN is promoted as a region fully integrated into the global economy.

Likewise, the ASEAN 2025 Forging Ahead Together (ASEAN 2015) envisions a peaceful, stable and resilient ASEAN Community with enhanced capacity to respond effectively to challenges, and as an outward-looking region within a global community of nations, while maintaining ASEAN centrality.

ASEAN embraces economic diplomacy by entering into negotiations for various economic agreements, such as the bilateral investment treaties (BIT) and preferential trade agreements (PTAs) (see Table 11.1), with the aim of enhancing ASEAN and ASEAN Member States' position as attractive investment destinations, either for natural resource seeking, market seeking, efficiency seeking or strategic asset seeking investments (Jusoh 2014; Chaisse and Jusoh 2016).

Table 11.1 ASEAN PTAs with dialogue partners

ASEAN + dialogue partners PTA	*Date of signing and entry into force*
Australia and New Zealand: ASEAN–Australia–New Zealand Free Trade Area (AANZFTA)	Signed: 27 February 2009 Come into force: 2010 for Australia, New Zealand, Brunei, Malaysia, Myanmar, the Philippine, Singapore and Viet Nam. 1.1.2011 & 4.1.2011 for Laos and Cambodia. 10.1.2012 for Indonesia
Korea: ASEAN – Korea Free Trade Area (AKFTA)	Signed: June 2009 Enter into force: 1 September 2009
China: ASEAN – China Free Trade Area (ACFTA)	Signed: 15 August 2009 Enter into force: 1 January 2010
Japan: ASEAN – Japan Comprehensive Economic Partnership	Signed: 14 April 2008 Enter into force: 1 December 2008
India: ASEAN – India Trade in Goods Agreement	Signed: 13 August 2009 Enter into force: 1 January 2010

Source: compiled by author.

Nevertheless, ASEAN as an organization does not have the competency to negotiate these agreements as a group, unlike the European Union. ASEAN instead negotiates these agreements through all of its members rather than as a unified organization.

One of the most important ASEAN instruments which can act as a tool in economic diplomacy for ASEAN and ASEAN Member State is the ASEAN Comprehensive Investment Agreement (ACIA). ACIA is the result of an evolution in the ASEAN framework on investment. ACIA was preceded by the ASEAN Agreement on the Promotion and Protection of Investments (1987) (ASEAN IGA) and amending Protocol as well as by the Framework Agreement on the ASEAN Investment Area (1998) (AIA) and its amending Protocol. ASEAN economic officials and trade diplomats may utilize the ACIA to attract investments into ASEAN as it contains provisions that are critical to businesses and investors. These provisions cover the liberalization of investment restrictions; the protection of investors and their investments; and the settlement of investment disputes (Chaisse and Jusoh 2016).

ACIA is an important economic diplomacy tool for ASEAN as it extends protection to non-ASEAN Member States' investors by allowing them to become an ASEAN Investor. This can be done first by a non-ASEAN investor establishing a juridical entity, which carries out substantial business in one of the ASEAN Member States. This entity can later become an ASEAN Investor by establishing another juridical entity in its target destination of investment in another ASEAN Member State. Thus, it is important for ASEAN Member States, especially the newer ASEAN Member States such as Myanmar, to adopt the standards set in the ASEAN agreements into their domestic policies.

Overview of Myanmar's investment climate

The Republic of the Union of Myanmar or Myanmar lies in a very strategic location between China to the northeast, India and Bangladesh to the west and northwest and Thailand and Lao PDR to the east. This makes Myanmar an important economic destination as it is situated in one of the most economically dynamic and important regions in Southeast Asia. In 2015, Myanmar has about 59 million people, with more than 135 ethnic groups. Many of the ethnic groups are Sino-Tibetan whilst the main religion is Buddhism, inherited from India more than a thousand years ago. Myanmar became a British colony in 1885 and was ruled directly from India, which also influenced the government and civil service system, the laws and policies and the court system in the country. Internationally, Myanmar is a member of the United Nations, the World Trade Organization (WTO) and ASEAN.

After more than 50 years in economic isolation, Myanmar, once a wealthy country in Southeast Asia, is now one of the poorest countries in Southeast Asia. The economy has largely stagnated since 1997 due to poor macroeconomic management, a large public sector debt, economic sanctions, and a sharp decline in foreign investment (Asian Development Bank 2014). In 2012, its GDP in current US dollars was estimated at $56 billion, making its per capita income $876 ($1405 in purchasing-power parity terms) one of the lowest in Asia (IMF 2014).

Agriculture dominates Myanmar's economic structure, accounting for 31 percent of GDP, but over 50 percent of employment (Asian Development Bank 2014). This indicates that productivity in the sector is significantly lower than the average for the economy as a whole. It also helps explain low urbanization, with only 33 percent of the population living in urban areas in 2012. Industry, which includes mining and natural gas and energy, and services respectively accounts for about 32 percent and 38 percent of GDP. In comparison, the average of ASEAN member states' shares of agriculture, industry and services in GDP are, respectively, 12 percent, 47 percent and 41 percent (Asian Development Bank 2014).

Prior to the closing of the country and after the opening up, Myanmar had been and continues to be an important trade and investment destination for natural resource seeking investment, as it is rich in natural resources. It also attracts market-seeking investment as it has a relatively large population, with increasing income. Efficiency-seeking investments are also attracted by the country's ambition to become an export hub while strategic asset seeking investments such as those seeking banking and financial services licenses also see opportunities in the expanding and growing economy.

The ASEAN Business Outlook Survey 2014 by the American Chambers of Commerce finds that Myanmar is one of the most attractive countries for new business expansion in ASEAN, apart from Indonesia, Vietnam and Thailand (US Chamber of Commerce 2015). Myanmar has been receiving a steady inflow of foreign direct investments (FDI) into the country, as shown in Figure 11.1.

Based on the UNCTAD data, Myanmar has seen the progress in FDI inflow between US$1.1 billion in 2011 to US$2824 billion in 2015. There is also an increase of inward FDI stock from US$15.6 billion in 2011 to US$20.5 billion at the end of 2015. Nevertheless, FDI inflow into Myanmar is still small compared with the overall FDI inflows into ASEAN (Figure 11.2). But, Myanmar is catching up fast with its peers in the region, especially compared with Cambodia and Lao PDR.

According to the figure released by the Directorate of Investment and Company Administration (DICA) of the Ministry of Finance and Planning of Myanmar, a great majority of the investments is still in the natural resources sector, led by oil and gas.

Nevertheless, investors will have to assess the political and legal risks when investing in countries such as Myanmar. As discussed in the 2012 Political Risk Survey conducted by The Multilateral Investment Guarantee Agency (MIGA) and the Economist Intelligence Unit (EIU), 'political risk' is now the most significant constraint on operation of FDI (MIGA 2012). Investors

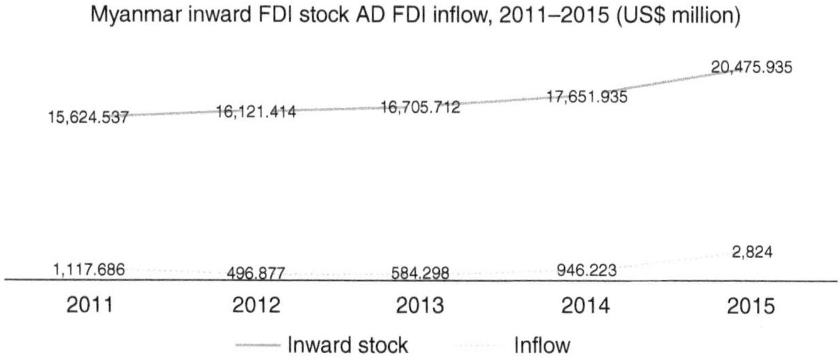

	Year				
	2011	*2012*	*2013*	*2014*	*2015*
Inward FDI stock (US$ million)	15,624.54	16,121.41	16,705.71	17,651.94	20,475.94
FDI inflow (US$ million)	11,17.686	496.877	584.298	946.223	2,824.00

Source: UNCTAD (2017).

Figure 11.1 Myanmar FDI inflow and inward stock, 2011–2015.

are mainly concerned with transparency and investment facilitation, investor protection and strength of institutions such as the legal system.

Investors' main question is whether Myanmar's investment policies are robust enough to overcome the concerns of the investors. Firms surveyed by MIGA – EIU identified several types of political risk as critical. These are, in order of preference: adverse regulatory changes, breach of contracts, transfer and convertibility restrictions, civil disturbance, dishonoring government guarantees, expropriation and nationalization in cases of terrorism and war. Political risk plays a more important role in the investment decision-making process over a longer period of time as compared with issues of macroeconomic stability and access to financing. The Economist Corporate Network survey finds that investors are concerned about uncertain legal environments, especially in the protection of domestic markets in certain ASEAN Member States such as Myanmar. The respondents are concerned that governments may change their mind over legal issues and important legislation with little warning and court decisions may be highly arbitrary.

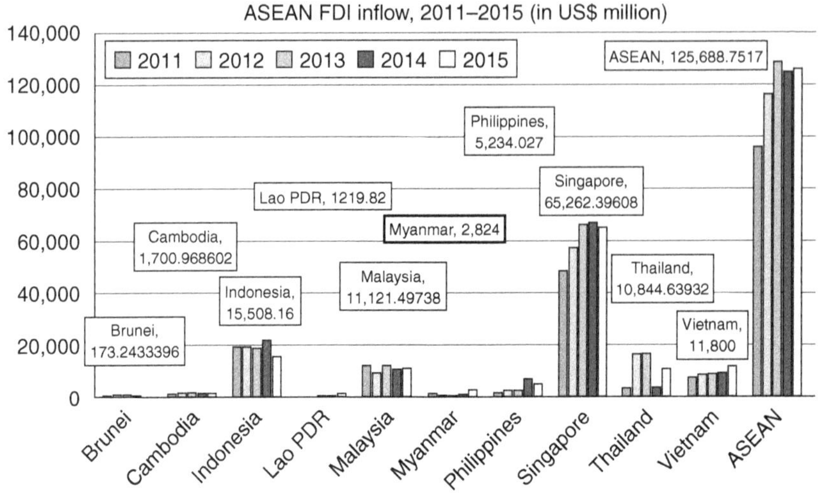

	Year				
	2011	*2012*	*2013*	*2014*	*2015*
Brunei	691.1703	864.9055	775.642	567.8897	173.2433
Cambodia	1,372.48	1,835.223	1,872.403	1,720.122	1,700.969
Indonesia	19,241.25	19,137.87	18,816.66	21,865.66	15,508.16
Lao PDR	300.75	294.38	426.67	720.84	1,219.82
Malaysia	12,197.58	9,238.831	12,115.47	10,877.35	11,121.5
Myanmar	1,117.686	496.877	584.298	946.223	2,824
Philippines	1,851.579	2,449.312	2,429.502	6,812.747	5,234.027
Singapore	48,329.04	57,149.75	66,066.89	68,495.56	65,262.4
Thailand	3,270.988	16,517.22	16,651.85	3,536.535	10,844.64
Vietnam	7,519	8,368	8,900	9,200	11,800
ASEAN	95,891.52	116,352.4	128,639.4	12,4742.9	12,5688.8

Source: UNCTAD (2017).

Figure 11.2 Myanmar FDI inflow compared with ASEAN, 2011–2015.

Myanmar and China economic diplomacy in investment

Myanmar and China's investment is linked with the trade relationship between the two countries. Trade and investment are interdependent in the age of global value chains (GVCs). At the same time, the traditional notions of investment and trade only relating to main sectors or tangible products are slowly being eroded by the increase in the cross-border trade in services, making investment in services through commercial presence ever more important. Thus, investment flow between countries must also be linked to the flow of trade in goods and trade in services as there are strong positive and self-reinforcing relationships between bilateral trade and FDI flows (Chaisrisawatsuk 2007).

For Myanmar and China, their trade and investment relation is part of the economic diplomacy within both country's economic and foreign policy objectives as both countries are considered as strategic partners with each other. Economic diplomacy for China and Myanmar include attracting investment and increasing trade, especially export from the country to the world market. Investment-related diplomacy involves all four types of investments, namely natural resource seeking, efficiency seeking, market-seeking and strategic asset seeking (Jusoh 2014; World Bank 2010).

In addition, Myanmar – being a newly opened economy – also seeks economic and technical aid, which is not normally practiced in the commercial diplomacy. Myanmar's economic diplomacy also focuses on increasing exports, attracting foreign direct investment and participating in work of the international economic organizations such as the WTO.

For China, economic diplomacy with Myanmar fits within its overall economic diplomacy goals. These goals have two main elements, namely promoting national interests and strategic economic goals by economic means through international contacts by the government, government agencies and officials (Zhou 1996). Chinese leaders have called for their country's transformation into a 'strong trading power' by working on reforms to deepen its integration with Asia as a region, modify international trade rules and standards, and secure needed technology, resources and markets to improve China's competiveness and national security (Heath 2016). It has been argued that China's approach to economic diplomacy evolved as its power grew and its needs diverged from those of its chief competitor, the United States. Medeiros (2009) defines the Chinese concept of economic diplomacy as the use of trade, investment, and, increasingly, finance policies to support China's diplomatic goals and the use of classic diplomacy to advance China's economic development, such as by ensuring access to foreign markets.

In its relation with Myanmar, China seeks to enhance its economic position by seeking resources that are abundant in its neighbor. Trade between Myanmar and China is heavily dependent on border trade, which makes-up the bulk of the bilateral trade. Border trade made up about 50 percent of China's exports to Myanmar and about 70 percent of its imports from Myanmar during the period 2000–2007, mainly with the Yunnan province (Ferrarini 2013).

According to Ferrarini (2013), up to 2010, more than one third of Myanmar's imports are sourced from China alone, with more than 70 percent of its in manufactured goods. Myanmar imports from China a broad range of capital and consumption goods and it relies up to 60–80 percent on China as a supplier of these goods, including motorcycles, cars and heavy goods vehicles. Myanmar's export basket is biased toward fuels (natural gas), food and other primary commodities (including precious stones and gems), which together constitute nearly 90 percent of total exports between 2006 and 2010. The top exports to China are timber, ores, pearls and precious stones, natural rubber, vegetables and fruit, fish and crustaceans, which broadly also resemble Myanmar's exports within ASEAN.

When Myanmar was under complete sanctions by the Western powers, it had to look for trade and investment from friendly neighbors, mainly China, Malaysia and Singapore. Between 2005 and 2012, FDI approvals have been dominated by investments from China, Thailand, Hong Kong (China) and Korea, and almost one half of total approvals occurred in 2010. Together with Hong Kong, Chinese firms represent 61 percent of realized investment or almost one half of total approved investment (OECD 2014b). Chinese investors may also be involved in projects financed in part by investors from other countries.

Only three OECD member countries, France, the United Kingdom and Korea are in the top ten in terms of total cumulative approved investments in Myanmar during the period. Chinese investment may well be understated, even if investment from Hong Kong, China is added, because some Chinese investment may go through the British Virgin Islands or the Cayman Islands (Ferrarini 2013). Some Chinese investment in joint ventures with military controlled enterprises may not be reported to the Central Statistical Office (CSO).

For China, the primary motive for investing in Myanmar is to meet the energy needs of Yunnan province where oil prices are, by one estimate, 30 percent above those of Eastern China (Ferrarini 2013).

Major Chinese investments include oil and gas pipelines, such as the Shwe Natural Gas Pipeline, numerous dams such as the Myitsone Dam and several mines, such as the Myanmar Taguang Taung Mine for nickel ore and the Letpadaung (Monywa) copper mine. The Letpadaung (or Monywa) open pit copper mine opened in 1980 with the largest deposit of copper in Southeast Asia and is a joint venture between Wanbao, owned by China's state-owned arms producer Norinco, and Myanmar Economic Holdings, a military-owned conglomerate. This investment had provoked protests from local residents on numerous issues such as alleged land grabbing, lack of compensation and damage to the environment.

The Shwe Natural Gas Pipeline and the Burma–China Oil Transport Project are to carry oil and gas from the Bay of Bengal across Myanmar to China. The US$29 billion project is a joint venture with the state-owned Myanmar Oil and Gas Enterprise (MOGE) and investors from China, India and Korea. In addition, the Yadana project to produce natural gas in the Andaman Sea 60 km offshore and to transport the gas via a 346 km subsea pipeline and then 63 km onshore to the Thai border is undertaken by Total (France) which has a 31.2 percent interest, with the rest held by Chevron (US), PTT (Thailand) and MOGE as the local partner.

The Taguang Taung Nickel Ore mine is the biggest cooperative mining project between China and Myanmar. It is a joint investment between the China Nonferrous Group and Taiyuan Iron and Steel Group (TISCO), two

Chinese companies, and it is expected to provide 85,000 tons of high grade ferro-nickel annually for supply to China.

In addition, China Power Investments Corporation plans to invest US$20 billion in a series of dams on the upper Irrawaddy River, including the Myisitone dam, which was suspended by the government in September 2011. Another series of six dams has been approved on the Salween River, involving predominantly Chinese investors but also local enterprises and the Electricity Generation Authority of Thailand. These six dams will provide an estimated 15,000 MW of installed capacity, including the TaSang dam, which will be the largest in Myanmar and the tallest in Southeast Asia.

Major issues with China's investments in Myanmar range from collaborations with the former military regime, land grabbing and a lack of respect for the rule of law, human rights and local culture. Many non-governmental organizations are against Chinese investments for the same reasons.

Myanmar's investment policy reform

As part of its international economic diplomacy, to ensure that Myanmar continues to attract quality investments that include those with responsible business conduct, Myanmar has started to diversify its sources of investment from countries in ASEAN, Europe, Japan, Korea and the USA. The economic diplomacy covers various activities such as investment promotion and taking part in internationally driven activities such as taking part in international surveys, for example Ease of Doing Business ranking by the World Bank Group, the Investment Policy Review by the OECD and the Trade Policy Review by the World Trade Organization (WTO 2014).

Most importantly, Myanmar is sending signals around the world, mostly outside China that investors and investments are welcome in Myanmar, and that Myanmar investment laws and policies are based on internationally acceptable standards of treatment, liberalization, protections and dispute prevention and settlement.

There are several activities conducted by Myanmar in order to gain the trust of investors. One is to review the investment law and policy with the assistance from the World Bank and the OECD, funded by the United Kingdom and Australia. Investment promotion activities are also undertaken, mostly sponsored by the host countries such as the United Kingdom, Japan, South Korea and the USA. The third type of activity is the direct engagement at the government-to-government level by entering into bilateral investment treaties and free trade agreement with investment chapters, generally known as International Investment Agreement (IIAs).

In reviewing its investment policies, Myanmar adopts the internationally acceptable standards, based on the OECD Policy Framework for Investments. Three principles apply throughout the Framework: policy coherence, transparency in policy formulation and implementation, and regular evaluation of the impact of existing and proposed policies (OECD 2014b). Myanmar, upon the recommendations of the OECD Investment Policy roped in the World Bank Trade and Competitiveness team to assist them in adopting the internationally acceptable standard in investment policy. Myanmar agreed to prepare a new investment law that covers both domestic and foreign investment that is clear, succinct and based on the principles of international best international practices, including principles that are already applicable to most foreign investment in Myanmar through IIAs that Myanmar has concluded.

The new Myanmar Investment Law, based on the best standard in terms of investor protection, investment entry and investment incentives, was passed by Parliament in October 2016. In terms of investor protection, the new law goes beyond what was included in the Foreign Investment Law 2012 and the Citizen Investment Law 2013. The new law adopts best practice standards for the treatment of investors, including a strong guarantee of currency (profit/capital) transfer, which normally applies only to foreign or non-resident investors. It also adopts the criteria on residency and not on nationality to define who is a foreign investor. This implies that a Myanmar citizen who is a non-resident and invests in Myanmar (i.e. an ex-patriate) will then enjoy the same benefits as a foreign investor based on that provision.

The new law further offers a strong protection against the risk of expropriation, both direct and indirect. In addition, the new law also offers a strong guarantee of non-discrimination. The strongest standard internationally is one that included national treatment (NT), most favored nation (MFN) and Fair and Equitable Treatment (FET). Including all three would be the highest and most desirable level of protection for a foreign investor in any country.

Myanmar is also working toward a high standard of judicial system, as the new law offers a strong dispute resolution provision. In the field of investment, a dispute resolution provision that does not offer many options to investors (from national courts, to domestic and foreign arbitration) is unlikely to be considered as best practice by the international and investor communities. Domestic citizens have constitutional rights to sue the State and foreign investors should at least be covered by the strongest guarantees possible. Finally, the new law extends these guarantees to investors without any need for prior agreement.

In addressing investment entry, the new law defines very clearly who can invest and where, what restrictions to foreign investment may exist either at horizontal or at sectoral level, on what is known as the Negative List. The Negative List will be attached to the law as a notification.

At present, what makes the Myanmar's investment policy subject to criticism is its Negative List as there are too many sectors subject to restrictions. Many sectors are also subject to foreign investment ceiling, which is, in effect, a forced joint venture. Many projects will have to undergo Myanmar Investment Commission (MIC) permits even for applying for a piece of land. To be able to invest in Myanmar, investors may have to require a permit if they invest in sectors requiring a permit under Section 36 of the Myanmar Investment Law; or to seek an endorsement if they seek to acquire land or fiscal investors when investing in sectors not requiring a permit. Investors investing in restricted sectors but not requiring permits or endorsement will be required to issue a notification of their investment to the MIC.

In addition to introducing a new investment Law, Myanmar has also started negotiating bilateral investment treaties with the European Union, in addition to existing bilateral investment treaties with China, India, Japan, Korea, the Philippines, Thailand, Israel, Laos and Vietnam. Myanmar has also engaged in investment treaty negotiations with Russia, Mongolia, Bangladesh, Iran, Serbia, and Hong Kong, China. In 2013, the United States and Myanmar signed a Trade and Investment Framework Agreement. The United States and Myanmar have not yet engaged in discussions on bilateral investment treaty or a free trade agreement.

Myanmar, through its membership in ASEAN, has also signed various preferential trade agreements with investment chapters such as the ASEAN–Australia New Zealand Free Trade Agreement, the ASEAN–China Free Trade Agreement and the ASEAN–Korea Free Trade Agreement.

China's investment policy reform

China is an important destination for international investment. China attracted US$118 billion in worldwide foreign direct investment (FDI) in 2013, second only to the United States, mainly due to its high sustained high economic growth rate prior to its economic slowdown in 2015 and its large domestic market. Compared with Myanmar, China attracts three main types of investment, i.e. efficiency-seeking, market-seeking and strategic asset-seeking. On the other hand, most of the natural-resource seeking investments are conducted by Chinese investors in their own country or by Chinese investors investing abroad. In 2013, China's outbound FDI amounted to a historic high of US$107.84 billion. By the end of 2013, 15,300 domestic investors have established 25,400 enterprises overseas to make direct investment around 184 countries and regions. China's combined outbound FDI stock totaled US$660.48 billion (Ministry of Commerce, China, 2014).

As in the case of other host economies, China has initiated several reforms of its investment policy, either through domestic measures or through international initiatives, including negotiating a high-standard International Investment Agreements (IIA) with the United States. The IIA negotiations with the United States is based on the US model Bilateral Investment Treaty (BIT), which covers both the 'pre-establishment' and 'post-establishment' phases of investment, and delineates a clear 'negative list' of negotiated exceptions. In addition, China has entered into the ASEAN–China FTA and China–Japan–Korea FTA and it is also involved in the negotiations of Regional Cooperation Economic Partnership (RCEP) Agreement, which includes ASEAN and its Plus partners.

Although China tries to show the world that the China is willing to accept internationally acceptable standards through IIAs, the national investment law is far from satisfactory, as it restricts foreign investments that are deemed not to be in its national interest or that might compete with state-sanctioned monopolies or other favored domestic firms.

Similar to Myanmar's Foreign Investment Law 2012 and the Citizen Investment Law 2013, China's investment laws are fragmented into several domestic laws. Such laws include Article 18 of the Constitution, which allows foreign enterprises and other economic organizations or individuals to invest in China; the China–Foreign Equity Joint Venture Enterprise Law 1979, which marked the beginning of the establishment of China's foreign investment legal regime; the China–Foreign Equity Joint Venture Enterprise Law; the China–Foreign Cooperative Joint Venture Enterprise Law, and the Foreign-Invested Enterprise Law, which includes the relevant administrative regulations issued by the State Council.[1] China also has special investment rules for the Central, Western, and Northeastern regions through the *Catalogue of Priority Industries for Foreign Investment in the Central-Western Regions*, which outlines incentives to attract investment in targeted sectors to those parts of China.

Nevertheless, Myanmar's mode of liberalization, as part of the ASEAN Comprehensive Investment Agreement (ACIA), allowing for easier access to investors and their investments, is not reflected in China's domestic law. Myanmar is undertaking a process of reducing sectors contained in the Negative List. On the other hand, China's *Catalogue for the Guidance of Foreign Investment in Industries* (Foreign Investment Catalogue, or Catalogue), most recently revised in December 2011, reflects China's higher level of restrictions on market access where there are more sectors included in the 'restricted' and 'prohibited' sectors.

Although investment in sectors not listed in the Catalogue is considered as permitted, transparency is a key issue in the China's investment laws. Transparency is a very important component in the reform taking place in Myanmar, while it is still an issue in China. China's Catalogue has inherent contradictions between it and other measures, such as a provincial sectoral negative list, and this has confused investors and added to the perception that investment guidelines do not provide a secure basis for business planning. Even in 'encouraged' and 'permitted' sectors, regulations apart from the Catalogue often detail additional restrictions on the specific forms of investment that are allowed. Chinese regulators have maintained the flexibility to ignore the Catalogue's guidance in some instances, and to restrict or approve foreign investment for reasons other than those specified. The government may also adopt new regulations or establish industrial policies that supersede the most recently published edition of the Catalogue.

Many investors feel that China does not offer a level playing field between domestic and foreign investors. This raises the need to have a national treatment provision in the domestic law as planned for the new Myanmar Investment Law, in addition to the same types of provision in the IIAs. Many investors find that China protects and promotes State-owned enterprises

(SOEs), imposes an equity cap, restricts foreign ownership in many industries, provides weak intellectual property protection, has not managed to reduce corruption and it has also an unreliable legal system. Investors also find it difficult to understand many regulations, which are mainly in the Chinese language and contain undefined key terms and standards, which are often applied in an inconsistent manner by different regulatory entities and localities. The complaints by investors are all too familiar as in the case Myanmar. However, during the reform process in Myanmar, most documents are now available in the English language in addition to the local Myanmar language. Most of the Myanmar officials are also able to communicate in the English language with foreign investors.

Another area that affects China's investment laws is the admission of investors and their investments, which is still subject to screening on a case by case basis and subject to review by multiple government agencies. China claims to provide national treatment after an investment has been established, but not before. Foreign investors may only invest where allowed by laws, regulations, and rules, in specified areas or industries, and are required to obtain ratification for planned investment projects and to establish companies. In some industries, such as the telecommunication industry, foreign investors are also required to obtain approval from relevant industry regulators. Separate approval processes also govern land use.

The admission process is very cumbersome and outdated compared with the new approach to be adopted by Myanmar. Under the new Myanmar Investment Law, as discussed above, Myanmar will do away with admission screening for most investments. To be able to invest in Myanmar, investors require a permit if they invest in sectors requiring permits under Section 36 of the Law; or to seek an endorsement if they seek to acquire land or fiscal incentives in sectors not requiring an MIC permit.

Nevertheless, Myanmar faces a big challenge in implementing the new Myanmar Investment Law. There is a shortage of experienced officers to review applications for investment Permits or endorsement. The move toward federalism under the new law also means that some decisions for endorsement for land rights and incentives for investors are to be made at the sub-national levels, by the state and regional government. This, at best, amounts to an experiment of federalism by the National League of Democracy (NLD) led Government. The MIC needs to develop a clear guideline on how the dual system of investment endorsement is going to work. The MIC needs to train and build capacity of its staff in Yangon, Nay Pyi Taw and other locations in the country. The MIC also needs to reduce discretion and increase predictability and transparency in the decision-making process in order to reduce the incidence of corruption, abuse of power or capture by interested stakeholders.

On the other hand, in China, as a result of many issues raised by the foreign investors, following the Third Plenum of the 18th Party Congress, the Chinese Communist Party issued a report which includes broadening foreign investment access in China, exploring the possibility of providing national treatment at all phases of investment, including market access (i.e. the 'pre-establishment' phase of investment), and using a 'negative list' approach in identifying exception and establishing more free trade zones such as the newly-established and still-evolving Shanghai Pilot Free Trade Zone.

In the Report, China intends to unify laws and regulations governing foreign and domestic investment. The reform is to support the *12th Five Year Plan for Utilization of Overseas Capital and Investment Abroad*, issued by the National Development and Reform Commission (NDRC), which promises to guide more foreign direct investment to an identified set of strategic and newly emerging industries (SEIs). Among the identified SEIs are energy efficiency and environmental technologies, next-generation information technology, biotechnology, advanced equipment manufacturing, new energy sectors, new materials, and new-energy vehicles, while 'strictly' limiting FDI in energy and resource intensive and environmentally damaging industries.

In January 2015, China issued a new draft for the Foreign Investment Law that intends to reform the primary foreign investment laws, i.e. the Law on Wholly Foreign-Owned Enterprises, the Law on Sino-Foreign Equity Joint Ventures and the Law on Sino-Foreign Contractual Joint Ventures. Although China's new approach is to set a unified investment law, as in the case of Myanmar Investment Law, the unified law only deals with foreign investors and their investments, whereas the Myanmar Investment Law deals with the rights and obligations of both domestic and foreign investors. In addition, China's new unified law will not reform the SOEs, which continue to dominate the economy. In contrast, the approach in Myanmar is to apply the same law to all forms of investors and investments.

In addition, the draft Foreign Investment Law of China refrains from regulating the corporate form of foreign-invested enterprises ('FIEs'). This suggests that FIEs, like Chinese domestic enterprises, will be subject to a generic body of Chinese corporate law, as currently embodied in such laws as the Company Law, the Partnership Law and the Individual Wholly-owned Enterprise Law, in terms of incorporation, corporate governance, liquidation and other corporate matters. The draft Foreign Investment Law also adopts a 'negative list' approach in regulating market entry of foreign investors. This is a practice already somewhat tested in the China (Shanghai) Pilot Free Trade Zone. The State Council (China's cabinet) will publish a 'negative list' to set out industries where foreign investment is restricted or prohibited as well as investments that exceed certain investment amount thresholds set by the State Council. Foreign businesses not operating in industries identified as 'restricted' or 'prohibited' in the negative list with proposed investments below the related investment amount thresholds may proceed to corporate registration without the need for any market entry approval. This is different from the reform process in Myanmar where there is no threshold imposed on investments. So long as investments are not within the restricted or prohibited sectors, investors may freely invest in Myanmar.

Chapter 4 of the draft Foreign Investment Law tries to reform the current national security review regime China created during Mr Wen Jiabao's tenure as China's premier. The scope of review ('where foreign investment infringes upon, or may infringe upon, national security', a formulation seemingly modeled on the US CFIUS approach) appears far broader than earlier references to the scope of such a review. For example, according to the Circular of the General Office of the State Council on Establishing the National Security Review System for Mergers and Acquisitions of Domestic Enterprises by Foreign Investors, the scope of national security review for Merger & Acquisitions transactions covers

> foreign investors' acquisition of domestic military manufacturing and related ancillary enterprises, acquisition of enterprises in the vicinity of key and sensitive military facilities, and acquisition of other enterprises related to national defense; foreign investors' acquisition of enterprises related to national security in such fields as involving important agricultural products, important energy and resources, important infrastructure, important transportation services, key technologies and major equipment manufacturing, which acquisition may result in foreign investors acquiring actual control of such domestic enterprises.

Article 149 of the Draft proposes imposing heavy penalties on contractual schemes that circumvent Chinese foreign investment restrictions, which again does not exist in the draft Myanmar Investment Law. Perhaps the most controversial is the so-called variable interest entity or 'VIE structure'. Currently, under some VIE structures, foreign investors have financed Chinese businesses in 'restricted' industries by owning and using a wholly foreign-owned vehicle to control a Chinese entity that possesses a coveted industry license, thereby receiving its economic benefits. As an example, many of China's high-growth companies in e-commerce employ the VIE structure in one way or another.

Under the Existing Foreign Investment Laws, some Chinese businesses would often have no way to raise international capital without employing the VIE structure. Article 45 of the draft Foreign Investment Law introduces a new concept whereby an entity incorporated in a foreign jurisdiction would nevertheless be certified by the Ministry of Commerce (MOFCOM) as a Chinese investor (not subject to foreign investment restrictions) provided that the foreign entity is 'controlled' by Chinese investors. 'Control' as defined in Article 18 covers three broad scenarios: (i) control of 50 percent or more of the voting rights; (ii) control of less than 50 percent of the voting rights but with the power to secure at least 50 percent of the board or with the voting power to materially influence the board or the shareholders meeting; and (iii) control through 'decisive influence' (via contractual or trust arrangements) over a company's operations, finances, human resources or technology.

China and Myanmar reforms: some comparisons

The above shows that both China and Myanmar seek to reform their investment policies in order to meet the internationally acceptable standards for investment policy. Reform in the investment policy may lead to a higher number of investments from abroad in the areas of interest of both countries. Both countries seek to liberalize foreign investors' market access to investment sectors. However, both countries take different approaches due to the different levels of development and other factors, such as the capacity of the officials in undertaking the market access reform.

One notable difference between them is that reform takes place in Myanmar with political reform. Reforms in investment law take place after Myanmar has opened-up its politics and economy toward the path of democratization and it is guided by the principles of rule of law as it is understood in the Common Law countries such as the United Kingdom and the United States and by the international principles as contained in international instruments such as the ACIA. This shows that as an ASEAN Member State, Myanmar adopts the standards set by ASEAN in order to bring the country forward globally and to place Myanmar as part of global value chains (GVCs). The adoption of the ASEAN economic diplomacy approach is important for Myanmar as it can ride on ASEAN's position as a potential regional economic power house in the world.

On the other hand, the reform process in China is purely for commercial and economic purposes without the willingness to reform its political system. The investment reform does not take place as a result of the political reform but rather out of the need by the Communist Party to continue exercising its version of economic diplomacy to attract new investors in a more challenging economic environment. China does not intend to democratize its investment regime as shown by the unwillingness to apply the same investment law to both domestic and foreign investments and the unwillingness to reform the SOEs' dominant position in the local economy. This fits very well within what is defined as 'State Capitalism' (Gallagher 2015), where the policies are both state-dominated and attuned to markets, which reflects a commitment to state power and national development for the attainment of 'wealth and power' at the national level.

Whilst Myanmar seeks to liberalize certain sectors, mainly in the efficiency seeking and natural resource seeking investment, China seeks to liberalize the investment sectors in the efficiency-seeking, market seeking and strategic asset seeking investment. Myanmar still lacks strategic assets as the economy is still at an early stage of economic development, compared with China.

Both countries recognize the importance of investment liberalization to attract FDI from the same home countries, although for different sectors or subsectors of investment and with different levels of legal and regulatory sophistication. A study by Berger *et al.* (2013), which examines the potential impact of liberalization and protection of foreign investment find that liberal admission rules, such as national treatment provisions in the pre-establishment phase promote bilateral FDI. Berger *et al.* (2013) further recommend a host country government seeking FDI to put a greater emphasis on providing more comprehensive and transparent admission guarantees negotiated with capital-exporting countries. In addition, Berger *et al.* (2013) suggest governments play an important role by providing for legal security and predictability at the admission phase through national treatment provisions in the negative list.

The view is supported by an independent study in Vietnam showing that liberalization provisions, such as more favorable definitions of investment, admission and establishment and national treatment, have a positive impact on FDI flow into Vietnam. Thus, liberalization of investment sectors and liberalization in the services sector will further encourage investments, especially at the admission phase.

China is negotiating with the US for a high-level and high-quality bilateral investment treaty comparable with the investment chapter in the just concluded Trans-Pacific Economic Partnership Agreement (TPPA), which provides for liberalization at both the pre-establishment and post-establishment phases, whilst adopting the negative list approach. The negotiation has not yet been concluded despite the duration taken and it is unclear what the outcome will be under the Trump Administration.

Myanmar, on the other hand, with the assistance mainly from the United Kingdom and the European Union, negotiated a lower standard IIA with market access for investors from the EU. Many European investors are looking for efficiency gains by investing in Myanmar either for domestic consumption or for the export market. Many are also investing in the oil and gas sector to secure the natural resources needed.

Assistance from the Western powers, technical assistance provided by the OECD and the World Bank ensures that Myanmar adopts higher standards of protection and new investment standards such as the promotion of the responsible business conduct, transparency and sustainable development. This is very much consistent with Myanmar's intention to further diversify its sources of capital and investment by seeking investors from other countries such as ASEAN Member States, the European Union, Australia and the United States.

For China to continue to play an important role in Myanmar's economy, especially in the natural-resource seeking sectors such as oil and gas and mining, China's investors and their investments must adapt to the changing political and economic environment in Myanmar. China's investors must be able to adapt to a rule-based investment law which respects the rule of law. This means China may have to change its approach in its current and future investments in Myanmar. For example, China's firms may have to adopt a more open and transparent environment where shady deals and corruption may be things of the past, especially when Western investors and the donors and international organizations such as the World Bank will demand major reforms in the way Myanmar conducts its investment approval process.

In addition, China's investors will have to adopt the responsible business conduct advocated in the Myanmar new investment law. Responsible business conduct is where investors abide by certain minimum standards such as paying attention to the local customs and culture, minimizing negative impact on the environment, and paying reasonable wages in the absence of a minimum wage. The main advocate of the responsible business conduct is the OECD and it is supported by the Myanmar Responsible Business Conduct Forum lead by Vicky Bowman, a former British Ambassador to Myanmar.

Conclusion

The above discussion shows that two neighbors, who rely on each other for trade and investment have taken different paths in their investment policy reforms. Although both Myanmar and China will continue to practice trade and investment as part of their economic diplomacy, Myanmar has decided to take a more pragmatic path in its investment policy reform.

Myanmar's pragmatic investment policy reform takes place as a result of the political reform toward a more democratic country, whereas the reform taking place in China is very much a policy reform to address concerns by investors. The reform taking place in Myanmar will assist in alleviating some of the country's political risk as it is part of an overall reform process taking place in the country. But the reform in China may not be linked to the political risk, which could remain the same due to the unchanged political structure in the country.

In conducting its reform, Myanmar is guided by the reports, criticisms and suggestions by international organizations such as the OECD and the World Bank, whereas China's reform process is internally driven based on a report commission by the Communist Party. China would have been conducting the reform differently had it engaged with the World Bank and the OECD in its reform process, where the country will probably have to seek a much more open investment climate with a higher level of transparency and much less discretionary policies and a more open admission process.

Nevertheless, Myanmar faces a challenge to implement the new Myanmar Investment Law 2016. Myanmar needs to develop internal administrative guidance on the implementation of the law due to a lack of administrative capacity and experienced staff. Myanmar needs assistance from development partners to conduct capacity building for the MIC staff. In addition, Myanmar needs to find a solution to how the National/Sub-National investment endorsement for land rights and incentives is to be implemented. Having the best of laws and policies is not equivalent to what is practiced as implementation is the weak point in all developing countries.

As a result of the reform process, Myanmar has learned to be selective in accepting investment from abroad. Myanmar under the current and future government will look for responsible investors and responsible investments to address the broader socio-economic needs of the country and not just net economic gains alone. Myanmar policy-makers – with the support of, or rather after being urged by, various interest groups – are looking at problems such as land grabbing and damage to the environment, which is mostly linked with investment from China or with Chinese interests, and which were mostly approved by the previous military government. Hence, the new approach by the Myanmar government used economic diplomacy as a tool to diversify sources of investment and to wean itself from the Chinese economic influence. Nevertheless, China – which is one of the main Myanmar's trading and investment partners – will continue to be a main player in Myanmar's economy for many more years to come.

Note

1 There are over 1000 rules and regulatory documents related to foreign investment in China issued by government ministries. They include, but are not limited to: the Guiding Catalogue of Foreign Investment Industries; the Provisions on Mergers & Acquisition of Domestic Enterprises by Foreign Investors; the Administrative Provisions on Foreign Investment in Road Transportation Industry; the Interim Provisions on Foreign Investment in Cinemas; the Administrative Measures on Foreign Investment in Commercial Areas; the Administrative Measures on Ratification of Foreign Invested Projects; the Administrative Measures on Foreign Investment in Distribution Enterprises of Books, Newspapers and Periodical; the Provision on the Establishment of Investment Companies by Foreign Investors; the Administrative Measures on Strategic Investment in Listed Companies by Foreign Investors. In addition, local legislatures and governments also enact their own regulations and rules to regulate foreign investments in their areas, in accordance with national laws and policies, including, for example, Wuhan's Administration Regulation on Foreign-Invested Enterprises and Shanghai's Municipal Administration Measures on the Land Usage of Foreign-Invested Enterprises.

References

ASEAN. 2015. *ASEAN 2025 Forging Ahead Together*. Jakarta: ASEAN Secretariat.

Asian Development Bank. 2014. *Myanmar Unlocking the Potential*. Manila: Asian Development Bank.

Bayne, Nicholas and Stephen Woolcock. 2007. *The New Economic Diplomacy: Decision-making and Negotiation in International Economic Relations*, 2nd edn. Farnham: Ashgate.

Berger, A., M. Buss, P. Nunnenkamp, and M. Roy. 2013. Do trade and investment agreements lead to more FDI? Accounting for key provisions inside the black box. *International Economics and Economic Policy*, 10: 247–275.

Chaisrisawatsuk, S. and W. Chaisrisawatsuk. 2007. Imports, exports and foreign direct investment interactions and their effects. In ESCAP, *Towards Coherent Policy Frameworks: Understanding Trade and Investment Linkages, Trade and Investment Studies*, No. 62 (pp. 97–115, Chapter IV). New York: United Nations.

Chaisse, Julien and Sufian Jusoh. 2016. The ASEAN comprehensive investment agreement: The regionalisation of laws and policy on foreign investment. Camberley: Edward Elgar.

Ferrarini, Benno. 2013. *Myanmar Trade and Its Potential*. ADB Economics Working Paper Series, No. 325. Manila: ADB.

Gallagher, Mary E. 2015. *The Social Relations of Chinese State Capitalism*. Oxford: Oxford University Press.
Heath, Timothy R. 2016. China's evolving approach to economic diplomacy. *Asia Policy*, 22: 157–191, http://asiapolicy.nbr.org.
International Monetary Fund. 2014. Myanmar: Second review under the staff-monitored program – staff report and press release. IMF Country Report No. 14/91. March. Washington, DC: International Monetary Fund. www.imf.org/external/pubs/ft/scr/2014/cr1491.pdf.
Investment Climate Advisory Services of the World Bank Group. 2010. *Investment Law Reform, A Handbook for Development Practitioners*. Washington, DC: World Bank.
Jusoh, Sufian. 2014. ASEAN investment agreements: A tool of economic diplomacy in meeting the objectives of ASEAN economic community blueprint. *Journal of Diplomacy and Foreign Relations* 14(1): 49–68.
Maehara, Seiji. 2011. Foreign Policy Speech by Minister for Foreign Affairs to the 177th Session of the Diet, 24 January 2011. www.mofa.go.jp/announce/fm/maehara/speech110124.html.
Medeiros, Evan. 2009. *China's International Behavior: Activism, Opportunities, and Diversification*. Santa Monica: RAND Corporation.
Ministry of Commerce, People's Republic of China. 2014. Joint report on statistics of China's outbound FDI 2013. Released 12 September 2014.
Multilateral Investment Guarantee Agency. 2012. *2012 World Investment and Political Risk: World Investment Trends and Corporate Perspectives, Sovereign Default and Expropriation and the Political Risk Insurance Industry*. Washington, DC: MIGA.
OECD. 2014a. *Southeast Asian Investment Policy Perspectives*, May. Paris: OECD.
OECD. 2014b. *OECD Investment Policy Review: Myanmar*. Paris: OECD.
Rana, Kishan and Bipul Chatterjee. 2011. *The Role of Embassies, Economic Diplomacy, India's Experience*. Jaipur: CUTS International.
Sudo, Sueo. 1992. *The Fukuda Doctrine and ASEAN: New Dimensions in Japanese Foreign Policy*. Singapore: Institute of Southeast Asian Studies.
UNCTAD. 2017. Foreign direct investment: Inward and outward flows and stock, annual, 1970–2015. http://unctadstat.unctad.org/wds/TableViewer/tableView.aspx?ReportId=96740.
US Chambers of Commerce. 2014. *ASEAN Business Outlook Survey 2014*. www.uschamber.com/sites/default/files/legacy/international/files/ASEAN%20Survey%202014.pdf.
World Bank. 201. Investment climate advisory services of the World Bank Group. World Bank.
World Trade Organisation 2014. Trade Policy Review Myanmar. W/TPR/S/293.
Zhou, Yongsheng. 1996. First exploration of Deng Xiaoping's thoughts on economic diplomacy. *Beifang Luncong* 1: 35.

12 Southeast Asia and China relations

Desecuritizing the South China Sea

Rashila Ramli

Introduction

The area known as the South China Sea, is a space occupying 3,500,000 square kilometers located at the fringe of the Pacific Ocean, straddling the Malacca Straits and the Straits of Taiwan. It sees the flow of a third of the world's shipping, mostly oil tankers carrying over 17 million barrels per day. The Silk Road of the Sea has a strong historical link with the Southeast Asian states. The first/classical oriental globalization witnessed the movements of Chinese traders, such as Zheng He who came to Melaka in the fourteenth century. Meanwhile, Indian and Muslim traders moved across the Straits of Melaka into Betawi (now known as Jakarta) and settled in the Yunnan province. These regional commons also witnessed voyages of galleons from Mexico to the Philippines, with a stopover in China, bringing corn, potteries, and silk in exchange for spices and other commodities, such as rubber and rice. The Ming dynasty connected with groups known as Malays in areas later known as the Philippines, Malaysia, Cambodia and Indonesia.

When occidental globalization occurred between the sixteenth and twentieth centuries, there was an increase in the traffic flow in the regional commons. The Dutch and British colonizers utilized the route between the Straits of Malacca and the Straits of Formosa (now known as Taiwan) for the purpose of resources removal (spices, goods, people) to be used by the colonial masters in their own countries. Up until the late nineteenth century, one can argue that the South China Sea was a regional commons used by traders and western colonizers as a passage way for the transference of natural resources. While there were issues of piracy, the maritime area was not regarded as a security matter until the twentieth century.

The debate surrounding sovereignty of the sea was prevalent during the occidental globalization where European powers were competing to gain influence at sea. Countries initiated taxes and levies, prevented sailing and fishing in maritime areas that they controlled. Two scholars or jurists, Grotius and John Selden, respectively wrote the *Mare Liberum* in 1606 and the *Mare Clausum* to justify their positions. Grotius proposed the freedom of the sea while John Seldon defended maritime sovereignty (Ye Qiang and Jiang

Zongqiang 2015). According to Ye and Jiang, China has always believed in an open sea policy. At the peak of China's navigation prowess, shown by Zheng He, China did not attempt to control the sea lanes. In fact, life by the sea and at sea was taken for granted by societies that inhabited the shores of the Malay Archipelago. The South China Sea was the regional commons to all. However, the Occidental international order grew in the eighteenth and nineteenth centuries, with the European powers' growing interest in developing international trade.

As trade bloomed, the middle of the twentieth century saw China gaining strength and actively pursuing an involvement in international affairs (Nederveen Pieterse 2014). In February 1948, China released the Map of the Location of South China Sea Islands. The objective of the Map is to clarify China's inherent territorial sovereignty under the post-war international order. By publicizing the map with the 'dash-line', China's intention was to claim sovereignty over all the insular features rather than the maritime jurisdiction (Ye Qiang and Jiang Zongqiang 2015, p. 3). China believed that the demarcation of territories was within the four conventions established in 1958 and the 1982 UNCLOS. The 'nine-dash' line sparked consternation among ASEAN member states in and also some major powers such as the US and Japan.

Much of the debate on the South China Sea (SCS) in the last six decades has been about securitization with very little on desecuritization. By examining the historical data, it can be argued that the SCS was not viewed as a security matter until the mid-1970s. Prior to that, the flow of sea traffic from the Indian Ocean into the Straits of Malacca had increased steadily as traders and colonizers moved goods between the regions. Then, when skirmishes between ASEAN member states and China started to increase, the South China Sea was tabled as part of the Second ARF agenda, without a protest from China. Thus, one can argue that securitization of the South China Sea, which began in 1948 was completed by the mid-1990s. The claimants of the contested territorial areas are China, Vietnam, the Philippines, Malaysia, Brunei, Taiwan and Japan. All states have indicated their stances.

This chapter takes the position that it is imperative to focus on the political–security dimension of the South China Sea dispute, i.e. the securitization of SEA and the promoters of peace first, before any claims into future gains through minimizing the gap of legitimacy of rule toward improving the governance of the common maritime area, i.e. the zone of interstate cooperation, with maritime economic development as a goal. Thus, three research questions are developed:

1 How did the South China Sea become a security issue and who are the actors involved in the process of securitization?
2 How do major actors, such as the six claimants, ASEAN as an organization, and interest parties, such as the European Union and the US, engage with China in mitigating the multiple territorial claims?

3 To what extent can desecuritizing SCS provide an alternative perspective toward interstate cooperation within SEA and China?

This chapter employs a qualitative approach from a constructivist standpoint, while being fully aware of the Realist approach, usually harbored by policy makers. From secondary sources, the author describes securitization of the SCS conflict and identifies the drivers of conflict. By desecuritizing the SCS through the identification of possible promoters of peace and stability, the author provides an alternative perspective of the SCS. Finally, several short-term and long-term options to promote interstate cooperation between SEA and China will be discussed.

The securitization of the South China Sea

Rethinking security is a project undertaken by the Copenhagen Peace Research Institute (COPRI). Barry Buzan, Ole Waever and Jaap de Wilde (1998) initially developed notions of securitization and desecuritization. Fundamentally, when an issue is deemed as a threat to a target object, then the issue begins to acquire a security dimension. This is stage one of the process (Figure 12.1). When the securitizing actor succeeds in convincing the audience that a target object is existentially threatening, then the process of securitization is successfully completed. The rhetoric, known as 'speech act' by different actors, becomes the units of analysis. Speech act may comprise official statements by statesmen, responses to official statements, resolutions of organizations such as ASEAN, and media portrayal of the issues. Actions that exhibit aggressive confrontation that threaten the lives of people can also be considered as part of the securitization of an issue.

Desecuritization, on the other hand, is the reversal of the two-stage process. It is the 'shifting of issues out of emergency mode' and into a normal space for negotiation (Oelsner 2005, p. 2). In other words, the issue is no longer seen as a threat. The author will proceed to desecuritize the SCS by looking at historical depictions of the maritime, using the Mediterranean Sea approach, as espoused by Fernand Braudel (1987) and the Nusantara Outlook, as proposed by Hans-Dieter Evers (2014a).

In studies of the South China Sea, they can be divided into three major themes. From the historical dimension, scholars such as He Tao (2015), and Westad (2012) tried to identify historical manuscripts and maps of South

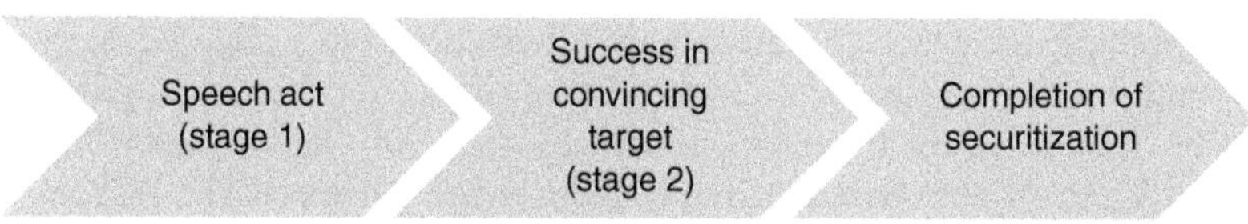

Figure 12.1 Two-step process of securitization.

Source: adapted from Buzan *et al.* (1998).

China Sea. The second theme is on ASEAN–China relations from the International Relations perspective – Amitav Acharya (2009), Johan Saravanamuttu (2010), John Ikenberry and Michael Mastanduno (2003) represent the group of scholars debating the interplay of China and major powers and its implication on ASEAN. Finally, the third group of scholars is an eclectic group, consisting of Jan Nederveen Pieterse (2014), Hans-Dieter Evers (2012), Dongyun Park (2010) focusing on Asia rising, the *longue durée* approach, and Asian capitalism respectively. The arguments put forth by the third group of scholars are most relevant in the effort to desecuritize SCS.

As stated earlier, China exhibited the Nine-Dash Line Map in 1948. For almost 30 years, limited attention was given to the stance because the states in the region were recovering from the aftermath of the Second World War. Hence, the states were focusing on internal developments while still under the impression that the sea is a regional common. However, things changed by 1974. The first recorded act of aggression was the military conflict between China and Vietnam that took place in 1974 when China seized Paracel Islands. Valencia *et al.* (1997) among others came to the conclusion that the continued aggression that recurred in 1988 could result in a flash-point leading toward greater tension. The Nine-Dash Line Map drawn by China in 1948, brought forth the initial wrath of countries in Southeast Asia, predominantly the Philippines and Vietnam, because of the encroachment of the regional commons.

The list of incidents given in Table 12.1 indicates a growing frequency of skirmishes and clashes between China and several members of ASEAN. It is observed that the periods between incidents have become shorter in the last decade. This also coincides with the deadline of the United Nations Convention on the Law of the Sea (UNCLOS) for states to submit claims on maritime territorial areas.

Under close scrutiny, the incidents could be categorized into two types. First, the covert, leading toward confrontational actions such as the seizing of the Paracel Islands by China from Vietnam, the arrival of Navy ships to Spratly Island, the cable cutting incident, and the deployment of the HYS981. Second, the diplomatic and conciliatory approach such as the claims and counter claims made by different states, the signing of DOC by China, and continued bilateral moves made by China with different claimants. The availability of using UNCLOS as a recourse in finding a solution can also complicate matters. The incidents and the availability of UNCLOS have led to multiple claims, some with different stances (Table 12.2).

The multiple claimants of the South China Sea, especially the Spratly Islands and the Paracel Islands, indicated various stances in their willingness to negotiate. Due to more frequent encounters with the Chinese, the Philippines and Vietnam tend be take a rather confrontational approach. The latest encounter between Vietnam and China is the ban on fishermen from entering the waters around Paracel Islands. That incident took place after the deadly protest in May 2014.

Table 12.1 List of incidents

1974	China seized Vietnam last toehold in the Paracels
1988	China's navy arrived among the Spratly Islands
1994	China built structures on stilts over Mischief Reef, part of Philippines continental shelf
2002	China signed the Declaration of the Conduct of Parties in the South China Sea (DOC) with ASEAN Check UNCLOS
2009	Claims and counter claims were submitted by states to meet the implementation of UNCLOS
June 2011	Cable Cutting Incident involving Oil exploration vessels
April 2012	Philippines warship tried to arrest Chinese fishermen around Scarborough Shoal
2013	Philippines formally notified Beijing that it was seeking international arbitration against the nine-dash line claims and its 'unlawful acts' in the South China Sea (*New York Time*, 4 December 2014)
May 2014	China deployed HYS981 to an area 17 nautical miles from southwestern most Paracel Islands, escalating into intense stand-off between Chinese and Vietnam law enforcement vessels and deadly riots in mid-May.
2015	Chinese vessels were spotted off the coast of East Malaysia. Malaysia sent a diplomatic note to register its protest
2015	In October, the US Naval Ship USS Lassen sailed within the 12 nautical miles of Subi Reef in the Spratly Islands
2016	On 10 May, China scrambled two fighter jets and three warships as the USS William P Lawrance sailed within 12 nautical miles of the Fiery Cross Reef
2016	On 12 July, A tribunal of Permanent Court of Arbitration rejects Chinese Nine-dash Line historical claims over South China Sea concluding it has no legal claim. It was a unanimous away in favor of the Philippines
2016	On 25 July, In Vientiane, Laos, ASEAN issued a joint statement regarding South China Sea dispute, which stated their commitment to ensure and promote the peace, stability and security in the region.

Source: www.bbc.com/news/world-asia-pacific-13748349.

In the Philippines, protesters took to the streets and picketed in front of the Chinese embassy in the influential Makati District on 12 June 2015. Headed by Renato Reyes, the Secretary General of the left-wing group New Patriotic Alliance, the protestors demanded the dispute be addressed in accordance with international law.

Table 12.2 Official position and stance of states

State	*Official position*	*Present stance*
Vietnam	Vietnam possesses sovereignty over the Spratly and Paracel archipelagos in accordance with UNCLOS.	Focus on strict implementation of the DOC between ASEAN and China in 2002; hopes that ASEAN members and China will launch official talks on a COC. Speaking at the Shangri-La conference in June, PM Dung wants an ASEAN-led Code of Conduct.
The Philippines	Chinese Nine-Dash Line violates UNCLOS provisions to which China and the Philippines are signatories; China has declined an invitation to use settlement mechanisms under Part XV of UNCLOS. Having exhausted almost all political and diplomatic avenues for a peaceful negotiated settlement of its maritime dispute with China, Secretary of Foreign Affairs Del Rosario stated that therefore the Philippines has taken the step of bringing China before the Arbitral Tribunal under Article 287 and Annex VII under UNCLOS.	International arbitration and joint development only after settling of dispute and clarification of claims; establish legally binding Code of Conduct (COC).
Malaysia	Claims that territory that falls within the economic exclusion zone to be under UNCLOS and to a small number of islands in the Spratlys.	Dialogue and cooperation, establish COC, no involvement of 'extra-regional states'; joint development of resources; no passing on of dispute to the next generation. Points to the example of the joint development zone in waters claimed by Thailand and Malaysia.

Brunei	Claims territory within its economic exclusion zone under UNCLOS.	Resolution through dialogue by states concerned and 'in accordance with universally recognised principles of international law', including UNCLOS; no international arbitration; implementation of DOC and efforts toward COC.
People's Republic of China	Paracel and Spratly islands for the last 2000 years an integral part of Chinese territory, reconfirmed by 1947 map. Arbitration started by the Philippines is illegal and founded on illegal occupation of Chinese islands and reefs, thus UNCLOS should not apply.	Does not want international arbitration but only by states directly concerned, joint development of the area; strict adherence to Declaration on Conduct of Parties in the South China Sea (DOC)
The Philippines	Chinese Nine-Dash Line violates UNCLOS provisions to which China and the Philippines are signatories; China has declined invitation to use settlement mechanisms under Part XV of UNCLOS. Having exhausted almost all political and diplomatic avenues for a peaceful negotiated settlement of its maritime dispute with China, Secretary of Foreign Affairs Del Rosario stated that therefore the Philippines has taken the step of bringing China before the Arbitral Tribunal under Article 287 and Annex VII under UNCLOS.	International arbitration, joint development only after the settling of disputes and clarification of claims; establish legally binding Code of Conduct (COC).

Source: EU-Asia Center (2015).

Drivers of conflict

In understanding the evolving conflict, previous studies have identified at least four drivers to the conflict in the South China Sea: (1) Assessing hydrocarbon movement and reserves; (2) declining fishing stock; (3) expanding military and law enforcement capabilities; and (4) growing nationalism.

Assessing hydrocarbon movement and reserves/declining fish stock

The shortest sea route between suppliers in African and the Persian Gulf and their Asian customers is the Straits of Melaka.

> The Straits is a critical transit chokepoint and has become increasingly important over the last two decades. In 1993, about 7 million barrels per day (bbl/d) of oil and petroleum products (20% of world seaborne oil trade) passed through the Strait of Malacca, according to the Center for Naval Analysis. EIA estimates that by the end of 2011, trade through Malacca was greater than 15 million bbl/d, or about one-third of all seaborne oil.
>
> (EIA 2013)

The importance of the South China Sea as a passage to transport seaborne oil, as indicated by the EIA report is one of the drivers that has turned the South China Sea into a security issue. More importantly, for the individual state, the claimants view access and ownership of the hydrocarbon reserve as a zero-sum game. Vietnam is planning to increase its maritime economy from 48 percent of its GDP to 55 percent in 2020. The Philippines is faced with a similar economic situation, with the belief that the contested Reed Bank has a large reserve of natural gas. Thus, the 2011 Reed Bank incident that took place between China and the Philippines. Both Malaysia and Brunei have decided to work on a joint development focusing on energy resource in the region (EIA 2013).

Declining fish stocks closer to the shores have forced fishermen from China, the Philippines and Vietnam to go beyond the EEZ, thus increasing the possibilities of offshore clashes. China has issued an annual fishing ban over some portions of the South China Sea. Some of the areas are considered as EEZ by the Philippines and Vietnam, thus inviting objections from these ASEAN members.

Expanding military and law enforcement capabilities and nationalism

The third and fourth drivers of conflict are related. The build-up of military capabilities including law enforcement vehicles and weapons are ways for states to project power and gain some recognition of strength. In the past decade, China has been increasing its military capabilities, much to the consternation of its neighbors, especially ASEAN member states (AMS). On the side of AMS, the Philippines, Vietnam, Malaysia and Singapore have also raised their military expenditure from 2010 to 2014. 'There has been a net increase for all countries, averaging 37.6 percent ... USD38.2 billion on defense in 2014' (Abuza 2015). In parallel, external major powers such as the USA tend to intervene either through naval exercises in the region, or through statements by military and political leaders.

With reference to the Nine-Dash Lines Map, when the lines are joined a U-shaped curve covering almost 90 percent of the South China Sea is formed. At this point, the concern of the US is clear. The US has been opposing China in China's effort to claim territorial sovereignty and there has been a number of incidents between China and the US.

China routinely intercepts US reconnaissance flights conducted in its EEZ and periodically does so in aggressive ways that increase the risk of an accident similar to the April 2001 collision of a US EP-3 reconnaissance plane and a Chinese F-8 fighter jet near Hainan Island. A comparable maritime incident could be triggered by Chinese vessels harassing a US Navy surveillance ship operating in its EEZ, such as occurred in the 2009 incidents involving the USNS *Impeccable* and the USNS *Victorious* (Glaser 2012).

Since the US has many allies among ASEAN member states, notably the Philippines and Vietnam, China does not take lightly threats by the US. 'Freedom of navigation and overflight should not be used as an excuse to flex muscle and undermine other countries' sovereignty and security' said Zhu Haiquan, the spokesperson for the Chinese Embassy in Washington on 26 October 2015. A day later, the USS Lassen sailed within the 12 nautical mile of Sibu Reef, China. Since President Obama proposed the 'Pivot to Asia', also known as Asia Pivot Policy, in 2012, the US has been seen to rebalance its relationships with the Asian state actors. The multidimensional approach embracing political, economic and security issues is meant to strengthen US engagement with Asian states. Nevertheless, ASEAN member states in dispute with China's sovereignty, have in general, welcomed the US navy in the South China Sea.

The hedging technique employed by ASEAN member states is obvious as they have secured their position against China ever since the escalation of tensions in the South China Sea. Vietnam and Malaysia are the two ASEAN member states leading a regional military build-up. Although the Philippines is lagging behind, it is counting on the US for assistance. There is also an increase in the number of submarines being deployed by the claimant states, although the topography of the South China Sea limits the navigational capabilities of submarines. However, rising nationalism can be seen as a possible provoker of conflict. The anti-Chinese sentiment in Vietnam, for instance, makes it difficult for its leaders to ignore China when sea disputes occur.

Notwithstanding the situation, all four drivers of conflict destabilize the region. Drivers of conflicts can be seen as agents of securitization since they assist in turning the SCS into a security issue. In the last decade, there has been an escalation of conflicts in the regional maritime commons. Numerous statements on SCS have been made by multiple actors. These statements can be considered as speech acts (Table 12.3). By 2015, speech acts have been

Table 12.3 Statements on SCS by multiple actors

State/organization	*Examples of excerpts reflecting perspectives of state*
Malaysia Hishammuddin Tun Hussein, Defence Minister of Malaysia at the Sixth Xiangshan Forum, Beijing, 17 October 2015	'There might be *counteractions by major powers* in the region, but sometimes it is beyond the control of small nations like Malaysia' Source: www.thestar.com.my/news/nation/2015/10/18/worry-over-unresolved-sea-disputes/
Vietnam President Truong Tan Sang, 28 September 2015, Voice of America	'The Chinese, in meetings with us, always claims that the islands belong to China, and it is undisputable. We would like to counter-argue that statement. *The Paracels and Spratlys belong to Vietnam* since ancient time, and it is also undisputable.' Source: www.voanews.com/content/vietham-china-spratly-islands/2984641.html
The Philippines Foreign Affairs Secretary Albert del Rosario at the 70th UNGA	'*The world cannot allow a country, no matter how powerful*, to claim an entire sea as its own nor should it allow coercion to be an acceptable dispute settlement mechanism.' Source: www.gmanetwork.com/news/story/539651/news/nation/philippines-tells-china-at-un-assembly-stop-coercion-and-intimidation
ASEAN Joint Communique 48th ASEAN Foreign Ministers Meeting 4 August 2015	Para 150: 'We discussed extensively the matters relating to the South China Sea and remained seriously concerned over recent and ongoing developments in the area. We took note of the serious concerns expressed by some Ministers on the *land reclamations in the South China Sea, which have eroded trust and confidence, increased tensions* and may undermine peace, security and stability in the South China Sea.' Source: www.eria.org/JOINT%20COMMUNIQUE%20OF%20THE%2048TH%20AMM-FINAL.pdf
China Vice Adm. Yuan Yubai, who commands the North Sea Fleet for the People's Liberation Army Navy	'*The South China Sea, as the name indicated, is a sea area. It belongs to China*' delivered by Vic Adm. Yuan at the London's Defence & Security Equipment International, or DSEI Conference Source: www.defenseone.com/threats/2015/09/defiant-chinese-admirals-message-south-china-sea-belongs-china/120989/

Table 12.3 Continued

State/organization	*Examples of excerpts reflecting perspectives of state*
USA President Barack Obama at the 70th UNGA, Sepember 2015	'Similarly, in the South China Sea, the United States makes no claim on territory there. We don't adjudicate claims. *But like every nation gathered here, we have an interest in upholding the basic principles of freedom of navigation and the free flow of commerce, and in resolving disputes through international law, not the law of force.* So we will defend these principles, while encouraging China and other claimants to resolve their differences peacefully.' Source: www.whitehouse.gov/the-press-office/2015/09/28/remarks-president-obama-united-nations-general-assembly

Source: compiled by author.

deeply embedded in the language of (non-)negotiation of the leaders. Table 12.3 gives examples of speech acts by multiple actors.

In the case of the SCS, securitization is not only a two-stage process. It is a dialectic process between the speech acts and actions undertaken by multiple actors. Actions and concerns over SCS were expressed by China, members of ASEAN, specifically the Philippines, Vietnam, Malaysia and Brunei; and external actors, such as the USA. The drivers of conflicts as agents of securitization have amplified the securitization process.

Desecuritization by promoters of peace and stability

While there are four drivers of conflict, this chapter identifies three promoters of peace and stability: (1) the efforts of national leaders and (several) parliamentarians; (2) role of ASEAN in shaping a state; and (3) the Nusantara or Mediterranean perspective. Promoters of Peace and Stability can be seen as agents of desecuritization of the South China Sea. The combination of top down and bottom up efforts from multilateral institutions, opinion leaders, media, scholars and NGOs assist in rethinking the importance of regional commons toward reclaiming South China Sea as a regional common.

Efforts of national leaders and (some) parliamentarians

As the Association of Southeast Asian Nations (ASEAN) works toward becoming the ASEAN Economic Community (AEC) by the end of 2015, many actions need to be taken in terms of governance. The ten member states with different levels of development are working to rationalize relations by concentrating on three pillars of activities: The ASEAN Political-Security

Pillar (APSP), the ASEAN Economic Pillar (AEP) and the ASEAN Social-Cultural Pillar (ASCP). Each area has contentious issues that ASEAN member states (AMS) must face together in the near future.

Within the political security community, AMS must also contend with the rise of China in the twenty-first century. One of the major contentious issues in ASEAN–China relations is the contestation over the South China Sea. In ASEAN–China relations, the dispute over the South China Sea is causing unwanted distress between ASEAN and China, and among member states. While the Philippines and Vietnam prefer a more aggressive approach, other members, including Malaysia prefer a more diplomatic approach. Under the ASEAN Political Security (APSC) Pillar, this issue became a political–security issue in 2002, which was the year that the Declaration on the Conduct of Parties in South China Sea (DOC) was signed between China and ASEAN. This can be considered as the first Speech Act toward desecuritization of the SCS. But what was the process that had taken place between the Southeast Asian states, ASEAN and China in implementing the DOC?

Stage two of the reversal process had taken place predominantly within ASEAN. As an organization, the Association of Southeast Asian Nations (ASEAN) has grown from a five-member state organization in 1967 to a ten-member state organization by 1999. The focus of ASEAN has been toward the creation of a stable region relying on the principles of non-interference, neutrality and peaceful coexistence. ASEAN has, since its inception, evolved into an organization focusing on the political-security, economic and social matters. These are the areas which have been focused on during the ASEAN Foreign Ministers Meeting and the ASEAN Inter-Parliamentary Assembly (AIPA).

However, while one can argue that there is inadequate attention to govern South China Sea, the Declaration on the Conducts of Parties in South China Sea (DOC) and a number of official documents adopted by ASEAN leaders and AIPA can be regarded as expressed intentions by AMS in promoting peace for the region. This section focuses on issues of good governance (or lack of it) and inclusiveness in settling the SCS issue. In the ASEAN Political-Security Blueprint 2025, section B. 6.1 specifically stated 'Maintain the South China Sea as a sea of peace, prosperity and cooperation'. There is a spectrum of political security threats. On the one hand, issues such as human trafficking, drug smuggling, haze, diseases, stateless children, generally known as non-traditional security issues, are cross-border issues that oftentimes require political solutions. On the other hand, traditional security issues such as border disputes, the multiple claims over the South China Sea, must also be handled with care. Here, there is a need to emphasize the importance of the Declaration on the Conduct of Parties in the South China Sea (DOC) and the Code of Conduct in the South China Sea (COC). The source of threat can be from within ASEAN or from external forces. Accordingly, the Crisis Group Asia Report N27, 7 May 2015 has outlined several short-term recommendations outlined below in order to achieve meaningful progress on formulating a Code of Conduct in the South China Sea:

1 To the government of China and ASEAN: Implement operational details of foreign ministry hotlines, and initiate a multi-agency consultation framework – modeled on the China–Japan high level consultation on maritime affairs
2 To the governments of China and Indonesia: Expand combined bilateral naval exercises on implementation of the Code of Unplanned Encounters at Sea, to include navies of all South China Sea littoral states
3 To external nations, other than China, and organizations with direct ties to ASEAN: Provide technical assistance and organizational support on incident-at-sea crisis management, for example by organizing and sponsoring workshops on best practices involving China and ASEAN

The ASEAN Foreign Ministers Meeting (AMM) is the space where political–security issues are dominant. AIPA, on the other hand is a bottom-up organization of concerned parliamentarians. As mostly elected members of the ten parliaments in ASEAN, the issues discussed at AIPA have a filtering effect into state mechanisms and communities at large. As discussed earlier, one of the areas focused on is on ASEAN political and security matters. The ASEAN Political Security Pillar (APS) is the basis for the formation of the community focusing on the well-being of the peoples by mitigating conflicts, maintaining peace and upholding neutrality and sovereignty of nation-states. One of the three pillars of ASEAN Community, APS provides the framework for monitoring the progress of AMS from 2006–2015. There are many mechanisms within APSC. Some of the mechanisms are the ASEAN Declaration on the Zone of Peace, Freedom and Neutrality (ZOFPAN), ASEAN Regional Forum (ARF), The Treaty for Amenity and Cooperation (TAC), the SEA Nuclear Weapon Free Zone (SEANWFZ) and the Declaration on Conduct of Parties in the South China Sea (DOC).

In the third and fourth paragraph of the DOC, it is stated that members of ASEAN Summit will:

> reaffirm their respect for and commitment to the freedom of navigation in and over flight above the South China Sea as provided for by the universally recognized principles of international law and to 'resolve their territorial and jurisdictional disputes by peaceful means, without resorting to the threat or use of force'.
>
> (DOC 2002, p. 1)

The members insisted that confidence building measures should include: (1) holding dialogues and exchange of views as appropriate between their defense and military officials; (2) ensuring just and human treatment of all persons who are either in danger or in distress; (3) notifying, on a voluntary basis, other parties concerned of any impending joint/combined military exercise; and (4) exchanging, on a voluntary basis, relevant information (DOC 2002, p. 2). Finally, members envisioned that pending a comprehensive and durable settlement of the disputes, member states could engage in cooperative activities that include,

> marine environmental protection, marine scientific research, safety of navigation and communication at sea, search and rescue operation, and combating transnational crime, including but not limited to trafficking in illicit drugs, piracy and armed robbery at sea, and illegal traffic in arms.
> (DOC 2002, p. 2)

The problem with the DOC is that while the intention is admirable, the deeds do not materialize easily. A paper by Carlyle Thayer (2012) dealt extensively with the follow-up activities leading toward the creation of the draft of the ASEAN Proposed Elements of a Regional Code of Conduct in the South China Sea based on the original Philippine Working Draft. It was at the 2012 AMM that the Joint Communique was not signed due to the disagreement of the Chair from Cambodia regarding the inclusion of the Scarborough Shoal.

As mentioned earlier, AIPA, with a strong bottom-up approach by parliamentarians, has a strong outreach to the public. AIPA, previously known as AIPO, held its first assembly in 1979. As elected representatives of the people, AIPA members, consisting of parliamentarians within ASEAN act as a link between the people and the government of AMS. At each assembly, resolutions are voted upon by AIPA members after much deliberation. Through the years, many resolutions have been adopted by AIPA. As such, resolutions passed by AIPA reflect such matters pertaining to harmonization of laws, global and regional security issues, promotion of human rights and interfaith dialogues.

The purpose of AIPA as stated in the AIPA Statute Article 2.4 is 'to study, discuss, suggest and solicit opinions to problems of common interests and express its views on the issues'. There was no mention of the non-interference principle that AIPA members must be bound to. Since AIPA is not a mechanism created by ASEAN, its members have greater leeway in discussing issues. All members are parliamentarians elected by their constituents to represent the interest of each parliamentary area. While there are a number of resolutions pertaining to supporting the ASEAN Political Security Pillar, there is one resolution that dealt directly with the South China Sea.

The resolution as stated in Table 12.4, which is a speech act, was passed in 2009, the same year where an increase in clashes was observed between the multiple claimants, and the year where China signed the DOC with ASEAN. It is noted that 2009 also coincided with the deadline given under UNCLOS to file claims for the Exclusive Economic Zone (EEZ), the 200 nautical mile area for maritime development.

Table 12.4 Resolution GA30/2009/POL-04

Code	*Resolution title*
GA30/2009/POL-04	Resolution on Global and regional Security Resolutions: 1 Promotion of Regional Peace and Stability 2 Strengthening Cooperation under TAC and confidence Building Measure 3 Ensuring full implementation of Declaration on the Conduct of Parties (DOC) in the South China Sea for peace and stability in South China Sea

Source: AIPA Secretariat (2009).

> As long as they take part in the resolutions, the countries are brought together because the laws then become more organized and easier to understand. That is the purpose of these resolutions. When the resolutions are passed, we do not expect all 10 countries to convert them into national laws.
>
> (Honorable Periosamy Otharam 2013)

The importance of good governance in achieving regional objectives, namely solving economic disparities and border disputes, cannot be repudiated. A regional community must be able to perform well in terms of leadership, integrity and competence. Hence, there must be an equilibrium between and among these three key components that propels an establishment of an ASEAN Community based on good governance.

Topics related to governance, such as the call to strengthen cooperation under TAC and to ensure full implementation of DOC, are aimed at spelling out the elements that make up good governance. Sound governance takes root in strong and visionary leadership, beginning at the top with the political level and coming right down to the community level, at the lowest possible strata of the society. Parliamentarians can help nurture leadership by bridging political elites and the peoples across the region. This will lead to a more active participation and contribution to the development of an inclusive ASEAN as a regional community.

Promoters of peace take into account the important role that the ASEAN Political Security Community plays in order to ensure that the Southeast Asian region remains relatively peaceful and neutral. The ASEAN Political Security community, in subscribing to a comprehensive approach to security, upholds a number of existing ASEAN political instruments, such as The Declaration on the Zone of Peace, Freedom and Neutrality (ZOPFAN) and the Treaty of Amity and Cooperation in Southeast Asia (TAC). ASEAN also has a number of mechanisms, such as the ASEAN Regional Forum (ARF) and Council of Security Cooperation in Asia Pacific (CSCAP), where AMS can discuss both traditional and non-traditional security threats to ASEAN.

Leadership by Heads of States or by ASEAN Foreign Ministers is insufficient to guarantee the accomplishment of the ASEAN Community that is inclusive in nature. The element of integrity needs to be infused into both leaders and followers (the peoples) with each and every one availing of the good values in order to achieve the common good. Responsibility and transparency ensure the sanctity and sustainability of the efforts toward collective engagement in forming the ASEAN Community.

Notwithstanding the nature of the security problems, a number of stakeholders are involved. The major complaint is the lack of a participatory approach involving relevant stakeholders including the victims, appropriate civil societies and the academes in finding viable solutions. Inclusiveness, as a process, must take into account the interest of all parties. The present sense of danger, especially the rise of the Islamic State (IS) and its influence in the region, must be curbed immediately. The existence of fundamentalist/conservative/repressive thinking and practices in the name of religion cannot be tolerated.

The ASEAN Political Security Community plays a very important role in identifying the locations of these threats, and must alert AMS on possible actions to be taken, in a concerted effort to ward off both internal and external threats. The APSC Blueprint is the guide to ensure the process toward inclusiveness has taken place. This resolution further calls for inclusiveness in order to ensure that all voices are heard.

Since ASEAN and China signed the 2002 Declaration on the Conduct of Parties in the South China Sea, there has been gradual positive development of engagement between ASEAN member states and China. The stances taken by AMS vis-à-vis China range from confrontational to acceptance of China's position. However, if one were to take a regional perspective, Acharya (2009) argues that it is important to analyze how China is embedded into the regional integration of Asia. Taking a constructivist point of view, one can argue that a strong and persistent regional organization such as ASEAN, can influence the behavior of a state.

From a regional perspective, China as a rising power (in the Second Oriental Globalization) needs to indicate power projection, provide public goods, push forth an ideology and gain regional legitimacy, i.e. acceptance by its neighbor. In all four categories, China has not met the expectations (Acharya, 2014).

First, China is not projecting a power that will challenge the US. It is also in a vulnerable position within the Indian Ocean. Second, China is not able to provide public goods extensively, such as aids and access to market. As for security public goods, most countries in Asia do rely on their alliances with the US, but China can be a challenge to the security of the region. Third, China is not exporting Communism to the region or the rest of the world, unlike the US with its brand of democracy and capitalism. Fourth, China has not gained regional legitimacy because of its aggressive actions, especially the construction of entities around the Spratly Islands.

ASEAN, on the other hand, has withstood almost 50 years of relationships. A socialization process that has taken place between and among the 10 member states, especially the newer members, has led to an internalization of values, roles and understandings. There has been a steady increase in trade, production, investment and finance. Furthermore, the number of multilateral structures leading toward cooperation and security such as the ASEAN Regional Forum (ARF) and the ASEAN Defense Ministers Meeting (ADMM) in 2010 have fostered multilateral solutions instead of a bilateral one in addressing conflicts (He Tao 2015).

While studies about socialization among ASEAN members showed that newer members are able to acquire values such as consensus building and the ASEAN Way, a study by Alastair Johnston (2003), which examines the socialization of China with ASEAN, put forth two interesting findings. First, China is able to adapt to the ASEAN process especially in ARF, where the SCS was discussed frequently. When the SCS was put on the Second ARF agenda in 1995, China did not oppose the Chair's declaration of consensus even though China preferred a bilateral approach in settling the matter (Johnson 2003, p. 136). Second, China began to practice multilateralism in Confidence Building Measures (CBM), such as organizing the Heads of Defense Colleges in a seminar of Defense Conversion Cooperation as well as exchanges in military law and environmental protection (Johnson 2003, p. 138). The study also indicated that China has found several ways to assert itself by making objections when issues or discussions passed its comfort level, usually in the language that they adopted in passing resolutions.

Overall, ASEAN's engagement with China has raised the level of confidence in finding amicable solutions on the SCS. Even though China believes in bilateral moves with various maritime territorial claimants, China is aware that it will not be able to establish control over all South China Sea islands in the near future. Moreover, China is also pressured by other members of ARF, such as India and the US to settle the dispute by abiding with international law. Here, India's role as a balancer in the Indian Ocean, and the US being the benign hegemon, will have an impact on China's posture. Thus, socialization coupled with persuasion can construct the behavior of a state, especially in a state's desire to gain regional legitimacy.

The Nusantara as a 'Mediterranean Sea'

Finally, desecuritization of the SCS can be continued through a perspective put forth by Hans-Dieter Evers in a project entitled, 'The South China Sea as a Mediterranean Cultural Area'. In his keynote address at the Ninth International Malaysian Studies Conference (MSC9) 2014, Hans-Dieter Evers questioned the lack of maritime governance, and the lack of a maritime development program by the Malaysian government especially, in relation to the South China Sea. He argued that there is a governance void in SCS, resulting in it becoming a contested maritime space. Drawing from the work of the 'longue duree' of history analyzed by Fernand Braudel (2001), Evers argued that there is a need to place the South China Sea within the Malay and Javanese conception of space better known as Nusantara. According to Evers:

> The Nusantara concentric *mandala* conception of space differs from the Chinese conceptions of bounded space. Fuzzy boundaries versus clearly defined boundaries, the Malay *hulu* of distant, undefined areas far from the centre versus the 'Great Wall' concept guide the perception of the South China Sea. The Nusantara concept is basically a maritime conception of free and undefined space, the Chinese appear to view the South China Sea as a bounded territory, possibly even as their exclusive sovereign territory. The two concepts of space are not compatible. As cultural concepts they are difficult to change.
>
> (Evers 2014b, p. 16)

Evers has taken a sociological approach in studying the conception of space in the Malay and Javanese communities. Both communities regard the sea as a focus of life, while land is considered as short passages connecting to the sea (Andaya 2000). The Malay conception of space focuses on water. The connection between *hulu* and *hilir* (upstream and downstream) has economic, political and geographical bearings on the Nusantara outlook.

Another important dimension argued by Evers is the intimate human connectivity between communities in the region (Table 12.5). Within this context, inter-island migration, also known as 'merantau' is common among inhabitants of the Nusantara. Evers followed through the idea developed by Denis Lombard (2012) on the Asian Mediterranean (*la Méditerranée Asiatique*). He contrasted classic connectivity to modern connectivity. These modern agents of connectivity have brought the communities closer through trades, marriages and travels.

By postulating that the South China Sea is a 'Mediterranean Sea' we imply that the surrounding lands and islands are closely connected. In recent decades the areas and nations around the South China Sea have become more and more tightly woven through migration and various forms of communication. Labor migration and the exchange of cultural traits from language phrases and eating habits to media and popular culture have increasingly created a common cultural area. Chinese influences have been strong, but so has been

Table 12.5 Classical and modern forms of connectivity

Classical forms of connectivity	*Modern forms of connectivity*
1 Patron–client relations	1 Multinational corporations
2 Family business networks	2 Production networks
3 Cronyism	3 Outsourcing
4 Diasporas	4 ITC networks

Source: Evers (2014b, p. 13).

the impact of Nusantara languages, religions and cultures (Evers 2012). In fact, the migration pattern has also been supported by DNA analysis. An extensive study by Nothofer (2013) on mapping the inter-linkages of migration indicated that there is a circular migration pattern where the Malays and their ancestors had migrated north.

Finally, desecuritization of the SCS is been accomplished by examining the early documents cited as historical evidence by China in recent publications on SCS. Bill Hayton (2015) argued that early works on the disputes were written without much reference to primary source material. Furthermore, local, empirical and historical data acknowledging that Nusantara predates the 1800 Chinese source document suggested by Fu (2013), give credence to the principle associated with the freedom of the seas, and the compatible conception of space upheld by the Chinese and communities in the Malay Archipelago.

The studies carried out by Evers, Nothofer, and Hayton can be seen as the second stage reversal process to desecuritize the South China Sea (Figure 12.2). It also has the possibility of offering an option for the promotion of peace and stability in the region. The argument is that different conceptions of space based on historical and sociological perspectives can provide a solution to governing the South China Sea in a cooperative manner. Instead of viewing SCS as a political–security matter, it will be more useful to view the SCS as a political–economic matter where close socio-cultural linkages precede claims of sovereignty. The Nusantara and the Chinese historic waters emphasize heterogeneous usage of the sea. However, more work needs to be done to provide possible governance maritime structures to manage the regional commons.

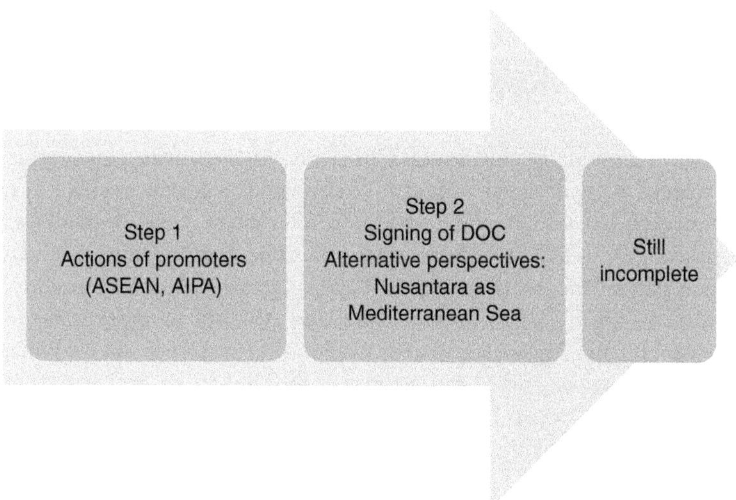

Figure 12.2 The two-step reversal process.

Source: adapted from Buzan *et al.* (1998).

Conclusion

Within ASEAN, the SCS issue gained prominence when China upset Vietnam by taking over the southern tip of the Paracel Islands. By 2002, the Declaration on the Conduct of Parties on the South China Sea offered the first sign toward a multilateral settlement of the matter. This shows that ASEAN as an organization is able to shape the behavior of China through its socialization and persuasion as China is now a dialogue partner of ASEAN. Since China wants to see the success of its 'Belt and Road Initiative', it now realizes the need to narrow the gap between words and actions.

This chapter identified the agents of securitization and desecuritization, i.e. drivers of conflict and the promoters of peace. Out of the four drivers of conflict, the data indicated that the demand for natural resources, namely hydro carbon and fishery stocks, may push states to redraw their maritime boundaries. The lull period between conflicts has also grown shorter over the years.

As a general strategy to managing the SCSC issue, Fravel (2003) suggested the delaying approach, the escalation strategy, and the cooperation strategy. All three approaches/strategies have been undertaken by various actors at different times. For example, China tends to use the delaying and escalation approach while ASEAN and ASEAN member states give weight to the cooperation strategy. As for the promoters of peace and stability, one can argue that the ability to shape the behavior of others usually takes a long time. Nevertheless, a regional organization such as ASEAN has the ability to engage with China at a multilateral level. Through documents and resolutions expressed by ASEAN leaders and AIPA members, we can foresee continuous intensified interaction between China and ASEAN member states. China realizes that it needs regional legitimacy in order to play a stronger role within the region. ASEAN, especially claimants such as Philippines, Vietnam, Malaysia and Brunei see the economic potentials of the SCS. Both China and ASEAN are also aware of the rebalancing act with external power, especially the US.

Despite the treatment of the South China Sea as a security issue, other possible perspectives, such as viewing the Nusantara as a Mediterranean Sea, is worth exploring because it will provide an alternative view on land–sea relations among communities in Southeast Asia. The South China Sea can also be seen as part of the ocean of Peace (Pacific Ocean). More importantly, desecuritization of the SCS will enable China and ASEAN member states to lessen the gap in finding an agreeable mode of governing the regional commons. In other words, desecuritization is important to ensure that there is a minimal development gap between countries and within countries as this regional commons can provide benefits for all states through negotiated plans for joint development.

References

Abuza, Zachary. 2015. Analyzing Southeast Asia's military expenditures. http://cogitasia.com/analyzing–southeast-asias-military-ependitures/.

Acharya, A. 2009. *Whose Ideas Matter? Agency and Power in Asian Regionalism*. USA: Cornell University Press.

Acharya, A. 2014. *Constructing a Security Community in Southeast Asia: ASEAN and the Problem of Regional Order*. London: Routledge.

AIPA Secretariat. 2009. Report of the 30th ASEAN Inter-Parliamentary Assembly. Jakarta, AIPA.

Andaya, Leonard. 2000. A history of trade in the Sea of Melayu. *Itinerario* 24: 87–110.

ASEAN:www.eria.org/JOINT%20COMMUNIQUE%20OF%20THE%2048TH%20AMM-FINAL.pdf.

Braudel, Fernand. 1987. *A History of Civilizations*. USA: Penguin Books

Braudel, Fernand. 2001. *The Mediterranean in the Ancient World*. London: Penguin Group.

Buzan, Barry, Ole Weaver, and Jaap de Wilde. 1998. *Securitization: A New Frame Work for Analysis*. Boulder, CO: Lynne Rienner Publishers.

China: www.defenseone.com/threats/2015/09/defiant-chinese-admirals-message-south-china-sea-belongs-china/120989/.

Crisis Group Asia Report. 2012. *Stirring up the South China Sea (II). Regional Responses*. 24 July 2012. Belgium: ICG.

Crisis Group Asia Report. 2015. *Stirring up the South China Sea (III). A Fleeting Opportunity for Calm*. 7 May 2015. Belgium: ICG.

DOC. 2002. Declaration on the Conducts of Parties in the South China Sea (DOC). http://aseansec.org/13163.htm.

Dongyun Park. 2010. The dichotomy between Northeast Asian capitalism and Southeast Asian capitalism. *Journal of the Asia Pacific Economy*, 5(3): 234–254. DOI: 10.1080/13547860050175035.

EIA. 2013. www.eia.gov/todayinenergy/detail.cfm?id=10671.

Evers, Hans-Dieter. 2012. Nusantara: Malaysia and the governance of the South China Sea. Keynote Address at the Ninth International Malaysia Studies Conference (MSC 9), Kuala Terengganu, Terengganu.

Evers, Hans-Dieter. 2014a. Governing maritime space: The South China Sea as a Mediterranean cultural area. *Southeast Asia Research Centre Working Paper Series*, No. 150, 2014.

Evers, Han-Dieter. 2014b. Nusantara: Malaysia and the Governance of the South China Sea. Keynote Address at the Ninth International Malaysia Studies Conference, 18–20 August 2014. Terengganu, Malaysia.

Evers, Hans-Dieter. 2016a. Nusantara Malaysia and the geopolitics of the South China Sea. The 11th Pok Rafeah Chair Public Lecture at IKMAS. Bangi, UKM.

Evers, Hans-Dieter. 2016b. Nusantara: Malaysia and the Governance of South China Sea. *Southeast Asian Social Science Review (SEASSR)* 1(1): 7–23.

EU-Asia Centre 2015. South China Sea: Background note. www.eu-asiacentre.eu/pub_details.php?pub_id=112.

Fravel. M.T. 2003. The long march to peace: Explaining China's settlement of territorial disputes. Thesis Dissertation. Los Angeles: Stanford University.

Fu, Kuen-chen. 2013. Safeguarding China's national interests in the South China Sea: Rectification, services, leadership, and maritime delimitation. *China Oceans Law Review* 1: 12–26.

Glaser, B. 2012. Armed clash in the South China Sea: Contingency Planning Memorandum No. 14. The Council for Foreign Affairs. www.cfr.org/world/armed-clash-south-china/p227883.

Hayton, B. 2015. The importance of evidence: Fact, fiction and the South China Sea. In Bill Hayton, ed. *The South China Sea: The Struggle for Power in Asia*. Princeton: Yale University Press.

He Tao. 2015. From bilateralism to multilateralism: Evolution and prospects of ASEAN defense cooperation. CIIS. 10 March 2015.

Ikenberry, John and Michael Mastanduno, eds. 2003. *International Relations Theory and the Asia Pacific*. New York: Columbia University Press.

Johnston, A. 2003. Socialization in international institutions: The ASEAN way and international relations theory. In G. Ikenberry and M. Mastanduno, eds. *International Relations Theory and the Asia Pacific* (pp. 107–162). New York: Columbia University Press.

Lombard, D. 2012. The concept of space and time in the Southeast Asian Archipelago. In Geoffrey Wade and Tana Li, eds. *Anthony Reed and the Study of the Southeast Asian Past* (pp. 85–100). Singapore: ISEAS.

Malaysia: www.thestar.com.my/news/nation/2015/10/18/worry-over-sea-disputes/.

Nederveen Pieterse, Jan. 2014. Asia rising: Welcome to the multipolar world. In Hyun-Chin Lim, W. Shafer, and Suk-Man Hwang, eds. *Global Challenges in Asia: New East Asian Developmental Models and East Asian Community Building* (pp. 31–62). Seoul: Seoul National University Press.

Nothofer, Bernd. 2013. Austronesian-speaking seafarers: Their settling of the South China Sea. In *Workshop Reframing the South China Sea: Towards a Mediterranean Understanding of Culture and* Resources, 11–13 November 2013. Institute of Asian Studies, Universiti Brunei Darussalam.

Oelsner. 2005. (De)securitization theory and regional peace: Some theoretical reflections and a case study on the way to stable peace. San Domenico Di Fiesola: EUI Working Paper, RSCAS, 2.

Periosamy Otharam, 2013. *The Brunei Times*. 23 September 2013.

Saravanamuttu, J. 2010. *Malaysia's Foreign Policy, the First Fifty Years: Alignment, Neutralism, and Islamism*. Singapore: ISEAS.

Thayer. Carlyle, 2012. ASEAN'S Code of Conduct in the South China Sea: A litmus test for community-building? *The Asia-Pacific Journal* 10(34), 20 August.

The Philippines: www.gmanetwork.com/news/story/539651/news/nation/philippines-tells-china-at-un-assembly-stop-coercion-and-intimidation.

USA: www.whitehouse.gov/the-press-office/2015/09/28/remarks-president-obama-united-nations-general-assembly.

Valencia, Mark, Jon Van Dyke, and Ludwig, Noel. 1997. *Sharing the Resources of the South China Sea*. Hawaii: University of Hawaii Press.

Vietnam: www.voanews.com/content/vietham-china-spratlyislands/2984641.html.

Westad, OddArne. 2012. *Restless China and the World since 1750*. London: The Bodley Head.

Ye Qiang and Jiang Zongqiang, 2015. China's 'Nine-dash Line' claim: US misunderstands. RSIS Commentary. No. 011, 14 January 2015.

Index

Page numbers in *italics* denote figures, those in **bold** denote tables.

For Product Safety Concerns and Information please contact our EU
representative GPSR@taylorandfrancis.com
Taylor & Francis Verlag GmbH, Kaufingerstraße 24, 80331 München, Germany

www.ingramcontent.com/pod-product-compliance
Ingram Content Group UK Ltd.
Pitfield, Milton Keynes, MK11 3LW, UK
UKHW020019200926
475702UK00014B/1964
* 9 7 8 0 3 6 7 3 5 9 9 0 4 *